WEST
Th
a
an
te

F

Ple

2

30.

2

SOVIET AIR FORCE FIGHTER COLOURS 1941–1945

SOVIET AIR FORCE FIGHTER COLOURS 1941–1945

Erik Pilawskii

Colour Profiles and Line Drawings
Chris Banyai-Riepl

Colour Schematics
Erik Pilawskii

First published 2003

ISBN 1 903223 30 X

Produced by Chevron Publishing Limited

Project Editor: Robert Forsyth

Cover and book design by Colin Woodman Design

Published by Classic Publications
an imprint of Ian Allan Publishing Ltd, Hersham, Surrey KT12 4RG, England

Printed by Ian Allan Printing Ltd, Hersham, Surrey KT12 4RG

Visit the Classic Publications website at www.classic-books.co.uk

Contents

Author's Introduction

Over the last ten years the study of VVS colouration during the Great Patriotic War has improved much, and many hitherto uncovered facts have at last been revealed. Not surprisingly, however, some uncertainty does indeed remain – not immoderately related to the enormous improvisation that characterised Soviet air operations during the War – but the picture is far more complete than it has been on this matter for all of the last half century.

Little did I realise, when I penned that sentence some years ago how extraordinarily true this statement might become. The matter of colour research with regard to the practices of the VVS during the Great Patriotic War (GPW) has undergone revolutionary progress over the last several years. Indeed so fast did even my own research on the matter evolve, that I was unable to keep any of my published documents entirely up to date at any time hitherto. Additionally, two *M-Hobby Magazine* authors – V. Vakhlamov and M. Orlov – located, reduced and published an amount of documentation that exceeds in volume everything ever before collected on the subject. This is a superb body of work; but it must be considered in context, just as with other sources of information on this fascinating subject.

This book, hopefully the first of several volumes, is the result of a 15-year odyssey to discover the truth about the Great Patriotic War. When I first had the chance to examine Soviet aircraft of this era in 1986, I was astonished to find that they did not in any way fit my expectations nor prejudices. Like most, I had grown up with the same old ideas about out-of-date Soviet contraptions which won through only by the application of massed numbers, all the while falling like flies in front of the German 'super-pilots'.

But, as a qualified pilot myself, and with some technical experience, I was able to see through that fog of propaganda. The machines I saw were *clearly* not related to any such conception. I had hitherto examined many Western aircraft of this period, and by comparison, I was immediately struck by the fact that a number of features of these Soviet machines appeared to be *superior* to those of often-lauded Western types, even upon first glance. After watching a flight demonstration of these Soviet aircraft, the reality was quite apparent; a disservice of enormous proportions had been done to the VVS in the Western historical record. It was at that moment, that I undertook to sort out the facts from the rhetoric, and became engrossed in this subject, resulting in this work.

A full account of conducting the research for this volume would probably make for a book on its own; but I was fortunate enough to have had access to archival sources before the dissolution of the USSR. In many respects this was critical, for at that time all of the relevant records and documents were still within their original locations in the archival collections that held them. Furthermore, the archival staff at these collections were thoroughly professional and of great assistance in the conduct of my research. These collections were also operated within the titanic Soviet bureaucracy, and thus once one had penetrated this bewildering maze of paperwork, the door was open (so to speak) for the successful navigation of that system. I was very lucky to have been fairly and generously treated by those bureaucrats.

I should note as well, that my own research has really been conducted in several 'phases', depending upon the interest and focus of the book I had planned to complete. I must admit that this focus did shift more than once, and so, therefore, did the type of information I sought to retrieve. As a result, one could really approach the information in this book in several ways; through the history of the aviation factories, the technical details of the aircraft, and the aircraft's finish and colouration. Upon reflection, however, I find that all of these considerations dovetail nicely together to form a unified picture of Soviet aircraft of that period.

Any attempt to research the VVS of the GPW must, in my view, rest upon the work of two giants in Russian aviation history. The first, and foremost, author must be Vadim Shavrov, and his thoroughly ground-breaking research on Soviet aviation, *The History of Aircraft Construction of the USSR*, in two volumes. It is the sheer detail of his work that leaves one breathless. To have included in a single work, an expansive understanding of development and factory politics within, say, *Zavod 1* in Moscow, alongside a schematic drawing of stabiliser attachment point flange joints, is almost beyond comprehension. And yet, for Shavrov, these factors flow together seamlessly and effortlessly, as if the picture of Soviet aircraft development was incomprehensible without them in tandem. Whatever errors or omissions that may now have been recognised in his works (and it must be said that these are indeed modest considering the scope of his writing), the overall picture is that Shavrov stands, quite properly, at the head of *all* VVS research.

The second giant in this area of research is the indefatigable figure of A.T. Stepanets. It is true that Stepanets' work revolves specifically around the Yakovlev OKB and its fighter aircraft designs. However, it must also be said that his work is an example of how aviation history should be written and published, *as such*. Not only was Stepanets a significant author on the matter of Yak fighters during the War (by dint of his testing position at the NII VVS), but his historical writing, research, and archival activities continued unabated thereafter, and with the utmost attention to detail and scholarly standards. His work in the collections of papers from Yakovlev, the Saratov factory No.292, and other primary sources is quite unmatched. Stepanets' latest resulting volume, *Yak Fighters from the Period of the Great Patriotic War*, is an innocuous, little green paperback, which upon examination, makes a mockery of every attempt to write aviation history hitherto. This outstanding work is unlikely ever to be surpassed in scholarship and authority by any other aviation author, including this one.

These canon of Soviet aviation research are richly supported by a new crop of outstanding historians, some likely, no doubt, to attain similar status in their time. Of this new breed of researchers, I would recognise authors such as Mikhail Maslov, whose work on Polikarpov aircraft (both in research and aircraft restoration) is quite unmatched. Authors Leypnik and Kuznetsov have taken up the Yakovlev mantle from Stepanets with outstanding additions to the history of this fighter family, and Gordon and Khazanov have been hard at work for years publishing excellent but relatively little known works on VVS aircraft. *M-Hobby* authors, Orlov and Vakhlamov, have advanced the study of VVS colouration so fully, that it must be said the matter would have been thrown backwards as much as *two decades* without their excellent research on the subject. In the area of pilot history and biography, no one has made further strides than German author Hans Seidl, and Russian historians Sultanov and Abramovits. It is to all of these fine historians, that a considerable debt is owed in the creation of this book, and in the conduct of my own research into this fascinating subject.

It is, alas, impossible even to contemplate listing all of the many persons here who have kindly assisted me in my ongoing research. Even if unnamed, I can assure them all that their contributions and assistance will not be forgotten or remain unappreciated. Above all, in gratitude, I would like to thank my dear old friend Matt Bittner, and less old (but not less dear) 'mate', Peter Vill, for their personal support and assistance in this long process; in Russia, a special thanks to my colleagues Valentine Parshin, Konstantin Malinovski, Vladimir Archipov, and Yuri Grechov; in Poland, thanks to the indefatigable Stanislaw Rominsky; in Latvia, my gratitude to the scholarly expertise of Alexander Ruchkovsky; and perhaps the biggest and most heartfelt thanks of all, to my dear friend, the keen-eyed and sharp-minded Ilya Grinberg, without whom this book would simply have been impossible.

To all, my warmest thanks and appreciation.

EP

Preface

On 22 June 1941, over 2,770 *Luftwaffe* aircraft, comprising four Air Fleets, swept down on the 'ill-prepared' and unsuspecting aircraft of the Red Army Air Forces. Within 12 hours they had inflicted upon the Soviet VVS the heaviest air strike in the history of aerial warfare; some '1,700' aircraft were destroyed on the ground with a further 250 in the air. Within a month, Soviet losses had climbed to '4,400' aircraft; by September the total was '7,500'.

Such appalling losses shocked an incredulous world, to whom the very idea of Soviet air-preparedness seemed a farce. The *Luftwaffe*, scarcely able to believe its success, found itself jovially reporting the appearance "...of the last few Soviet machines" all throughout the Autumn. Everyone was convinced that the 'Paper Tiger' had been exposed, that the Soviets were finished in the air, as well as on the ground.

Yet, perceptibly for many, there was a growing number of inconsistencies in these ideas. Despite these alleged losses, Soviet machines continued to appear... and continued... and continued. The great number of machines found "destroyed" on the ground were, in fact, discovered to have been abandoned, and furthermore were almost all obsolescent types, most of which were not even airworthy at the moment of invasion. Their pilots, far from routed, were increasingly aggressive and many were quite experienced. Furthermore, new aircraft types began to arrive in combat, seemingly in disregard of the fact that the Russian aviation industry was largely forced to pull up its roots and retreat 1,500 km to places like Kuibishev during that very autumn and winter. Moreover, German losses of aircraft had been far from moderate, exceeding 2,700 by 1 December. Then, as often, things were certainly not as had been seen.

The history of the Soviet Air Forces during the Second World War – what Russians often refer to as the Great Patriotic War (and unusually, for this is also the name given to the Napoleonic War of 1812-14) – is the story of their dramatic transformation of fortunes from 1941 to 1945. How could any military organization suffer such catastrophe, only months later to re-emerge as a forcefully powerful arm, and within a further year, decisively defeat the very same enemies who had battered them before? As well, we are left to marvel at the sheer courage of the early Soviet aviators, who despite the tragedy, continued to hurl themselves at the German air formations ferociously, and, most amazingly, with more than a little success. It is, more than any other, their own story.

It is also the story, sadly, of how such admirable achievements could possibly have gone without recognition – both inside and outside of the USSR – for so long. The consistent desire to discount and gainsay all Soviet accomplishment is very well known in Western history (and in 'modern' Russian history as well), and is conditioned largely by propagandistic and ideological bias, or perhaps a desire in Russia, specifically, to leave the past well behind. However, the effort expended to minimize and rationalize the heroic Soviet victory in the Second World War goes *way* beyond even this tired agenda, setting wholly new standards in concealment and discredit. The reason for this puzzling behaviour is, I am quite certain, sheer incredulity.

All historians of that enormous war worthy of the name have at last, and not a little reluctantly, had to admit that the Second World War by all rights could be – and perhaps should be – known as 'The Great German-Soviet War, et al'. Put simply, the Soviets prevailed against the Germans largely single-handedly, by their own effort and means, and in no way were dependent on the late-arriving materiel (and, quite often, of questionable quality as well) afforded them by the Lend-Lease Act. This means, then, that the enormous and somewhat costly efforts of the United States and Great Britain had, in fact, little real impact on the outcome of the War. The vast majority of German forces were faced and destroyed on the Eastern Front, and simply could not have been defeated by the armies of England and the United States.

Such a realization is clearly *not* acceptable to Westerners – including, one must recall, the Germans – nor their Governments and their interests, and thus we have the conditions described above. This is nowhere more evident than with the history of the Soviet VVS. Though considerably smaller than the American Army Air Force, and lacking in almost all of the resources lavishly available to it, the Red Army Air Force, nonetheless, accomplished infinitely more than all of the Allied Air Forces combined. Not only that, but the VVS performed under the most appalling conditions, and while facing the majority of the *Luftwaffe* in the process. It is little wonder, indeed, that the RAF and USAAF are more than mildly chastened.

The result has been an attempt to discredit all VVS activity during the war. Its aircraft have typically been referred to in the most unflattering light (though, albeit, there are some happy exceptions to this), and its tactics felt to have been crude, backward, and ineffective. In fact, the opposite could not have been more true. But it is for the Soviet pilots themselves, that the most vitriolic attacks have been saved, curtly accused of having been doltish, brainwashed sheep, who achieved little more than affording targets for the various German aces, who accumulated enormous scores. Every type of amateurish pop-psychology has been proffered to rationalize such insidious nonsense, including allegations that the pilots were rendered incompetent by 'Communist' ideology! It is simply impossible to impart on such stupidity the level of repudiation and disgust it deserves.

Why examine the markings and colouration of Soviet aircraft? It has always been my intention to study the Soviet (and Russian) Aviation *industry* as a whole. Perhaps differently from other historians of this subject, I began my search by looking at the economic and industrial factors and operations that led to the manufacture of these aircraft. It has always been my view, that only by studying the factories and production of aircraft, can one glean a true picture of the *modus operandi* of their design and development, and of course, then, of their true nature.

This relates to a second avenue of interest on my part. As a pilot myself, I have always been interested in the flying properties and characteristics of historic aircraft. In many cases, we have to rely in the modern world on anecdotal accounts; the number of surviving authentic *and* airworthy machines from history is rather small. But, as to which any historian can attest, anecdotal evidence – such as it is – tends to be rather sketchy, at best. It is vastly preferable and more scientifically valid, in my mind, to view all written and orally transmitted accounts through the lens of engineering and aerodynamics. This, of course, is yet another reason why I have sought to study the design and production forces behind these aircraft; understanding their engineering helps to understand their behaviour.

The recognition of the importance of historical colouration is – in my opinion – simply a logical development of history and historical survey. Perhaps this conclusion might be dismissed as logical only in light of our modern, more image-conscious mentality; I disagree. During the 1950s, 1960s and 1970s, the world was subjected to museum exhibits featuring authentic historical aircraft, that were presented in the most dour, extraordinary, perplexing, and generalized paint schemes. Even in the most prestigious collections, aircraft were routinely repaired and 'restored' with bits casually fabricated in the staff workshop, or taken from other derelict machines, even those of dissimilar types. None of these modifications were noted with any great accuracy or import – after all, what was the point?

Shifting priorities and an expanded sense of historical authenticity during the 1970s put an end to these practices. In the modern era, such behaviour would be utterly unthinkable – every repair or modification is undertaken with the utmost documentation and quality. Replicated parts and items are so marked and clearly noted, and where at all possible original items are located. And so it has come to be with all things relating to historical aircraft – authenticity is the standard against which all work is held accountable. Today it is true, that at least for the last 10 years or so, even in collections that do not enjoy an international reputation, this standard of authenticity is to include *colouration*.

In a modern aviation museum of any repute, no aircraft could possibly be restored without first conducting a detailed painting analysis. Layers of paint are carefully stripped away to reveal the original lacquers, and to the degree possible, the machine is re-finished after restoration to look as close as can be determined to its original appearance during service. Colour matches are carefully blended, primers are examined, colour research is consulted if available, and photographs are inspected, all in an effort to execute the camouflage and markings to the greatest degree of accuracy that can be achieved.

It is precisely in this vein that this book was conceived. Of course, the value to hobbyists, modellers, restoration staff, artists and researchers of various kinds, should be self-evident. The main thrust of the work, however, is history, pure and simple. To me, there is no bias in any usage of this kind of material, and it serves as all historical work tends to do – in many roles.

Lastly, this book is also an examination of what role historical photography can play in modern analysis. Turning to black and white images may not seem like an overly logical place to begin an examination of *colour*. But now attitudes are changing, and we have – as a historical community – begun to realize that *in combination* with other sources of information, these pictures can be quite illuminating. The greatest advance, of course, in this area has been in the museums – nothing has shed such light on historical colouration as the accurate restoration of surviving specimens. It is to this work, whether performed by myself or by other staff around the world, to which my colour research and this book are most indebted.

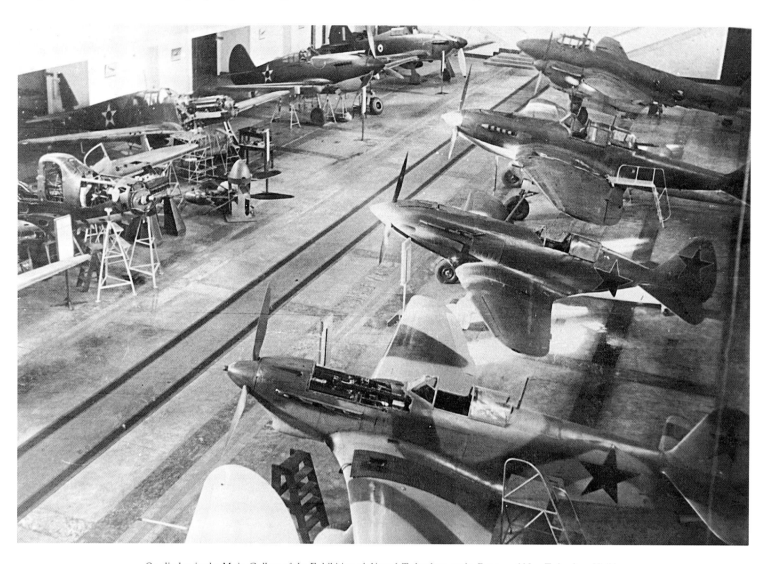

On display in the Main Gallery of the Exhibition of Aircraft Technology at the Bureau of New Technology. Visible are, left to right: P-39, P-51A, Kittyhawk IIB, Hurricane II, Pe-2, Il-2 AM-38F, MiG-3, Yak-9 (in an AII lacquer 'loops' scheme), and an La-5FN. (Photo: G.Petrov)

Abbreviations and Glossary

In this volume the reader will encounter many acronyms and abbreviations relating to the Soviet Air Force, the Soviet Government, and governmental ministries. The very number of such acronyms is telling – it reflects the monumental size of the Soviet bureaucracy during (and after) the Great Patriotic War. The most common of these are listed here, along with Russian words appearing regularly in the text.

ADD
(Aviatsiya Dal'nevo Destviya)
Long-Range Aviation, later the 18th Air Army

AMT *(Aerolak matoviy)*
An all-purpose aviation-use lacquer featuring a matt surface

AON
(Aviatsionnaya Armia Osobovo Naznachenya)
Special Purpose Aviation Army

Aviatsionniy Park
(also, *Aviapark*)
Aviation Depot (Airpark)

Aviakhim
(Obshchestvo Druzey Aviakhimicheskoy Oboroni i Promishlennosti SSSR)
Society of Friends of the Aerial and Chemical Defence and Industry of the USSR

Aviatrest
(Gosudarstvenniy trest aviatsionnoy promishlennosti)
State Aviation Industry Trust

BAP
(Bombardirovochniy Aviapolk)
Bomber Air Regiment

BF
(Baltiskiy Flot)
Baltic Fleet

Bombardirovschik
Bomber

Byuro Konstruktsiy
Design Bureau

ChMF
(Cherno-Morskiy Flot, also given as ChF*)*
Black Sea Fleet

Dal'niy
The word means 'distant', but in the context of aviation its meaning is better equivalent to 'long-range'. In the Yakovlev OKB, the suffix D was often used to denote *dal'niy* fighters.

Dal'niy Deystviya
Literally, 'distance enhanced', but in context it can be used to mean 'extended long-range'. In the Yakovlev OKB, the suffix DD was often used to denote *dal'niy deystviya* fighters.

DBA
(Dalno-Bombardirovochnaya Aviatsiya)
Long-Range Bomber Aviation (see ADD)

Delta Drevesina
Literally, wood-plastic. A timber product in which the wood itself was impregnated with a birch resin mixture (including phenol-formaldehyde) and heat-cured to produce a durable, fire-resistant structure for load-bearing use (i.e. as in wing spars, etc).

Diviziya Aviatsionnaya
Aviation Division

DVK
(Diviziya Vozdushnykh Korabley)
Division of Flying Ships

EON
(Eskadril'ya Osobovo Naznachenya)
Special Purpose Squadron

Eskadril'ya Aviatsionnaya,
or just *Eskadril'ya*
Aviation Squadron

FAB
Fugasniy aviabomb
High-explosive aviation bomb

Glavaviaprom or **GUAP**
(Glavnoe Upravlenie Aviatsionnoy Promishlennosti)
Chief Directorate of the Aviation Industry

Glavvozdukhflot or **GUVF**
(Glavnoe Upravlenie Vozdushnovo Flota)
Chief Directorate of The Air Fleet

GKO
also *Narkomat Oborony*
(Gosudarstvenniy Kommitet Oboroni)
State Defence Committee

GROSS
(Grazhdanskoye Opitnoye Samoletostroenye)
Civil Experimental Aircraft Construction

GUGVF
(Glavnoe Upravlenye Grazhdanskovo Vozdushnovo Flota)
Chief Administration of the Civil Air Fleet

GVF
(Grazhdanskiy Vozdushniy Flot)
Civil Air Fleet

IAD
(Istrebitel'niy Aviadiviziya)
Fighter Air Division, usually comprising four to six Regiments

IAK
(Istrebitel'niy Aviakorpus)
Fighter Air Corps, usually comprising three to five Divisions

IAP
(Istrebitel'niy Aviapolk)
Fighter Air Regiment, usually comprising three to four Squadrons

IA PVO
(Istrebitel'niy Aviapolk Protivo-Vozdushnovo Oborona)
Fighter Regiment of the Anti-Air Defence

Istrebitel' (**I**)
Fighter

Istrebitel'naya Aviaeskadril'ya (**IAE**)
Fighter Squadron, usually comprising 9 to 15 aircraft

KOSOS
(Konstruktorskiy Ot'del Opytnovo Samoletostroenia)
Experimental Aircraft Construction Development Team

Korpus
Corps (or main body)

Krasnaya Armiya (**KA**)
Red Army

Krasniy Vozdushniy Flot (**KVF**)
Red Air Fleet

LBE
(Legko-Bombardirovichnaya Aviaeskadril'ya)
Light Bomber Squadron

LII
(Letno-Islyedovatel'skiy Institut)
Flight Research Institute

NACA
National Advisory Committee for Aeronautics (US)

NKAP or *Narkomaviaprom*
(Narodniy Kommisariat Aviatsionoy Promishlinosti)
People's Commissariat for the Aircraft Industry

NKVD
(Narodniy Kommisariat Vnutrennikh Del)
People's Commissariat for Internal Affairs—in fact, Stalin's state secret police

NII VVS
(Nauchno-Ispitatel'niy Institut Voyenno-Vozdushikh Sil)
Scientific Test Institute of the Army Air Forces

NIPAV
(exact full Russian name unknown)
Scientific Fighter Aircraft Armament Range

ODVF
(Obshchestvo Druzei Vozdushnovo Flota)
Society of Friends of the Air Fleet

OKA
(Otdel'naya Krasnoznamennaya Armia)
Independent Red-Banner Army

9

OKB
(*Opitnoe Konstruktorskoe Byuro*)
Experimental Design Bureau

OKB
MS (*Opitnoe Konstruktorskoe Byuro Morskovo Samoletostroeniya*)
Experimental Naval Aircraft Design Bureau

OKO
(*Opitniy Konstruktorskiy Otdel*)
Experimental Design Group

ORAP Detached Reconnaissance Regiment
(*Otdel'naya Razvedivatel'naya Polk*)

Otryad
Group (large flight)

PARM
(*Polevie Aviaremontnie Masterskie*)
A forward maintenance and repair workshop

Polk (**AP**)
Regiment (Aviation Regiment)

PTAB
(*Protivo-Tankovaya Aviatsionnaya Bomba*)
A hollow-charge anti-tank bomb

PVO
(*Protivovozdushnogo Oborona*)
The Anti-Air Defence Forces

Razvedchik
Reconnaissance Aircraft

SAP
(*Smeshanniy Aviapolk*)
Composite Aviation Regiment

ShAP
(*Shturmoviy Aviapolk*)
Assault Air Regiment

Shpon
A timber product consisting of cross-grained layers of birch strip impregnated with phenol-formaldehyde resin, heat-bonded on one or both sides to bakelite film

SF
(*Severnoe Flota*)
Northern Fleet

STAVKA
(*Shtab Glavnovo Verkhovnovo Kommandirovaniya*)
Headquarters of the Supreme High Command

Shturmovik
Assault Aircraft

TsAGI
(*Tsentral'niy Aero-Gidrodinamicheskiy Institut*)
Central Aero-Hydrodynamics Institute

TsARB
(*Tsentral'naya Aviatsionnaya Remontnaya Baza*)
Central Aviation Repair Base

TsIAM
(*Tsentral'niy Institute Aviationovo Motorstoeniya*)
Central Institute of Aviation Motors

TsKB
(*Tsentral'noe Konstruktorskoe Byuro*)
Central Design Bureau

UTI
(*Uchebno-trenirovanniy istrebitel'*)
Fighter-Trainer Aircraft

UVVS
(*Upravlenie Voyenno-Vozdushnikh Sili*)
Directorate of the Air Forces

VIAM
(*Vsesoyuzhniy Institute Aviatsionnikh Materialov*)
All-Union Institute for Avitation Materials

VMF
(*Voenno-Morskoy Flot SSSR*)
Naval Forces of the USSR

VVA
(*Voenno-Vozdushnaya Akademiya*)
Air Forces Academy

VVS
(*Voyenno-Vozdushne Sili*)
Army Air Forces

VVS VMF
(*Voyenno-Vozdushne Sili Voenno-Morskogo Flota*)
Naval Air Forces

Zavod (*Zavoda* pl.)or earlier **GAZ**
(*Gosudarstvenniy Aviatsionniy Zavod*)
State Aviation Factory

Zveno
Flight

Common Unit Abbreviations

IAP	Fighter Air Regiment
GIAP	Guards Fighter Air Regiment
IAP VVS-ChF	Naval Fighter Air Regiment of the Black Sea Fleet
IAP VVS-SF	Naval Fighter Air Regiment of the Northern Fleet
IAP VVS-KBF	Naval Fighter Air Regiment of the Baltic Fleet
IA-PVO	Fighter Air Regiment of the Anti-Air Defence
OIAE	Independent Fighter Aviation Squadron

Table of VVS Rank Equivalents

VVS	(abbv)	USAAF	*Luftwaffe*
Lotchik	*Ltck.*	Private	Flieger
Efreytor	*Eftr.*	PFC	Gefreiter
Mladshiy Serzhant	*M.Szht.*	Corporal	Unteroffizier
Serzhant	*Szht.*	Sergeant	Feldwebel
Starshina	*Stsh.*	Staff Sergeant	Oberfeldwebel
Mladshiy Leytenant	*M.Lt.*	2nd Lieutenant	–
Leytenant	*Lt.*	Lieutenant	Leutnant
Starshiy Leytenant	*St.Lt.*	–	Oberleutnant
Kapitan	*Kpt.*	Captain	Hauptmann
Mayor	*May.*	Major	Major
Podpolkovnik	*Podpolk.*	Lt. Colonel	Oberstleutnant
Polkovnik	*Polk.*	Colonel	Oberst
General Mayor	*G.May.*	Maj. General	

The names of certain cities widely mentioned in this book have changed in the years following the Great Patriotic War. As well, many common names have been anglicized, such as "Moscow" for the Russian name *Moskva*. In this volume the city names of the period will be employed, but they can be cross-referenced on a modern atlas with the following list:

Great Patriotic War era name	*Current name*
Alma Ata	Almaty
Bochkarevo	Belogorsk
Frunze	Bishkek
Gor'ki	Nizhniy-Novgorod
Königsberg	Kaliningrad
Krasnogvardesk	Gatchina
Kuybishev	Samara
Leningrad	Sankt Peterburg
Leninsk	Chardzhui
Lomonosov	Oranienbaum
Stalingrad	Volgograd

Transliteration

For the purposes of this book, a modified Rimskiy Standard method of transliteration has been used. The Rimskiy Standard does not seek to phoneticize the English spelling as do some other transliteration systems, and this method has been employed as closely as possible, with one exception. Russian words with the transliterated ending "ogo" are actually pronounced "ovo", but to avoid confusion these have been left in their native spelling in the text. The following table gives the Rimskiy Standard Transliteration used in this book.

А	A	И	I	Р	R	Ш	Sh
Б	B	Й	Y	С	S	Щ	Sch
В	V	К	K	Т	T	Ъ	^
Г	G	Л	L	У	U	Ы	I
Д	D	М	M	Ф	F	Ь	'
Е, Ё	E	Н	N	Х	Kh	Э	Eh
Ж	Zh	О	O	Ц	Ts	Ю	Yu
З	Z	П	P	Ч	Ch	Я	Ya

The Russian letter Ё is also given as E, as it is rarely defined in Cyrillic text. As well, the often seen phonetic "Ye" and "Yo" for the Russian E and Ё are not used.

A Treatise on VVS Colour Systems

Colour Systems, Old and New

One of the truly perplexing aspects about GPW-era colour research is the host of incongruous designations, nomenclatures, and naming conventions applied to the finishes relevant to this period. It seems at times, as if no one can agree on any aspect of paint and varnish identification, and the surviving physical evidence is almost always at odds with the documentation available. For example, for years I regarded the existence of the 'AMT' nomenclature to be spurious; a post-war invention at best. The reason here was that none of the papers, maintenance unit records, nor production diaries from the GPW that I have managed to locate, mention this naming convention. No paint was known as 'AMT-1' in the *Zavod* 18 Production Diary, for example; it was known simply as 'earth brown'.

In retrospect, this may not seem so surprising after all – under such difficulties, it is more than understandable that factory personnel may have been unfamiliar with the new aerolacquer paint specifications, nomenclatures, and procedures. Also, supply of the new finishes must have been problematic, and stocks of the older lacquers would certainly have been used when required. Similarly, why would a Forward Maintenance Brigade care what a can of new paint was called, or whether or not its appearance conformed to the latest official TU (technical specification) from Moscow? In some cases, perhaps they did; but it occurs to me that in most cases, these workers really did not bother with such minutiae. Overall, the introduction of a whole new system of coloured finishes during the middle of many factories' evacuations to the east and south could not possibly have helped matters; confusion at the factories must have been near total. To help with the proper identification of colours in the documentary record, I have drawn up the following table listing the paints by their common names and references, as used by various parties; the official nomenclature or designation (where known) is also given in Cyrillic.

Official Designation	Common Factory Name	Common Field Name
AII Blue АИИ Голубой	'blue', 'light blue'	'blue', 'underside blue'
AII Green АИИ Зеленый	'green'	'green', 'olive green'
AII Black АИИ Черный	'black'	'black', 'black-green'
AII Dark Green АИИ Темно-Зеленый	'dark green'	'green', 'dark green'
AII Light Brown АИИ Светло-Коричневый	'sand brown', 'southern brown'	'light brown'
AII Brown АИИ Коричневый	'ochre brown', 'red', 'red-brown'	'red-brown', 'earth-brown'
A-14 (A-14F) Steel А-14 Стальной	(unknown)	(unknown)
AII Aluminium АИИ Алюминии	'AII(al)', 'aluminium dope'	'aluminium dope'
AEh-9 АЭ-9	'light grey'	'light grey'
(none)	'Tractor Green'	(unknown)
(none) Possibly AEh-5	'Factory Green'	(unknown)
(medium grey) likely AEh-8	'Medium Grey'	'Medium Grey'
Wood Aerolak Аэролак Деревяний	'wood aerolak', 'blue-grey primer'	(unknown)
ALG-5 (unknown) Гунт Металлический АЛГ-5	Metal Primer	'metal primer'
Industrial Metal Use Primer Гунт Металлический	'Metal Use Primer', 'blue-green primer'	'blue-green primer'
AMT-6 Black АМТ-6 Черный	'black'	'black'
AMT-4 Green АМТ-4 Зеленый	'green'	'green', 'olive green'
AMT-7 Blue АМТ-7 Голубой	'blue', 'light blue'	'blue', 'underside blue'
AMT-11 Grey-Blue АМТ-11 Серо-Голубой	'blue-grey', 'medium grey'	'grey', 'blue-grey'
AMT-12 Dark Grey АМТ-12 Темно-Серый	'grey', 'dark grey', 'dark blue-grey'	'blue-grey',
AMT-1 Light Brown АМТ-1 Светио-Коричневый	'earth brown', 'grey-brown'	'earth brown', 'grey'
A-24m Green А-24м Зеленый	'green', 'metal green', 'dark green'	'green'
A-21m Light Brown А-21м Светио-Коричневый	'dark brown', 'grey-brown', 'green-grey'	'dark brown', 'dark earth'
A-33m Grey-Blue А-33м Серо-Голубой	'blue-grey'	(unknown)
A-32m Dark Grey А-32м Темно-Серый	'dark grey'	(unknown)
A-28m Blue А-28м Голубой	(unknown)	(unknown)
A-26m Black А-26м Черный	'black'	'black'

From the above table, it is clear why so much confusion over the identification of colours has ensued over the last 60 years or so. While the factory and field personnel quite sensibly gave descriptive names to the paints in use, these did not in many cases match the official designations for the lacquers. These official nomenclatures were presumably made within the Moscow bureaucracy, for indeed many of them are not related to the actual appearance of the colour at all; it is difficult to understand the name *Light Brown* for the colour A-21m, for example. Moreover, some of the descriptive names given to the paints are redundant, or even contradictory, resulting in further confusion. One suspects as well that the nomenclatures in use also contributed to many of the spurious colour ideas that circulated in the West for so long. The term 'Brown' does not immediately conjure in one's mind a red-ochre colour, and the common use of the term 'black-green' in field units to refer to AII Black is quite misleading (there is no hint of green in its appearance).

The second part of this conundrum is the extraordinary revelation that there were, in fact, two distinct paint and varnish systems in use during the Great Patriotic War. All VVS aircraft up to the winter of 1941 were camouflaged according to the standard pre-war 1938-1940 applications, using pre-war AII lacquers manufactured at *Zavod*

30 in Moscow. In the Autumn and Winter of 1941, a series of specifications was drawn up for a new type of aviation finish known as 'AMT' (*aerolak matoviy*), for use on mixed construction aircraft, and A-?m (*aerolak maslyaniy*) for use on all-metal aircraft. At least some of these new finishes were placed into production at *Zavod* 36 with the most extreme difficulty that winter, and allegedly were distributed to various factories (*Zavoda* 21, 292, and 153 seem to be mentioned here in particular), in rather variable quantities for incorporation into manufacture during the Spring of 1942. Given the catastrophic dislocation of production during this time in the Soviet aviation industry, and the resulting shortages in supply of every description, it is certainly understandable, that these new finishes were introduced only gradually in many cases. Indeed, in many instances it appears that the two types of finishes were used together on the very same lines, perhaps even deliberately, and in some cases for the duration of the war. Moreover, examples of the pre-war finishes were being applied – presumably at various factories – right up to 1945; Vakhlamov and Orlov found documented requests to use these varnishes throughout 1943, for example, and manufacturing records for them from 1946-47. As a result, the record is very far from clear. This condition is also exacerbated by the fact that some finishes cannot be distinguished on black and white film (such as AII Blue and AMT-7), and in other cases the shades are so close that only where the photographic exposure and conditions are very evident (which is true, sadly, in a minority of the photographs we see) can the various appearances be determined.

It should be noted that not all of the new paints were a distinctive colour. Aircraft were being camouflaged with a Black over Green disruptive application, for example, as much as three years before the 1941 Directive establishing this scheme as a recommended pattern for Fighter and Tactical Aviation; that is, years before the invention of AMT finishes. The primary reason for the new paints was their improved chemistry and other properties, and the fact that they featured a uniform satin finish. One might notice that all of the original AMT finishes matched in colour the AII lacquers which they were intended to replace – Black, Green and Blue.

The similarity in appearance, it turns out, was not a mere coincidence; new evidence shows that this was quite deliberate, and quite logical. In a letter between the Deputy Director of the NKAP and the Director of Aviation Factory 199, it has emerged that the early AMT finishes were in fact manufactured utilizing the very same pigments as used in the earlier AII shades. When one considers the matter, one is forced to ask why they might do otherwise – clearly this is quite logical; I cannot suggest why the idea has never circulated before. It also explains, quite logically, why the initial AMT and AII colours often cannot be distinguished on film. Only later were entirely new colours introduced, and even those bore a close resemblance to previous aero paints in use throughout the USSR.

New Research and Findings

The documentary material unearthed by Vakhlamov and Orlov has proved very exciting for those interested in VVS colouration. The existence of these documents was known for a number of years, and indeed a summary of the information contained therein was widely circulated. For example, William Green and Gordon Swanborough were shown a copy of this summary in 1973 while they were compiling *Soviet Fighters Parts 1 and 2* [Macdonald and Janes, 1977 and 1978] (the origin of the use of the 'AMT' colour nomenclature in the West), and most of my Russian colleagues are familiar with it as well. However, apparently no one actually saw the original material itself until the two *M-Hobby* authors located it, and this included not only copies of the Directives and TU (*tekhnicheskie usloviya* = 'technical specifications') for the paints, but also the much suspect colour booklet as well.

This large body of documentation – which was stamped '*Secret*' for some unfathomable reason – was compiled by the NKVD ('Ministry of the Interior', but in fact, the State Secret Police). It was published in 1948, and appears to have existed in several volumes including a book of sample

colour chips and photographs. However, this fact in itself raises an immediate problem – a collection of documents compiled in 1948 could not possibly describe the wartime practices of colour use in full, nor in any semblance thereof. Such a report must, by definition, represent an after-the-event attempt to catalogue previous practices, many of which were conducted both with extreme urgency and improvisation under dire wartime conditions, and also were the products of apparently unremarkable pre-war standards. Other possibilities, such as local factory applications, are completely beyond the documentation in these collections, and this, of course, is fine. The material unearthed by Vakhlamov and Orlov was not intended (so far as I can determine) as some type of comprehensive and authoritative guide to GPW colours – simply, it describes the official specifications that were issued, demonstrates the details of these measures, and shows examples of their implementation.

Pre-War Lacquers: Camouflage to 1942

In June 1941, the only existing colour schemes for use in all aircraft camouflage, whether via production or field expedient, were the extant pre-war applications of 1939-41. However, this demonstrates in many ways the difficulties of discovering the various details of VVS colouration. If the two systems – AII and AMT/Am – looked the same, how could they be distinguished?

Before the war, the VVS was widely utilizing a series of aerolacquers known as 'AII'-type finishes. These purpose-use aviation lacquers were preceded by several formulations of aerolacquer, including the AM-, AE-, A-, and AEh- series finishes, the most important of which were the AEh lacquers, as they continued to be used in civil aviation (i.e. Aeroflot) for some time further on. AII lacquer is basically clear (it has a slight 'obsidian' tint to it); it is pigmented to produce the various coloured versions of the finish (i.e. Aluminium, Green, Blue, etc.), and features a fairly glossy sheen when new. This finish, however, does not appear to last very long, and under exposure to the sun and elements it quickly becomes satin, and then flat in appearance. AII lacquer did not appear to adhere well to unprepared surfaces (though much better to wood than to metal), and the idea seems to have been (ideally) to apply a coat of primer underneath applications of AII *aerolak*.

Since AII *aerolak* was usually pigmented, it was very easy to produce new colour variations of this finish for experimental or other uses. The various experimental 3-colour schemes of 1940 (see *M-Hobby* 1/99) are a good example of this type of practice, and many were executed using AII lacquers.

Given that AII was pigmented in this way, one might suppose that in use AII lacquers would have featured quite a range of variation in colour. Surprisingly, this appears not to be the case. In fact, of the many samples, of AII Blue (*goluboi*) that I have collected – examples dating from 1938 up to 1946 – there is virtually no variation in colour. This indicates that this version of AII lacquer was produced by making use of some automated or other standardized manufacturing method that assured consistency, thus meaning that it was almost certainly manufactured in vast quantities (in this case at *Zavod* 30, and possibly at *Zavod* 36, as well). The same condition may be noted for AII Green, Aluminium, and other variants.

In 1941, most VVS aircraft featured one of a series of new camouflage schemes invented and applied during 1939-40. Indeed, in 1940 there was a series of directives issued by the NKAP and UVVS that all un-camouflaged machines would have a 'military' livery applied to them (these are referred to in aggregate as the '*Maskirovochnaya Direktiva*'). Along with this Directive, the NKAP issued a series of recommendations to the aviation factories on correct procedures for aircraft finish and priming, *in addition* to camouflage matters. Three major 'options' were put forward, but sensibly the NKAP also allowed for individual practices and exceptions where required. Perhaps intended to be helpful at the time, these recommendations are understandably the cause of much confusion in the matter of VVS colouration and aerolacquer use today.

As it happened, none of the recommended procedures for wooden construction aircraft came to fruition. There was the idea to use

AII(Al) over a proposed primer known as DD-113; there was another idea to use a similarly proposed DD-118 primer for all surfaces; the maroon-coloured finish developed for use over *delta-drevesina* surfaces, VIAM-B3, was suggested as a general wood use primer. In the event, the DD- primers were not mass-manufactured due to unspecified 'defects' with the paint, and only a few prototypes (for example, the I-301 and I-26) were painted with VIAM-B3, which was also not produced in quantity.

For metal structures, the recommendation was to use the pre-war primer ALG-1 (yellow), and later ALG-5 (grey-green) prior to the application of various aerolacquers. There is some evidence in the post-1940 period (essentially the GPW) of the appearance of ALG-1 primer on metal panel areas; it is easy to identify, being 'dirty yellow' in colour. The use of ALG-5, however, is more obvious. This colour easily falls into the range of specified shades (greenish grey) which were, for years, identified as an alternative, later 'dull' version of Industrial Metal Use Primer (IMUP). This fact should have led to the identification of this lacquer, because ALG-5 is a metal primer, and began its major distribution in 1942-43, which corresponds fairly well to the appearance of the 'dull' IMUP shade in 1943-44. Be that as it may, most researchers are now confident that this paint is indeed ALG-5 metal primer.

Lastly, *Narkomaviaprom* suggested at the end of this lengthy documentation that some 'alternative' paints could be used for priming, etc., were the suggested lacquers not available. In this way they recommended the use of AII Blue, AMT-7 Blue, a proposed aluminium dope known only as '*aerolak* No.17' (never mass-produced), or even out of date and unobtainable, old lacquer AS. This may well describe why certain Polikarpov designs at *Zavod* 1, Moscow, had their interiors painted in AII Blue (likely, they were primed entirely in the colour). Also, recommended mixtures of ALG-1 were proposed, these intended to give different shades of 'yellowish-brownish' colours. One mixture in particular which is very interesting is the NKAP recommended shade of 50 per cent ALG-1, with 50 per cent A-14 (see 'Interior Colours'). This mix results in a bronze coloured paint; it is remarkable that many odd VMF camouflages are described as including 'bronze' colouration.

There is no doubt, for example, that some curious pre-1940 finishes persisted in use throughout the early *Barbarossa* period (for example, the 'dazzle' applications). These oddities will be dealt with in a later volume; our purpose in this book is to describe the more common wartime patterns.

1940-1941

Frontal Aviation

Within Army Aviation ('Frontal') the most common camouflage applications began with an overall coat of AII Green lacquer on the aircraft's uppersurface, and AII Blue on the lower; this pattern was basically standard for machines manufactured after 1938. Bomber and transport machines quite often were left in this single-colour livery, though the intent certainly appears to have been to use a two- or three-colour scheme when possible. Earlier aircraft surviving in service that were painted with AEh-9 light grey seem also to have been repainted thus. However, machines previously finished in AII(Al) aluminium were usually left in this condition and 'supplemented' with green and other colour applications. Thus, SB bombers were seen to carry wavy Green line camouflage over Aluminium, as did a few I-153s, but most machines wore a solid Green uppersurface over Aluminium unders. Some of these aircraft were further modified by more typical two-colour uppersurface schemes later in 1941.

An alternative single-colour scheme appeared, often seen at *Zavod* 1, where a dark green colour known only as Factory Green was used in lieu of AII Green for a number of fighter aircraft. During the GPW era, the MiG-3 was the usual recipient of this colour application, and in the pre-war era the I-152, early I-16s, and many Polikarpov OKB prototypes wore this finish. However, some very new evidence suggests

that this lacquer might have been in use elsewhere, perhaps at *Zavod* 21 (Gor'ki), even into 1942 on the I-16 programme; the matter continues to be a mystery. In fact, nothing further is known about this paint nor its properties; it is not known if this was an AII lacquer or another finish. New research suggests that this finish might be the 1930s aerolacquer AEh-5, which it closely resembles on black and white photography. The *Zavod* 1 diary specifically mentions the use of the colour on occasions, but it does not explain why it was used. However, photographs showing aircraft from *Zavod* 1 concurrently wearing AII Green and Factory Green sitting next to each other do exist, so we can be sure that it is not a misinterpretation of AII Green.

Fighters, especially newly-manufactured examples, were prone to wear the new and fashionable two-colour scheme consisting of AII Dark Green applied in a disruptive pattern over the basic Green/Blue finish. Many bombers also wore this colour pattern, the Pe-2, TB-7 (Pe-8), and Er-2 chiefly amongst these. A common alternative to this application, especially in 1941, was to apply AII Black over Green instead of Dark Green. This colour scheme is evident in photographs as early as 1937 (on TB-3s), but it seems to have gained momentum in use on certain Assault Aviation machines (I-152s, I-153s, Il-2s) during this time. It was very common on TB-3 and Er-2 bombers, and also on tactical and reconnaissance machines such as the U-2 (Po-2) and R-5, but not on SB bombers. Fighter aircraft began to wear the Black/Green livery increasingly during 1941, but photographs earlier than this often show a Dark Green/Green colour scheme.

For Tactical Aviation there was another, classic, two-colour scheme during this time consisting of AII Brown over the basic Green/Blue pattern. For some reason, this colour seems to be closely associated with certain aircraft and/or factories, and not with others. This camouflage appeared occasionally on the DB-3, and also on U-2s (Po-2s) during 1939, and it was applied to the pattern Li-2 pre-production machines. However, there is no photographic evidence that Brown was used for Fighter Aviation, nor Assault Aviation before 1943, except on the Su-2 (see below). There are pictures of a few SB 2M-103s (of the later Series, [perhaps 201 plus]) wearing this scheme in 1941 and also some Yak-2/-4 aircraft in addition to a number of early manufacture Pe-2s.

Three-colour schemes did indeed exist during this period, more even than the experimental work mentioned earlier. The Su-2 programme was perhaps foremost in this regard; a large number of photographs of this machine demonstrate three-colour camouflages (those that have two-colour schemes usually wear Black/Green or Brown/Green). The Su-2's scheme usually consisted of Dark Green and Brown applied over the standard Green/Blue template, though some also seem to include AII Light Brown, or sometimes Black, in place of Brown. Three-colour applications (using Black) can be seen on DB-3 bombers, Po-2s, and some R-5s, from the 1940-41 period, but they were not yet common.

One last point for this period revolves around the use of Army 4BO Green on VVS aircraft schemes. This green colour was the same as used on Army tanks, cannon, and other equipment, was 'greyer' when new than AII Green and more 'bronze' in colour than AMT-4 when aged, and featured a matt finish. It is also a very unstable colour, and it darkens considerably with age. The nature of the use of 4BO is hard to pin-point with any exactitude. Some reports claim that production was carried out during 1941 using 4BO Green, and this may be so, but the use of this colour seems somewhat ad-hoc. My assumption (and that is all it is) is that 4BO was probably used during the period of production dislocation, between the Autumn of 1941 and the Summer of 1942. I doubt that 4BO would have been used in lieu of AII Green where the latter was available, and the surviving physical evidence seems to confirm this idea (in that 4BO is unknown on surviving examples and is evident only on machines dating from early 1942, and that AII Green is common).

Naval Aviation

The VVS VMF, or Naval Air Forces, operated in a very independent and often eccentric manner with regard to aircraft colouration during the GPW. This distinctive tendency to do things in their own way was evident from the period even before the War and it blossomed considerably as the situation became more desperate.

For aircraft that were newly constructed and supplied directly to the VMF, the colour applications in 1940-1941 were fairly typical. A large number of Naval machines were finished in overall AEh-9 grey and AII Aluminium during the pre-war era, and their 1941 appearance reflects this fact (i.e. lots of solid-colour surfaces and meander-line applications). However, field application was the norm (apparently) in the VMF rather than the exception, and all manner of curious examples abound in the photographic record. Green lines over AEh-9 finish seem not to be uncommon, and the manner and extent of 'blotching' over Aluminium is extraordinary.

Three-colour camouflage on VMF DB-3s from even this early period appear to be the norm, and are distinct from Frontal Aviation examples. Many of these applications seem to include Black and possibly Brown over Green, but some pictures demonstrate colour shades that are still undetermined (and may include areas of exposed AII Aluminium and/or Wood *Aerolak*). However, as a group the most extraordinary of all VMF schemes appear on the various MBR flying boats in service at this time. Two-, three-, four- and even five-colour schemes can be seen on these machines, and the colours utilized appear to include Green, Wood *Aerolak* (Blue-Grey), exposed areas of AII(Al) or AEh-9, Black, and possibly another lighter green or similar colour. The only surviving example of such a scheme of which I am aware exists in the collection (fuselage only) of the *Voenno-Morskoy Musey* in St. Petersburg, which I examined in 1988. The colour pattern in this case was comprised of AII Green, Wood *Aerolak* and AII Black applied over a base coat of AEh-9, leaving some of the light grey areas exposed (four-colour scheme).

Interior Colour

The matter of VVS interior colouration has grown very much in complexity over the years. Some examples have provided confirmation of existing ideas, and yet others have challenged these same hypotheses. In reality, the matter is more complicated than my earlier studies[1] would tend to suggest, and also appears to be more related to the materials of construction in some cases – and not in others – than I had previously thought.

Some new evidence (largely the work of the *M-Hobby* authors), and recent examination of physical samples, has revealed that in the 1930s, many VVS aircraft were finished with an interior aviation lacquer named A-14 and there was a *nitrolak* version dubbed A-14F. A-14 lacquer was labelled 'steel', and it had a dark grey colour somewhat like AMT-12, with a hint of green.

The use of A-14 in the pre-war era is interesting, and telling. When in the late 1930s some factories began to paint their interiors – especially on aircraft with unfinished metal surfaces or painted with aluminium dope – with AII Aluminium lacquer, this practice must have been a left-over of previous procedures. The 1940 Camouflage Directive and the NKAP recommendations that accompanied it, must have thrown the matter into utter confusion at some factories. True, steel tubing, armour plate, and other metal structures were being coated with Metal Use Primer far back into the 1930s (or even before) and continued to be so; but when factories decided to paint the interior surfaces a uniform colour, the NKAP recommendations were a muddle.

During 1940 and 1941 the NKAP issued several new recommendations about the correct priming techniques for metal and wooden surfaces. Its specifications were somewhat voluminous, but can be summarized essentially in the following categories:

For Priming Metal Surfaces
ALG-1 mixed with 6 per cent aluminium powder, or
ALG-1 mixed with A-14 lacquer, or
A layer of ALG-1, ALG-5, and A-9 lacquer (each)

For Priming Wooden Surfaces
Two layers of AII Aluminium over DD-113 primer, or

Two layers of DD-118B primer, or
Three layers of DD-188A primer, or
Two layers of A-14, or
One layer of VIAM-B3, or
The factories may also use the existing lacquers AII Blue and AMT-7, or
A clear lacquer known as 17-A, or
Lacquer AS, or
On amphibious and other hydroplanes, AEh-9, AEh-10, or AEh-15 may be used.

Having been primed, the only specification which was given for the surface of the cockpit interior was a coat of A-14, as in the pre-war style. No doubt, it is this type of language that has led to the stereotypical colour citation for VVS aircraft over the years as 'grey'. Additionally, as usual, there seems to have been the typical NKAP 'language' about factories continuing their current practices in the face of shortages or other difficulties.

These myriad varnishes are also not explained by appearance. DD-113 and DD188A/B are simply described as 'grey', unless they are mixed with aluminium rather than zinc powder, in which case they are 'silvery-grey'. ALG-1 is said to be 'yellow' (a 'dusty' mustard colour), ALG-5 is described as 'green-grey', and A-9 is a dark blue lacquer. In fact, since their appearance is unknown, how they might look when mixed together or layered is also impossible to say. Based purely on a logical guess, the mixed colour for ALG-1 and A-14 would end up looking like FS(2)6559.

Obviously, to test for the occurrence of all of this vast number of practices on the surviving collection of GPW-era aircraft would be well beyond impossible. What can be said by way of examination of the surviving interior surfaces, is that these NKAP recommendations seemed to have been followed in the manner of all other similar specifications from this Ministry – to a degree, but not a large degree. When taking paint down to the surface on surviving GPW aircraft, one does run into a very thin layer of yellow primer which is quite translucent on some metal surfaces, usually dural or aluminium ones, and rarely on steel. This may well be ALG-1. Wooden surfaces, when painted, do wear grey primers of some kind, usually one with a cool, 'bluish' hue, but not always. Some are slightly warmer, and the interior of Kozhedub's La-7 at Monino appears to be A-14.

The bluish shade of grey seems to be a lacquer known only as Wood *Aerolak*, dating from the early 1940s. The only surviving container of this lacquer was manufactured at *Zavod 30*, and, unusually, has virtually nothing on the can's label except the factory, production lot number and the description '*Aerolak, Derevyanniy*' ('wood aerolacquer'). There is some speculation that Wood *Aerolak* might be the pre-war *aerolak* AE-10 (not to be confused with 'AEh' lacquers), simply re-packaged; its appearance on black and white film is similar. It might well be one of the DD primers, or some other unknown finish. But, even if these are different paints, the colours are similar, and distinguishing them would be tricky some 60 years on. It has also been noted that Wood *Aerolak* was widely used on aircraft *exteriors*, and thus may not be used internally to any great extent.

It is my theory that the various primers and lacquers for use on wood are probably hard to distinguish from each other. In a condition where one is examining a wooden surface that is 60-plus years old, it might not be possible to tell in some – or most – cases what finish is present. The colours for Wood *Aerolak* and A-14, for example, are different enough that they might be obvious, but for the other primers there is simply no good description of them upon which to make a determination. As a result, in this volume we will refer to these wood primers in aggregate as the Wood Finishes; the specific finish in question will have to rely on individual estimation or better future research.

As for metal surfaces, the record is slightly less murky. The finish ALG-1 has been mentioned, and seemed to have been used on dural and aluminium surfaces as a primer. There is no known case where this was the surface finish – another varnish always seems to have been applied. Another primer found commonly on steel and sometimes on dural and aluminium surfaces is an old industrial primer known only as Industrial Metal Use Primer (IMUP); the designation for this finish is unknown. IMUP was employed widely in Soviet manufacture; it was not an aviation use varnish. IMUP has been located on buses, ventilation grilles, steel piping, and also on the steel and dural sheet and tubular structures in aircraft. Hitherto, two variations of this finish have been mooted, but it is now thought that the 'duller' of the two is in fact ALG-5 *aerolak*.

In addition, the colour resulting from the ALG-1+A-14 multi-surface primer mixture may resemble FS(2)6559. This is tantalizingly close to the colour that is usually associated with ALG-5. From the above, it seems that this grey-green colour could also be a mixture of ALG-1+A-14. Or it could be both. This matter will have to await better research to be resolved in full.

These questions may seem overly esoteric, but in fact they are not. When the factories were manufacturing aircraft, the usual procedure seems to have been to leave much of the internal structure as it was delivered to the assembly line. This means that areas that had been primed upon completion (either as a sub-assembly from another plant, or from another station in the current factory) demonstrated the primer's colour inside the crew compartment. The surviving physical record seems to substantiate this idea.

Therefore, when aircraft constructed largely of metal were finished, the cockpit usually appeared in one of the metal primer colours. In many cases, this is the 'bright' industrial MUP, meaning a blue-green colour. It is important to recall here that many aviation factories either obtained a large amount of their sub-assembly work from sub-contractors (welded steel frames were commonly so acquired, as were steel armour plate and engine components), or were engaged in the manufacture of non-aviation products before the War. 'Industrial' MUP seems to have been ubiquitous. ALG-5 was also seen, especially after 1943. A-14 is very much less common in the surviving record; in fact, the only surface that I would immediately identify thus is the cockpit of Kozhedub's La-7. The reason for this seems logical – A-14 was probably employed as it had been pre-war, i.e. in a single, overall coat for the cockpit. Since this procedure was less common during wartime manufacture, it may have been seen less often as a surface finish. It is also possible that some surfaces identified hitherto as the Wood Finishes are also, in fact, A-14. There are also many cases where no priming of metal surfaces took place, this being especially notable on steel and armour pieces.

Surviving wooden surfaces in cockpits tend to be finished either not at all, or in one of the Wood Finishes. The precise shade of this grey colour is described above. When the wood areas were not painted, as such, they were given a sealant in the form of a layer of 17-A clear varnish. The interior surface of fabric areas also seems to have been given a coat of 17-A, or possibly of non-pigmented AII lacquer.

There were, of course, a number of unusual factory specific practices with regards to interior colouration. At *Zavod* 1, Moscow, AII Blue was sometimes used to coat the cockpit interior, probably in cases where it was then being used as a primer (as per the NKAP recommendation). *Zavod* 18 (and later *Zavod* 1, after evacuation) in Kubishev often finished the cockpit of an Il-2 with a uniform coat of IMUP, noting that most of the interior was built around a tub of steel armour, which was probably painted in this way to begin with. Factories such as *Zavod* 1 (during 1938 and 1941) and 166 (Omsk) also indulged in having uniform colour cockpits, and these were often completed in A-14 or one of the Wood Finishes. On the Yak-3 and La-7 programmes, ALG-5 was usually employed as an interior cockpit colour, despite the fact that these aircraft had largely wooden structures. It should also be noted that AII Aluminium was sometimes used as a cockpit interior finish in the immediate pre-war (and probably into the early war) period, regardless of the primers in use.

In the broadest possible terms, then, to clarify the matter, there were three main approaches at the factories to finishing aircraft interiors (cockpits and crew compartments):

1. *Do Nothing.* No repainting of any interior area was completed during production. If certain sub-assemblies (like armoured chairs, steel tubing, control sticks) were painted by a sub-contractor or a separate workshop, these were left as they were delivered. Wooden structural areas would have a 'natural' appearance, save for a thick glossy coat of 17-A clear sealant. Metal areas and panels would appear unpainted. The various control and instrument panels were almost always supplied to the line as components, so these would be painted as they were finished elsewhere. The result was something of a mixture of colours and textures. The armoured chair might be steel or IMUP, as would be the steel tube framing; the side panels might be wood or silver or blue-grey; the radio, pressurized tanks, control knobs and columns would be painted as per their usual manner; and so on.

2. *Finish the factory work.* All items built and added by the factory – namely, the structure itself – would be finished according to the practice then in use. These practices changed quite often, so the specific colour in question is a matter of examination, but the idea would be not to have unpainted surfaces (clear doped fabric was considered to be properly finished). Sub-assemblies or delivered components that were painted would be left 'as is'; those that were not, would be finished upon assembly. The factories themselves, regarded the appearance of unpainted surfaces as shabby, and described such work as 'unprofessional'. The idea was not to have all the surfaces *match*, but simply to be finished in some way. This was probably the manner in which the majority of Soviet aircraft were completed during 1941-45.

3. *Paint everything.* Some factories – or even some specific employees within a factory – felt that a uniform cockpit finish was desirable. No doubt this was a hold-over from pre-war manufacture of some kind, or sheer preference. In these cases, virtually everything was painted in a uniform colour after primary assembly. Instruments and other control apparatus were not painted, neither were various gas or fuel tanks (these were specifically to be left in their designated colour for recognition). There are even cases of painting over interior doped fabric surfaces, as well; everything was done to have a uniform finish. *Zavod* 1 in Moscow and *Zavod* 18 at Voronezh were famous for this type of procedure, as were specific employees at Novosibirsk, Omsk, Gor'ki, Ufa, and Ulan-Ude. Generally however, such uniform painting was the exception and not the rule during 1941-1945.

Internal Structures, Engines and Sundry Items

A brief word is in order on the colouration of internal structures, engines, and the like. I say 'brief' quite literally, for the NKAP specifications and recommendations on these paints could fill volumes on their own; it is endemically indicative of Soviet bureaucracy that minutiae such as engine block painting could occupy reams of documents.

Aircraft interiors were largely completed as per the above recommendations on primer usage. The interior of wooden wing structures, for example, were either not painted, or occasionally, with one of the Wood Finishes. Metal internal structures are similar, and when painted, seem to show such finishes as A-14. However, when painted, the interior surfaces of moveable metal panels (such as engine access panels, etc), appear to have been finished either by the sub-contractors or the factories in IMUP (or ALG-5); few appear to be dark in photographs as with the appearance of A-14.

Other components were finished typically as follows:

Compressed air (also Carbon Dioxide) tank – black (A-12 primer)

Control Stick – black (A-12 primer), IMUP, or unpainted

Engine block – unpainted, dark blue-grey (MV-2 primer), or black (MV-6 primer)

Engine heads, valve covers – black (MV-6 primer)

Fire extinguishers and other anti-fire gear – red (A-13 primer)

Fuel cell and tubing – yellow (DM, or A-6 primer)

Instrument panel – black, also sometimes coated with padded leather (brown to black)

Landing gear/oleo struts – as underside (AII Blue, AMT-7, A-28m)

Nitrogen tank – dark blue (A-9 primer), or white

Oil tank and lubrication system – brown (A-8)

Oxygen tank – medium blue (A-10 primer)

Propeller – black (AMT-6, AII Black, A-26m, AEh-11)

Radiator and coolant ducting – medium to dark green (A-7 primer)

Radio – black (A-12), or dark green (A-7, 4BO, or other)

Undercarriage wells – as underside (AII Blue, AMT-7, A-28m), or unpainted

Factory Post-Production Colours

After aircraft were completed on the production lines a few more details were still to be attended to at the plant before the machine was handed over to the military. When the aircraft was rolled out of the factory, it was usually finished with some identifying numeral. The type and meaning of the numerals, not to mention their placement, depended on each factory. At Novosibirsk, a number making up part of the aircraft's Production Number was applied to each machine on the fin/rudder in white (i.e. '24-36', which would indicate Series 24, example No.36). At Gor'ki, a tactical number (of the type used in the field) was applied on the fuselage, made up of the last two digits of the Production Number (i.e. the aircraft's number of that Series). *Zavoda* 1 and 18 often painted a small arbitrary number on the fin which had no further significance. On some occasions, some factories used three digit numbers – Tbilisi was famous for doing so.

The factories often applied the national markings to finished aircraft. These varied from plant to plant and also evolved over time, and a full listing of these markings can be found in the Appendix 'VVS National Markings'. The factories employed four major colours for their post-production markings: red, black, white and yellow. There are no known photographs showing colours other than these *at factories* applied to post-production markings. Red was used for the national insignia, and also for numerals, and was the colour of choice for the various maintenance stencils applied. White was the usual colour for numerals, and also was employed as a trim for numbers and for later national markings. Black was used similarly, but as a trim colour for the star insignia, it fell out of use during 1942-43. Yellow was the least common colour, but its use can be seen right through the war, both as a numeral colour and also as a trim for national markings until 1945. The specific colour to be used was decided at the time of application, and presumably was selected on the basis of easy visibility and the paints to hand.

However, once the finished aircraft left the factories, the usual VVS variations set in at once. Many field units applied their own tactical numbers (to identify aircraft), of their own design and colour. Usually the preferred location in the field was on the fuselage, and many of these numbers were quite large. Some units applied their own national insignia, or embellished the stars applied at the factories. Once again, the four basic colours of red, black, white, and yellow predominate. That said, odd colouration for these markings is certainly known. In some Northern units (Navy and Army), silver colours such as AII Aluminum are alleged to have been used for both numerals and trim colour, though there is currently no evidence for such practices. There is an example of an I-153 which appears to have a MUP coloured numeral (Biskup's '102'), and a well-known SB bomber from 1942 with its numeral rendered in 'negative' over the camouflage, so that the green area of the scheme has black numerals and the black area, green ones. Various other trim colours, (spinners, flashes, borders, rudders, stripes, etc.) were similarly completed.

In an effort to help identify the colours in question, many possibilities have been considered. Colour chips were dismissed early on, since the fidelity of colour reproduction is simply not accurate enough to date to produce the desired results, and the cost is equally prohibitive. Instead, several standard colour references exist, and these are thought to be a more ideal solution. One system, the Methuen Colour Index, is quite useful, but this is largely an extrapolation of the CMYK printing system, and thus certain bright blue colours are impossible to represent. However, the Munsell artists' colour system was determined to be outstandingly accurate, and this reference was chosen as the primary vehicle for colour identification.

The US Federal Standard (FS) is listed also as a general guide (and no more) for its ease of use and wide-spread popularity, but alas, this system is quite limited in the number of colours offered in the book (FS 595b is employed in this table). To supplement this system, I have also chosen to give colour references in the Pantone Colour Printing system. This system is virtually universal, is currently in use by graphics houses, printers, publishers, and other art-related enterprises, and is fairly accurate; many computer graphics software packages can utilize Pantone references, as well.

The following table lists each VVS paint, gives its nearest match in the FS colour system, the Pantone Colour system, the *Methuen Book of Colour*, and the specific colour match in Munsell reference. The value listed for the typical shade of the finish is the normal appearance of the lacquer on VVS aircraft in service. The values given for old and worn finishes are provided to describe the lacquer's appearance as it weathers and the surface deteriorates, and would be seen on examples demostrating considerable wear.

COLOUR TABLE

Finish	FS Colour Range	Pantone Equivalent	Methuen Colour Book	Munsell Colour Match
AII Blue	FS(1,2,3)5466 or slightly less brilliant; old and worn looks more like (3)5550 (the amount of glossy sheen decreasing rapidly with exposure for all AII lacquers)	There is no even close approximation in the Pantone system; the closest match in any colour printing system is ANPA 735-6 AdPro; as a last resort, examine CMYK 60/0/17/0	There is no even close approximation in the Methuen system; 23A6 has been suggested as approaching the correct hue, but no more than this	(H/V/C – Hue Value Chroma) 1.00B/8.0/12.0 (typical) 9.2B/8.6/5.5 (old and worn)
AII Green	FS(1,2,3)4258 when new; darkens when older and worn to FS(3)4151	Pantone 383 (new) Pantone 377 (old)	29C8 (new) 29D8 (old)	5.5GY/7.5/11 (factory fresh) 6.0GY/7.0/10.5 (typical appearance) 6.2GY/5.7/10.65 (old and worn)
Army 4B0 Green	FS(3)4257 (or slightly lighter) when new; darkens when older and worn to FS(3)4095	Pantone 366 (new) Pantone 371 (old)	28C6 (new) 28E7 (old)	8GY/7.0/7.5 (new) 9.5GY/5.5/6.0 (old)

Factory Green (*Zavod* 1)	FS(2)4058	Pantone 357	26F8	9.5GY/2.5/8
AII Dark Green	FS(1,2,3)4062 - 4066	Pantone 355 - 356	27D8	0.5G/4.0/10.0
AII Black	FS(1,2,3)7038	Pantone Black-7	23F2	4.75PB/1.0/0.75
AII Brown	FS(1,2,3)0111 when new; lightens when very old and worn to FS(3)0206	Pantone 174 (new) Pantone 695 (old)	10E8 (new) 10D4 (very old and worn)	9.5R/2.10/8.80 (typical) 7.0R/5.5/5.0 (very old and worn)
AII Light Brown	FS(1,2,3)0260 when new; darkens when older and worn to FS(3)0480	Pantone 129 (new) Pantone 612 (old)	There are no good colour matches in Methuen; 3B7 comes closest	7.0Y/8.0/10.5 (typical) 7.0Y/7.0/6.5 (old)
AII Aluminium	FS(1)7178	Pantone Cool Grey 2	3B1	2.25G/9.13/0.95
A-14/A-14F Steel	FS(2)6187	Pantone 424	28E4	5.0G/4.0/2.0
Wood *Aerolak*	FS(2)6320 - 6176	Pantone 5483	There are no good colour matches in Methuen; 23D4 is closest	5.0B/5.0/4.15
Metal Use Primer (Industrial) 'Bright'	FS(3)4664 - (3)5622 (there is no good match in the FS system for this colour; if white and grey is added to FS34350 it may be possible to mix the correct shade)	There are no good colour matches in Pantone; 3245 is closest	There are no good colour matches in Methuen; 25A3 is closest	10.0G/9.10/6.0
ALG-5 Metal Primer (or ALG-1 + A-14)	FS(3)4670 (there is no good match in the FS system for this colour)	Pantone 344	There are no good colour matches in Methuen; 26A3 is closest	3.0G/8.0/5.0
AMT-7 Blue	FS(2)5550	There is no close approximation in the Pantone system; the closest match in any colour printing system is ANPA 735-6 AdPro; as a last resort, examine CMYK 53/0/16/0	There are no good colour matches in Methuen; 24A4 is closest 8.54BG/8.83/5.47	
A-28m Blue	FS(3)5250	Pantone 313	23A7	6.0B/6.0/6.0
AMT-4 Green	FS(2)4151	Pantone 377	29E8	5.25GY/4.5/8.0
A-24m Green	FS(3)4098 - 4102	Pantone 371	29F8	5.5GY/3.5/8.0
AMT-6 Black	FS(2)7038	Pantone Black-7	23F2	4.75PB/1.0/0.75
A-26m Black	FS(3)7038	Pantone Black-7	23F2	4.75PB/1.0/0.75
AMT-1 Light Brown	FS(2)6306 -(3)0372	Pantone 402 - 403	2C2 (lightest) to 4D2 (darkest)	5.88Y/4.48/1.75 (dark shade) 10.0YR/6.39/.31 (light shade)
A-21m Brown	FS(3)6350 - 4201	Pantone 133	3E3 (typical)	Varied from 8.0Y/5.0/2.0 to 0.5GY/4.5/3.0
AMT-11 Grey-Blue	FS(2)6375 - 6300	Pantone 5435	21B3	9.45BG/6.7/1.92
A-33m Grey-Blue	FS(3)6463	Pantone Cool Grey 3	21C3	7.5BG/7.5/1.0
AMT-12 Dark Grey	FS(2)6187 - 6081	Pantone 431	25E4	9.0G/3.25/2.3
A-32m Dark Grey	FS(3)6251	Pantone 425	24F3	7.0G/4.05/1.0
Tractor Green (*Zavoda* 153, 18)	FS(2)4666	Pantone 359	28A7	0.25G/8.25/10.2
AEh-9 Lacquer	FS(2)5630	Pantone Cool Grey 1	17B1	2.25G/9.13/0.95
Medium Grey (AEh-10?)	FS(2,3)6493	Pantone 5645	There are no good colour matches in Methuen; 10C1 is closest, but too dark	9.0GY/7.1/1.2

1940-41 CAMOUFLAGE

Refinished Schemes

Original camouflage	*New camouflage*
AII Aluminium overall (option 1)	AII Green solid colour uppers over Aluminium undersurfaces AII
Aluminium overall (option 2)	AII Green or Dark Green applied in wavy lines or blotches over Aluminium, Aluminium undersurfaces
AII Aluminium overall (option 3)	AII Green and AII Black 2-colour disruptive scheme over Aluminium undersurfaces
AEh-9 Light Grey overall	Solid AII Green uppers over AII Blue undersurfaces

Factory-Applied Single-Colour Camouflage Schemes

AII Blue lowersurfaces, AII Green uppersurfaces
I-16
I-152/I-153
U-2 (Po-2)
DB-3/Il-4
Pe-2/Pe-3
Li-2
Yak-2/Yak-4
TB-3
Pe-8
MiG-1/MiG-3
SB

AII Blue lowersurfaces, Factory Green uppersurfaces
MiG-1/MiG-3 (*Zavod* 1 only)

Factory-Applied Two-Colour Camouflage Schemes

AII Blue lowersurfaces, AII Dark Green over AII Green uppersurfaces
I-16
I-153
Pe-2/Pe-3
Pe-8
Yak-1
Il-4

AII Blue lowersurfaces, AII Black over AII Green uppersurfaces
I-16
I-152/I-153
Pe-2/Pe-3
Pe-8
Yak-1
Yak-7
Il-2
Su-2
Yak-2/Yak-4
DB-3/Il-4
Li-2
U-2 (Po-2)
SB
R-5

AII Blue lowersurfaces, AII Brown over AII Green uppersurfaces
DB-3
U-2 (Po-2)
Su-2
SB
Pe-2

Factory-Applied Three-Colour Camouflage Schemes

AII Blue lowersurfaces, AII Brown and AII Dark Green over AII Green uppersurfaces
Su-2

AII Blue lowersurfaces, AII Black and AII Light Brown over AII Green uppersurfaces
U-2 (Po-2)
Su-2
R-5

The New System and the Old: AMT/Am and AII

In the Autumn of 1941 – with the German advance threatening and the dislocation of production taking shape – a decision was made to introduce a whole new range of aircraft finishes known as 'AMT', at this seemingly impossible moment. There were numerous reasons why such a new type of finish came to be utilised – AMT could be reliably applied without the need for any primer over all sorts of surfaces, even of mixed construction. Also, AMT varnish was very hardy, and had a very hard finished surface of satin sheen; indeed, it almost had a 'plastic' look about it. At the same time it was decided to make use of a second type of new finish, – Am – intended for use on all-metal structures. Logic and surviving evidence suggest that this paint was thinner and lighter than AMT, and thus represented a weight saving. It would then almost certainly be less robust and have inferior adhesion properties over wooden surfaces, and therefore was restricted for use over metal areas only.

Production of the new aerolacquers commenced in the Winter of 1941 at *Zavod* 36, which hitherto had manufactured only limited quantities of such paints. The conditions under which production began could not have been more difficult, but great insistence was made on the part of Moscow officials so that quantities of the new finishes appeared as soon as possible.

Sometime around the beginning of 1942, these new AMT paints began to be delivered to *Zavoda* 21 (Gor'ki), 153 (Novosibirsk), and 292 (Saratov), essentially for the LaGG and Yak fighter programmes. The first AMT finishes to be distributed were allegedly AMT-4 (green), AMT-6 (black) and AMT-7 (blue), corresponding to the officially recommended camouflage scheme of black over green in a two-colour disruptive application, at the same time that the older AII lacquers were being used increasingly for this colouration. Of course, in the photographic record AMT-4, -6, and -7 are difficult to distinguish from AII Green and Black. Certainly we see plenty of Black/Green schemes from this period, many of which can indeed be identified as AMT applications.

However, a significant problem arises when we consider AMT-7. The citation of 'FS 25190' by Orlov and Vakhlamov for the 1948 NKVD report's colour chip does not fit any of the surviving physical evidence. Of the thousands of photographs examined by the author, none shows a corresponding appearance to such a colour, nor anything close to it. In the photography of the period, all of the undersurface finishes are similar in appearance. With the revelation that AMT colours utilized the same pigments as the preceding AII paints, we can understand that AMT-7 in fact would have looked extremely similar to AII Blue when new, being perhaps just a shade 'greyer'. It is just possible, by way of explanation, that the colour chip presented in the NKVD booklet was in fact from a sample of A-28m, or some other post-war blue colour.

During a visit to Moscow, the author inspected samples of what was purported to be AMT-7 from the Monino U-2; it corresponds in this case to something more like FS 25183. This is the only blue colour that I have recovered from any VVS aircraft of the 1938-46 period that does not look like AII and AMT Blue, and certainly it was not the original colour on this aircraft. These samples do not have the characteristic AMT appearance and finish, or the foul odour of AMT varnishes when ground up or sanded. More interestingly still, this colour – 25190 – would be extremely obvious in the black and white photographic record on Soviet films. The standard Soviet Army K-16 and K-39 film would show the colour as somewhat dark, indeed darker than AMT-11; 16 mm film would look similar. Nowhere in the photographic record do we see anything like this. Indeed, this colour could also not replicate the curious behaviour of AII and AMT Blue on K-16 film, where they appear consistently, without exception, to be rather washed-out in appearance.

A shade corresponding to FS 25183 does appear on VVS aircraft beginning in 1947. This colour can be seen in photographs of La-9s and La-11s, on Tu-2s, Il-10s, various early jet prototypes and is ubiquitous on surviving aircraft from that time in various museums in Russia, Poland, Romania and elsewhere. This fact is all the more significant because these photographs were taken on K-16/39 film, just as were the majority of pictures taken during the GPW. Thus, one can make a direct comparison between the appearance of these lacquers on various aircraft, and therefore establish that these shades do not match – and therefore cannot be – the wartime colours. It is also the case that all of the other known Am lacquers are very dark in appearance. This fact is so consistent that I would submit that this is a defining characteristic of this type of *aerolak*, no doubt the result of its particular chemistry. FS 25183 conforms to this observation very well, and I am convinced that this dark colour is the genuine appearance of A-28m.

The colour chips as presented in the 1948 NKVD report examined by Orlov and Vahklamov are very suspect. Firstly, no colour chips are offered for any of the older AII lacquers, and as these were ubiquitous in production and use even after the War, the thoroughness of this report becomes immediately questionable. Secondly, the authors of the report clearly did not examine any of the relevant factory records. To have missed altogether the enormous body of language in these sources about the use of various colours, their odd and contradictory nomenclature, and the corresponding documentation in the records of the NKAP which attempted to sort out this muddle, would seem to be impossible. Thirdly, many of the colour chips in this NKVD report do not match to any satisfactory degree any authentic surviving example of aircraft lacquer of the GPW period. Out of more than 100 examples of this type, such an incongruity is especially damning.

I am compelled to submit that the 1948 NKVD report's colour chips are nothing more than a bureaucratic exercise. It seems to me to have been an after-the-fact attempt to make a report on the colouration of the GPW. Such an endeavour would have been quite impossible in 1948 for virtually anyone, let alone an NKVD functionary with no expertise in aviation finishes nor access to quantities of them. The colour chips presented in this report are probably all post-war chips of varnishes from the 1947-48 time frame, such as then existed, and a number of which are not even aviation use lacquers. It is interesting to note, for example, that the chips for the colours which were still in regular use at the time of the report seem to be authentic. The colour for A-24m Green is given as being in the range FS 34151–FS 34102, and that seems to be in satisfactory agreement with known examples. However, the chip for A-28m Blue, which had been replaced by the colour A-36m Grey by 1948, seems completely spurious. The range FS 34533 agrees with *no* evidence – whether photographic or physical – of any colour in use during the GPW. It does, however, match a shade (the number of which is unknown to this writer) being introduced by the Yakovlev OKB (which was described as "blue" in their documents) in 1948 for certain jet prototypes. The same case is true for the NKVD report's colour chip for AMT-7 Blue (also replaced in 1948 with AMT-16); again, it is impossibly out of agreement with any evidence, and certainly not correct.

1942-43

Frontal Aviation

Throughout 1942 and 1943, the use of Black over Green camouflage (whether AMT or AII) became increasingly common on VVS fighters, though by no means did it supplant the application of Dark Green over Green schemes. Possibly 4B0 was perhaps *occasionally* seen during 1942. Additionally, at *Zavod* 153 there was a chronic shortage of 'regulation' varnishes during late 1941 and into 1942, and as a result some Yak-7s and the reputedly last Novosibirsk LaGGs were completed wearing a green colour rescued from stocks of paint for tractors and farm equipment. At one point, a batch of this colour was also shipped to *Zavod* 18 at Kuybishev for temporary use on the Il-2 programme.

In Assault Aviation, the trend appeared to revolve around the equal use of AII Dark Green or Black (AII or AMT) over Green (again, probably both) throughout 1942, though in the Il-2 programme, the use of Black was more common overall. Beginning in 1943, there was a fundamental shift in Il-2 camouflage with the introduction of various three-colour schemes, these usually comprised of Black and Brown over Green. A three-colour Southern scheme (see below) was also employed during 1943 using Black and AMT-1 or AII Brown over AII Light Brown. By the second half of the year, these applications had blossomed into several colour variations, including AMT-1/Black/Green, Brown/Black/Green, Brown/AMT-1/Green, and later AMT-1/AMT-12/Green liveries. In addition, there were Light Brown/AMT-1/Green applications undertaken at unit level in the field (notably by the 194 ShAP). At *Zavoda* 1 and 18 it appears that most two-tone Il-2 schemes were completed in AII Brown over Green, and that these seem to be common through to the end of the War.

The continuing use of AII lacquers was also much in evidence with regard to bomber production. During 1942-43, Pe-2s were equally common in both Dark Green and Black over Green schemes, and on Il-4s the AII finishes appear to have predominated. U-2s (Po-2s) were commonly finished in various three-colour applications, though Black over Green schemes were very common as well. In 1943 a whole new series of three-colour schemes appeared on the Il-4, these usually comprising AMT-1 and a combination of AII Brown, AII Light Brown, or A-21m over Green. Pe-2s also began to wear new three-colour schemes during this period, AMT-1 and AMT-12 over Green seeming to predominate amongst these, though two-colour applications appear to be more common in the photographic record. Also at this time, bombers began to feature Black undersurfaces for nocturnal operations, though by no means were all aircraft so employed finished in this manner. Bomber aircraft of the Long Range Bomber units (the ADD) also began to wear black undersurfaces in increasing quantities, especially for night operations.

Regional Camouflage

A further innovation in VVS colouration occurred during 1942-43 with the use of specialized regional scheme applications completed at the aviation factories. There is indeed some documentary – and even anecdotal – evidence for the use of specialized schemes prior to this time, but there is no indication at any of the aviation factories that such schemes were applied there, and I suspect that any 'regionalization' in the colour schemes prior to 1942 was probably undertaken by units in the field of their own accord.

Typically, regional camouflage was applied at the factories for an entire Series, or part of a Series, often at the behest of the branch of the Army or Navy interested in the machines. For example, the Navy (VMF) might pass a request through the NKAP for a number of Il-2 aircraft with regionally appropriate camouflage. Should they wish, the Naval unit(s) involved could even specify (or perhaps request) what colours were to be used, or other details of the scheme. *Zavod* 18, for example, might then receive the request from the NKAP, but also with instructions to contact some representative from the requestor (the Navy) should any questions arise. When disputes or disagreements broke out between the factory and the requesting parties (which was often), the NKAP was usually called to resolve the problem by specifying a procedure.

South Front schemes are probably the best known of this type of camouflage, and aircraft were finished in small batches in two- and then three-colour schemes featuring a base application of AII Light Brown (or later A-21m), with disruptive patterns of AII Brown or Black over that. Some machines may even demonstrate 4B0 green or AMT-4 in these applications, but such cases are rare. One further difficulty is that only two aviation factories – *Zavod* 18 at Voronezh and *Zavod* 292 at Saratov – made detailed entries of regional colour applications in their factory records. Though a photograph may show a LaGG-3 fighter that is clearly finished in a regional scheme, the corresponding area of the factory's records (*Zavod* 21, for example) often say nothing of the matter at all. Therefore, one is then left to estimate the colours utilized by analysis, and in some photographs it is impossible to determine if the unusual colouration is a feature or film error.

There were specialized Naval schemes developed during this time for use on the Northern Fronts (on the Il-2 and Il-4, and possibly some Pe-2s), but their colours and execution are still unknown (however, given the surprising number of complaints at the factory level, they must have been extraordinary in appearance). Details of an 'Eastern Scheme' at *Zavod* 18 for aircraft operating in Mongolia and the Far East have begun to emerge at the time of writing and some photographs have also emerged showing this application, thought now to consist of AMT-1, AII Light Brown, and A-21m.

Winter Applications

Winter applications became common during 1942 and 1943, these making use of several finishes, especially at unit level. However, a white water-based paint known as MK-7 became available early in 1942, and this was the preferred Winter finish when available. MK-7 was thick and caused some drag penalty when applied, and was later replaced by modified versions of the finish: MK-7Sh (said to be similar to plaster), and MK-7F (with an alcohol-based solvent). MK-7 remained in use, though decreasingly, in Bomber and Transport Aviation, and to a lesser degree Assault Aviation, well beyond the end of 1943, but on fighter aircraft a new Winter finish was mooted in the late autumn of that year. From November and December 1943, fighter aircraft began to appear in a 'Winter' (see below) finish consisting of a single colour application of Wood Use *Aerolak* or AMT-11 on the uppersurface. At many factories, this application seems to have been made in lieu of the normal summer camouflage, though there are examples that clearly appear to have been applied in the field over the temperate finish as well.

Naval Aviation

The VMF continued to make use of specialized and very curious camouflage schemes during 1942-43. There is written evidence in a unit journal (1 MTAP) in the Voenno-Morskoy Musey (The Military Naval Museum) that in 1943 Il-4s wore a scheme of 'dark blue, green, and bronze'. Sadly, I have no idea what colour, exactly, these may correspond to (A-28m? AMT-4? ALG-1 mixture?), nor am I certain that the claim is correct. However, in the same collection there are photographs of darkish-looking Il-4s of 1 MTAP taken in 1943, whose colours cannot be identified to date. Further, anecdotal material exists stating that Pe-2s were seen to wear a scheme that was 'mostly black, with grey and dark blue colour above', and a scheme made up of 'mixtures of green'. I have, unfortunately, not yet located any photos that might show either of these alleged applications. However, it is also true that the majority of VMF aircraft continued to be allocated directly from the production factories, and most of these wore standard camouflage types. It also seems to be the rule that by and large, the more curious schemes appeared on bomber and reconnaissance aircraft, and not usually on fighters, whose schemes in 1942-43 look to be entirely normal.

Interior Colour

No significant changes appear to have been made during 1942-43 with regard to aircraft interior finish. Metal structures continued to wear Metal Use Primer, and wooden areas the Wood Finishes. The practice of over-coating the entire cockpit in Wood Finish grey during assembly seemed to remain common in Moscow, Gor'ki, and Omsk factories, but not elsewhere. Fabric surfaces were still mostly unpainted. However, the practice of leaving metal skinning unfinished on interior surfaces seemed to decrease in popularity, these often receiving a coat of Metal Use Primer.

1942-43 CAMOUFLAGE

Factory-Applied Single-Colour Camouflage Schemes

AII Blue lowersurfaces, AII Green uppersurfaces
Li-2

AII Blue lowersurfaces, Wood *Aerolak* uppersurfaces
LaGG-3
Yak-1
Yak-7
Yak-9

AMT-7 Blue lowersurfaces, AMT-11 uppersurfaces
LaGG-3
La-5
Yak-1

Factory Applied Two-Colour Camouflage Schemes

AII Blue lowersurfaces, AII Dark Green over AII Green uppersurfaces
Pe-2
Pe-8
Yak-1
Yak-7
Yak-9
Il-4
Il-2
Po-2 (U-2)
Er-2

AII Blue lowersurfaces, AII Black over AII Green uppersurfaces
Pe-2/Pe-3
Yak-1
Yak-7
Yak-9
Il-2
Il-4
Li-2
U-2 (Po-2)

AII Blue lowersurfaces, AII Brown over AII Green uppersurfaces
Il-2 (two-seaters only)

AII Blue lowersurfaces, AII Brown over AII Light Brown uppersurfaces
Yak-1 (South Front Regional scheme)
Yak-9 (South Front Regional scheme)
LaGG-3 (South Front Regional scheme)
Il-2 (South Front Regional scheme)

AII Blue lowersurfaces, AII Black over AII Light Brown uppersurfaces

LaGG-3 (South Front Regional scheme)
Yak-9 (South Front Regional scheme)
Il-2 (South Front Regional scheme)
Li-2 (South Front Regional scheme)
Yak-6 (South Front Regional scheme)

AMT-7 Blue lowersurfaces, AMT-6 Black over AMT-4 Green uppersurfaces

Pe-2/Pe-3
LaGG-3
La-5
Yak-1
Yak-7
Yak-9
Il-2
Il-4
Li-2

AMT-7 Blue lowersurfaces, AMT-12 Dark Grey over AMT-11 Grey-Blue uppersurfaces

La-5 (unconfirmed)
LaGG-3

Factory-Applied Three-Colour Camouflage Schemes

AII Blue lowersurfaces, AII Brown and AII Black over AII Green uppersurfaces

Il-2
Po-2 (U-2)

AII Blue lowersurfaces, AII Black and AII Light Brown over AII Green uppersurfaces

U-2 (Po-2)
Il-4
Pe-2

AII Blue lowersurfaces, AII Black and AMT-1 Brown over AII Green uppersurfaces

U-2 (Po-2)
Il-4
Pe-2

AII Blue lowersurfaces, AMT-1 Brown and AII Green over AII Light Brown uppersurfaces

U-2 (Po-2) (South Front Regional scheme)
Il-4 (South Front Regional scheme)
Pe-2 (South Front Regional scheme)

AII Blue lowersurfaces, AII Brown and AMT-12 Dark Grey over AII Green uppersurfaces

Il-2

AMT-7 Blue lowersurfaces, A-21m Brown and A-26m Black over A-24m Green uppersurfaces

Pe-2 (Naval North/Baltic Front Regional scheme)

AMT-7 Blue lowersurfaces, AMT-1 Brown and AMT-12 Dark Grey over AMT-4 Green uppersurfaces

Pe-2
Il-2
Il-4
Po-2 (U-2)
Yak-6

The NKAP Templates – 1943

Along with the introduction of new aerolacquers in 1943, NKAP and the UVVS also issued a series of specific camouflage recommendations. These recommendations – and they were *recommendations*, not requirements – actually took the form of a number of painting templates for most VVS aircraft, specifying not only the colours to be used, but the patterns as well. In this regard, the 1943 templates were unique – never before had a Government bureau issued such detailed documentation on aircraft finish, and during the GPW, rarely would they again (perhaps noting the response to the 1943 suggestions).

As with many such official recommendations, the factories' reaction to the new templates was uninspired. Some manufacture did, unquestionably, take place using these colour templates, but photographs of such schemes are rare. Many aspects of camouflage after 1943 did demonstrate, at least, elements of the NKAP patterns, especially in Fighter Aviation where the typical early 1944 schemes bore similarities to the NKAP templates (later, they deviated). It is also untrue, as has been asserted elsewhere, that these NKAP templates were an order, or an official policy on camouflage; this was not the case. Indeed, the NKAP documentation specifically states that the templates were 'suggestions' and 'proposals' (*predlozhenie*), intended for use as a standard scheme where desirable (one can easily imagine that conflicts between field units and the factories' painting teams had a lot to do with these NKAP recommendations). As usual, the typical NKAP phrases permitting individually appropriate procedures and regional camouflage are replete in these documents.

At least one pattern template was issued for each of the following types: Il-2, Il-10, Pe-2, Il-4, Po-2, Pe-8, Tu-2, Yak-6, Single-Seat 'Fighters' (Yak-1/-7/-9, La-5), Li-2 and Er-2. Others may exist. The specific camouflage template for each aircraft, and its employment, will be illustrated in their respective sections elsewhere in this book, but in general the templates all made use of the new AMT and Am lacquers, and for bombers/transports/attack machines they are all three-colour schemes. This latter fact is interesting in that it probably shows *Narkomaviaprom*'s approval – or, at least acknowledgement – of the tremendous rise in three-colour scheme development at the factories during 1942-1943. This behaviour reveals the usual relationship between the NKAP and the aviation factories, in that the NKAP not only issued specifications, but also codified many of the factories' current practices into their own documentation.

1944-45

Frontal Aviation

The year 1944 seems to have been pivotal for VVS aircraft colouration. Throughout 1943, VIAM and the UVVS had been mooting a new series of colour schemes for aircraft, paying particular attention to Fighter Aviation. It does not appear, both from the written and photographic record, that any significant headway was made before the end of the year in this regard, but during November and December 1943. Lavochkin and Yakovlev fighters began to roll off the lines at *Zavoda* 21, 153 and 292 in a new scheme of solid colour uppersurfaces covered in Wood *Aerolak* or AMT-11. This blue-grey (or Grey-Blue) finish was a significant departure from the standard appliqué coat of MK-7 white, and it also seems to have been adopted by various units in the field at roughly the same time.

Interestingly, there is no written evidence that this application was considered to be a Winter finish, as such. Indeed, as a seasonal finish, it might be more accurate to describe this scheme as a 'wintertime' application. The use of grey uppersurfaces does not seem logical in snow conditions, but then again, snow does not lie on the ground all over Russia 100 per cent of the time during winter months, and also a white aircraft is woefully visible in mid-air. It may be that the VVS, too, rejected the use of MK-7 finishes for Fighter Aviation because of the significant drag and weight penalties of this paint; in this case, an alternative would have to be found. Additionally, it may have been felt that if white was not used, then a single-colour application was better than a two-colour disruptive scheme under Winter conditions. Whatever the reasoning, the practice seemed to have been consistently applied over both winters (interestingly, several modern camouflage experts have insisted that a colour like AMT-11 – next to white – would have been an excellent Winter livery).

In the Summer and Autumn of 1943, orders were issued for manufacture of new AMT varnishes at *Zavod* 36: AMT-11 medium grey-blue, and AMT-12 dark grey, plus their metal-surface equivalents A-33m and A-32m. This may have meant that the new single-colour scheme had been developed about this time, and that implementation of the new application was simply carried out with the closest colour match at hand, but later events seem to cloud this issue. There is evidence that even before the winter moved towards the beginning of 1944, some La-5s (perhaps not all, nor even most) at *Zavod* 21, were being finished with one of the new AMT paints in lieu of Wood Use *Aerolak*, thus giving an AMT-11 single-colour uppersurface. However, photographs from neither Novosibirsk nor Saratov tend to show this condition in early 1944.

As the winter ended and temperate camouflage was again applied to fighter aircraft (late March 1944), a new and thoroughly classic colour scheme emerged on Soviet fighters consisting of two grey colours in a disruptive application over blue undersurfaces. The precise nature of these colour applications remains a matter of protracted debate. The confusion arises from the all-too-familiar Soviet practice during the GPW of employing new finishes at the same time as, or even alongside, the older ones. This was absolutely the case during 1943 and 1944. The first examples of the new grey/grey scheme were created by applying a medium grey paint (which is now thought to be the pre-war lacquer, AEh-8) over the single-colour finish of Wood *Aerolak*, seemingly in reverse order from the logical manner. This application can be seen very clearly in many photographs, and always when looking at these non-AMT colours one sees the lighter shade applied over the darker. The identity of this medium grey varnish is unknown; it has been suggested that it may be AEh-8 lacquer, and on balance this seems likely. What does seem certain, though, is that this colour is the very same shade that is routinely found on some Aeroflot and other civilian aircraft during this time period; some flying boats seem to wear it also. The samples of this finish that I obtained appear to have very similar characteristics to AEh lacquer, but I consider the matter to remain unresolved at the time of writing.

Vakhlamov and Orlov discovered that the official recommendation at this time was to make use of the older varnishes until the new AMT finishes became available. This is extremely interesting, in that it provides very strong clues about the distribution and availability of earlier varnishes. Even at the end 1943, Wood *Aerolak* and the Medium Grey finish must have been universally available and distributed widely; a fact, of course, which is powerfully supported by the surviving physical and photographic evidence. However, at *Zavod* 21 (Gor'ki) and *Zavod* 31 (Tbilisi), the new AMT finishes seem to have been adopted almost at once; it is exceedingly difficult (if not impossible) to locate any photograph of an La-5FN (i.e. newly manufactured) in late 1943-early 1944 wearing a scheme corresponding to the earlier finishes, nor demonstrating the lighter grey over darker application. This fact may have much underlying logic to it, as it seems that production at Gor'ki was always heavily involved in the introduction of AMT finishes (i.e. the experimental 3-colour LaGG schemes from *Zavod* 21 in 1942). The AMT version of the new grey/grey camouflage consisted of a base coat of AMT-11 with AMT-12 applied in a disruptive pattern over that. *Zavod* 292 at Saratov seemed to follow suit shortly thereafter; the Yak-1 and Yak-3 programmes in 1944 usually demonstrate AMT type colour schemes. However, at *Zavod* 153 – the bothersome conglomerate at Novosibirsk – the older non-AMT finishes seemed to be not uncommon. One can, for example, locate examples of Yak-9s manufactured at *Zavod* 153 even in 1944 that feature Wood *Aerolak* and the unidentified medium grey colour. Yak-9 production at Omsk, meanwhile, appears to have been conducted

exclusively with AMT finishes. This is not to say, though, that Novosibirsk made exclusive use of non-AMT paints; wartime photography does not support this interpretation at all, and the exact proportion of each practice at *Zavod* 153 is simply not known.

All of this brings to the fore one of the last enduring mysteries of these new AMT colours – when were they first employed? It is a fair guess to assume that Gor'ki or Tbilisi would have been the first factories to receive and make use of the AMT grey paints. This means that the La-5 or LaGG-3 programmes would have been the recipient of these colours, and the search has focused on these aircraft. There are suspicious and controversial photographs of grey/grey La-5Fs dating from the latter half of 1943 that *may* show an AMT-11/-12 application. However, none of these pictures are very clear, and are of poor quality. On the other hand, there are no good views of La-5s wearing the older grey lacquers in a two-colour scheme, and so if the colours in the pictures are indeed grey, it must be assumed that they are AMT paints. Also, AMT-11/-12 LaGG-3 schemes are certainly known, and as production of this aircraft finished with the end of the year, we know that this scheme must have been applied during 1943. Even so, on the Yak programme at Saratov there are many factory production pictures dating from the latter half of 1943, and almost all of these show Black/Green painted aircraft on the lines (albeit, in AMT colours). Similarly, the Yak-7 seems to have worn the older grey paints quite commonly, as did some Yak-9Ts, both products of Novosibirsk.

When AMT lacquers were first mooted in 1941, it took the production and supply apparatus about six to nine months to widely distribute the first AMT finishes (AMT-4/-6/-7). During this time there were early applications of the colour at *Zavod* 21 (Gor'ki), but elsewhere AII finishes seemed to be the standard for some months more. Even then, after these AMT paints were widely available, the older AII lacquers were not discarded, but rather remained in widespread use alongside their newer counterparts. My deep suspicion is that this is analogous to the situation at the end of 1943. As such, it is possible – or perhaps even probable noting the Factory's usual behaviour – that Gor'ki (or even Tbilisi) may well have produced machines wearing AMT paints as early as the late summer of that year; but the photographic evidence seems to show that most aircraft did not receive these AMT greys until sometime during 1944.

During the Winter of 1944-45, single-seat fighters were finished according to the single-colour grey scheme, though now making use of the new AMT colours. AMT-11 is thought to have been more common (not standard) for this purpose, but the surviving photography and physical evidence demonstrates many AMT-12 covered examples (especially Yak-3s and La-7s), as well.

One last interesting fact involves the appearance of fighters at the front in 1945. Aircraft that were manufactured after March appear to be finished in the standard AMT-11/-12 temperate livery, but most fighters in service in the field at this time almost never seem to be so (at least, those that received a single-colour finish), and retained their single-colour application well into 1945-46. It is probable that this practice had everything to with the hubbub surrounding the Victory and its related matters, but it is also intriguing to ponder the effect that this may have had on later VVS fighter finish; in 1947-48 the standard camouflage became a solid application of A-36m grey colour overall.

Bomber Aviation continued to develop the use of three-colour schemes during 1944-45, but this is not to say that two-colour applications disappeared from the scene altogether. In fact, the Pe-2 programme developed little in the way of camouflage during this period; schemes executed in 1945 differed little from those of 1943 – either in pattern application or colour – save for an apparent reduction in the use of Black (Dark Green over Green AII schemes were still common in 1945). Il-4s were much more common in the metal use Am finishes (such as A-24m, A-26m, and A-21m) in 1944, but AMT-1 was still enthusiastically employed in this programme as well. Other bombers and transport/liaison aircraft of smaller manufacture series (such as the Li-2 and Er-2) seem to appear commonly in older camouflage colours, Black over Green predominating. Po-2s sported a host of colour schemes during 1944-45, many of these three-colour types, but again the use of Black/Green applications is not uncommon.

In Assault Aviation – essentially the Il-2 and Il-10 – some curious developments were seen during the latter war period. Il-2s were still very common in two-colour AII Brown and Green schemes, but increasingly so in three-colour camouflages. In these three-colour Il-2 applications it is alleged that AMT-11 was used as a component colour. My only response to this hypothesis is that there is simply no existing evidence at all that this is true; neither the photographic, written, nor physical evidence supports the claim. However, much evidence has emerged for the use of AMT-12 in three-colour schemes. Indeed, it is possible – even probable – that some schemes previously identified with AII Brown/AMT-1/Green colours were in fact completed with AMT-12 and AMT-1 over AMT-4. Black, however, seems not to have been typically used with AMT-12; or, at least, examples of this type of finish in the *surviving* record are non-existent.

Even more curious, though, are the camouflage finishes of the Il-10 programme. Visitors to the Russian Air Force Museum at Monino are usually baffled by the bizarre green mottled scheme to be found on the collection's Il-10. Remarkably, and utterly unexpectedly, surface penetration testing proved that not only was the paint scheme indeed the original and unretouched finish, but that it was applied in AII Dark Green over AII Green. Revisiting the photographic record, one is forced to conclude that prejudice has clouded modern interpretative efforts in this regard; there are plenty of perfectly clear surviving photographs of this odd scheme (see, for example, p.58-59 in *Soviet Combat Aircraft*, Vol.2) on Il-10s from 1945 (and interestingly on no other aircraft). It is also true as well, that some Il-10s do seem to wear a solid application of a dark green colour, most probably A-24m. The origination and extent of employment of this mottled application is completely unknown, as are the details of the concurrent use of A-24m.

Winter and regional schemes continued in use during 1944-45, but with significantly reduced frequency. Bombers and assault machines still received a coat of white MK-7 finish during periods of snow in certain cases, but apparently they did not wear the application during the entire season, and many partially removed white applications can be seen. South Front colour schemes were still applied at some factories upon request (at Kuibishev in particular), but most photographs show only a Black over Light Brown livery in these cases, or perhaps AMT-1 instead of Black. The surviving record indicates that standard three-colour camouflage replaced many hitherto regional applications in most units by 1944.

Naval Aviation

The camouflage practices of the VVS VMF during 1944-45 are unfortunately not particularly well known. The available photographic record seems to show schemes that correspond to 'typical' VVS patterns and colours, and indeed this is probably true in most cases. However, it is difficult to believe that the VMF discontinued its use of individualistic and curious Naval schemes, despite the notable lack of discussion of these at factory level. One interesting development during this period, however, seems to be a larger than usual number of Il-4s in VMF service with Black undersurfaces, as was seen earlier on ADD machines. Some of these Il-4s might even have been painted at the factory, and a special matt black finish called MK-6 *noch'* ('night') was issued in small quantities for this purpose (the ADD is said to have used it as well). It is a matter of speculation that perhaps the Navy was engaged in more frequent nocturnal operations in 1944-45 in general – it seems that this was indeed true for the Il-4 – or if the colouration represented another shift in VMF colour choices? Continued investigation of this matter is certainly required.

Interior Colour

The various practices for interior colour finish remained relatively unchanged through to the end of the war, but starting in 1944, some evidence exists to suggest certain changes in Fighter Aviation production. Many surviving fighter aircraft from 1944-45 have had their interiors repainted in grey. In most cases, collecting samples of these interiors reveals that the finish is in fact A-36m Grey. Such examples can be dismissed out of hand as having been 'refurbished' after the War; the interiors would have appeared during the GPW in the standard fashion (i.e. Wood Finishes, Metal Use Primer, clear dope, A-14, etc.).

Factory-Applied Single-Colour Camouflage Schemes

AMT-7 Blue lowersurfaces, A-24m Green uppersurfaces
Il-10

AMT-7 Blue lowersurfaces, AMT-4 Green uppersurfaces
Tu-2
Li-2

AMT-7 Blue lowersurfaces, AMT-11 Grey-Blue uppersurfaces
LaGG-3
La-5
La-7
Yak-1
Yak-7
Yak-9
Yak-3

AMT-7 Blue lowersurfaces, AMT-12 Dark Grey uppersurfaces
La-7
Yak-1
Yak-3

AII Blue lowersurfaces, Wood *Aerolak* uppersurfaces
Yak-7
Yak-9

Factory-Applied Two-Colour Camouflage Schemes

AII Blue lowersurfaces, AII Dark Green over AII Green uppersurfaces
Pe-2
Pe-8
Il-4
Il-10
Po-2 (U-2)
Er-2

AMT-7 Blue lowersurfaces, AMT-6 Black over AMT-4 Green uppersurfaces
Pe-2
Li-2
U-2 (Po-2)

AII Blue lowersurfaces, AII Brown over AII Green uppersurfaces
Il-2

AII Blue lowersurfaces, AII Brown over AII Light Brown uppersurfaces
Yak-1 (South Front Regional scheme)
Yak-9 (South Front Regional scheme)
Il-2 (South Front Regional scheme)

AII Blue lowersurfaces, AII Black over AII Light Brown uppersurfaces
LaGG-3 (South Front Regional scheme)
Yak-9 (South Front Regional scheme)

AII Blue lowersurfaces, Medium Grey over Wood *Aerolak* uppersurfaces

Yak-7
Yak-9

AMT-7 Blue lowersurfaces, AMT-6 Black over AMT-4 Green uppersurfaces

Il-4
Li-2

AMT-7 Blue lowersurfaces, AMT-12 Dark Grey over AMT-11 Grey-Blue uppersurfaces

LaGG-3
La-5
La-7
Yak-1
Yak-7
Yak-9
Yak-3

Factory-Applied Three-Colour Camouflage Schemes

AII Blue lowersurfaces, AII Black and AII Light Brown over AII Green uppersurfaces

U-2 (Po-2)
Il-4

AII Blue lowersurfaces, AII Black and AMT-1 Brown over AII Green uppersurfaces

U-2 (Po-2)
Il-4

AII Blue lowersurfaces, AII Brown and AMT-12 Dark Grey over AII Green uppersurfaces

Il-2

AII Blue lowersurfaces, AII Brown and AII Black over AII Green uppersurfaces

Il-2

AII Blue lowersurfaces, AMT-1 Brown and AII Green over AII Light Brown uppersurfaces

U-2 (Po-2) (South Front Regional scheme)
Il-4 (South Front Regional scheme)
Pe-2 (South Front Regional scheme)

AMT-7 Blue lowersurfaces, AMT-1 Brown and AMT-12 Dark Grey over AMT-4 Green uppersurfaces

Pe-2
Il-2
Il-4
Po-2 (U-2)
Yak-6
Tu-2

The 'Last Minute' Regulation

As if to complete its remarkably annoying habit of clouding the VVS colour picture to the maximum possible extent, the NKAP issued a new set of recommendations at the end of 1944 (incorporated in part in order No. 5590/0207) for Air Force camouflage. In these 'last minute' recommendations, the NKAP sought to simplify matters by suggesting that virtually all VVS aircraft should be finished in the 1944-45 standard fighter colours of AMT-12 over AMT-11. Specifically, the following types were mentioned for this procedure: Il-2, Il-10, Pe-2, Tu-2, Il-4, Pe-8, Li-2, Po-2, UT-2, Yak-6.

The effect of these recommendations was minuscule, if it existed at all. There is much doubt as to whether these recommendations were circulated to any of the aviation factories; no factory records give mention of them (which would be almost unprecedented), and there is no current evidence that these instructions were ever distributed. Certainly, the photographic record does not demonstrate that these procedures were ever put into effect. Indeed, the production records for *Zavod* 18, Kuibishev, clearly show that no quantities of AMT-11 lacquer were ever ordered, nor received by the factory, and that AMT-12 was ordered in small quantities only (mainly for the Il-2 programme). A series of well-known photographs were taken at *Zavod* 22, manufacturer of the Pe-2 and Pe-8, on 1 May 1945 (a mere week before the Victory), which show all of the machines on the huge lines being finished in a three-colour pattern, possibly one of the 1943 NKAP templates, or the older two-green AII colouration. No two-tone grey examples can be seen.

In short, there are simply no photographs to show that these recommendations were ever put into use. There is a series of pictures taken of an Er-2 manufactured in 1945 that is said to be finished in this way (from examination, it seems possible), and just *possibly* one single Tu-2 (this photograph is very poor in quality and unclear), but in the main they do not exist. The record on the finish of Il-2s, Il-10s, Po-2s, Pe-2s, and Il-4s in particular is quite clear, and a grey/grey 'fighter' type scheme was never used on these programmes. If these 'last minute' recommendations ever did circulate to the aviation factories, they must have gone little further than the waste basket.

Summary

The accumulation of large numbers of physical paint samples over recent years has contributed greatly to unravelling the complexities of wartime VVS colouration. This work, combined with the excellent written documentation unearthed in *M-Hobby*, has finally cast light on a topic which for too long has been shrouded in mystery.

After a quantitative re-examination of my own notes and findings on VVS colouration, I discovered that the early War period AII Green/Dark Green scheme was not as common as I had thought, and that the Black/Green livery was far more typical. It is possible that my perception was 'steered' by the curiously large number of surviving examples featuring Green/Green schemes, but the photographic and written record is clear, and perhaps this was after all only a prejudice on my part. Still, it is useful to note that the use of this camouflage persisted right through the entire War.

The matter of the specifics of paint and varnish production at both *Zavoda* 30 and 36 remains to be fully explained. It would be very useful to obtain a comprehensive understanding of how and where the supply chains operated from either facility, and what varnishes, exactly, were produced and distributed from each. For example, Vakhlamov and Orlov discovered written requests from several factories throughout the War to continue using earlier AII varnishes (this is significant, in that the factories rarely asked for official permission to do anything of such specific detail, except in the case where the matter was either controversial, or if they hoped to codify what they were doing currently as the new 'policy').

Certainly the supply of the older paints was widespread, because VIAM, the NKAP, and the UVVS kept recommending their use in cases where AMT/Am stocks were not available. It is also known that production making use of AII finishes continued to the end of the war (and after); the Pe-2, Il-2 and Il-10 programmes being examples of this. There are many clues as to how this worked, but the full 'logic' of the operation is still unknown, and only documentation of this type is likely to provide these answers.

Material *has* come to light on this point. Some clues have recently surfaced which shed new light on some of the questions regarding Soviet aerolacquer manufacture during the GPW. For example, we know from a document issued by the NKAP that *Zavod* 30, in Moscow, stopped manufacturing AII Aluminium finish during 1940. However, at the end of the War, in 1945, a similar document comments upon the manufacture of this finish at *Zavod* 36 for some years previously. *Was it then the case that varnish and lacquer production was slowly phased out in Moscow and transferred to* Zavod *36?* The answer is, alas, at the time of writing, unknown. However, the clue here is that in 1946 – i.e. *after* the war – *Zavod* 36 reported that it manufactured 430.3 tons of AII aerolacquer. This compares to 1,243.5 tons of AMT lacquer in 1945, and 927.1 tons in 1946. As can be seen, *very* substantial quantities of the 'old' lacquer were still being produced, even as late as 1945-46.

Some researchers have raised complaints thus far about the material presented by Vakhlamov and Orlov, in that their language on the matter of non-AMT/Am paint usage is "slippery" and "nebulous". That may or may not be – such a claim seems subjective to me. My own feeling is that these authors have chosen to publish the documentary evidence as it is, without interpretation. This is both academically satisfactory and interesting historically, in that it provides some perspective on the relevance of wartime-era documentation to the actual practices then underway. Any historian working in the field of Soviet wartime production will know that most of the respective practices, solutions and improvisations of entities at factory or unit level were never documented in an official capacity at all; in wartime, this should be expected. On the other hand, it is true that some factory personnel would have sought to follow the official guidelines as closely as possible. Thus, one sees an interesting dichotomy arise in which some factories operate with very great independence, while others try to embody in production the exact phraseology of each official specification. *Zavoda* 153 (Novosibirsk) and 166 (Omsk) are possibly classic examples of both types of behaviour, but the actual history of each factory is much more complicated than such a generalization.

The material in the 1948 NKVD report does not offer anything significant on the use of non-AMT/Am varnishes, and documents their employment only indirectly or through general statements. As a result, Vakhlamov and Orlov's work does not offer anything significant on the use of non-AMT/Am varnishes during 1941-45, either. The familiarity of these practices as contained in the 1948 NKVD report – and the continuing and wide-spread use of AII lacquers during the GPW – is not clear to these authors, and they have written nothing illuminating on this point. On the other hand, it may be that Vakhlamov and Orlov believe that their superb work on the pre-war use of AII lacquers speaks for itself, and that the reader should be expected (or encouraged) to extrapolate the resulting meaning on his own.

It is true, furthermore, that the 1948 NKVD report is not especially helpful in establishing wartime camouflage schemes. The report offers some photographs of aircraft demonstrating the small number of pattern applications, which are discussed in the report itself. However, I have worked personally within the archival collections from which these photographs were taken. To describe the examples offered in the report "representative" is impossible. It is clear that the authors of this report searched diligently for photographs giving examples of the patterns which they had in mind, and that they simultaneously ignored the *vast* majority of prints which either failed to show these few schemes, or contradicted them altogether. Quite literally, the authors carefully selected some twelve or so photographs from some three or four *thousand*. Moreover, upon investigation, many of the views are revealed to have been of prototype aircraft, often photographed at one of the aviation factories. Such views are misleading, in that the report claims in many cases that these pictures were of operational units in the field; this was demonstrably not the case.

Notes on Colour, Chips, and Techniques

First, a word of caution: the US Federal Standard (FS) system is far too limited in scope to describe accurately complex colours in use with the Red Army during the GPW. The listed numbers should be viewed only as my personal attempt to explain the appearance of the original colours, which naturally would have varied slightly from batch to batch, and sometimes even more than that. Second, colours on small chip samples can appear rather different – usually darker – from a colour when applied to a large, three dimensional object. This occurrence has to do with the simple facts of light reflection, ambient value, and other factors, and should not deceive the modeller or historian. Moreover, the original paint samples left to us are over 50 years old, and it can take an act of analytical chemistry to understand how they might have appeared when originally applied.

Hitherto, it was the general misconception that no sense of order could be ascribed to the painting and camouflage of Soviet aircraft during the GPW; that the enormity of Soviet improvisation in the factories obviated any attempt at normality. Certainly, with respect to improvisation and fluid factory conditions, there was much; however, the supply and availability of paints and varnishes was indeed finite, and their use did have some rules and guidance. In fact, a whole range of technical specifications grew up around the employment of different varnishes, and there were even some officially recommended camouflage scheme pattern applications, as well. And, despite the fact that individual factories often developed patterns and colour schemes of their own, and quite obviously demonstrated very significant license and discretion in matters of aircraft camouflage, the surviving record indicates that many of the varnish employment rules were, in fact, adhered to in the main.

All paints and varnishes in use in all Soviet State Aviation Factories were produced at a limited number of factories, *Zavod* 30 (Moscow) and *Zavod* 36 predominating. Production of aerolacquers had begun in 1925 at *Zavod* 30 (then GAZ 16 *Aerolak*), and continued until 1946 or 1947, at least. *Zavod* 36 began to manufacture aviation paints sometime before 1937, and quickly assumed a leading role with VIAM and the NII VVS in the development of new aerolacquers. Large scale manufacture of AII finishes seems to have taken place before the War, but the decision to produce the new AMT lacquers here in 1941 really launched the period of mass production for this facility.

There were a number of exceptions to the standard supply practice, the largest occurring at *Zavod* 153, Novosibirsk. This gigantic complex became an arm of State Production unto itself, partially due to its size, and also, in part, due to its extreme isolation. In 1941-42, Factory 153 found itself at the end of a very tenuous supply line, and varnishes did not always rate in the top categories of necessity when packing supply trains in Moscow. As a result, during 1942 manufacture was forced to improvise, and being entirely pragmatic the plant made do with what was at hand. Amongst the bewildering number of items produced at Novosibirsk prior to the outbreak of War were tractors, carts, and grain carriages. All of these items had been finished with a cheerfully bright green paint, which was no longer in production, but of which there were still enormous stocks at hand. Also on hand were large quantities of black paint, and so *Zavod* 153 took to producing its own camouflage finish for aircraft that were manufactured from late 1941 and throughout 1942, consisting of Black applied over Light Green.

The second exception occurred in the field. It was not unknown for certain pilots, or even certain units, to apply camouflage patterns of their own design. Presumably, the majority of these inventions were executed using widely available paints, i.e. the standard types. Wartime photography confirms this theory, and even in the oddest cases the colours used can, in fact, usually be identified. However, there are exceptions, and in particular one sees them when examining the aircraft of the VVS VMF (Naval Aviation). It is not impossible that some types of custom paint colours could have been used in some cases, and there are VMF aircraft that do truly defy any colour analysis. It should be stressed however, that such cases – if true – were the exception, and never represented any kind of consistent practice or scheme.

Lastly, there were colour applications that seemed to be associated with certain factories or even aircraft programmes. *Zavod* 1 in Moscow, for example, made use of an unknown paint of forest green colour (AEh-5?) in its solid colour camouflage schemes during 1939-1941. No explanation for this behaviour has ever been given. Likewise, at Kuybishev the various Ilyushin OKB programmes (Il-2 and Il-4, primarily) made enthusiastic use of the older AII Brown finish, throughout the war. This is odd, in that most other factories seemed not to use the colour, except perhaps for *Zavod* 22, and in Il-2 production at *Zavod* 30 (Moscow) where this paint was manufactured.

A note on black and white photographic film is in order. During the GPW, the Soviets made use of a large number of film types. Of the commonly identified types, the State magazines and newspapers seemed to use out of preference, several film types widely available to commercial customers. These films are often overly sensitive to red light, and critically sensitive to exposure, meaning that in most cases the pictures taken with them are very hard indeed to analyze usefully. The standard film issued to Soviet military photographic personnel was a type of monochrome film designated K-16 and K-39. These two films seem to have identical properties, save for the fact that rolls of K-16 have 22 shots, while those of K-39 usually have 27 (the nomenclature 'K' has widely been assumed to mean '*Kamera*', but I recently examined some film from the 1930's manufactured by Kodak with similar properties; interestingly, the rolls came in 22 and 27 exposure varieties). K-16/39 film gives a fine image, one that is quite modern in appearance. The one odd characteristic of these films is their sensitivity to light blue colours; these often appear to be washed out. Darker blue colours, however, do not demonstrate this effect, and darker green colours (such as a fir tree) appear to be rather dark.

The investigation of black and white photography can reveal much, especially when using the power of modern personal computers and advanced software. However, the proper use of these tools for such analysis is upon the photographic *negatives*. All too often I have discovered that modern computers can digitally manipulate prints of photographs to such a degree, and with such subtle variance, that one simply cannot extract the original information out of the picture's current appearance. This fact has been proven again and again during the last five years.

However, even 'amateur' investigation can offer revelations. Different colours rendered in greyscale (black and white) tend to have different and unique appearances, even to the naked eye. Obviously, computers, analytical software, spectrographic machines, and other devices enhance these properties to an extraordinary degree; but a trained eye, with experience, can discern much on its own.

Two colours that do not appear as they are seen on K-16/39 film are AII and AMT Blue, the underside shades. On period photography it appears to be somewhat light; is this shade – specified in this book and seen widely on surviving examples – too 'brilliant'? I admit that this point is not settled to the complete satisfaction of all VVS

historians, but it is unquestionably true that every aircraft in Russian, Polish, Hungarian, Czech and Rumanian collections from which I have managed to collect physical samples, has yielded a colour of blue which concurs with the colour which I cite in this book. These discoveries span the whole GPW and beyond, from an R-5 built in 1938 to a Yak-9U completed in 1946. The appearance of this colour in black and white GPW-era film is a well-known characteristic of K-16/39 – lighter blue colours tend to look quite light on this kind of film, often even somewhat washed-out in appearance. Confirmation of this odd characteristic is evident in almost every photograph: look at the sky. Anyone who has been to Russia can appreciate the bright – and in summertime, quite vibrant – blue colour of the summer sky, and the permutations of this shade through the seasons. In virtually all cases, you will see a very light, often washed-out looking sky in these photographs, even in shots clearly taken during the summer months on a perfect day. Note, also, how the shade of the sky looks very much like the underside blue colour? This is one of the classic properties of K-16. One final confirmation can be found in photographs taken from Soviet 16 mm movie film, which did not share this odd behaviour. Look for example at Grib's famous Yak-9D '22'; this still is from a section of widely-seen film. Notice the colour of the AMT-7 underside now – it is hard to distinguish from the upper grey colours, and looks remarkably like a greyscale image of such a scheme. In still photos taken on K-16/39, Grib's '22' appears to have a washed-out light looking underside, as usual.

I am not claiming that simple exercises like this one can illuminate the entire picture (as it were) on VVS colouration from the GPW. However, it does give some idea, however superficial, of the possibilities of photographic interpretation. Imagine subjecting pictures – and better yet, picture negatives – to sophisticated software analyses that can compensate for lighting, ambient discolouration, and hosts of other effects. The discipline of photographic interpretation uses these tools very well. In the last several years, photographic analysts from both inside and outside of Russia have successfully identified very many colours to high precision through black and white photo interpretation, all of which were subsequently confirmed by physical evidence on unrestored aircraft of known and documented authenticity.

1 See www.Kithobbyist.com/VVS/

An Introduction to Soviet Aircraft of the Great Patriotic War

The aircraft of the VVS during the GPW were an interesting amalgam of design needs and considerations, often seemingly in contradiction to one another. Typically smaller, lighter and less complicated than their Western contemporaries, these machines, nonetheless, were painstakingly crafted with the greatest care and imagination to exceedingly difficult standards of function and reliability – indeed, often very much beyond those of other countries' efforts. Furthermore, they rarely represented the sort of compromise – either in performance or handling – that one might expect in view of the somewhat dire limitations imposed on the use of metal alloys, and the like. It is this fact, perhaps more than any other, that truly demonstrates how brilliant were the engineers and designers of the Soviet OKBs were.

During the war years, many Russian aircraft were constructed in a wood-plastic product known as *delta drevesina*. This material was enormously strong, and if somewhat heavier than a similar section made of duraluminum, it was also much cheaper to produce, consisted of ubiquitous raw materials, and was extremely simple to repair under even the most primitive field conditions. Many Soviet aircraft designers leapt on the material even *before* the need for economy in strategic metals was realized, recognizing its superb suitability and pliability in producing a robust field design. Soviet aircraft structures were often covered in another wood laminate product known as *shpon* – cross-grained layers of birch strip impregnated with phenol-formaldehyde resin, heat-bonded on one or both sides to Bakelite film over a plywood or spruce core. This type of skinning material featured a very fine surface when properly constructed, and could be polished to form a very low drag finish.

The Russians, at peace for nearly two years more than their European contemporaries, fell somewhat behind in the development of increasingly powerful aircraft engines (just as the Americans did, under identical circumstances). In 1939 there were three primary avenues of development in this regard, the 1,100 hp upright vee 12-cylinder M-105 of Viktor Klimov, genealogically related to the Hispano-Suiza V-12; the 1,300 hp upright vee 12-cylinder AM-35 and -38 of Artem Mikulin, featuring a larger capacity and high compression; and a series of 1,500 hp twin-row 14-cylinder radials by Aleksandr Shvetsov, all entirely original and modern designs not related to his earlier work with the Wright Cyclone based M-25, and later M-62 and -63. Of the three, Shvetsov's radials were the most complex, and consequently available the latest. But in time, one of these – the M-82 – would be shown to be a classic in aviation engine design, and even today, models that were manufactured as long as 60 years ago can be found humming along, still earning a living after six decades of use.

Soviet engines during the war period were 'rated' in terms of maximum horsepower in a somewhat atypical manner, leading to confusion as to their actual performance. The standard practice in this regard was similar to the British system, in which the motor's *maximum sustained* rating was given in its type designation. Thus, the 1,050 hp M-105P engine was actually capable of 1,100 hp (take-off and emergency) at 2600 rpm (much as the Rolls-Royce Merlin II, rated at 1,030 hp, actually produced 1,310 hp using 100 octane fuel). However, there were occasionally exceptions to this rule, in that the Shvetsov M-82 radial, in its boosted variants, often was given at its true maximum output in the designation. The reason for this difference in practice is unknown. The standard Soviet aviation fuel types were rated at 87-, 90-, 94-, and 97-octane, though some quantities of US-supplied 100/130 gasoline also made it to the front.

In the matter of aircraft armament and weaponry, the Soviets led the world. First appearing in 1932, the 7.62 mm ShKAS (Shiptal'niy-Komaritsky Aviatsionniy Skorostrelniy – Shiptal'niy/Komaritsky Aviation high-speed gun) KM-35 was *still* the finest rifle-calibre aircraft machine gun in the world during the Second World War. It fired a powerful cartridge, giving the gun excellent ballistic and destructive characteristics, possessed a cyclic rate-of-fire of almost 1,800 rounds per minute, and was basically reliable. However, by 1939 the rifle-calibre gun was increasingly considered to be ineffective against modern aircraft, particularly against all-metal multi-engined bombers, and so two lines of pursuit developed with regard to increased striking-power. One idea incorporated the use of heavy machine guns, usually of 0.5 inch (12.7 mm) calibre. In this regard, the Soviets developed the superlative 12.7 mm UBS (Universalniy-Berezin Skorostrclniy – Universal Berezin High-Speed gun, often referred to as simply 'UB'). Supremely reliable, and weighing only *half* as much as its Western counterpart, the American .50 cal M2, this gun fired a shell comparable to the American gun at the same velocity (2,800 fps), though at the much improved rate of 850-900 rounds per minute. The other major movement was a gradual shift to aircraft cannon, and here again the Soviet weapon was one of the finest of its day. The 20 mm ShVAK (Shpital'niy-Vladimirov Aviatsonaya Krupno-Kalibernaya – Shpitalniy/ Vladimirov Aviation large-calibre gun), first produced in series in 1938, weighed only 92 lb (25 lb less than the Hispano-404), yet fired a 3.5 oz explosive shell at a muzzle velocity of 2,821 fps. At 800 rounds per minute, it featured an ingenious geared feed mechanism that kept it from jamming at nearly any g-force. Later, in 1944, an improved model (designed by Berezin) known as the B-20 emerged. This weapon weighed almost half as much as the original ShVAK, but retained all of the earlier gun's ballistics and striking power, making it a most fearsome proposition.

Several further aircraft cannon were developed by the Soviets, these in anticipation of ground-attack duties in addition to air-to-air fighting. Volkov and Yartsev's 23 mm VYa-23 gun possessed outstanding penetration capabilities (3,170 fps), though a somewhat modest rate-of-fire (450-550 rounds per minute). Finally, there was the Nudelman-Suranov team, whose work focused largely on airborne anti-tank guns, the NS-37 and -45 (of 37 mm and 45 mm size, respectively), both of which were utterly formidable and used to great effect against German armoured targets. It is interesting to compare, for instance, the NS-37 to the Oldsmobile 37 mm M-4 gun, which it out-performed by nearly double the muzzle velocity – with a similar weight shell – and with three times the penetration ability and at 90 per cent of its gross weight.

In terms of aircraft ordnance, the VVS was the first of the world's air forces to operationally deploy aerial rockets, both in air-to-air and air-to-ground applications. The RS-82, an 82 mm solid-propellant rocket, was originally designed as an anti-bomber weapon. Short and stubby, with only spot-welded, sheet-metal fins for guidance, and a velocity of 1,200 fps, the RS-82 was never a particularly accurate

Above: *Two standard aircraft weapons of the Great Patriotic War: the 7.62 mm ShKAS (above), and the 12.7 mm UBS (below). (Photo: Author's collection)*

Right: *Aircraft cannon of the GPW era. From left: 37 mm NS-37, 23 mm VYa-23, 20 mm BT-20 and 20 mm ShVAK. (Photo: Author's collection)*

missile, though its warhead was lethal should it encounter its target. Its first employment occurred during the Khalkhin-Gol incident of 1939 against the Japanese Imperial Army, with only moderate success. In the event, the RS-82 was used primarily as a ground-attack weapon, as was the later RS-132 rocket – a larger, 132 mm, development. In the hands of a practised pilot, these tiny missiles were extremely potent when fired in a scattering volley, often being so employed against Flak positions, and other such targets. Even so, many pilots did, in fact, fire them successfully at enemy aircraft – especially bombers – and the RS rocket was employed in this manner well into 1943. Specialized anti-armour versions existed of both RS missile types, these sometimes being referred to as BRS rockets.

Another specialized anti-armour munition in widespread use in the VVS was the PTAB (*Protivo-Tankovaya Aviatsionnaya Bomba*) Hollow-Charge Armour-Piercing Bomb series, available in 1.5 kg, 2.5 kg, and 10 kg sizes. These tiny bombs were dropped in bundles, usually *via* a disbursement canister, and were quite effective 'tank-killers' despite their size – the charge of the larger model being quite sufficient to punch a hole in any German vehicle up to and including the PzKw VI Tiger. The most typical VVS aircraft bomb was the FAB (*Fugasniy Aviabomb*, or high-explosive aviation bomb) series of 'general use' HE munitions. These came in a variety of sizes, from 50 kg, 100 kg, 250 kg, 500 kg, 1,000 kg and 2,000 kg weights, to the 'blockbuster' 5,000 kg weapon which could only be lifted by the Pe-8. The ZAB (*Zazhigatel'niy Aviabomb*) series were magnesium-based incendiary bombs of many sizes, ranging from 2.5 kg to as much as 500 kg in weight. Another of the larger series were the anti-personnel fragmentation bombs of the AO (*Aviabomb Oskolochniy*) type, in many sizes from 2.5 kg to 250 kg, and including large anti-structure fragmentation OFAB (*Oskolochniy-Fugasniy Aviabomb*) bombs. In addition, there were liquid-phosphorus incendiary bombs of the XAB (*Khimicheskiy Aviabomb*) family; BETAB rocket-bombs; SAB illumination flare bombs; BRAB armour-piercing bombs; several versions of anti-shipping mines ranging up to 2,000 kg in weight, and featuring all manner of fuses (including magnetic, chemical and contact); and a series of air-dropped torpedoes weighing from 850kg to 1,450 kg.

It is often in the matter of aircraft equipment and features that the machines of the VVS are so unfailingly derided in Western texts. The reader is assured over and again that Soviet aircraft of the Second World War were crude, ill-finished, and quite inferior to Western designs. Curiously enough, one is rarely told just *how* they were supposedly inferior – the reason being plain enough, in that the statement is utterly false. The standards of manufacture, and the fit of various panels, ranged from poor to outstanding, as was the case in manufacture everywhere. Certainly, the early examples of some Soviet machines of certain programmes dating from MiGs in 1940-41, for

example, were of a rather poor standard. This is hardly surprising in light of the astronomical expansion programme then underway which made use, of course, of what was then completely unskilled labour, and by the calamitous dislocation of the aviation industry as a whole when it was forced to uproot itself and move thousands of kilometres to the rear. By 1943, however, the fit and finish of Soviet aircraft was to be compared to any other nation's in the world.

In the matter of cockpit instrumentation, it is true that most VVS machines were not equipped with a gyroscopic artificial horizon. For the hard-pressed Russians, such an expensive and delicate instrument was fitted only to specialized all-weather machines (such as the Yak-9DD), being regarded as essentially unneeded[1]. Their cockpits often lacked effective cabin heaters, and the instrument panel lighting was said to be somewhat mediocre. The standard Soviet reflector sight, the PBP-1, was quite rudimentary, if serviceable, and not entirely popular with VVS pilots. One area in which the Russians *did* trail their contemporaries was that of aircraft wireless. Most early VVS aircraft were fitted with an unreliable, single-channel device, that could only with a certain amount of qualification, be referred to as a proper military radio. Later, improved sets such as the RSI-4 became standard, though they were still inferior in range, frequency, and channel selection to their Western counterparts.

On the other hand, the cockpits of VVS aircraft were typically, *extremely* well protected by a fully-armoured steel seat, armour plating of 8-10 mm thickness, and usually by a 55 mm sheet of armour-glass fore *and* aft. There was also a simple and effective anti-fire system (based on diverting inert gases from the exhaust to the fuel cells), which kept deaths of Soviet aircrew resulting from burns to nine per cent of the British and American figure. Pilot safety was regarded above all other considerations, and promising designs were routinely rejected on the grounds of unsafe handling or flight characteristics, insufficient crew protection, or the inability of the crew to exit the machine in an emergency. It is painfully ironic that Soviet aircraft – brutally derided in Western print as piloted by 'robots' without concern for individual life – were built to much greater standards of safety and crew protection than Western machines.

One of the more interesting, and at times frustrating, aspects of Soviet aviation of the Second World War is that of aircraft type designation and nomenclature. The more than considerable amount of confusion generated by attempting to pinpoint the correct names of various VVS aircraft is, in part, a product of Soviet bureaucracy. But this is not the only cause, for even within a single factory or Design Bureau (OKB) there were often conflicting designations for the same aircraft or variant. Indeed, at times the situation became so grave that *Narkomaviaprom* issued its personnel with a conversion table, giving the appropriate designations for each machine indexed with its relative name, depending on the party generating the document!

In the event, the 'Official Designation' appears to have been the nomenclature assigned to the machine in the State Production Contract, which was issued jointly by *Narkomaviaprom* and the State Commissariat for Defence (GKO). This aircraft designation was usually employed by the NII VVS (the Scientific Research Institute of the Air Forces), only with rare exceptions, and subsequently in all material generated by them. The correct designation formula for any Soviet aircraft consisted of Aircraft/Type/(Number)Engine/(Series), though occasionally ones sees the engine suffix and even the series omitted in State documents. Thus, the precise nomenclature of the initial production block of Yak-1 fighters is 'Yakovlev Yak-1 M-105P Series-1', while that of a late-production *Peshka* might be 'Petlyakov Pe-2 2M-105PF Series-305'. Unfortunately, however, this designation may very well have been used nowhere else, being either too unwieldy – or even too unfamiliar – for use in Forward Maintenance Brigades, in the factories, or even amongst the design staff, any or all of whom may have had their own designation for the machine in question. Infrequently, the year of manufacture was appended (unofficially, of course) to the aircraft designation, where this was seen to be convenient for differentiating variants (for example, there were differences between the 1942 standard Yak-1b and the 1943 standard).

Perhaps the most illuminating example of this phenomenon is the veritable host of designations given to those aircraft making up the transition from the in-line LaGG-3 fighter, to the radial-powered La-5. To the design staff in Moscow (led by Gudkov), the radial-engined LaGG airframe was the 'Gu-82' (M-82-powered design by Gudkov), while the staff at Gor'ki called the machine the 'Type 37' which was used by the Lavochkin OKB staff only after the Gor'ki workers flatly refused to refer to the aircraft in any other way. Furthermore, when the pre-production model was handed over for service trials, the NII VVS adopted the 'LaG-5' designation, based on the NKAP's *draft* Production Contract. The first designation recognized on the revised and standardized Contract is 'Lavochkin La-5', albeit this relates to the proposed Production Standard for the first 'normal' series. Moreover, once these machines reached the field they became know alternatively as 'LaGG-5', 'LaGG-3 M-82', 'LaGG-3(Radial)', or even 'Lavochkin/ M-82'. Finally, it is almost certain that all such machines retroactively received the La-5 designation once series manufacture got into stride. The resulting problem for the aviation historian, here, is palpable.

These one- and two-letter type codes, were initially derived from a word demonstrating the purpose of the machine. 'I', for example, stood for *Istrebitel* – or 'Fighter' – as in the Polikarpov I-16; 'DB' for *Dal'niy Bombardirovchik* – 'Long-range (Distant) Bomber' – as in the Ilyushin DB-3. Early in 1940, however, along with a great many other changes, the designator coding process was changed with regard to aircraft to signify the Chief Designer responsible for that particular design. A two-letter code was used to specify the primary designer responsible for the aircraft (often the Bureau Head), a one-letter code indicating a significant contribution from another Chief or Assistant Designer. Thus,

the DB-3 became the Il-4 (Ilyushin); the I-26 became the Yak-1 (Yakovlev – being a single letter in Cyrillic); the I-301 became the LaGG-3 (Lavochkin, Gudkov, Gorbunov). Throughout the War, in fact, all types of Soviet coding began to change over to the new system. Engine designations, for example, were finally reorganized in early 1944, so that the M- (for *Motor*) was replaced with a suitable two-letter designer's code (i.e. 'VK' for Viktor Klimov, etc.), based on the first and last name.

As a result, perhaps, a number of the aircraft designations that have been in use in Western texts for some *60 years* are entirely spurious. The variant of the Yak-1, for example, with the cut-down rear fuselage and Yak-9 type armament is often referred to as the 'Yak-1M'. The *correct* nomenclature of this type, however, is simply 'Yak-1', or, more precisely, '*Yak-1 s Uluchshennim Obzorom, Bronirovanem, i Vooruzhenem*' – 'Improved Vision, Armour, and Armament'. In service units it was sometimes also given as 'Yak-1 1943', or 'Yak-1B'. Indeed, there was a 'Yak-1M' – exactly two of them – both were hand-built prototypes of the Yak-3 model, and were never built in series. Some writers have tried to refer to the I-211 (the MiG-3 development featuring an M-82 radial) as the 'MiG-5', but actually this nomenclature was reserved for a twin-engined machine that never, in the event, saw production. The Tupolev ANT-40 has forever been mislabelled in the West as the 'SB-2', whereas it is, in fact, simply the SB bomber. The error occurred by adding together part of the engine suffix (indicating *two engines*) from the long name (i.e. SB 2M-100 Series-32). It is indicative of the West's general ignorance of the VVS that the correct names for its various aircraft are often, even now, still unknown.

One final matter is critical if one is to understand the history of Soviet aircraft manufacture during the GPW – any notion of Western style linear manufacture must be abandoned immediately. Western manufacturers (say, Curtiss for example) were obsessed with defining even the tiniest modification to their finished products by issuing a host of suffixes to the aircraft's designation. Thus, one has 'C' and 'K' and 'M' variants, and '-15' and '-25' block production, and so forth. No such requirement existed in Soviet manufacture, and suffixes were rarely issued for even the most significant modification within a manufacturing programme (the Yakovlev OKB, as an exception, seems to have cornered the Russian market in suffixes). An Il-2 produced in 1941 with a single crew member, straight metal wings, and an AM-38 engine, was *still* an 'Il-2' in 1943 (the often-repeated '-M' and '-2M3' suffixes are spurious), but by this time with swept wooden wings, two crew members, and an AM-38F motor. There was never any official change in nomenclature, and one was never seen to be needed.

In the factories, production was fluid. A small modification could be devised even by the lowliest member of a production line team, and if the modification was deemed worthy of examination it might be ordered to be applied on a single line to try it out. This type of improvisation was common. Successful changes were, of course, reviewed by the Design Staff, and if they became permanent new drawings would then be completed and distributed to the other factories manufacturing the machine in question (at least usually, but not always). Chief and head designers had almost unlimited license to experiment within their OKB's factory, and many did so. The situation regarding production of the LaGG-3 fighter is illustrative of this point, wherein *Zavoda* 21 and 31 would both make local modifications to their version of the fighter, only occasionally informing the other factory that they had done so, and even less frequently issuing drawings on the modification. Some of the changes made at *Zavod* 21 would then be rejected by the staff at *Zavod* 31, and they would simply not incorporate them into their manufacture, or vice versa. As a result, machines of a similar Series number issued by both factories in fact often had no similarity whatever between them.

Local shortages of parts or materials often exacerbated this fluid condition. To keep production moving, improvisations were often used, sometimes resulting in a permanent change to the programme. Other such improvisations were temporary, but in view of the German advance it was often not acceptable (at least in the early days) to halt production for any cause, so desperate were the needs of the hour.

In the end, the technological accomplishments of the Soviet Union in the air war are legendary. Names like the Yak-1, the Yak-9 and the La-5 may not roll off the tongue of the Western reader like those of the Spitfire, the Mustang and the Hellcat. However, in terms of sheer accomplishment, in their achievements, in their remarkable contributions, in the monumental scale of the titanic struggle in which they fought and prevailed, they are unequalled. Moreover, to have completed these feats under the extreme conditions of duress which the Russian people then found themselves – below the heel of a ruthless, inept and paranoid dictator, and directly at risk of subjugation and genocide at the mercy of crazed, racist murderers almost defies belief.

The names of Soviet aircraft may not always be familiar to Western readers. But, as their story and the history of their achievements emerge from the mists of prejudice and confusion by which they are now clouded, they will do so.

Camouflage Application Techniques

The term 'application theme' relates to the methodology of camouflage application in the VVS during the GPW. Templates, pattern masks, and other forms of painting guides were not in use by the Soviets during the 1941-45 period. Rather, all painting was accomplished by hand, usually using a spray gun, and the exact patterns to be applied were simply executed by the worker on duty in the finishing bay at that particular time.

Because no templates existed, the patterns varied quite widely. There are no known cases of factories issuing diagram schematics for a camouflage pattern, nor are there any notes on the subject typically available in factory records. Therefore, it seems obvious that the schemes were passed on orally, or by examining the previously painted examples prior to a given shift. Sometimes, individuals simply painted aircraft during their working hours in the manner of their own choosing, and as long as there were no objections from the Line Foreman or other supervisory personnel, this behaviour seems to have been tolerated to a large degree.

It is much more useful to regard any VVS camouflage pattern as a 'theme', rather than a set pattern – the general features were likely to be the same, but the exact finish was often a matter of individuality, or simple non-linear application (inevitable when such things are replicated by hand). Therefore, I have used the expression 'application theme' to refer to the various camouflage patterns. It was quite rare for any two examples to be *exact* replicas of one another. Rather, individual aircraft

showed at least small dissimilarities in their finish, and quite often very much more than 'small'. Indeed, individual anomalies within a defined camouflage pattern are legion, and sometimes changes were quite radical, such as the use of different colours from shift to shift, while employing the same basic application.

One last point must be made: the camouflage schemes presented in this volume cannot tell the story of VVS camouflage from 1941-45 comprehensively. Such a work, including all possible factory applied schemes, would be impossible at this time. The patterns described in this volume rather describe the *known* factory-applied schemes, those that are documented in sufficient numbers of photographs to both draw in three dimensions and to be fairly convinced that they are not unit-specific liveries. The idea, essentially, is that readers will be able to identify many of the camouflage patterns that they see in various period photographs, and indeed, the more one examines, the clearer these patterns will emerge.

Notes on Camouflage Illustrations

The camouflage three-view plates in the following section are not intended as scale drawings. These are general arrangement drawings only, and some of the detail therein may be generic or misplaced. Please refer to the scale line drawings for each aircraft type for true detail, shape, and planform information. Also, the printing process may not result in colouration that is entirely authentic of the desired shades, and therefore should be regarded as representative, only. Please refer to the Treatise on VVS Colour Systems for colour identification.

The same caveat must be made for the colour profiles in this book. Sadly, it is true that the CMYK colour printing system has certain properties, which can serve as a limitation when rendering some colours. Unfortunately, the colours that CMYK does not represent well – bright greens and blues – are very much in use in VVS camouflage. Therefore, while every effort has been made to ensure that the appearance of the colours in this book are as close as possible (and that means these are *not* exact) to their actual appearance, the resulting colour shade should not be taken literally. This fact is exacerbated by variations within printing batches, and so forth. In all cases, proper colour identification must be undertaken by referring to Chapter One.

---

1. In fact, as any competent pilot can attest, an artificial horizon, while convenient, is hardly a necessary flight instrument. In the event, the Soviet pilots did quite well without them, and were able to operate in weather conditions in which the *Luftwaffe* categorically could not (and whose aircraft were all so-equipped!).

Lavochkin LaGG-3

932

Chapter 1

Lavochkin LaGG-3

One of an entirely new generation of Soviet fighters designed in 1938-39, the I-301 prototype, the result of an amalgamated team comprising designers Semen Lavochkin and Mikhail Gudkov, under the direction of NKAP Department Chief Vladimir Gorbunov, was unique. Whereas most other monoplane fighter designs around the world were increasingly of all-metal, stressed-skin construction, the I-301 was built largely of compressed laminate wood, reinforced with resin (a type of wood-plastic known as 'delta-wood', or delta-drevesina). The ply skinning, known as 'shpon', was bonded and lacquered with a strong resin over delta drevesina spars and formers. Though the method was known to be heavier than an all-metal lay-out, the twin advantages of robust strength and extraordinary ease of maintenance in the field were seen to be far more important than any resulting weight penalty. Furthermore, the method conserved the few alloy resources possessed by the Soviet Union at the time, a subject of intense concern for Gorbunov who had been charged by VIAM and the NKAP to examine alternative materials suitable for aircraft production.

During the 1938 design specification conference held by the NKAP and the UVVS, Vladimir Gorbunov proposed an all-wood fighter that would have sufficient performance as a modern monoplane, yet not consume any of the USSR's supply of strategic materials. Lavochkin, a young and talented designer, was tasked with formalizing the conceptual study of this machine, and in time Gudkov, another NKAP designer joined the project. Under Gorbunov's direction, Lavochkin's design eventually crystallized as the 'Type K'. The 'Type K' was an all-wood semi-monocoque design of exceptionally clean lines, save for the installation of the engine which apparently was not particularly satisfactory. However, the basic characteristics of the 'K' were obviously advanced, and Lavochkin and Gudkov were ordered to the *Zavod* 301 facility in Moscow to complete two initial prototypes.

Lavochkin would lead the staff in practical terms (logically, since the Type K was largely his design), but powerplant matters were almost exclusively in the hands of Gudkov, while Gorbunov was in overall charge of the programme, coordinating very effectively with the Factory 301 plant staff and Director Yu. Eskin. This somewhat extemporary design team was officially recognized as OKB 301, and its prototype machine became known simply as the 'I-301' after the factory itself.

The I-301 design featured a double-spar wing of all-wood construction with *shpon* skinning, the spars themselves being manufactured out of the new compressed resin-wood *delta drevesina* product developed by L. Ryzhkov. The airfoil was of classic Clark YH section, and the tapered wings featured large, internally balanced ailerons positioned well outboard. The fuselage was a wooden semi-monocoque structure with birch stringers and *shpon* outer surfaces, as were the fin and stabilizer, except for the forward metal panels covering the engine. All control surfaces were of dural framework construction and were fabric-covered. The prototype's canopy was originally designed as a hinged unit, but Pilot-Engineer Aleksei Nikashin, one of the factory's most experienced pilot-engineers, argued that this was completely unacceptable, and a sliding unit of somewhat hasty manufacture was fitted. The rudder was externally balanced by means of weighted horns along both the top and bottom, and included an adjustable trim tab. The I-301 featured widely spaced landing gear, but was dogged by ineffective oleo dampers that resulted in a tendency to bounce decidedly upon any, but a well-executed three-point landing – a problem that would haunt the basic design over most of its life. The 1,050 hp Klimov M-105P 12-cylinder upright vee was chosen to provide power, and 350 litres of fuel was distributed through three cells, one under the seat, and one in each inner wing section. Provision was made in the first prototype to accept a 23 mm Taubin MP-6 cannon firing between the cylinder banks, and no fewer than four machine guns were mounted above and below the engine. Provision was also made for a sheet of 8 mm armour plate aft of the pilot's seat, though this was not fitted until the second prototype.

In an effort to accelerate testing Aleksei Nikashin was assigned to head the flight programme. The No.1 prototype first flew on 30 March 1940, and was delivered to the NII VVS for evaluation on 14 June. The I-301 was found to be quite impressive, offering extremely low drag, good aileron response, and a worthy turning circle. Performance in the new fighter was impressive, the aircraft's superb surface finish allowing it to achieve the outstanding maximum speed of 614 km/h at 4,930 m, though its climb performance was markedly inferior to that of the I-26, giving the impression of being somewhat under-powered. The aircraft demonstrated mediocre handling in the air, possessing heavy – though well coordinated – controls, unhappy stalling characteristics, directional instability, and a tendency for the nose to rise unexpectedly at low airspeeds. As with other VVS prototypes, the hydraulic system was prone to failure early on, and NII test pilot Stefanovski damned the hastily contrived canopy as grotesquely unacceptable, demanding that a better unit be fitted. Further, the I-301's visibility on take-off was poor, it had an incipient tendency to bounce on landing. Altogether, the various test pilots judged the machine to fall within the capabilities of the average VVS pilot, but the need for various improvements was highlighted as well.

Along with testing of the initial machine, construction of the second prototype continued throughout August and September. This aircraft was essentially similar to the first I-301 prototype, except that it featured a revised, single-spar wing structure which was intended to reduce the aircraft's weight. A better sliding canopy section had been fitted, and a similar unit was attached to the first prototype while it was being repaired in September. Some minor improvements had been incorporated into the second aircraft following the initial factory and NII testing, this largely with regard to the arrangement of hydraulic tubing and difficulties with the deployment of the armament. However, just as both prototypes were ready to return to flight testing, the NKAP and the UVVS issued a specification arbitrarily stating that all Soviet fighters should have a range of 1,000 km. This came as an unpleasant setback to the I-301 programme and considerable scrambling then took place to attempt to meet the new requirement. The resulting modifications were entirely ad hoc; in the first prototype, provisions for a 65 litre fuel cell to be squeezed in between the spars of the outer wing panels on each side were developed, but the delay that would have resulted in the programme (to static load and other testing) was unacceptable, and thus a supplementary tank was installed behind the pilot. The second prototype could not be so modified (due to the single-spar wing), and also received a small 15 litre supplementary tank behind the pilot's seat.

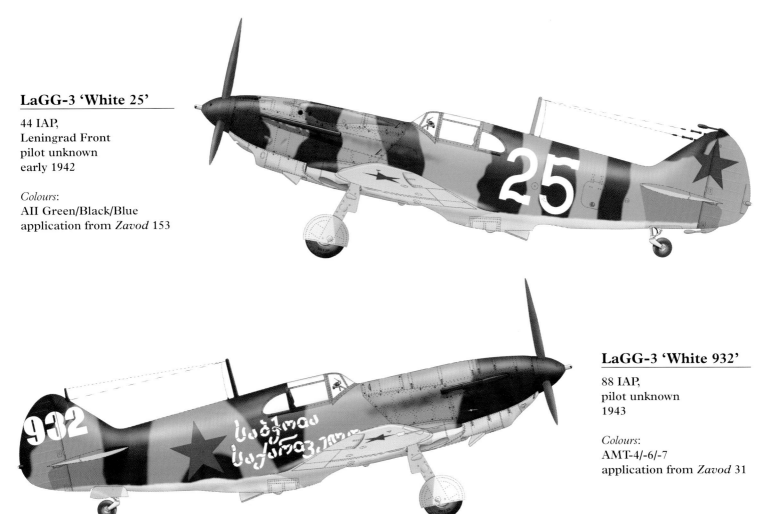

LaGG-3 'White 25'

44 IAP,
Leningrad Front
pilot unknown
early 1942

Colours:
AII Green/Black/Blue
application from *Zavod* 153

LaGG-3 'White 932'

88 IAP,
pilot unknown
1943

Colours:
AMT-4/-6/-7
application from *Zavod* 31

After a handful of flights demonstrating the apparent range of this new configuration, the NKAP took the extraordinary step of ordering the I-301 into production based on the No.1 prototype as the LaGG-1 (this nomenclature was derived from the new Soviet designation system incorporating the various designers' names), despite the complete lack of testing of the new long-range modifications. The sheer urgency of the need to field more modern fighters and the consequent need to prove the new wooden production methods for which the LaGG fighter was a flagship programme, must have weighed heavily upon the NKAP decision, and indicated that the Government was prepared to take risks to introduce improved aircraft types in the face of growing evidence of impending German hostility. To facilitate production, the design team was split up, Gorbunov heading to *Zavod* 31 at Taganrog, and Lavochkin to Gor'ki to establish the primary LaGG lines and programme centre at *Zavod* 21. Meanwhile, Gudkov remained in Moscow at *Zavod* 301, ostensibly to become Chief Designer for OKB-301.

Actual production of the LaGG-1, however, never took place. As the various lines were in the process of tooling, and the respective designers relocated, the decision was taken to initiate production based upon and including the extended range modifications to the first prototype. The new production model was re-designated LaGG-3, and featured the outer wing tanks of the modified No.1 prototype in addition to a host of minor improvements and modifications from the second prototype machine. The NKAP issued a new Production Contract for the improved variant on 2 November, ordering production from several factories throughout the country.

The first production model LaGG-3 rolled off the factory floor of *Zavod* 23 (Leningrad) early in December, 1940. The new fighter

featured an 8 mm armour sheet behind the pilot, and carried the heavy armament of two 12.7 mm UBS and two 7.62 mm ShKAS guns – the breeches of which were covered by a large blister fairing – above the engine, each with 220 and 325 rounds, respectively. Provision was made for a 23 mm Taubin cannon firing through the spinner with 80 rounds, but as none of these weapons was available at Leningrad, a 12.7 mm super-heavy BK machine gun was fitted instead. The PBP-1a gunsight was standard, along with an RSI-3 radio. Performance in the Leningrad LaGG-3 was very close to the pre-production models, 357 mph being attained at 5,000 m, and an initial climb of 895 m/min was common.

Despite the successful (albeit slow) instigation of production at *Zavod* 23, the decision in retrospect by the NKAP to launch mass-production of the LaGG-3 without proper testing of the revised No.1 prototype, nor even the flight characteristics imposed by the additional weight of the extra wing fuel tanks, seems incredible. The NKAP reasoned that, although the design was clearly immature, the need for any necessary modifications could be ascertained in the field under service conditions, and put into effect on the production line in due course. In the event, such a rationale proved wrong. Production of the new fighter at *Zavod* 21 floundered as numerous defects persistently materialized on the pre-production machines, these of so serious a nature that the NII VVS refused to certify them for service introduction. These problems had everything to do with the difficulties associated with the reorganization of production at Gor'ki, where hitherto the I-16 had been manufactured, and with the rapid expansion of the facility, requiring the use of large numbers of unskilled workers.

During January and February, the *Zavod* 21 staff worked frantically to resolve the LaGG's difficulties. Throughout these many hardships

Chief Designer Lavochkin proved to be a first-class plant and design bureau leader. Working ceaselessly, he addressed each new problem with calm understanding and determination, always resisting the considerable urge to panic or lose control of his temper. Indeed, so thoroughly impressive was Lavochkin, that the old plant guard who had initially resisted his introduction soon rallied around the programme, and heroic efforts were undertaken to redress the LaGG-3 production situation.

Persistent problems with the Taubin MP-6 cannon resulted in the abandonment of this weapon in favour of the VYa-23 gun of similar calibre, but which was just then becoming available. As a result, many early LaGG-3s simply had a UBS gun mounted in the spinner in its place, though the armament had been reduced to four guns (one of the 12.7 mm guns above the engine was omitted) to make room for the larger bulk and weight of the Volkov-Yartsev cannon. The landing gear hydraulic system was improved with new lock valves, revised cowl panel hinges were designed and changes were made to the sliding canopy. The list of modifications seemed insurmountable, and indeed, by February 1941, numbered 2,228 recommended design changes.

Above: *A very early (possibly a Gor'ki Series 2-4), Zavod 21-built five-gun LaGG-3 in flight, probably armed with a 12.7 mm BK machine gun firing through the spinner. Note the unpainted cockpit framing, which was occasionally seen in 1941 Soviet aircraft finishes. This aircraft is seen while in service with the 44 IAP, on the Leningrad Front in 1942. (Photo: G.Petrov)*

As a result of these difficult conditions, the early model LaGG-3s from *Zavod* 21 were quite poor in manufacture, largely defeating the type's aerodynamic cleanliness with ill-fitting panels, poor finish, and even inaccurately executed tolerances. Though the control surfaces of the LaGG-3 were effective at all speeds, stick pressure was disappointingly heavy. Furthermore, the type suffered with continuing failures of the hydraulic system, and some production batches of Soviet Plexiglas for the canopy at this time were so opaque that many pilots were forced to fly with the hood open in order to see out clearly. Worse still, engine overheating remained a serious problem that seemed to defy every solution put to it.

On a positive note, the production LaGG-3 was equipped from the start with an ingenious safety device developed by engineers at VIAM and the LII in the mid-1930s. The need to reduce the hazard of fire in a combat aircraft was seen to exceed the protection offered by self-sealing fuel cells. In test after test, the prototypes of the new 12.7 mm UBS gun and 20 mm ShVAK cannon would rip such giant holes in a standard, rubber-lined, self-sealing fuel tank that the petrol would immediately mix with oxygen and explode in flames. No amount of reinforcement, it was found, save for unacceptably heavy armour plate could prevent this. As a result, the engineers at VIAM hit upon the idea of denying oxygen to the resulting gash, thus preventing combustion. A simple system of tubes directed inert gases from the engine's exhaust manifold to the fuel cell, the pressure inside of which was regulated by a simple ball type valve with a spring. The resulting system was superbly effective, and simple in the extreme. Later, most VVS machines would supplement this tubing system with the ability to direct nitrogen from the craft's flap and landing gear emergency N_2 bottle to the fuel cell, should damage occur to the tubing or valve.

The early production Gor'ki LaGG-3s featured a four-gun armament of two ShKAS and one UBS gun mounted above the engine, and one 23 mm VYa-23 cannon (or UBS in its place) firing through the spinner. During the summer of 1941, the 23 mm gun was often replaced by the lighter 20 mm ShVAK cannon, which later became standard. Power was provided by the M-105P engine driving a VISh-61P three-blade airscrew of 3 m diameter. All-up weight had now increased to 3,287 kg, and in this configuration performance was disappointing, maximum speed falling to 458 km/h at sea level and 535 km/h at 5,000 m. Initial climb also suffered, this being reduced to 829 m/min., with a service ceiling of 9,300 m, and wing loading had

risen in the Gor'ki-built machines 3.81 kg/m2, dramatically higher than the pre-production models.

In the meanwhile, production of the LaGG-3 was spooling up at both *Zavod* 31 at Taganrog, and *Zavod* 153 at Novosibirsk. At Taganrog, Gorbunov—now Head Designer—faced considerable difficulties in launching production of the LaGG fighter. Though the staff at *Zavod* 31 were much more experienced than at Gor'ki, they were not used to working with wooden construction techniques. Even more serious a difficulty were the perpetually revised drawings sent to Taganrog by the Lavochkin staff at *Zavod* 21. In fact, Gorbunov complained bitterly that lines could scarcely be established for production when the blueprints were revised three or four times per week – this did indeed occur! However, Gorbunov was a masterful organizational genius, and by March the factory had turned out their first completed fighter, despite all difficulties. Simultaneously, Gorbunov and his staff were exploring ways to lighten the production aircraft, and indeed the staff at *Zavod* 31 were undertaking local modifications to the fuselage of this type on their own initiative, despite the perpetual objections of the NKAP.

As a result of these bewildering conditions, at no time did production of the LaGG-3 at the various factories actually resemble any sort of standard. Revisions were being executed on the lines at *Zavod* 21 by the Gor'ki staff, then transmitted to Taganrog as drawings were prepared, by which time new modifications were often being applied on the lines again. At *Zavod* 31 these revisions would be incorporated into production as the drawings were disseminated, but these were applied in addition to any local modifications which were under investigation by Gorbunov. Furthermore, neither of these factories ever produced a LaGG fighter similar to those manufactured at Leningrad. The situation for maintenance units in the field must have been excruciating.

The establishment of production at Novosibirsk, meanwhile, was dramatically behind schedule. The first LaGG-3 did not emerge from the *Zavod* 153 lines until July 1941, and these aircraft were beset by the same problems as early-manufactured fighters from Gor'ki – namely, poor finish and construction. Units in the field were not at all impressed by this condition, and Lavochkin increasingly bore the brunt of vociferous complaints from all directions. Indeed, in some circles, Lavochkin's name was increasingly invoked in vain, much to his personal discomfort. But Lavochkin realized that production of the fighter under the dire threat of the German advance on Moscow could not be stopped to permit a complete overhaul of the LaGG-3 programme; all modifications were therefore tempered by the need to facilitate their rapid and seamless deployment on the production lines.

This type of solution was certainly a compromise, but there was no other possibility under the conditions at hand, though this realization did nothing to bolster Lavochkin's reputation.

The LaGG-3 was not available in service in the Western military districts during the early *Barbarossa* period. Even though some 322 examples had been completed prior to 22 June 1941, only about 50 machines had been delivered to units in the field; the remainder were still at the factories awaiting corrective repairs and re-fits. LaGG-3s began to enter combat with German forces during the autumn, pilots of the 33 IAP completing sorties in their Gor'ki-built LaGGs in August. In service, the LaGG-3 was unpopular with some re-fitting VVS units, even though it was found to be possessed of heavy firepower, as well as being extremely robust and admirably simple to repair and maintain in the field – a quality imparted by its tough laminate construction. It did, however, demonstrate an alarming tendency to flick into a violent spin during tight turns, the stall coming on at high speed and without warning. The problem was greatly exacerbated by the fact that many of the LaGG pilots received only the briefest conversion training, having previously flown such light and nimble types as the Polikarpov I-153. After a number of machines had been lost in this way, Soviet pilots produced an unflattering sobriquet for the LaGG, the *'Lakirovanniy Garantirovanniy Grob'* – the Varnished Guaranteed Coffin!

The early series LaGG-3 demonstrated clearly its good and bad characteristics, though unhappily for the average VVS pilot, often the latter, as it required a pilot of considerable skill and élan to evoke the former. These LaGGs did not possess a turning circle dramatically superior to the Bf 109, and in comparison with its German rival, it was clearly under-powered. Control harmony was good, however, and VVS

Below: A ski-equipped LaGG-3 outside the Tbilisi facility, spring 1942. The aircraft is probably undergoing factory testing and has been painted with MK-7 white distemper, which is badly worn. This pattern of wear is typical for the finish; MK-7 adhered slightly better to wooden surfaces, and could be easily removed in areas receiving more handling. This aircraft also carries four RO132 rocket rails. (Photo: G.Petrov)

pilots skilled in dog-fighting made the most of this attribute, even though stick forces in the LaGG-3 were still too heavy. The fighter's firepower in the earlier four and five-gun models was quite formidable, but pilots complained that the reduced two-gun arrangement was inadequate. In fact, virtually the only characteristic of the LaGG not to receive criticism at this time was the type's outstanding survivability; LaGG-3s could be shot to pieces and still return the pilot safely home.

In combat, the early LaGG-3 demonstrated very mixed results. The experienced pilots of the 21 IAP performed well in the new fighter, despite the fact that no rear echelon conversion training was offered them, and also that they were equipped with Gor'ki built aircraft of poor manufacturing standards. Between 11 October and 30 November 1941, the 21 IAP accounted for no fewer than 39 enemy aircraft, seven tanks, and a sizeable number of other vehicles, all for the loss of 15 LaGGs and six pilots. *Kapitan* I. Nestov gave the premiere performance during this period of activity and demonstrated the exceptional striking power of the new VYa-23 cannon, destroying three He 111 bombers in only two firing passes with his four-gun model LaGG-3 on 21 October. However, the regiment's pilots had difficulty combating the German Bf 109F fighter, and achieved few successes against it. Battling the Messerschmitt, the LaGG pilots would have to manoeuvre in the horizontal plane to their utmost ability, emphasizing their turning advantage and control harmony to effect, but with the German fighter able simply to climb away out of danger at any time. The result was a frustrating situation for the VVS pilots, and a tactical stalemate at best.

On the Leningrad Front, the 157 IAP was turning in even more spectacular results in their *Zavod* 23-built LaGG-3s – three pilots each scored 'triples' against Bf 109s during a single week in October, 1941. Even so, the majority of converting VVS units found themselves at a loss with the new wooden fighter. The equally experienced 145 IAP – operating in the very same area as the 157 – suffered immoderate losses in the LaGG for little result, (some 50 Gor'ki-built aircraft in total) before being withdrawn for refit in April 1942. Of these, at least

ten LaGG-3s were lost when they stalled at high-speed and low-altitude whilst dog-fighting, killing the pilots. The Regiment considered the Lavochkin fighter to be a curse, and its pilots much preferred piloting their surviving obsolete I-16 Type 10s in battle. Having suffered similarly, the frustrated commander of the 44 IAP actually forbade his pilots to enter a turning dog-fight below 2000 m, regardless of conditions. At this low point, the LaGG programme was far from reaching its maximum potential.

Back at *Zavod* 21, the Lavochkin design staff were at work on the LaGG's armament. Eight underwing RO82 rails accommodating eight RS-82 rockets were fitted to LaGG-3s beginning in about the eleventh series. To counteract the resulting increase in weight, armament was reduced to a single 12.7 mm UBS above the engine on the port side, and a 20 mm ShVAK firing through the spinner. LaGGs at Novosibirsk, however, continued to be completed with the four-gun arrangement into early 1942. Work was also completed on a proposed variant mounting the formidable Shpital'niy 37 mm Sh-37 cannon between the cylinder banks. A production machine was removed from the lines and thus modified during October 1941. Testing of the LaGG-3-37 did not reveal any significant difficulties, and early in 1942 a batch of 20 machines was sent to the Bryansk front for evaluation under service conditions by *Polkovnik* Fedor I Shinkarenko's 42 IAP. Though heavy, and with reduced performance, the striking power of the LaGG-3-37 was extraordinary, and further development of a 37 mm cannon-armed LaGG fighter was urged.

Early in 1942, production of the all-wooden fighter was thrown into disarray. The German advance had necessitated the evacuation of many factories to the east in the autumn of 1941 and *Zavoda* 23 and 31 were so affected. The Leningrad factory was disassembled and relocated to Omsk, ending LaGG-3 production by this enterprise. *Zavod* 31 was relocated to Tbilisi, but the great distance of the move, combined with all manner of hardships experienced at this stage of the war, meant that LaGG production did not resume at the new location until January, 1942. Simultaneously, Alexandr Yakovlev's position and reputation had strengthened, and the NKAP took the decision to increase Yak fighter production. *Zavod* 21 at Gor'ki was designated as a production site for the Yak-7, and in April the Lavochkin design staff were ordered to relocate to Tbilisi and centralize LaGG-3 manufacture at the *Zavod* 31 facility. Furthermore, manufacture of the LaGG-3 was terminated at the Novosibirsk plant at the same time – again in favour of the Yak-7. For the remainder of their lives, a considerable amount of ill-feeling passed between Lavochkin and Yakovlev; one has to assume that this episode was directly connected to that situation.

With manufacture again under way in Tbilisi, several modifications appeared on the production LaGG-3 fighter in 1942. The external balance horns for the rudder were replaced by internal units of superior effect. The M-105PA engine was now the standard power plant for series manufacture and featured redesigned exhausts with three separate vents on each side. The RSI-4 radio became increasingly common and improved supplies of canopy units allowed for the rejection of inferior examples on the production line. Armament standardized on one UBS above the engine with 225 cartridges, one ShVAK cannon firing through the spinner with 120 cartridges, and six underwing RS-82 rockets. Finally, there were a host of minor improvements to the cooling system and radiator piping, at last mitigating the engine overheating problem. The new standard production model could achieve 455 km/h at sea level, 550 km/h at 5,000 m, and had an initial climb of 878 m/min, reaching 5,000 m in 7.2 mins with a ceiling of 9,300 m.

With the developmental impetus of the LaGG-3 programme now transferred to *Zavod* 31 under the direction of Gorbunov (production of the La-5 at Gor'ki meant that Lavochkin and most of his OKB never relocated from that facility), three major elements of the LaGG-3 programme were recognized as being in need of immediate attention. The first problem revolved around the fighter's unhappy high-speed stall under g-force loading. This condition was patently unacceptable, as the LaGG-3's only performance advantage over the

Messerschmitt Bf 109F lay in horizontal manoeuvrability; the severe stalling behaviour was restricting the dog-fighting capabilities of the Soviet machine to a point where inexperienced pilots were left with no advantage against the German fighters. Throughout 1941, Lavochkin had resisted the introduction of leading edge slats as a solution to the problem, despite the obvious success of these controls on aircraft such as the tricky MiG-3 fighter. However, before the relocating elements of the Lavochkin OKB staff had arrived at Tbilisi, Gorbunov – in a typical move – simply outfitted a LaGG right off the production lines with Handley-Page-type slats, as on the MiG. The modification was something of a *fait accompli*, for when Lavochkin's team examined and tested the machine with these slats, it was clear that the problem had been solved. Production incorporating leading edge slats was ordered immediately as these units became available.

The second major problem involved the LaGG-3's weight – simply put, the fighter was too heavy. Chief Designer Gorbunov had been experimenting with lightened airframes since 1941, and when this work was combined with the efforts of Lavochkin team members Strutsel and Ulechkov, a host of weight savings were realized. The rear fuselage was lightened at no cost to structural strength, the outer wing section fuel cells were removed, and other modifications carried out. Some aerodynamic improvements were also applied to the new model, a revised oil cooler intake under the aircraft's 'chin', and a radiator exhaust of improved profile and design were developed. Production examples incorporating this work soon appeared, these being known as LaGG-3 (Obl) – *Oblegchenny*, or 'lightened' – and were some 150-232 kg lighter than the standard production model (depending on its build and the type modifications made to the specific series). Powered by the M-105PA engine, a standard *Oblegchenniy* could attain 468 km/h at sea level, and 571 km/h at 5,000 m. Initial climb rose dramatically to 960 m/min, and the service ceiling reached 9,756 m. Manufacture of the lightened LaGG-3 began in the summer of 1942, and it was warmly received by service pilots at the front.

The third major area for improvement in the programme was the need for increased engine-power. The first development in this regard involved the availability of the improved M-105PF boosted engine. The new Klimov motor developed 1,180 hp (1,260 hp for take-off and emergency boost), and the supercharger gearing was arranged to provide maximum performance at lower altitudes, where aerial combat was most likely to occur. Performance improved dramatically with the new power plant, the non-lightened LaGG-3 of 1942 could achieve 498 km/h at sea level and 565 km/h at 5,000 m, climbing initially at 982 m/min. As the LaGG-3 (Obl) supplanted the earlier series, it was also manufactured with the M-105PF driven by a new VISh-105 prop featuring a revised spinner, and could attain 515 km/h at sea level and 565 km/h at 5,000 m, and its climbing ability shot upwards to 1,053 m/min. VVS pilots soon discovered that the M-105PF-powered *Oblegchenniy* could more than hold its own against the German Bf 109G, and the reputation of the LaGG-3 began to rebound during the latter half of the year.

An example of the new LaGG's abilities can be found amongst the records of the famous 31 IAP, who turned in their motley assortment of Novosibirsk and Gor'ki machines for a new batch of LaGG-3 (Obl) fighters from Tbilisi in July-August, 1942. Having scored only 28 victories in all on the LaGG in the half-year hitherto, the 31 IAP doubled that figure in the first month of operation with the *Oblegchenniy*, and in the following month doubled this impressive performance yet again. Total losses over the period were a mere eight machines, with not a single pilot lost in combat, demonstrating the type's robust survivability. Indeed, during a combat on 4 August, *St.Lt.* Bikhmukhametov's port wing struck a Bf 109G, which immediately broke in half and fell to earth fatally. The Soviet pilot returned to base untroubled, where his LaGG's port leading edge slat was replaced and damage to the paint finish repaired; Bikhmukhametov successfully flew the very same machine later in the afternoon. This type of extraordinary sturdiness, and the improving performance of the new LaGG-3 models, dramatically reversed the perception of the type amongst front-line combat pilots during 1942.

Earlier in 1942, the Lavochkin staff had experimented with an M-107-powered LaGG fighter variant. Though the new Klimov offered much greater horsepower than the M-105 engine, it was clearly underdeveloped at this point, and insurmountable cooling problems arose in the type. Indeed, factory test pilot Mischenko was forced to make 33 emergency landings due to cooling failures in 33 flights, and development of the LaGG-3 M-107 was halted, much to Lavochkin's disappointment. However, another engine solution was at hand. As far back as September 1941, Gudkov, still at the OKB-301 in Moscow, had been experimenting with the installation of Arkadiy Shvetsov's M-82 14-cylinder two-row radial engine into various airframes then powered by Klimov in-line motors. Amongst these projects was a LaGG airframe that had been fitted with the big radial, and was known as the Gu-82. Despite Lavochkin's apparent incredulity, the Gu-82 was demonstrating performance that should have brought it immediate attention – it achieved 626 km/h on one flight in October 1941. So exceptional was this performance that the NKAP actually considered a production programme for the machine, even before it had been submitted to the NII VVS for evaluation.

At the beginning of 1942, with the relocation of his OKB to Tbilisi and the impending termination of the entire LaGG programme looming large, Lavochkin at last agreed to the advice of his OKB Chief Engineer, S. Alekseev, who strongly supported the M-82 as a possible solution to the matter of increased horsepower. Shvetsov, too, was frustrated by a lack of customers for his new radial, and seeing the opportunity dispatched his OKB Deputy, Senior Engineer Valedinski, to Gor'ki to assist with the development of an M-82-powered LaGG. Working in close contact with power plant specialist Slepnev, the two engineers worked heroically to overcome the exceedingly complicated task of fitting the large radial engine to such a thin fuselage. As well, Alekseev (and later, Lavochkin) worked tirelessly on this matter despite the other responsibilities that were supposed to have taken precedence at this time, and undoubtedly the progress of the new radial LaGG was accelerated by the intensive efforts. At last, in February 1942, the new LaGG-3 M-82 rolled off the workshop floor, and factory test pilot Yu. Stankevich made the first flight on the 14th. Even during the initial evaluation flight it was patently obvious that the performance of the new machine was vastly improved over the standard LaGG-3, and Valedinski was said to have phoned Shvetsov immediately after the flight in triumph. The wheels of Soviet procurement now swung into furious action, and the prototype was flown successively by pilot-engineers Nikashin, Yakimov and Kubishkin, all of whom enthusiastically recommended the aircraft for production. The result was the famous April 1942 NKAP conference (described in the following section) which led to production of the La-5 fighter.

Development of the LaGG-3 fighter continued unabated, however, as it was clear that manufacture of the La-5 would take some time to supplant it. During the summer of 1942 a new series of LaGG-3-37 machines was constructed, these also mounting the Shpital'niy gun between the cylinder banks of the engine, but with the ammunition supply increased from 20 to 23 rounds. Power was provided by the M-105PF engine, and the second series LaGG-3-37, based on the *Oblegchenniy* airframe, could reach 502 km/h mph at sea level and 560 km/h at 5,000 m. Combat testing with the 291 IAP in the autumn and winter of 1942 was quite successful, and plans to manufacture a standardized LaGG-3-37 fighter were adopted at Tbilisi. By December, a production series standard was at last agreed with the NKAP, and manufacture of the LaGG-3-37 began in limited quantities during that month. Performance was largely unchanged in the standardized variant, but the Shpitalniy cannon was replaced by the lighter and more reliable Nudelman-Suranov NS-37 gun with 33 rounds available, and the single UBS above the engine was retained with 220 cartridges.

Delivery of the LaGG-3-37 continued well into 1943, albeit in limited numbers, and machines of this type served with several notable units. One *eskadrilya* of the famed *Normandie-Niemen* Regiment was amongst those so-equipped during 1943, and it flew the type with considerable success. The French pilots were enormously impressed by the fearsome power of the NS-37 cannon, and considered the LaGG to be a stable and accurate platform for this weapon. Indeed, on 5 June *Cpte.* Doret, illustrating the point, struck a Ju 87 dive-bomber from 500 m with a single round of 37 mm fire. The Junkers exploded in mid-air, downing an escorting Messerschmitt fighter nearby. In service, squadrons of LaGG-3-37s were often escorted by an equal number of standard LaGGs with the intention of shielding the heavier 'gun-ships' from the attention of enemy fighters, and this arrangement proved most effective when employed in a coordinated manner.

During 1942 and 1943 a few LaGG-3 fighters were completed at *Zavod* 21 with the AFA-I or -M tactical reconnaissance camera and armament was reduced to a single 20 mm gun firing through the spinner. Essentially a *Razvedchik*, or 'scout' aircraft, these machines received no distinctive designation. There was at least one LaGG fitted with an M-106 motor for high-altitude testing, and a two-seat training model was mooted, but apparently never completed. During the summer, the LaGG-3 *Oblegchenniy* was modified with underwing mounting brackets which could accommodate either an 80 litre drop tank or FAB bomb up to 100 kg in size, and this outfit became standard for manufacture at Tbilisi.

Further aerodynamic improvements to the LaGG-3 continued throughout 1942 at *Zavod* 31. The Lavochkin design bureau modified one of the new *Oblegchenniy* airframes with a retractable tailwheel, an internal radio aerial (allowing the removal of the mast aft of the cockpit), and the oil cooler intake was revised further, and could be identified by a subtle change in appearance. Further improvements were made to the flaps, the internal rudder and elevator counter-weights, and to the control surface linkages. Additionally, gearing changes to the M-105PF's supercharger were aimed at providing increased performance at even lower altitudes than had been achievable previously, as the LaGG was certainly envisaged as an escort and strike machine by this time in its development. The resulting 'improved and lightened' (*Uluchshenniy i Oblegchenniy*) LaGG-3 – known to the Lavochkin staff as the 'G' prototype – was outstanding. The modifications to the airframe not only resulted in higher performance, but the 'G' featured very much improved handling and control force characteristics than even the *Oblegchenniy* LaGG, and Pilot-Engineer Mischenko was thrilled with the aircraft. The NII VVS examined the 'G' only briefly during early April 1943, and immediately cleared the variant for manufacture. The production LaGG-3 *Uluchshenniy i Oblegchenniy* series had a maximum speed of 626 km/h at sea level and 598 km/h at 3,810 m, with initial climb reaching to 1,122 km/h and taking only 5.1 minutes to achieve 5,000 m. Termination of LaGG-3 production during the autumn of 1943 undoubtedly meant that the number of 'improved and lightened' LaGGs to enter service was relatively small, but these were enthusiastically received by service pilots wherever they were delivered, and found to be very much more than a match for any Messerschmitt fighter.

The outstanding proponent of the late-model LaGG fighter was probably Yuri Shipov of the 9 IAP VVS-ChMF. Shipov's *eskadrilya* was entirely equipped with LaGG-3 *Uluchshenniy i Oblegchenniy* models, and excelled at 'free-hunt' missions intended to counter German fighters over the Krim and Novorossiysk regions (Crimean Front). During 1943-44, Shipov downed eight Bf 109s from JG 52, his squadron accounting for nine further Messerschmitts, all without loss of its own. To the amazement of the regimental commander, Shipov demonstrated in a mock combat during 1944 that the 'improved and lightened' LaGG could successfully complete combat turns with a Yak-9D (universally recognized throughout the VVS as a turning dogfighter) and even climb better than it. Indeed, so outstanding were the last LaGG-3 models that the 9 IAP VVS-ChF had no difficulties encountering the formidable German Fw 190 after it was transferred to the Baltic Front in late 1944. It continued to operate these machines until the end of the war, ending with a sterling record against enemy fighters.

The final development in the LaGG programme involved yet another weight-saving course, largely under the direction of Gorbunov and engineer I. Ulechkov during the beginning of 1943. After a searching analysis, the machine was ruthlessly stripped of all extraneous weight, even the leading edge slats being removed to save precious kilograms. The oil cooler intake was further refined aerodynamically and made more shallow in profile, giving the machine's nose a more streamlined appearance. Power was provided by the M-105PF-2 engine which was capable of 1,240 hp. (1,310 hp for take-off and emergency boost), and the armament consisted of a single UBS gun above the engine and a 23 mm VYa-23 cannon firing through the spinner. This new LaGG development, the Type 105, represented a nearly complete re-design of the aircraft's structure, despite the external similarities in planform and configuration. The rear fuselage was cut down as on the La-5, and on the second Type 105 prototype, the oil cooler intake under the 'chin' was removed altogether and repositioned to the wing-root intakes. Though the Type 105 was formidable, protracted delays in development had meant that the aircraft did not reach the NII VVS until May 1944, by which time it was completely outclassed by the Yak-3 and La-7 fighters which were already in production. The NII VVS confirmed the type's fine handling, but rejected the 105 for series production and with that, the last chapter in the development of the LaGG-3 fighter was closed.

In all, 6,528 LaGG-3 fighters were manufactured during three years of production, from the beginning of 1941 to the end of 1943. The LaGG family were respectable dog-fighters, but they were at a considerable disadvantage to the Bf 109F and G in speed, and especially in the climb, particularly at heights above 5,000 m where the Messerschmitt could simply 'walk away' at will. Great effort was expended to improve the performance of the LaGG, and the later 'mature' versions of the wooden fighter were formidable. Control harmony was always outstanding in the type, and in the lightened versions the response was equally impressive. The LaGG-3 had nothing to fear in turning and horizontal manoeuvrability from German fighters, and this attribute was indeed key to its successful employment in combat, but the liquid-cooled LaGG had reached the limit of its performance potential, and this resulted in a switch to the much more powerful M-82 radial and the La-5.

	LaGG-3 1941 Zavod 23	LaGG-3 1941 early	LaGG-3 1941 mid	LaGG-3 1941 Zavod 153	LaGG-3-37 1941	LaGG-3 1942
Weights						
Empty:	2537 kg	2578 kg	2615 kg	2557 kg	2677 kg	2536 kg
Loaded:	3263 kg	3353 kg	3287 kg	3350 kg	3416 kg	3106 kg
Wing Area:	17.51 m.sq	17.51 m.sq	17.51 m.sq	17.51 m.sq	17.51 m.sq	17.51 m.sq
Engine	M-105P	M-105P	M-105P	M-105P	M-105PA	M-105PA
	1050 (1100) hp	1050 (1100) hp	1050 (1100) hp	1050 (1100) hp	1050 (1100) hp	1050 (1100) hp
Maximum Speed						
At Altitude:	576 km/h at 5000 m	535 km/h at 5000 m	540 km/h at 5000 m	532 km/h at 5000 m	532 km/h at 5000 m	550 km/h at 5000 m
Sea Level:	498 km/h	458 km/h	466 km/h	453 km/h	460 km/h	471 km/h
Climb						
Initial:	900 m/min	829 m/min	848 m/min	823 m/min	838 m/min	878 m/min
Time to Height:	6.8 min to 5000 m	8.5 min to 5000 m	7.9 min to 5000 m	8.7 min to 5000 m	8.2 min to 5000 m	7.1 min to 5000 m
Service Ceiling	8521 m	9300 m	9300 m	9300 m	8567 m	9300 m
Armament	2 x UBS	1 x UBS	1 x UBS	1 x UBS	1 x UBS	1 x UBS
	2 x ShKAS	2 x ShKAS	2 x ShKAS	2 x ShKAS	1 x Sh-37	1 x ShVAK
	1 x BK	1 x VYa-23	1 x ShVAK	1 x ShVAK		6 x RS-82

	LaGG-3 1942 Lightened	LaGG-3 1942 Boosted	LaGG-3 1942 Boosted and Lightened	LaGG-3 1942	LaGG-3-37 1943 Improved and Lightened	LaGG-3 Type 105
Weights						
Empty:	2278 kg	2636 kg	2322 kg	2838 kg	2226 kg	2155 kg
Loaded:	2871 kg	3106 kg	2911 kg	3370 kg	2777 kg	2755 kg
Wing Area:	17.51 m.sq	17.51 m.sq	17.51 m.sq	17.51 m.sq	17.51 m.sq	17.51 m.sq
Engine	M-105P	M-105PF	M-105PF	M-105PF	M-105PF	M-105PF-2
	1050 (1100) hp	1180 (1260) hp	1180 (1260) hp	1180 (1260) hp	1180 (1260) hp	1240 (1310) hp
Maximum Speed						
At Altitude:	571 km/h at 5000 m	565 km/h at 5000 m	576 km/h at 5000 m	560 km/h at 5000 m	598 km/h at 3810 m	619 km/h at 3415 m
At Sea Level:	468 km/h	498 km/h	515 km/h	502 km/h	545 km/h	555 km/h
Climb						
Initial:	960 m/min	982 m/min	1053 m/min	1019 m/min	1122 m/min	1158 m/min
Time to Height	6.7 min to 5000 m	6.6 min to 5000 m	6.0 min to 5000 m	6.4 min to 5000 m	5.1 min to 5000 m	4.8 min to 5000 m
Service Ceiling	9300 m	10215 m	10215 m	10215 m	10700 m	11220 m
Armament	1 x UBS	1 x UBS	1 x UBS	1 x UBS	1 x UBS	1 x UBS
	1 x ShVAK	1 x ShVAK	1 x ShVAK	1 x NS-37	1 x ShVAK	1 x VYa-23
	6 x RS-82					

**Early series
four-gun LaGG-3
Gor'ki production**

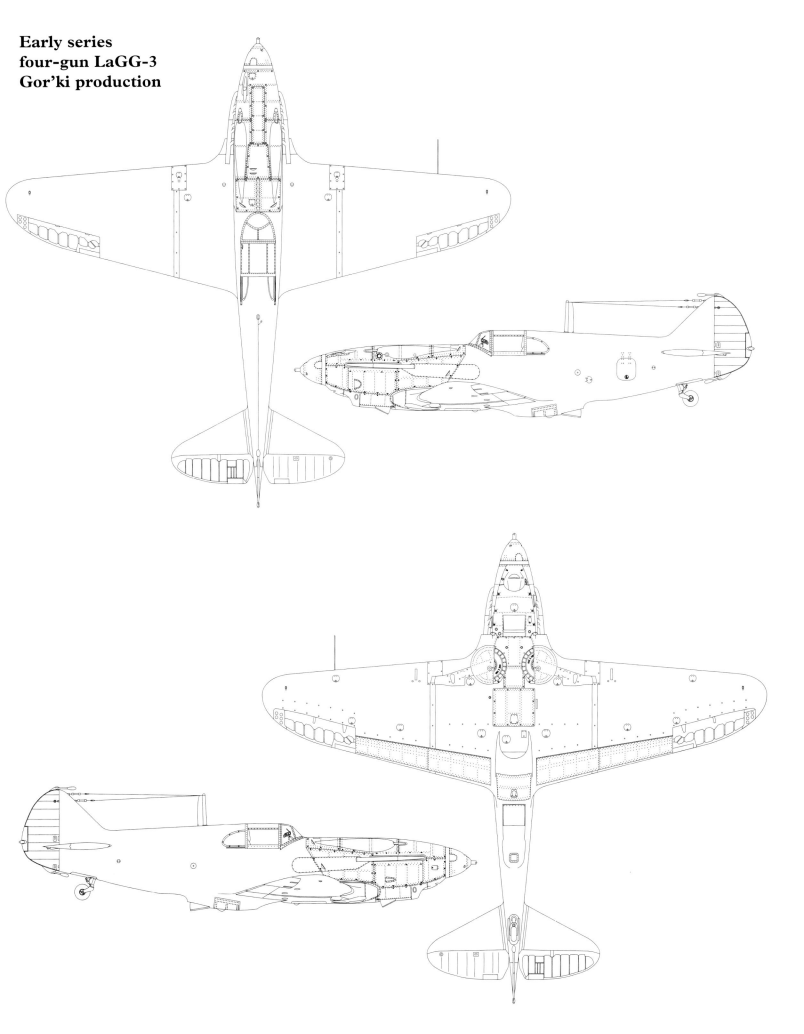

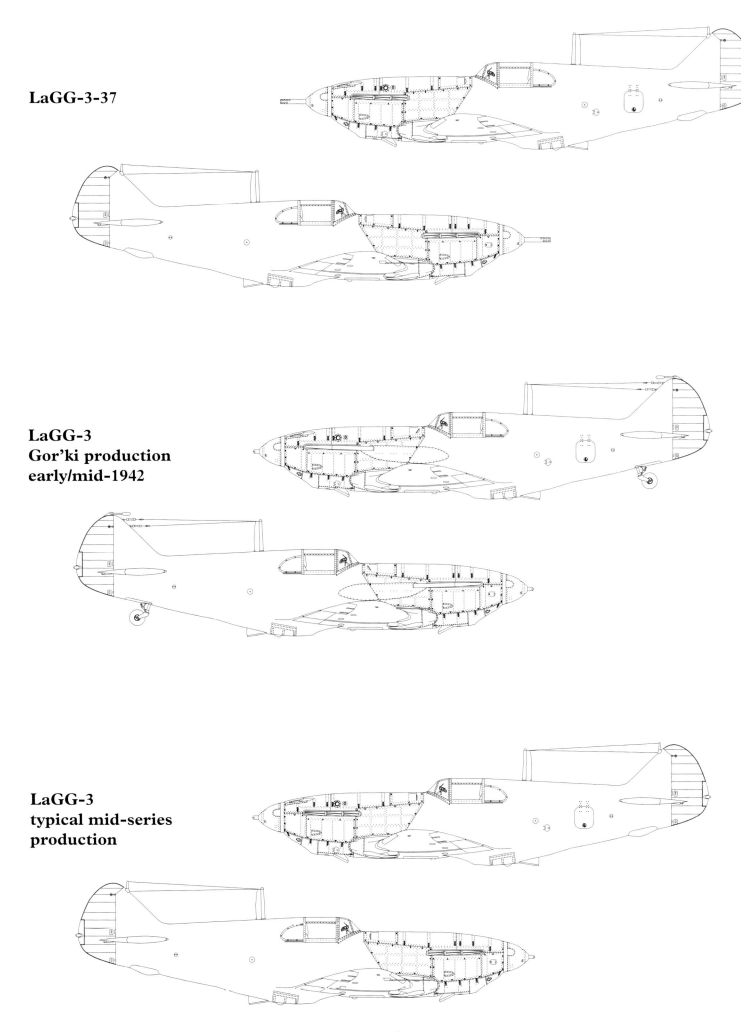

LaGG-3-37

**LaGG-3
Gor'ki production
early/mid-1942**

**LaGG-3
typical mid-series
production**

**Late series
LaGG-3** *oblegchenniy*
Tbilisi production

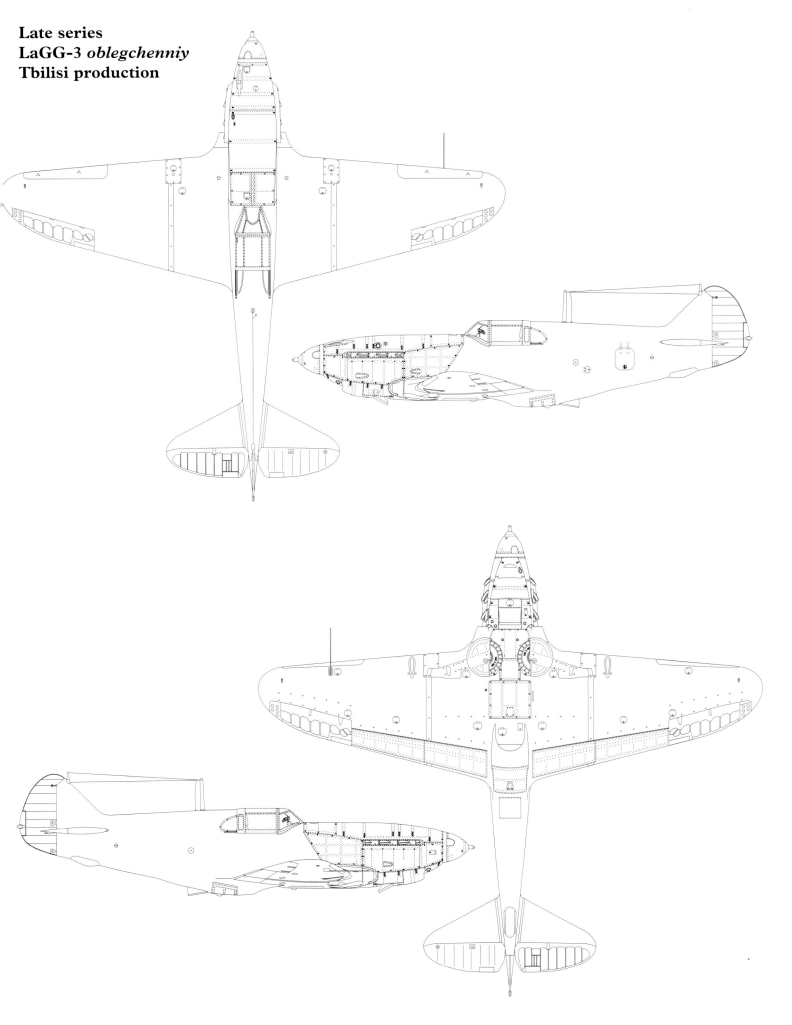

THE DEVELOPMENT OF CAMOUFLAGE ON
THE LaGG-3 FIGHTER

LaGG-3 Production... Everywhere

Following a complicated and often difficult development, the LaGG-3 fighter at last entered production in December 1940. Though the programme was based at *Zavod* 21, Gor'ki, various delays would result, and the initial examples of the aircraft would roll out of the *Zavod* 23 facility in Leningrad. Manufacture of the LaGG-3 fighter at Leningrad was brief. In that time, however, the plant produced aircraft of very high quality, and as if to identify its products visually, utilized a camouflage application of its own design. A total of 54 LaGG-3s were completed in Leningrad, and it is thought that only these machines wore this pattern (see Fig. 1).

Fig. 1

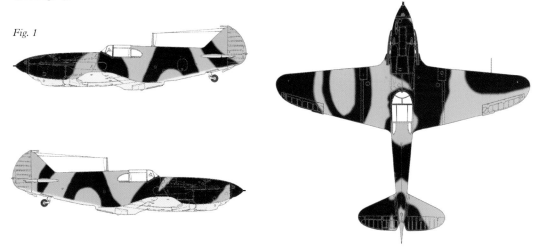

The pattern on the starboard wing sometimes resembled small bands of colour, but often it expressed what is nearly a 'loops' type application. If, indeed, this is what the staff had in mind, it is the first 'loops' feature known to have appeared in VVS camouflage. The port wing features are largely unknown, and have been re-constructed from a single, clear photograph. However, evidence visible in other pictures makes me confident that this was the usual pattern in use on this scheme. The fuselage pattern is not particularly noteworthy, and consists mostly of two hump features and a black nose. All colour demarcations appear to have been semi-hard, but very sharp-edged examples are known.

Another simplified pattern application was seen on products from *Zavod* 21 during early 1941. Completed in AII Black over AII Green on the upper surfaces, the scheme featured both hard and semi-hard colour demarcations (as illustrated here – see Fig. 2).

Fig. 2

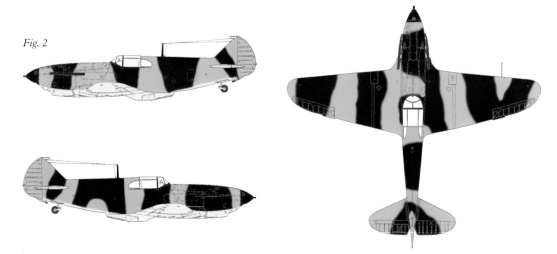

There were 'reversed' applications of this scheme in which the fuselage patterns on the port and starboard sides were switched. These 'reversed' versions are not seen frequently, but they do appear consistently throughout the usage of this camouflage scheme.

At the time of writing, the camouflage patterns of the early LaGG-3 examples from *Zavod* 31, Taganrog, are not known. There was apparently no major series of photographs taken at this plant by the Government prior to its evacuation in September-October 1941. When the factory resumed production in Tbilisi in 1942, it began to turn out an improved version of the fighter, one which had a different appearance and camouflage.

The last of the early series LaGG-3s was completed at *Zavod* 153, Novosibirsk. In keeping with this factory's reputation for extreme individualism and eccentricity, the machines built from the summer of 1941 until the end of manufacture in early 1942 featured a unique and quite interesting scheme. Although widely known and recognized – the result of an extensive Army photographic visit to the 44 IAP around Leningrad – this scheme was used only at Novosibirsk (see Fig. 3).

Fig. 3

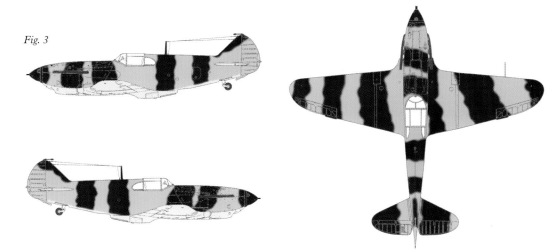

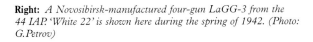

Above: *Photographed in late 1941, this is what appears to be a four-gun LaGG-3 of the 44 IAP wearing the Zavod 153 'banded pattern'. 'White 25' has had its sliding canopy removed as well as its wheel covers, probably to cope with the mud . (Photo: G.Petrov)*

Right: *A Novosibirsk-manufactured four-gun LaGG-3 from the 44 IAP. 'White 22' is shown here during the spring of 1942. (Photo: G.Petrov)*

Once again the colours in use were the AII lacquers of the period, Black over Green on the uppersurfaces with Blue underneath. The simplified application was completed in AII Black over AII Green, and with AII Blue undersurfaces. The pattern consisted mostly of simple bands of colour, these applied somewhat casually and with a soft colour demarcation. In fact, the Black is something of an appliqué, as it appears that the base coat of Green was applied carefully, showing a typical upper/lower colour demarcation.

At the time of writing, there is no definitive information on the interior colouration of these early LaGG-3s. The anecdotal evidence is that aircraft manufactured at Novosibirsk and Leningrad had their cockpits left unpainted. Given the brevity (Leningrad) and difficulty (Novosibirsk) of production at these facilities, that claim seems to be quite likely. The I-16 fighters manufactured at Gor'ki were probably the recipients of pre-war practices in cockpit finish, and probably had a uniform coating of A-14, AII Aluminium, or Wood finishes. One can only speculate as to the effect of these practices on the LaGG-3.

1942 – Production Matures

With the new year came improved variants of the LaGG-3 fighter, and of course new camouflage patterns. During the winter months of 1941-42, only *Zavod* 21 seemed to have finished its LaGGs in a white winter coating of MK-7 distemper (see Fig.4).

Fig. 4

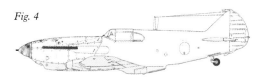

Right: *A winter-camouflaged five-gun LaGG-3 of the 3 GIAP VVS KBF (ex-5 IAP VVS KBF) running up on a snow-covered airfield on the Leningrad Front during the winter of 1941-42. This machine is thought to be one of the Zavod 23-manufactured models (note the unusual cowling shape). (Photo: G.Petrov)*

The other factories either halted manufacture before the onset of winter camouflage, or simply never applied any. As a result, many remarkable field-applied winter examples can be seen on early LaGG-3s.

Zavod 21 again led the way with a revised camouflage pattern on its temperate scheme. The pattern was not overly distinctive, and was applied in AII Black over AII Green (see Fig. 5).

Fig. 5

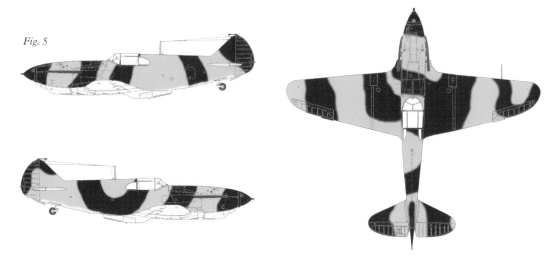

All uppersurface colour demarcations were semi-soft, reflecting the new trend of 1942. The upper/lower colour demarcation was semi-hard, and not as neatly executed as had been seen previously.

Zavod 31, now at Tbilisi, also issued its revised LaGG fighters with an updated camouflage. This scheme was completed in AII lacquers, as before, but with a very thick and attractively-applied fuselage meander (see Fig. 6).

Fig. 6

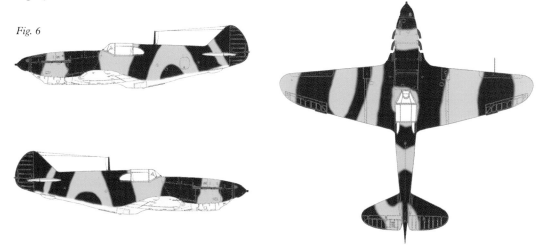

Right: *A Zavod 31-built LaGG-3 photographed near Moscow, summer 1942. This aircraft demonstrates the work of NKAP Department Chief Vladimir Gorbunov and his team, and shows unique aerodynamic improvements, such as a reshaped non-standard spinner; revised wing root inlets; reshaped oil cooler chin intake; new armament scheme; internally-balanced rudder; improved cowl panel sealing; improved forward windscreen installation and revised gas scavenging exit. This aircraft is already fitted with leading edge slats, despite the early date. (Photo: G.Petrov)*

The colour demarcations tended to be somewhat soft, ranging from semi-soft to semi-hard.

During 1942, the usual practice vis-à-vis cockpits seems to have been to finish them in the usual manner. Wood *Aerolak* was applied to the numerous wooden surfaces at the factory, but this colour was not used to give an overall uniform appearance, and components supplied by sub-contractors appear to have been left as they arrived. Unfinished cockpits are not usually seen in the photographic record on the LaGG-3 after 1941, and these were probably the exception to the rule.

AMT Colour

During the summer of 1942, *Zavod* 21 began to abandon the use of AII aerolacquer in favour of the new NKAP system, *Aerolak Matoviy*. Indeed, the LaGG-3 programme at this facility led the way, and AMT-only schemes were evident even before AII paints were abandoned on the same factory's La-5 fighter.

The first of these applications in AMT was very similar in pattern to many La-5 schemes. AMT-6 Black was applied over AMT-4 Green, and the undersurfaces were AMT-7 Blue (see Fig. 7).

Fig. 7

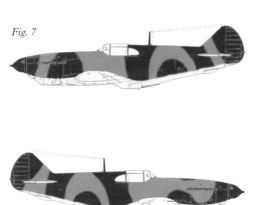

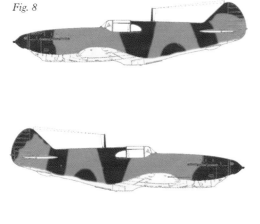

The colour demarcations in all locations were usually semi-hard, though a very few hard-edged examples are known. The fuselage pattern was a thin and simplified meander, but the upper view pattern was very neatly done. This scheme persisted at Gor'ki until the LaGG-3 programme – which was clearly winding down during 1942 – came at last to an end in the Spring of 1943.

However, at Tbilisi manufacture of the LaGG-3 would last until the very end of that year, and several more camouflage innovations were to come. The first of these new patterns appeared in the summer of 1942, this involving the new AMT colours in a two-tone scheme. AMT-6 was applied over AMT-4, and the undersurfaces were, of course, AMT-7 (see Fig. 8).

Fig. 8

This pattern application was very neat, and seems to show an influence from the concurrent Gor'ki pattern of the same time frame on the upper surfaces. The execution of the fuselage meander features was usually quite exact, and this is regarded as the hallmark of this pattern. The colour demarcation lines can range from semi-hard to semi-soft, but the latter are far more common.

Another typical modification to this application was also seen at *Zavod* 31. Again in AMT colours, it appeared at roughly the same time, though was less frequent in use (see Fig. 9).

Fig. 9

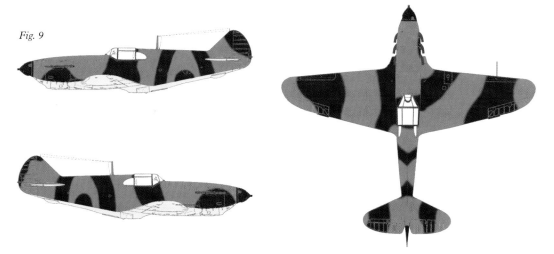

Harder-edged colour demarcations were known on this scheme in addition to semi-soft types.

These new Tbilisi patterns were well received by units in the field, and seem to have been the camouflage of choice for PARMs and other maintenance units repairing LaGG-3s. Without any significant modification, these pattern applications survived into the latter half of 1943.

During the winter of 1942-43 both factories were in the habit of finishing their LaGG-3s in MK-7 white. The application was usually professional, and always accomplished over the temperate camouflage of the time period (see Fig. 10).

Fig. 10

Right: *'Red 52', a typically white-camouflaged LaGG-3, was the personal mount of Hero of the Soviet Union Ivan Kaberov of the 3 GIAP VVS KBF and is seen here on the Leningrad Front in 1942-43. The MK-7 distemper was probably applied quite heavily, but has worn away in its usual manner. (Photo: G.Petrov)*

South Front Schemes

During 1942 and 1943 several batches of regionally appropriate camouflage schemes were applied at *Zavod* 21, Gor'ki. There are hints that this practice might have been adopted at Tbilisi in 1943, as well, but no definitive evidence has yet come to the fore.

In the 1942 version, the colours in use appear to be AII Black applied over AII Light Brown; the undersurfaces were probably AII Blue (see Fig. 11).

Fig. 11

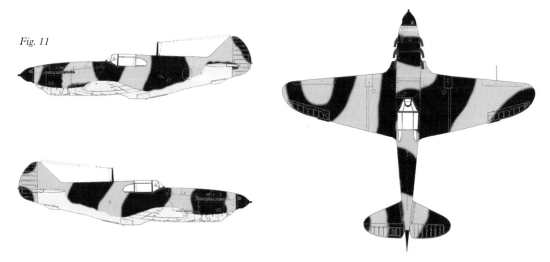

The pattern was very striking, and on the port wing there is an unmistakable 'loops' feature. The colour demarcations appear to have been semi-soft, but some photographs show a quite loosely-applied camouflage. Also, the upper/lower colour demarcation line is invariably irregular, and this is quite unique on the LaGG-3 programme.

During 1943 the colours seemed to have changed. First, there was no further regular use of AII lacquer at that time, and speculation is that the undersurface colour must have been AMT-7. The only known surviving photograph would tend to support that theory. However, the most consistent explanation for the upper surface colours are AII paints – Brown and Light Brown. No AMT and/or Am colour combination equates to the photograph (the negative of this print has been examined, as well). Therefore, a best estimation would be that these machines were finished with a mixed lacquer scheme (see Fig. 12).

Fig. 12

Unfortunately, as there is only one known view, no information on the starboard nor upper view is available. Despite the lack of photographic coverage, the better part of an entire Series were so finished, some 70-80 aircraft.

Turning Grey in 1943?

The debate over the first employment of the new NKAP two-tone grey camouflage scheme is a recurrent theme in this book. Two factories (Gor'ki and Tbilisi) were very aggressive in the introduction of AMT aerolacquers. It is no coincidence that both enterprises manufactured Lavochkin OKB designs, and it is true that these factories exchanged personnel and information regularly.

The key factor in this however, is that it is known when LaGG-3 production halted at each factory, particularly with respect to *Zavod* 31. As a result, it is beyond question, that since there are examples of LaGG-3s in AMT-12/-11 camouflage, this scheme was applied at *some point* during 1943. In general, this seems to be earlier than at other factories, where the practice mostly came into fashion during early 1944.

But, when exactly? As previously mentioned, photographs of some La-5Fs from *Zavod* 21 are under investigation, but no conclusion has been reached at the time of writing. On the LaGG-3, the new colour scheme appears only on machines of late manufacture – essentially the lightened variants with improved aerodynamics. It is therefore very unlikely that any machines at Gor'ki were painted in this way and it seems that Tbilisi introduced the new scheme on the LaGG-3 programme. The exact date at which this occurred is not known, but any date after the summer of 1943 is possible. Unfortunately, at the time of writing, there are no known photographs of LaGG manufacture at Tbilisi during this period. Such photographs will be necessary to pin-point the date, and at present the best *estimate* must remain the autumn/winter of 1943.

Advocates of an earlier date for the application of the new scheme point to a curious development on the LaGG-3's colouration. Since there were at least two major camouflage pattern applications, does this not then require an extended amount of time to develop them? The answer is unknown.

Be that as it may, the first pattern was an attractive, if somewhat generalized, application. The colours were AMT-12 over AMT-11 and the undersides in AMT-7 (see Fig. 13).

Below: Late model LaGG-3s of the 9 IAP VVS ChF serving in the Kuban region during the autumn of 1943 or the winter of 1943-44. These machines were probably amongst the earliest to wear the new AMT-11/-12/-7 camouflage. (Photo: G.Petrov)

Fig. 13

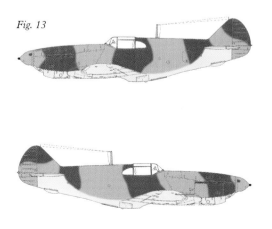

Right: Late model LaGG-3s in service with the 9 IAP VVS ChF, late 1943. (Photo: G.Petrov)

The uppersurface view was quite clever and neat in execution, while the fuselage applications were somewhat generic. All colour demarcation lines were semi-soft, and no undersurface colour was allowed to extend onto the rudder. The rear fuselage upper/lower colour demarcation 'ramp' feature was classically curved.

A second significant AMT grey application occurred at *Zavod* 31, possibly concurrent with the previous example. This pattern was clearly a version of the NKAP template, as one might well expect from this factory (see Fig. 14).

Fig. 14

Left: An unknown pilot of the VVS ChF stands next to his curiously-finished LaGG-3. Somewhat resembling a late Zavod 31 AMT-11/-12 pattern, this camouflage was probably applied in the field following the introduction of these new colours (some of the underlying darker areas, probably black, seem to be evident beneath the AMT-11 lacquer). Such repainting was particularly common on La-5s and surviving LaGG-3 aircraft in 1944. (Photo: G.Petrov)

Usually no AMT-7 colour was seen on the rudder in this scheme, but exceptions to this practice are known. The colour demarcations were semi-soft, and being a rather standard application, nothing more remarkable can be said about it.

Some of the very last LaGG-3s that were manufactured during the final winter months of 1943 wore a single-colour scheme. Typical for the time, this was completed in AMT-11. The rear fuselage 'ramp' feature tended to be quite casual, and the demarcation somewhat soft (see Fig. 15).

Fig. 15

Unusual LaGG-3 Camouflage

In the 168 IAP several LaGG-3s wore a makeshift camouflage during the winter of 1942-43. Some of these aircraft had what appears to be MK-7 applied over the Black area of the scheme, making them into two-tone white/green examples. Others sport wild patterns of white over the temperate camouflage, and one aircraft appears to have been painted with MK-7 over the upper and lower surfaces entirely.

Exceedingly intricate and colourful winter camouflage patterns were applied to the LaGG-3s of the 145 IAP (19 GIAP) during the winter of 1941-42. The photograph below can only hint at the extent of this appliqué work.

Right: *An early Series LaGG-3 of the 19 GIAP in the winter of 1942. Note the unusually rounded colour patterns on the horizontal stabilizer, and the hand-applied disruptive pattern over the fuselage. This is thought to be the personal aircraft of Hero of the Soviet Union Viktor Mironov (centre) of the 19 GIAP. (Photo: G.Petrov)*

Above: *A remarkable LaGG-3 of the 3 GIAP VVS KBF, summer 1943. This aircraft has been re-painted with a solid coat of AMT-4 Green, and has an unusual band in black (possibly AMT-6) seemingly to highlight the tactical number '59'. The plain red star is hand-drawn, and badly out of proportion. The pilot (unknown) is reporting to Eskadrilya Commander I. Kaberov. (Photo: G.Petrov)*

Right: *A LaGG-3 of the 19 GIAP (ex 145 IAP) wearing the famous 'hissing cat' emblem, 1942. (Photo: Author's collection)*

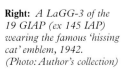

Above: *This LaGG-3 is interesting. It is an early four-gun model, and in the corner of the photograph the written date of '10 July 1941' is just visible. The aircraft seems to have an unpainted rear, wooden fuselage portion, which has been covered with meandering lines of AII Green lacquer. The rudder appears to be plain doped linen. The wings, however, do appear to have been finished and they show what seems to be the Novosibirsk 'banded' application. There have always been anecdotal reports that the last 20 or so LaGG-3s manufactured at Zavod 153 were delivered in such haste (apparently to make room for the Yak-7) that they left the factory unpainted. This photograph may well show one of these machines, but if true, the date must have been recorded in error – since these would have been completed in January-February 1942. (Photo: G.Petrov)*

Lavochkin LaGG-1, La-5, La-7

Chapter 2

Lavochkin La-5, La-5FN, La-7

In the annals of aviation history, there are a number of machines that have successfully made the transition from in-line to radial power plants, but perhaps none so fitfully as Semen Lavochkin's all-wood I-301 fighter. As sturdy and workman-like as the V-12-powered LaGG-3, the later radial engined versions of the La-5 and La-7 were transformed into superlative interceptors of outstanding performance, and wrought destruction on German formations they encountered. Ironically, Lavochkin resisted the development of the M-82-powered LaGG from the outset, and in fact came very close to preventing construction of the type altogether. Indeed, it was not until an impressive prototype machine was constructed virtually behind his back, and at the very moment that the future of his entire fighter programme was at stake, that Lavochkin at last embraced the concept. And yet, despite all of this, it must be said that Lavochkin's influence was keenly felt in the development of the La-5 and La-7 programme, and that in the end, these wonderful aircraft deserved to wear the stamp of Lavochkin's name and Bureau.

During the autumn of 1941, Gudkov – still at work in Moscow and always deeply interested in aircraft power plant matters – was searching for a means by which to improve the performance of several in-line powered fighter prototypes by fitting them with Arkadi Shvetsov's M-82 14-cylinder radial engine. Gudkov's work was in part seen as an insurance policy of sorts, offering an alternative engine scheme should supplies of the Klimov V-12 suddenly fall into jeopardy. But Gudkov was convinced that if the big radial could be properly mounted to the airframe, the resulting moderate increase in weight and drag would be offset by the much higher power rating of the motor, and thus would result in great advances in performance. Work of this kind with the Yak-7 and MiG-3 essentially came to nothing (though production of a Yak-7 M-82 was mooted for a time), but his radial creation using a LaGG-3 airframe, dubbed Gu-82, was more successful.

Gudkov created the Gu-82 in a relatively short period by taking a completed engine and cowling unit from the dormant Su-2 production lines in Moscow and installing this into one of the pre-production LaGG-3 airframes left in the OKB 301 workshops. His flare for power plant matters was shown to great effect, for although the machine was a pure lash-up, the fit of the cowl unit and the fairing skirts into the fuselage looked entirely professional and well-designed. In fact, however, the internal arrangement of cowling baffles and mounting hardware were a complicated maze of hand-built items, completely impossible to replicate in any type of mass production. This meant that the Gu-82 was really more of a concept demonstration machine than a production prototype, a fact that would result in consternation later on in the programme. Gudkov had also provided a solution to the problem of arming the fighter by neatly installing two synchronized 20 mm ShVAK cannon above the engine, and the Gu-82 appeared to be a very sound package when it rolled off the workshop floor in July 1941.

Propeller and engine troubles, and Gudkov's assignment to improve the mounting of the 37 mm cannon in the LaGG-3, kept the machine grounded until September. However, at last taking to the air, the Gu-82 immediately began to register flight performance figures that seemed extraordinary. Indeed, on 7 October of that year Factory Test Pilot Grishin flew the Gu-82 to a maximum speed of 629 km/h at 5,000 m after having reached that altitude in only 5.5 minutes. These figures were sensational and were immediately brought to the attention of the NKAP by Gudkov and Factory Director Eskin. Perhaps frustrated by the current difficulties besetting the LaGG programme, the NKAP began to consider a Production Contract for the Gu-82, despite the fact that almost nothing further was known about the prototype! Indeed, Gudkov and Eskin had certainly not transmitted the remainder of Grishin's report on the Gu-82, because he also noted that the aircraft's centre of gravity was precariously far forward, resulting in

poor handling and exceptionally difficult landing behaviour, that the engine would both overheat seriously at full power and over-cool (shock-cool) dangerously in a dive, and that the M-82's severe torque effect drastically limited aileron response when banking to the right.

In late October and November 1941, the evacuation of the *Zavod* 301 facility was ordered, interrupting the new machine's flight evaluation programme, and Gudkov was transferred to *Zavod* 153 at Novosibirsk along with the Gu-82 prototype. Once in place at the new factory, Gudkov found himself with a host of new assignments involving aircraft armament and engine cooling, and the NKAP ordered Gudkov to hand over the development of his creation to the Lavochkin OKB staff at Gor'ki. The Gu-82 was subsequently moved by rail to that facility, but while in transit, Lavochkin's staff was ordered to relocate to *Zavod* 31 at Tbilisi. The resulting confusion, no doubt exacerbated by Gudkov's disappointment at having his most significant achievement taken from his control, seriously delayed work on the M-82 powered LaGG prototype, much to the delight of Yakovlev, who was busy trying to monopolize Yak-7 production at *Zavod* 21. Furthermore, the arrival of the Gu-82 at Gor'ki must have reinforced Lavochkin's prejudices against the use of the M-82 radial in his programme, not only in the prototype's shortcomings in handling, but also in the fact that it in no way resembled an aircraft suitable for mass production.

It was at this critical juncture that Shvetsov's OKB Deputy Valendinski arrived at *Zavod* 21. Despite Lavochkin's objections, Valendinski was warmly received by Chief Designer S. Alekseev, and an ad-hoc group materialized to first study the Gu-82 prototype, then construct an entirely new prototype using a production LaGG airframe and an M-82 mock-up engine brought by Valendinksi. Aircraft Motor Engineer Slepnev and Gor'ki Armament Brigade Leader Shabanov were also drawn into the process by Alekseev. The tasks facing this development group were complicated in the extreme, and it soon became apparent that the entire forward fuselage would have to be redesigned from scratch, including the engine mountings. Working with extraordinary determination and skill, the ad hoc team built a new prototype machine in less than 40 days, rolling the new LaGG-3 M-82 off the workshop floor on 10 February 1942. The new prototype featured completely redesigned engine mounts and an all-new cowling, incorporating revised internal baffling and components and supplemented by two large cooling flaps on either side of the unit's trailing edge.

Highly impressed by the work on the LaGG-3 M-82, Lavochkin now reversed himself and became an active proponent of the type. On the 14th, the new prototype made its first flight with Factory Pilot Mischenko at the controls, Lavochkin looking on anxiously. Despite over-heating problems with the engine, the M-82-powered machine was clearly an advance over the in-line LaGG fighter in performance, and Mischenko's impressions were very favourable overall. Lavochkin

La-5 'White 60'

Location and assignment uncertain

Colours:
AMT-4/-6/-7 application from *Zavod* 21

La-5F 'White 10'

41 GIAP
Aleksandr Pavlov, 1944

Colours:
AMT-11/-12/-7 field application

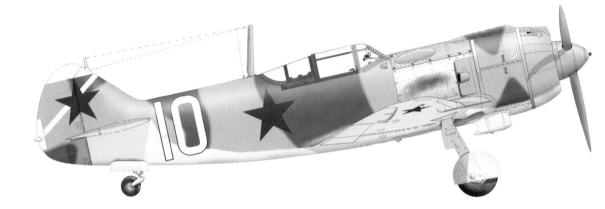

La-5F 'White 11'

2 GIAP
Pilot unknown
1944

Colours:
AMT-11/-12/-7 field application

La-5F 'White 45'

3 GIAP VVS KBF
Lavensaari, Leningrad Front
Kpt. Ivan Tsapov
1944

Colours:
AMT-11/-12/-7 application from *Zavod* 21 or 99

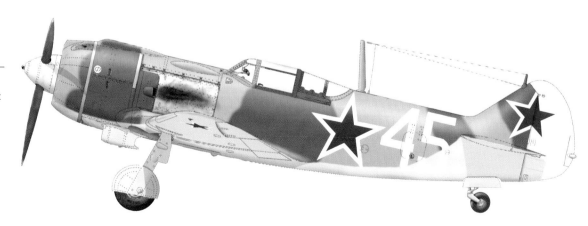

was now convinced that the LaGG-3 M-82 represented the salvation of his development programme, whose future at that moment seemed to be in question. The result was nothing short of a lobbying campaign directed at Stalin, reports from various authorities within the Soviet defence establishment (including Factory Administration Head Gostintsev, Regional Secretaries Gusarov and Rodinov, and Factory Pilot Nikashin) all reaching the State Defence Committee the following month.

The resulting political machinations were indeed significant, but the performance of the new LaGG-3 M-82 – known to the Lavochkin staff as the Type 37 – spoke for itself. Seeing the obvious potential, the Government established a joint commission to examine the new prototype at the end of April, comprised of pilots and engineers from the NII VVS, TsAGI, and the LII. This commission, often recalled as the famous 'La-5 Committee', worked under difficult conditions and with a very tight schedule, flight test evaluations being scheduled for a mere six days, and with the demand that a recommendation be forwarded to the State Defence Committee immediately upon completion of the test course! Eleven flights were made by the Committee Pilot-Engineers Kubishkin, Saginov and Yakimov, and this data was supplemented with performance analyses collected by previous evaluation flights by Kubishkin and Mishchenko. The Committee confirmed the earlier flight data and impressions of the LaGG-3 M-82, and save for difficulties with engine over-heating, regarded the type as very successful. The resulting report to Moscow listed a maximum speed of 518 km/h at sea level and 604 km/h at 6,402 m, with an initial climb of 1,072 m/min., and requiring only 5.2 minutes to reach 5,000 m at full boost. Handling was said to be good, and essentially unchanged from that of the standard LaGG-3, save for the effects of engine torque on aileron rolls to the right. The joint commission formally recommended the LaGG-3 M-82 type for series production based on the evaluation course, and submitted these findings to the State Defence Committee.

Now, the NKAP swung into furious action, and issued no fewer than three Production Contracts in as many days for manufacture of the new fighter at *Zavod* 21. The aircraft was noted on the second document as the type 'LaG-5', and it is under this nomenclature that production commenced at Gor'ki. Meanwhile, Lavochkin and his OKB staff were instructed to remain at *Zavod* 21 to oversee the development of the new machine, work on the LaGG-3 programme being left under Gorbunov's dynamic direction at Tbilisi. Production of the new fighter at Gor'ki was skilfully handled by the plant staff, and the new programme was seamlessly integrated into the operation of the factory, supplanting the production programme of Lavochkin's old rival, Yakovlev, and his Yak-7 – this time much to the delight of Lavochkin.

The initial production LaG-5s were powered by the Shvetsov M-82A radial delivering 1,330 hp (1,510 hp for take-off and emergency boost), and driving a VISh-105V propeller. Armament comprised two synchronized 20 mm ShVAK cannon mounted above the engine, each supplied with 140 rounds of ammunition. The PBP-1a gunsight was standard, and all sundry equipment was similar to the standard, early 1942 LaGG-3 fighter, whose airframes were utilized in manufacture. Fuel was divided into five cells with a capacity of 430 ltr, as on the concurrent LaGG-3, and some of the very early examples were seen to lack leading edge wing slats. All up weight for the production LaG-5 was 3,367 kg, which led to a reduction in flight performance. The early LaG-5 could achieve only 512 km/h at sea level and 583 km/h at 6,250 m, climbing initially at 983 m/min.; figures significantly lower than that of the LaGG-3 M-82 prototype.

The introduction of the first such machines into combat was less than auspicious, pilots of the

49 IAP noting that the performance of the LaG-5 was considerably less than they had been led to expect. Worse, these machines were based on LaGG-3 airframes that had already been rejected from production in their respective programmes, because they suffered from insufficient internal balance units for the control surfaces. This fact, combined with the powerful torque of the M-82A, resulted in poor control and a considerable physical workload for the LaG-5 pilot – very unhappy flight characteristics for combat use. Furthermore, cooling difficulties were reaching untenable proportions, a full 50 per cent of the machines on hand being unavailable for operations due to such defects. The 49 IAP's first battle accounts revealed the destruction of 16 enemy aircraft for the loss of ten LaG-5s and five pilots, and upon hearing of this situation the State Defence Committee dispatched a commission from TsAGI to *Zavod* 21 to investigate matters.

The TsAGI team quickly determined the nature of each difficulty, and recommendations from this group were effected immediately upon the production lines. TsAGI Deputy, Prof. Polinovski, worked especially successfully on the most serious of these problems, this involving excess drag generated by the cowling's internal cooling baffles. Polinovski's modifications resulted in the relocation of the supercharger intake on the outside of the cowling structure, being placed along the top of the unit (similar to what had been done by Slepnev and Valendinski on the LaGG-3 M-82), but aft of the forward cowl ring, giving a truncated appearance. A series of radially disposed louvres were installed just inside the forward cowling face, these deploying outwards from the central reduction gear housing boss similar to a child's pinwheel. These units were designed by TsAGI during wind tunnel testing, and were outstandingly successful in regulating airflow over the engine. The internal baffles were also completely redesigned, and the result was drastically superior cooling for the motor, and also reduced drag at the same time. Finally, manufacture resumed making use of the current LaGG airframe only, all earlier examples being shipped by rail to Tbilisi for refurbishment.

The revised, or 'Standard' LaG-5 began to reach combat units in August and September of 1942. These aircraft typically reached 525 km/h at sea level and 588 km/h at 6,250 m, and could climb initially at 1,021 m/min. Though these figures were an improvement over the earlier versions (such as the Series 4 machine tested at the NII VVS), they still did not represent the quantum jump in performance over the LaGG-3 that had been promised, and indeed some units had already been flying the LaGG-3 (Obl) for some months, which could generally out-perform the LaG-5! In September, the NKAP again revised the Production Contract to codify the detail changes made to the cowling and other sundry areas, and the fighter's nomenclature was revised at the same time to La-5.

Above: *A very early series LaG-5 (note the early cowling details) photographed in 1943 in the Orel-Kursk area. The cowl bands have been painted over, but the stainless steel exhaust plate has not. The poor fit of this item is a sure sign that this aircraft was a LaGG-3 airframe converted to La-5 production. (Photo: G.Petrov)*

In November, further improvements were applied to a standard production La-5 when the rear fuselage decking was cut down, and the canopy replaced by a clear teardrop-shaped rear section. For protection, a 55 mm sheet of armoured glass was fitted behind the pilot's head, and the 8 mm armour sheet behind the pilot's chair was widened. The ammunition boxes for the ShVAK cannon were also enlarged, 170 rounds being provided for each weapon. Performance was not measurably affected by these modifications, and changes to the production line were expected to be carried out with no stoppage in manufacture. These modifications resulted in very greatly improved visibility, and this machine was submitted for evaluation by NII pilots at once.

The debut of the La-5 in numbers during the Stalingrad Campaign has been the subject of debate and over-simplification. The overall picture is one of successful employment, at least in combat. Units equipped with the older LaG-5 did not perform as well as those flying the La-5 variant, while the units that were equipped with the improved La-5s (such as the 3 GIAP) wrought havoc on the *Luftwaffe*. All manner of variables came into play – not least the experience level of the units involved – but generally the newer La-5s performed better, and some units flying the LaG-5 were quite mediocre. However, maintenance and engine cooling problems[1] were by no means banished at this time, and it seems that no regiment managed to keep more than about 60 per cent of its strength of La-5s in the air at any one time, an appalling reliability rate for a VVS aircraft.

The experiences of two similar units gives a good flavour of the La-5's performance at Stalingrad. The 3 GIAP, equipped with factory-fresh La-5 *Massoviy* (Standard) fighters, began operations over the North Stalingrad Front during December 1942. Here, they performed extremely well against the Bf 109 F-4s and G-2s of JG 53. On 15 December, P. Bazanov led 18 La-5s into combat against 31 Bf 109s, destroying seven without loss, including one personal victory. Again, on 22 December, the 3 GIAP found itself badly outnumbered, Commander Propenko attacking 25 Messerschmitts with a single *eskadrilya*, and claiming five destroyed with a 'double' for himself. During the Campaign, the 3 GIAP engaged in 53 encounters with enemy fighters and destroyed 42 enemy aircraft for the loss of five La-5s and two pilots. Numerous bomber and transport aircraft were also destroyed, and the 3 GIAP was singled out for its outstanding performance by Corps Commander Eremenko. Meanwhile, the 437 IAP, part of the very same Division, fared much worse in their LaG-5s. On 7 January 1943, the unit clashed with JG 52 and lost five fighters and two pilots for one Messerschmitt, with two pilots seriously wounded. On 1 February, a large encounter developed with aircraft from JG 53 over Pitomnik airfield, which involved about 25 fighters from both sides. Four Bf 109s were destroyed along with two He 111s and two Ju 52 transports, but at the heavy cost of six LaG-5s, plus several damaged, with all of the downed pilots either killed or captured.

Meanwhile, the Shvetsov OKB at Perm (*Zavod 19*) had been hard at work with a commission from TsIAM to correct certain problems with the M-82 engine, and its installation in the La-5 fighter. For this purpose, the last four machines (including, for example, Production No.37210853) of Series 8 had been allocated to a joint development team featuring representatives from TsAGI, the LII and TsIAM for development work of this type. These four machines were finished together by factory personnel and the commission, and featured several notable improvements, including cowling panels that were tightly sealed by redesigned joints, a new and more streamlined oil cooler, improved supercharger intake design, and modifications to the exhaust manifolds. The resulting increase in performance was quite notable, No.37210853 reaching 604 km/h at 6,250 m, and demonstrating equally improved climb performance.

Next, the M-82's major faults were rectified by Shvetsov and the TsIAM team alongside these airframe developments. The problem with spark plug erosion was cured, the cylinder heads were re-designed for superior cooling, the oil cooler pump improved, and exhaust gas ducting revised. The resulting modifications extended the M-82's combat lifespan to 150 hours, and operation at maximum power could now be sustained with no further fear of damage to the motor. Further, the improved temperature control properties and cylinder head design meant that the M-82 could be operated without fear at full over-boost, and in the second supercharger gear, increasing emergency and take-off horsepower to 1,700 hp. The improved engine was designated the M-82F (*forsirovanni*, or 'boosted'), and was placed into immediate manufacture at *Zavod 19*.

Consequently, the NKAP ordered that all La-5 production was to include the new motor at the earliest possible moment, this new variant later being designated somewhat retroactively as the La-5F. Production examples of the new version began to roll off the Gor'ki lines during January, 1943. The new La-5F could be identified externally by neater, more streamlined cowlings, revised oil cooler housing shape, and a new supercharger intake featuring an inlet on the cowling lip as well as a fairing aft of the main cowl ring. With a gross take-off weight of 3,365 kg, the La-5F could achieve 554 km/h at sea level and 601 km/h at 6,250 m, and initial climb rose to 1,125 m/min. Furthermore, beginning with the Ninth Series manufacture of the La-5F, the fuselage and armament modifications reviewed by the NII the previous November were incorporated into the programme, and the La-5F began to appear with the cut-down rear decking and fully glazed canopy. The new variant's performance remained unchanged, but the improvement in visibility was extremely popular with VVS pilots, and even greater successes mounted immediately.

At this juncture the Lavochkin OKB staff began work on a lightened La-5, known as the Type 39. Much has been made in Lavochkin's surviving papers about the Type 39, but the Production Diary for *Zavod 21* strongly suggests what had long been suspected – namely, that the Type-39 was nothing more dramatic than a La-5 based upon an LaGG-3 *Oblegchenniy* airframe dispatched from Tbilisi. Indeed, since the *Oblegchenniy* had successfully been in production for at least six months prior to work on the Type 39, the question must be asked why the La-5 had not *initially* been based on this standard? Be that as it may, development of the Type 39 moved ahead with predictable speed. The outer wing fuel cells were removed and the empennage lightened, as on the La-3(*Obl.*), and revisions were made to the control linkages in the wing and tailplane. A major improvement was effected with regard to the landing gear, however, when the gear shock struts were welded directly to attachments on the forward wing spar, and modified in overall length. This clever engineering improved the incipient bouncing characteristic of the La- series fighters whilst landing, and represented a major advancement in safety for inexperienced pilots.

The resulting Type 39 aircraft was a great improvement upon its predecessor's handling and manoeuvrability, and with dramatically increased performance. Testing at the factory was accomplished in a few flights during February 1943, and all of the modifications were recommended for series manufacture. The revised La-5 airframe was simply introduced onto the La-5F production lines as it became available, no designation change of any kind signifying the new variant. In this form, the La-5F (Type 39) weighed 3,226 kg at take-off, and its maximum speed rose to 559 km/h at sea level and 616 km/h at 5,709 m. Climbing ability improved even more dramatically, an initial value of 3,745 ft./min. being achieved, reaching 5,000 m in only five minutes. Better still, horizontal manoeuvrability and turning circle were significantly improved by the lightened airframe, aileron response now exceeding even that of the Yak-9.

With the new La-5F entering frontline service in March 1943, VVS pilots at last had a La-5 capable of the kind of performance they had been promised. At once, pilots reported the outstanding capabilities of the new La-5F over the Bf 109 G, being superior to the enemy in-line fighter in every performance category below 6,100 m. Control harmony was excellent, and for the first time Soviet pilots felt that Lavochkin's fighter had equalled the formidable Fw 190. Pod. Pokrishev's 159 IAP set the tone early in the new La-5F (Type 39) when, on 20 May, it became embroiled in a huge contest with over 50 Bf 109s. Thirteen Messerschmitts were destroyed for the loss of a single La-5F, this belonging to the Regiment's most novice flyer, and

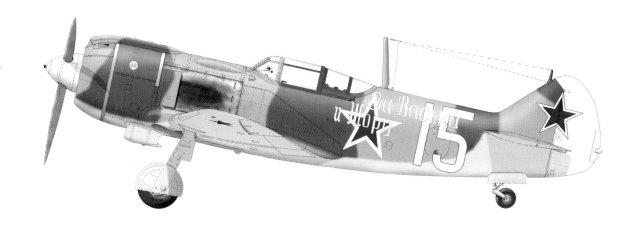

La-5FN 'White 15'

159 IAP
Petr Likholetov
Leningrad Front
Summer 1944

Colours:
AMT-11/-12/-7 from
Zavod 381

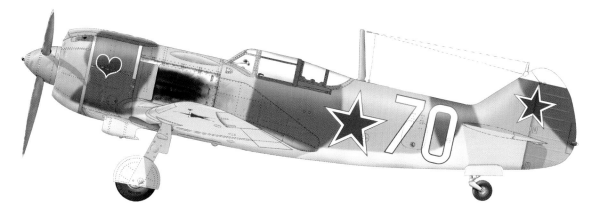

La-5FN 'White 70'

41 GIAP
St.Lt. Sementsov
Ukraine
Summer 1944

Colours:
AMT-11/-12/-7 application
from *Zavod* 21 or 99

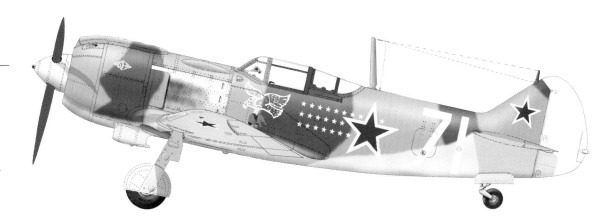

La-5FN 'White 71'

254 IAP
Pilot unknown
Poland
Autumn 1944

Colours:
AMT-11/-12/-7 application
from *Zavod* 21 or 99

La-5FN 'White 95'

Location and ownership
uncertain
ca. 1944

Colours:
AMT-11/-12/-7 application
from *Zavod* 21 or 99

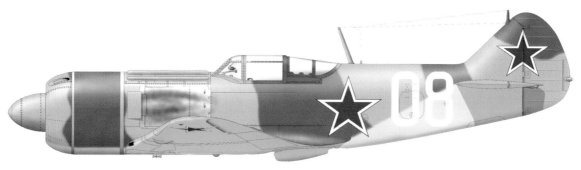

La-7 'White 08'

Moscow factory
1945

Colours:
AMT-11/-12/-7 application
from *Zavod* 381

La-7 'White 14'

Unit unknown
Lt. A.A. Bivalov
Gor'ki factory
1945

Colours:
AMT-11/-12/-7 application
from *Zavod* 21

La-7 'White 24'

9 GIAP
Sultan Amet-Khan
Germany
February 1945

Colours:
AMT-11/-12/-7 application
from *Zavod* 381

La-7 'Yellow 06'

Unit and pilot unknown
Baltic Front
1945

Colours:
AMT-12/-7 application
from *Zavod* 381

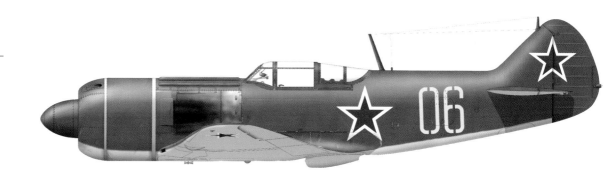

with *Lts* Serov and Likholitev both claiming 'doubles'. Despite holding a two-to-one numerical advantage, the enemy formation was routed in the course of the action and was seen to flee at full boost. On 27 May, the new La-5Fs experienced their first major encounter with the Fw 190, 11 Lavochkins of the 31 IAP engaging a similar number of enemy Focke-Wulfs. The ensuing combat was bitterly contested by both sides, virtually none of the VVS fighters returning undamaged. In the final tally, three La-5s were lost for six Fw 190s, all of the Soviet pilots surviving the ordeal to fight again.

The No.2 Type 39 prototype was further modified back at *Zavod* 21, meanwhile, this machine exhibiting additional refinements. To save weight, the wing's twin *delta-drevesina* spars were replaced by

duralumin units of similar shape and configuration. Another round of aerodynamic improvements was carried out on the airframe surface, around the cowling, the oil cooler housing, and again on the supercharger intake, which was now lengthened to the front of the cowling. In April, an early version of the new M-82FN motor was installed in the Type 39 No.2, this power plant featuring direct fuel injection, which could reliably deliver 1,470 hp (1,850 hp for take-off and emergency boost). With all modifications, the Type 39 No.2 weighed 2,130 kg in its loaded condition, and fuel was now housed in a main fuel cell in the fuselage, all wing tanks having been discarded.

Factory Pilot Nikashin flew the new machine later in the month, still designated as Type 39 to the staff, and confirmed Lavochkin's own calculations regarding the additional improvements. The revised Type 39 No.2 reached 599 km/h at sea level and 653 km/h at 6,250 m, climbing initially at the exceptional rate of 1,241 m/min; and taking a mere 4.8 minutes. to reach 5,000 m. Noting these outstanding results, the NKAP issued an immediate Production Contract for the new La-5 machine based on the FN motor, this to be designated La-5FN. Noting the various performance difficulties that plagued the introduction of previous Lavochkin fighter variants, the NKAP specifically decreed that production of the La-5FN was to feature comparable flight characteristics to the factory evaluation prototype.

At the same time, manufacture of the La-5F was getting fully underway at two additional factories, *Zavod* 99 at Ulan-Ude and the refurbished and expanded *Zavod* 381 facility in Moscow. Instigation of production at both factories was achieved with great success, largely on the basis of extensive drawings and tooling instructions assembled at Lavochkin's personal direction. This operation was very much in contrast to the LaGG fighter programme, and Lavochkin must have certainly learned his lesson in this regard during difficulties with production the previous summer. Both facilities produced La-5F machines of high manufacturing standards and in June 1943, the LII examined Ulan-Ude machine No.99391160 and recorded a flight performance of 561 km/h at sea level and 619 km/h at 5,790 m at a gross weight of 3,202 kg.

Unfortunately, at Gor'ki the requirement for uninterrupted La-5 production meant that Lavochkin's staff was left to introduce the new La-5FN modifications piecemeal on the first production examples as they rolled off the lines late in May 1943. In this condition, early La-5FNs featured performance that was completely unchanged from the current La-5F models, and in frustration, a Government investigation of Lavochkin's OKB ensued that summer. Lavochkin and his team were subsequently cleared of wrongdoing and incompetence, especially in light of the improving performance of production examples during the summer and autumn, but the episode was yet another blemish on the designer's reputation.

The La-5FN model fired its guns in anger for the first time over the massive Kursk salient in June 1943, many of these in service with the 32 GIAP under *Polk.* Davidkov. So urgent was the introduction of these aircraft for service evaluations under combat conditions, that some of the machines were said to have been rushed to the Front in a partially unpainted condition, and many appear to have lacked proper Soviet national markings. These fighters represented an immature batch of production models. Davidkov recorded that virtually none of the La-5FNs delivered to the Regiment featured entirely similar performance characteristics. However, despite these difficulties, the new La-5FN performed very well with the 32 GIAP, the Regiment destroying 33 enemy aircraft (including 21 Fw 190s) for the loss of six of its own number in 25 combats. Some pilots, such as Babkov and Shishkin, apparently received La-5FNs of very high performance with all of the new improvements built in, and regarded their aircraft as 'completely untouchable' by German fighters. Shishkin, in particular, demonstrated his aircraft's capabilities on 17 July by single-handedly annihilating an entire *Schwarm* of Focke-Wulfs in one bitter 15 minute dogfight. On 6 July 1943, Artem K. Gorovets entered the annals of military aviation legend when he spotted a flight of Ju 87s and attacked them single-handedly. Despite the frantic evasive manoeuvring of the German dive-bombers, Gorovets downed nine of the Stukas before several unseen Fw 190s fell on him from above. Gorovets was hit fatally and crashed near Zvorinskie Dvori.

By September 1943, the standard La-5FN was being completed in substantial numbers with all the design refinements in place, as supply of the M-82FN motor finally improved. However, at both Gor'ki and Moscow the La-5F model continued to be manufactured alongside the newer La-5FN well into the autumn and the winter months at *Zavod* 99. Some of the later La-5F models were in fact hybrids, featuring the revised and improved –FN airframe but mounting the M-82F motor, these being particularly common in manufacture at *Zavod* 381. Such aircraft must have sported improved performance, but there do not

Above: *A photograph which depicts the transition from La-5F to La-5FN. On the left, a late model La-5F with all of the 'Type 39' improvements; to the right, an early La-5FN. These 159 IAP pilots are assembled in front of the Regimental Commander Petr Pokrishev in 1944. (Photo: G.Petrov)*

seem to be any surviving measurements of the type's characteristics. A typical 'standardized' La-5FN of late 1943 weighed 3,329 kg at take-off and retained the normal armament of two 20 mm ShVAK cannon above the engine, but the supply of ammunition was increased again, the port (and at Moscow, the starboard as well) gun's box now containing 200 cartridges. Maximum speed [2] rose to 577 km/h at sea level and 638 km/h at 5,945 m (without boosting the engine fully, the figures were measured at 337 mph and 385 mph, respectively), the aircraft climbing initially at 1,214 m/min and reaching 5,000 m in only 4.6 minutes (five minutes without boosting). Control harmony and response were outstanding in the La-5FN, stick forces remaining light and effective right through the flight envelope.

Despite the limited numbers of La-5FNs introduced into service during 1943 (about 1,500 altogether), the type had an effect on the air war over the Russian Front out of all proportion to its availability. The *Luftwaffe* was exasperated by the fact that the various models of the La-5, La-5F and La-5FN could not be distinguished in combat, and thus German pilots were forced to respect all La-5s as potentially devastating FN models. The situation was analogous to that occurring on the Western Front vis-à-vis the Spitfire Mk.V and Mk.IX, but to even more dramatic effect, and enemy fighter activity was drastically curtailed – and often completely neutralized – by the arrival of La-5FNs to the Front. Indeed, many VVS aces began to compile impressive scores on the La-5FN, including Popkov, Kozhedub, and Golubev, to name only a few, and losses in the type were equally modest in combat.

The widespread introduction of the La-5 fighter into service during 1943 drew the attention of the NKAP to the various difficult landing characteristics of the type. The La-5 was subject to not inconsiderable torque-swing on take-off and landing, and the oleo struts and compression forks were insufficiently designed, resulting in an annoying tendency to bounce, unless a three-point landing was executed. For an experienced pilot these tendencies were easily mastered through the use of the aircraft's superb control surfaces, but occasionally novice pilots were known to flip the Lavochkin over onto its back by the sudden and untoward application of power, or to literally bounce off the runway during a landing. The NKAP determined that a tandem-seat training machine was needed to improve pilot familiarization and conversion procedures, and work began at *Zavod* 21 during the summer of that year on such a variant. Using a standard La-5F airframe, a second, instructor's position was added behind the pilot's seat with a lengthened greenhouse-type canopy installed. All armour protection was removed, along with the oxygen and nitrogen systems, and armament was reduced to a single ShVAK to port with a 120 round magazine. The La-5UTI dual-seat trainer was tested successfully by the NII VVS in September 1943, and a small series of these machines was manufactured at Gor'ki.

Above: *Handsomely-marked La-5FNs of the 41 GIAP, Ukraine, 1944. To the right is Hero of the Soviet Union, Aleksandr Pavlov, striking a confident pose, while to the left is the gregarious Hero of the Soviet Union, Aleksandr Lobanov. La-5FN '70' (with the red heart emblem) is thought to have belonged to St.Lt. Sementsov. Note also the yellow, and yellow-and-red nosed Lavochkins at the rear of the line, one of which is thought to be Lobanov's personal mount, 'White 26'. (Photo: G.Petrov)*

Also during the Summer of 1943, development of a La-5 powered by the new Shvetsov M-71 radial was undertaken. This powerplant weighed some 273 kg more than the M-82 and had a slightly larger diameter, but was shorter in length. The M-71 produced 2,200 hp at sea level with full boost, and was equipped with a two-stage supercharger and direct fuel injection. The La-5 M-71 prototype was based on the standardized La-5FN airframe, but had it's air intake moved to the bottom of the cowling, almost as if the La-5FN cowling was turned upside down, and the oil cooler was moved aft underneath the pilot. The performance of the M-71-powered machine was impressive, reaching 613 km/h at sea level and 689 km/h at 4,400 m, and handling was said to be good. However, the M-71 was still immature, and inevitable problems arose in cooling and operation with the power plant. These problems, and the successful further development of the Type 39 (leading to the Type 45 and the La-7), resulted in the abandonment of the powerful M-71 variant.

Lavochkin's OKB at Gor'ki, however, were by no means finished with development of the La-5 fighter. Further aerodynamic improvements were studied, and Lavochkin and Alexeev can be credited with working very closely with TsAGI and the LII during these efforts. Indeed, La-5FN No.39210206 was handed over to the LII, who completely rebuilt the aircraft under the direction of Engineer Molochayev, introducing a host of refinements. The air intake trunking was moved to the bottom of the cowling, as on the M-71 prototype, and the oil cooler reduced in profile and moved aft to a position below the pilot. This simple modification had been derived directly from TsAGI wind tunnel testing, and was found to reduce overall drag by an extraordinary 1.3 per cent. Considerable attention was also paid to the engine cowling, which was redesigned to incorporate fewer panels for improved sealing. The wing's dural spars were lightened further, and individual exhaust pipes were provided for each cylinder head.

The improved LII prototype demonstrated outstanding performance, Test Pilot Adamovich reaching 689 km/h at 2,075 m at a weight of 3,452 kg during January 1944. The NKAP was very impressed by this work, and Lavochkin was ordered to prepare a pre-series example incorporating these refinements at *Zavod* 21. The improved variant, known to the OKB staff as the Type 45, was developed with the close co-operation of the TsAGI testing facility and the LII, and was quite advanced. The Type 45 featured all-metal wing spars of reduced weight (as on the LII machine), the improved M-82FN installation with individual exhaust stacks, and a VISh-105-V4 propeller featuring stiffer blades. The supercharger intake was modified again, this time being removed from the cowling altogether and replaced by two smaller intakes, one in each wing root. The wing centre-section was improved and featured a slightly reduced aspect ratio, though still of Clark-YH section, and demonstrated a revised

planform from above, in addition to improved wing fillets. The armament was also modified, comprising three of the new lightweight Beresin B-20 20 mm cannon, two located to port and one to starboard.

The finished Type 45 was immediately dispatched to the NII VVS for testing, and despite problems with the engine and local structural defects, performance was found to be breathtaking. Pilot-Engineer Kubishkin achieved 599 km/h at sea level and 684 km/h at 6,250 m with only *normal* engine power, no testing of boosted flight attainable. Such performance was unheard of in Soviet testing, and the NKAP again spiralled into frenzied action. A Production Contract for the new fighter, to be known as the La-7, was issued with all speed, *Zavod* 381 at Moscow even being authorized to interrupt manufacture of the La-5FN if necessary to expedite the introduction of the type. At Gor'ki, Lavochkin had been hard at work streamlining the production of the La-5FN, and was well advanced on the process of re-tooling for what he expected to be the 1944 standard La-5 series. However, the NKAP decision to move directly to production of the La-7 sent Lavochkin back to the drawing board, and credit must be given here for the significant reduction in production man-hours effected by the Factory staff during 1944, both for the La-5 and La-7 programmes. In fact, so large was the manufacturing impetus at *Zavod* 21 that La-5FN machines continued to be manufactured here well into the autumn, until the supply of specific La-5FN components was consumed.

As a result of these factors, the first La-7 series was completed at *Zavod* 381 during March and April 1944, and these machines were handed over to the pilots of the 63 GIAP for operational trials during the summer. The initial La-7 aircraft were, once again, found to be inferior in performance to expectations, maximum speed often falling to 664 km/h or below even at combat power, with climb performance suffering equally. Engineers from the LII moved quickly to resolve these problems on the production lines, mostly involving the improved installation of the ASh-82FN engine and cowling, and by the autumn the production examples were demonstrating proper performance characteristics once again. The production La-7 also lacked the powerful armament of the Type 45 prototype since quantities of the B-20 cannon were not yet available for incorporation into the programme. The fitting of two 20 mm ShVAK guns with 200 rounds per gun remained standard, but an improved PBP-1V gunsight was installed.

Despite the reduced performance of the initial La-7 fighters, the pilots of the 63 GIAP were thrilled with the aircraft. During September and October 1944, the unit destroyed 55 enemy fighters (many of which were Fw 190s) for the loss of four La-7s in combat, despite being very heavily outnumbered in the area. However, this performance in the air was marred by an unexpected problem with the ASh-82FN motor, which began to fail catastrophically under service conditions. The 156 IAP for example, had nearly one half of its La-7s grounded simultaneously by engine failures during October, and four aircraft were lost in the 63 GIAP to engine difficulties. Worse, a spate of wing spar failures occurred during the same month, and in desperation, Marshal Novikov was forced to step in and order all La-7s in front line service to be grounded.

An investigative board was formed immediately with representatives from TsAGI, the NII VVS, VIAM, and the Lavochkin OKB. This committee worked skilfully and with great determination, and within only two weeks had determined the various items of failure. The wing spar troubles had been caused by the improper execution of lightening holes in the structure at *Zavod* 381, and this was rectified at once on the production line.

Failure of the otherwise usually reliable ASh-82FN was traced to the relocation of the air intakes to the wing roots. Under service conditions, dirt and other material was ingested into the supercharger intake whilst taxiing, a problem that had not been realized during testing on the paved strips at the NII VVS and LII. A screen device was installed into each intake just below the supercharger to redress the matter, and the problem was effectively solved.

With all production irregularities dealt with, manufacture of the La-7 resumed at once in November with considerable vigour. The resulting 'standard' La-7 fighter was one of the finest fighters of the

	LaG-5 1942 Standard	La-5 1942 Early Series	La-5F 1943 Type 39	La-5F 1943 Early Series	La-5FN 1943 Standard	La-5FN 1943
Weights						
Empty:	2686 kg	2677 kg	2605 kg	2595 kg	2683 kg	2655 kg
Loaded:	3365 kg	3357 kg	3366 kg	3226 kg	3326 kg	3329 kg
Wing Area:	17.51 sq.m	17.51 sq.m	17.51 sq.m	17.51 sq.m	17.51 sq.m	
Engine	M-82A	M-82A	M-82F	M-82F	M-82FN	M-82FN
	1330 (1510) hp	1330 (1510) hp	1350 (1700) hp	1350 (1700) hp	1470 (1850) hp	1470 (1850) hp
Maximum Speed						
At Altitude:	581 km/h at 6250 m	585 km/h at 6250 m	598 km/h at 6250 m	613 km/h at 5795 m	618 km/h at 5795 m	635 km/h at 5945 m
Sea Level:	510 km/h	523 km/h	552 km/h	556 km/h	565 km/h	574 km/h
Climb						
Initial:	983 m/min	1021 m/min	1125 m/min	1142 m/min	1175 m/min	1215 m/min
Time to Height:	6.0 min. to 5000 m	5.9 min. to 5000 m	5.4 min. to 5000 m	5.0 min. to 5000 m	4.8 min. to 5000 m	4.6 min. to 5000 m
Service Ceiling	9450 m	9450 m	9530 m	10090 m	10670 m	11000 m
Armament	2 x ShVAK	2 x ShVAK	2 x ShVAK	2 x ShVAK	2 x ShVAK	2 x ShVAK

Second World War; indeed, it was unmatched at low- and medium-level by any aircraft of its day, and may very well have been the most successful dogfighter ever known in Europe. Handling and control harmony were superlative, its rate of roll equalled that of the Fw 190, and its turning circle second to no enemy fighter. The late 1944 La-7 weighed 3,322 kg in its loaded condition, and could reach 614 km/h at sea level and 680 km/h at 6,275 m. Climb performance was spectacular, especially for a machine of its weight, the initial rate exceeding 1,311 m/min and requiring only 4.2 minutes to reach 5,000 m at full boost.

To the *Luftwaffe*, the La-7 was the most feared of all Soviet types, being regarded with not a little admiration – and incredulity. Few aircraft could stay with the La-7 at low to medium altitudes, and by comparison its acceleration, climb, and manoeuvrability left German fighters behind.

Success in the La-7 was almost total, and in comparison with its superb counterpart, the Yak-3, the loss rate for the Lavochkin was half that of the Yak. Indeed, the combat record of the La-7 is legendary, and rightly so, a mere 115 La-7s were lost to all military causes (less than half of these in aerial combat), while at the same time unquestionably accounting for more than 3,100 aerial victories (and perhaps many more). Entire formations of German aircraft were routinely decimated by flights of La-7 fighters, as in the case of the 31 IAP during the Lake Balaton campaign. Between 16 and 22 January 1945, three entire German fighter *Geschwader* were removed from the enemy Order of Battle by the 31 IAP, each in a single combat engagement, and all for the loss of one La-7. In the 9 GIAP, many of this elite unit's aces compiled the greater part of their scores very rapidly after switching to the La-7 despite their long service in the Airacobra previously, Amet-Khan, Alelyukhin, and Golovachev amongst them.

During February 1945, the supply of the Berezin B-20 cannon at last materialized, and La-7s at both *Zavoda* 381 and 21 were manufactured in series with the intended three-gun armament specified in the Production Contract. In this form, two weapons were deployed on the port side, and one to starboard, each with a supply of 170 rounds. The teardrop-shaped fairings above the cowling were replaced with three longer, squarish fairings, giving a distinctive appearance. The B-20 was a superlative weapon, having all the performance of the ShVAK at only half the weight, and was extremely reliable. VVS pilots clamoured for the three-gun La-7, whose striking power was indeed formidable, (though the total weight and performance of the aircraft so armed being completely unchanged).

	La-7 1944 Early Series	La-7 1944 Standard	La-7 1945
Weights			
Empty:	2627 kg	2646 kg	2641 kg
Loaded:	3256 kg	3222 kg	3223 kg
Wing Area:	17.59 sq.m	17.59 sq.m	17.59 sq.m
Engine	ASh-82FN	ASh-82FN	ASh-82FN
	1470 (1850) hp	1470 (1850) hp.	1470 (1850) hp.
Maximum Speed			
At Altitude:	660 km/h at 6160 m	677 km/h at 6160 m	677 km/h at 6160 m
Sea Level:	582 km/h	615 km/h	615 km/h
Climb			
Initial:	1220 m/min	1310 m/min	1310 m/min
Time to Height:	4.6 min. to 5000 m	4.2 min. to 5000 m	4.2 min. to 5000 m
Service Ceiling	9450 m	10500 m	10500 m
Armament	2 x ShVAK	2 x ShVAK	3 x B-20

A number of experimental developments of the La-7 appeared early in 1945, the most interesting perhaps being the La-7PVRD and La-7R with a liquid-fuel rocket installed in the rear fuselage. The idea was to employ the rocket for needed bursts of 'emergency speed', but in the event only 747 km/h was attained, while the aircraft's performance was otherwise seriously affected by the unit's extra weight, and by the shift in the centre of gravity to the rear. As a result, any plans to deploy the device operationally were dropped (though, indeed, the arrangement appeared again in both the La-9 and La-11). A two-seat training model was also developed, the La-7UTI, and was built in series after the War until 1947. Another La-7 was modified to mount the M-71 motor, but again this version was not considered for manufacture.

Production of the La-5 and La-7 was a triumph for Lavochkin and his OKB, and during 1944 surpassed that of any other Soviet fighter, save for the Yak-9. These designs were so impressive that Lavochkin was twice awarded the Stalin Prize (of 100,000 Roubles) during the course of the manufacturing programme, much to the delight of Lavochkin who at last enjoyed the reputation he had felt he deserved. By the end of the GPW, 10,009 La-5s and 5,753 La-7s had been completed; an exceptional achievement in industry. With the advent of the La-7, Lavochkin demonstrated that his Bureau was at the very pinnacle of piston-engined fighter development, and work of this kind would continue after the GPW with the La-9 and La-11 interceptors of the late 1940s.

**La-5
standard production**

La-5F

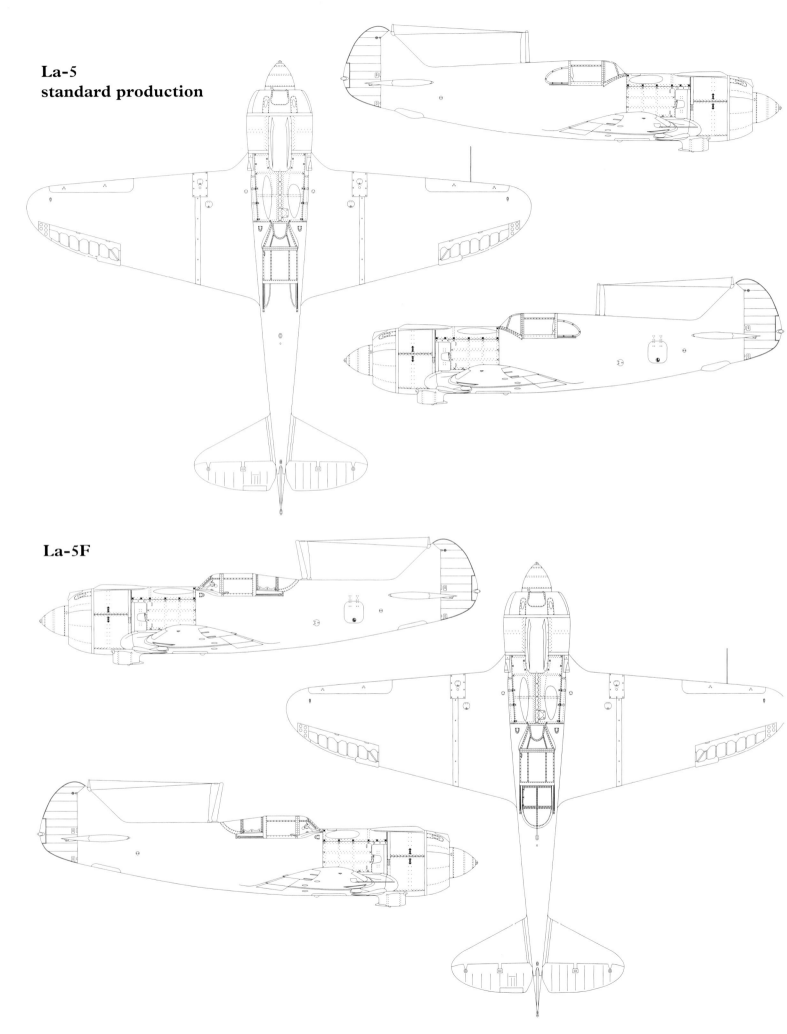

**La-5
early manufacture**

La-5FN

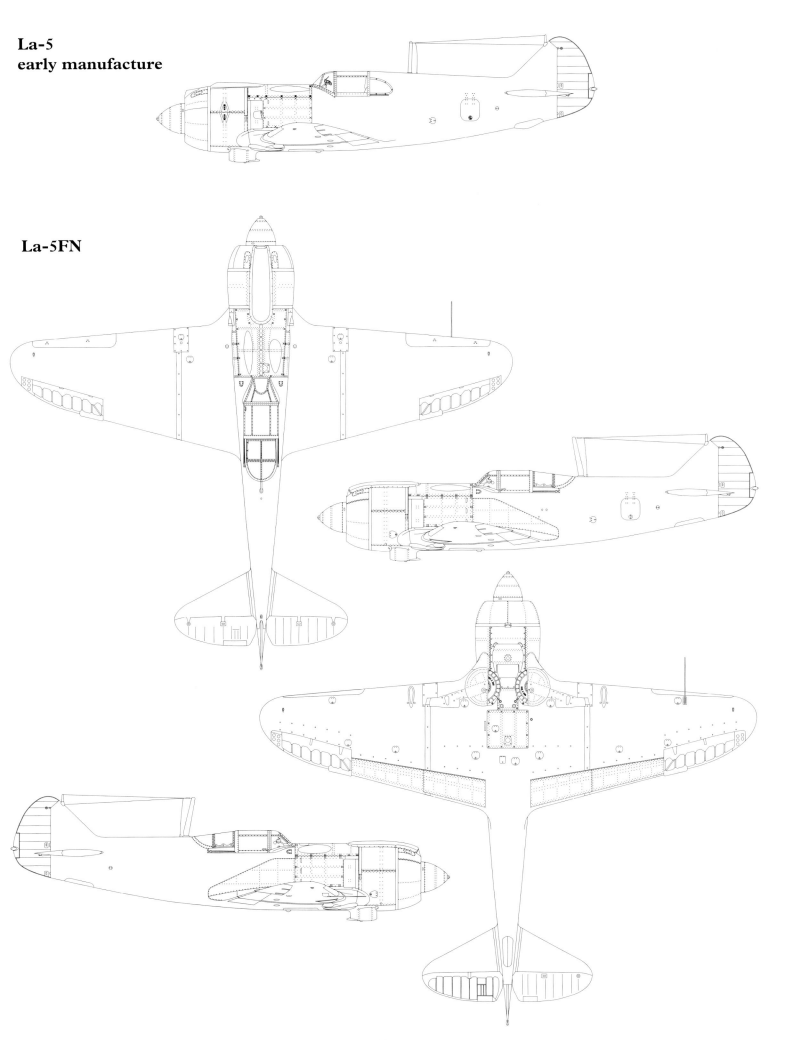

La-7

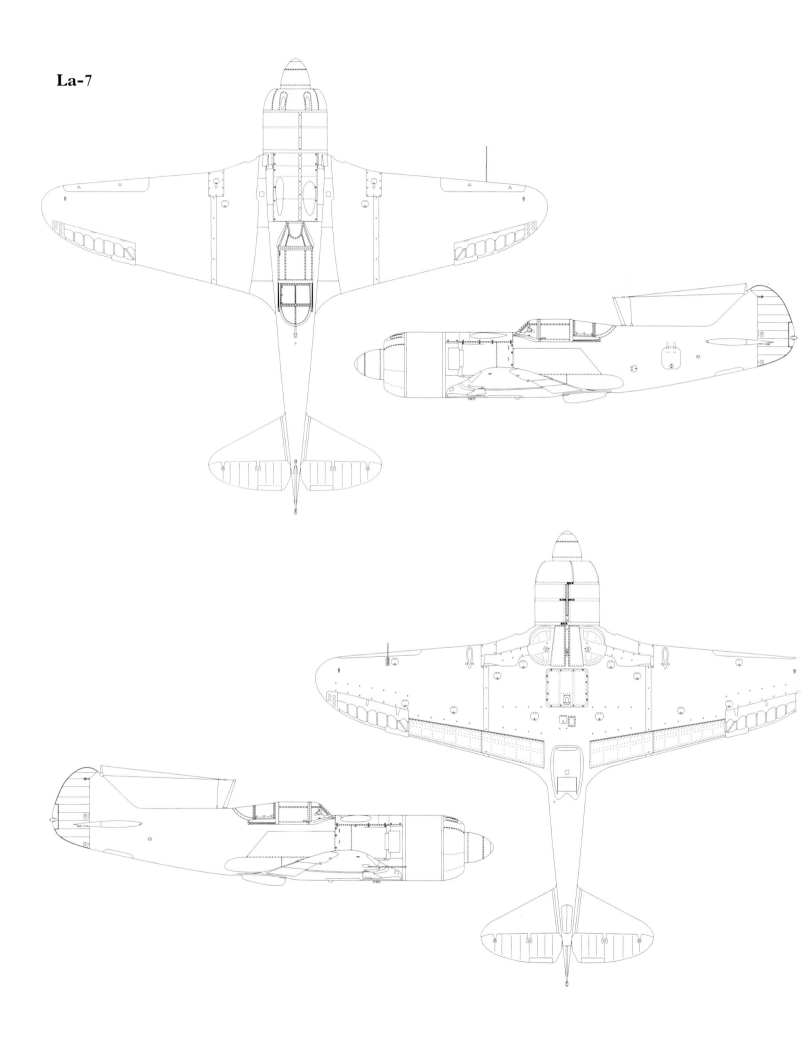

THE DEVELOPMENT OF CAMOUFLAGE ON
THE La-5 AND La-7 FIGHTERS

The Radial Lavochkin

During the late spring of 1942, manufacture of a new, radial-powered aircraft got underway at the Gor'ki facility, *Zavod* 21. The new aircraft was the progenitor of a whole series of classic Lavochkin fighters, and was named LaG-5 by the NKAP contract.

The camouflage of the new LaG-5 was clearly influenced by the concurrent LaGG-3 programme. The very first machines were completed at Gor'ki in a two-colour scheme of AII Black over AII Green uppersurfaces, and AII Blue lowersurfaces. The pattern was virtually identical to the LaGG-3's application then in use, but the forward area of the camouflage was unique, and consisted essentially, of two large 'blobs' of colour (see Fig. 1).

Fig. 1

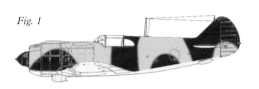

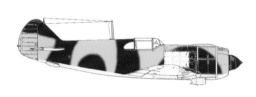

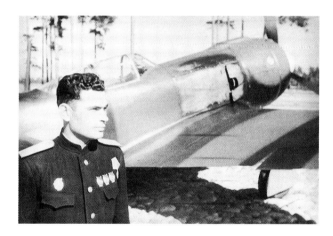

Above left: *An early La-5F of the 4 GIAP VVS KBF belonging to Hero of the Soviet Union, Kpt. D.M. Tatarenko, in July 1943. Note that the aircraft is in immaculate condition. The 'F' engine emblem is clearly visible, and the cowl bands have been overpainted at the factory with the camouflage scheme; the paint would soon wear off them. (Photo: G.Petrov)*

Above: *La-5s photographed in the Orel-Kursk area, 1943. The nearest machine has the Shvetsov 'F' logo on the engine cowl, denoting an M-82F engine. This might well indicate one of the very rare initial examples of the La-5F model without a cut-down rear fuselage (early examples from Series 9). (Photo: G.Petrov)*

Left: *An La-5 wearing the 'Eskadrilya Valeriy Chkalov' (Valeriy Chkalov Squadron) inscription in what appears to be yellow. 'White 60' has been associated with many pilots over the years, and in the case of this photograph, the original caption attributes the aircraft to the commander of the 3 IAK, G.May. Savitskiy. Note the Yak-6 liaison machine in the background, wearing a very intriguing three-colour camouflage. (Photo: G.Petrov)*

This pattern application was very symmetrical over the fuselage sides, and not so on the uppersurfaces. The colour demarcations tended to be semi-hard, and the upper/lower demarcation was extremely neat and tidy.

However, there was at least one major innovation. One some models, the upper/lower colour demarcation was entirely unlike the LaGG-3's; it abandoned the old lower and tidy demarcation in favour of a new 'ramp'-type feature (see Fig. 2).

Fig. 2

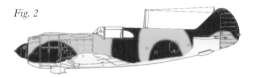 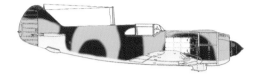

The upper surface pattern did not change, but often in these cases the uppersurface colour demarcation lines were semi-soft. Both of these innovations were clear movements towards more modern camouflage practices.

Internal Colouration

In all early La-5s, the interior colour practice was typical for the 1942 period. There do not seem to have been many cases of unpainted interiors in the La-5. The typical *Zavod* 21 method was to finish the cockpit, but not in a single, uniform colour. Metal use primer was common on metal and steel surfaces, and Wood Finish on the wooden panels and structural members. Because of the very large quantities of wood in the La-5 cockpit, it was not uncommon to encounter cases where all surfaces were completed in a uniform colour with the Wood Finishes or Wood *Aerolak*, even throughout 1943.

The La-5 and New Colours

With the reorganization of the Production Contract for the Lavochkin radial fighter, the aircraft was now re-titled the La-5. At this time there was an interesting adoption of some new colour schemes.

The initial La-5 scheme appeared similar to the immediately preceding applications. However, in addition to symmetrical patterns, there were now just as commonly asymmetrical patterns. Furthermore, the new AMT lacquers were almost always employed from this point with the Black/Green uppersurface application (AMT-6 over AMT-4), and in the case of AMT finishes the undersurfaces would be AMT-7 (see Fig. 3).

Fig. 3

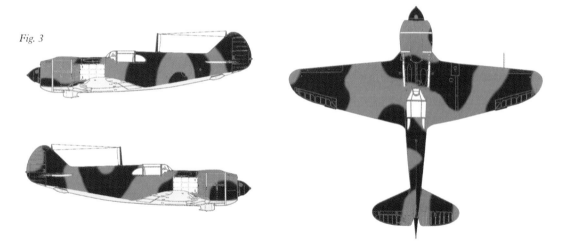

Left: *An 'Eskadrilya Valeriy Chkalov' La-5, this aircraft belonging to Hero of the Soviet Union, Petr Likholetov of the 159 IAP. The tactical number of his aircraft is unknown. (Photo: G.Petrov)*

The colour demarcations were typically semi-soft. It is worth noting at this point, that the stainless steel cowl bands around the engine cowling were not *routinely* painted over, and were left unfinished and shiny. However, there are many examples of aircraft where the bands were certainly painted over at the factory, and this seemed to be not at all uncommon well into 1943. The stainless steel plate aft of the exhaust was originally painted over on the LaG-5 and early La-5s, but gradually, through 1942, this became less common, and by 1943 seemed not to occur at all.

At the same time, there was a continued use of the older AII lacquers. Using again both symmetrical and asymmetrical applications, these were very similar in appearance to the first schemes (see Fig. 4).

Fig. 4

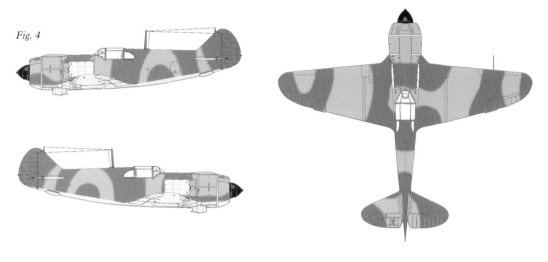

Above: *An La-5 of the 4 GIAP VVS KBF in 1943. Note the simple bands of colour making up the wing surface's camouflage. Such simplified applications were quite common at Gor'ki at this time. (Photo: G.Petrov)*

Fig. 5

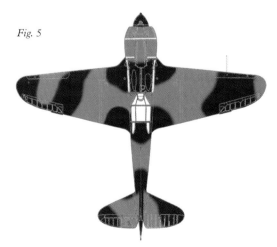

For the AII examples, only Dark Green over Green colours have been identified to date. From the summer of 1942, all of the La-5 camouflage patterns incorporating Black seem to be AMT lacquer examples. Consequently, there was an AMT colour version of this same pattern, with extremely similar features (see Fig. 5).

One last AII lacquer pattern was seen before the end of 1942, this again in Dark Green over Green. The new pattern application retained the tidy upper/lower colour demarcation line of the earliest applications, and in this way was somewhat outdated. However, the uppersurfaces demonstrated semi-soft, even soft and not particularly regular demarcations, as if they were applied very casually (see Fig. 6).

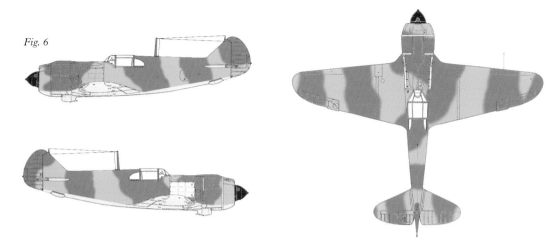

Fig. 6

During the winter of 1942-43, the usual practice at *Zavod* 21 was to apply a coat of MK-7 white distemper at the factory. MK-7F was the preferred variant of this paint, and usually the coverage was quite thorough and professionally applied (see Fig. 7).

Fig. 7

1943 – AMT

With the new year came a new model of the Lavochkin fighter, and an entirely new look – in more ways than one. The new La-5F variant featured a cut-down rear fuselage and clear aft canopy section, thus imparting on the type its more 'classic' appearance. As so often happened with VVS colouration, this change in exterior appearance seemed to demand a similar shift in camouflage practices.

The first La-5Fs were completed in a scheme somewhat reminiscent of the previous La-5 patterns, always in Black over Green. AMT lacquers were in use exclusively by this time, and no further AII paint examples can be found in the photographic record (see Fig. 8).

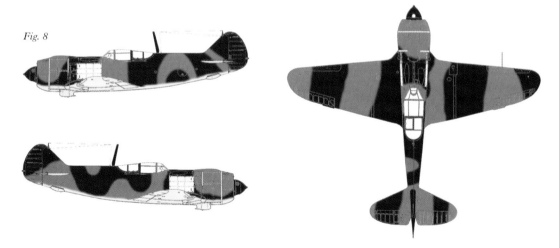

Fig. 8

Uppersurface colour demarcations were usually semi-soft, as was the upper/lower colour demarcation line. The old lower demarcation was still in use, though usually with a less regular – and not particularly straight – line. The upper surfaces look to have been simplified, which was certainly a change from the later 1942 schemes.

This pattern application was also quite common at the new La-5 factories, *Zavod* 99 at Ulan-Ude and the refurbished and expanded *Zavod* 381 facility in Moscow. There are no clear photographs which show AII-painted La-5 aircraft from either enterprise, and the older upper/lower colour demarcation seems to be usual at these factories.

However, not soon thereafter, and at least by early summer 1943, a radically new pattern appeared. The scheme was extremely simplified over all surfaces, both on the upper and fuselage views. This pattern application was always completed in AMT-6 over AMT-4, with AMT-7 unders. More significantly, however, the old upper/lower colour demarcation was discarded dramatically by introducing a very bold 'ramp' feature on the rear fuselage, basically forming a straight line from the stabilizer to the wing root.

This shift in upper/lower camouflage appearance was quite dramatic, and one has to assume that this was an influence on practices elsewhere. Furthermore, *Zavod* 21's well-known association with the introduction of AMT lacquers is evident – no other factory eliminated AII lacquers so completely from their inventory, and certainly not as early as 1943. Gor'ki was serving – intentionally, or not – as a springboard for the NKAP recommendations (see Fig. 9).

Fig. 9

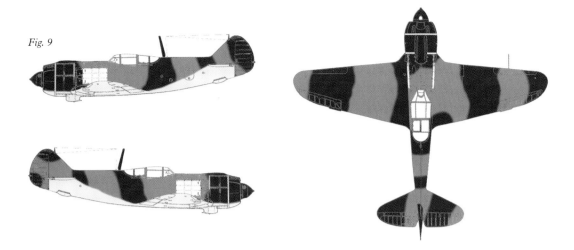

There are few photographs of La-5FNs wearing a Green/Black livery. Nevertheless, there must have been a number of these aircraft so painted – about 1,500 were completed prior to 1944, some as early as May-June 1943. The only known examples in this colouration all appear at Kursk, but the writer suspects that the pattern they wear was probably relatively standard for Green/Black La-5FNs (see Fig. 10).

Fig. 10

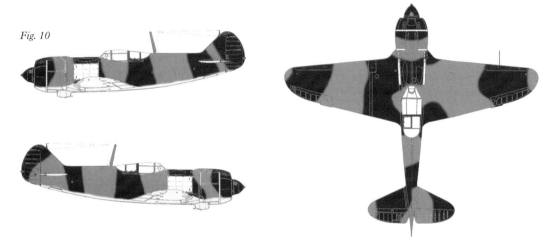

These were Gor'ki-built machines but with the La-5F the two new factories showed a tendency to follow *Zavod* 21's painting routine, and this may have been true in this instance, as well.

Grey is Your Master

The precise moment at which the use of the NKAP's new grey colours – AMT-11 and AMT-12 – came into use is still a matter of heated debate. What does not seem to be in question is the location of the first usage of this scheme, and there are two possibilities; one of these is certainly at *Zavod* 21, with Gor'ki (*Zavod* 31 at Tbilisi) being the other. Unfortunately, this factory did not record such details as aerolacquer orders and supply in their Directorate papers, nor in the Production Diary, as did Saratov and Kuybishev for example. The result, then, is that we must rely only on the surviving photographic record for guidance.

The distribution of AMT paints during 1943 is questionable. As has been discussed previously, there is simply no photographic evidence to show many of the relevant practices. However, two types of application are conspicuous by their absence. Firstly, there are no known cases of non-AMT colour La-5Fs or La-FNs at Gor'ki. Secondly, there are no known factory photographs of all-white La-5s during the winter of 1943-44 (though there is one of such a machine at TsAGI). If white MK-7 overall was not in use, and there were no earlier grey colours to make up the application, what was being done at *Zavod* 21 during the winter months of 1943-44?

There *are* photographs that show machines under construction at Ulan-Ude from this time in single-colour schemes. In a widely circulated series, La-5Fs can be seen in production during December 1943. The colours are impossible to determine with complete accuracy due to the poor quality of the exposures, but in my judgement they seem to show Wood *Aerolak* upper surfaces. This would be plausible in my own view due to the continuing utilization of this lacquer in cockpit finishing well after this date (see Fig. 11).

Fig. 11

The photographs show a colour demarcation which is very loosely applied on the upper/lower demarcation. The concurrent practice at *Zavod* 381, Moscow, is not known, but the writer suspects that this colour might also have been in use there, noting that the manufacturer of Wood *Aerolak* – *Zavod* 30 – was located just 10 km away from this factory.

However, there are some photographs which depict partially MK-7-coated La-5Fs of quite new manufacture from December 1943. In these pictures no weathering is visible, and thus the aircraft must have been completed recently. Of course, the receiving unit might have applied the white distemper themselves; there is no way to know. It would appear, though, that the application of MK-7 white is very uniform (always applied to the forward part of the aircraft). But, which of the three factories might have been responsible, and to what degree, can only be speculated (see Fig. 12).

Fig. 12

Somewhere during this time period – broadly from September-October 1943 to January-February 1944 – the use of the new NKAP two-tone scheme did come into use at Gor'ki. The new camouflage was faithfully based on the NKAP template, and consisted of the colours AMT-12 over AMT-11; AMT-7 remained the underside finish (see Fig. 13).

Fig. 13

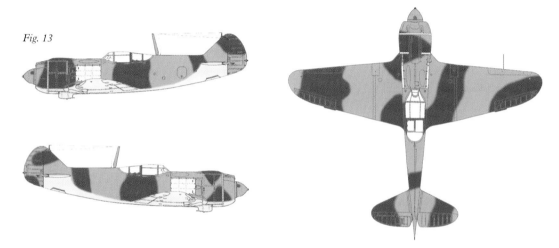

Above: *A good aerial shot of an La-5F of the 41 GIAP, flown by Hero of the Soviet Union, Aleksandr Pavlov in 1944. This photograph was taken with 'journalist'-type film, and demonstrates the classic misrepresentation that occurs over-sensitivity to exposure and red colours. The camouflage here is an unusually-applied (probably in the field) NKAP template of AMT-11/-12/-7. (Photo: G.Petrov)*

All colour demarcations were semi-soft, as per the new style, and the rear fuselage wore a large 'ramp' feature. Machines manufactured at *Zavod* 99 were very similar, and are usually impossible to distinguish in the photographic record.

The same pattern was also applied *very* widely to the La-5FN (see Fig. 14).

Fig. 14

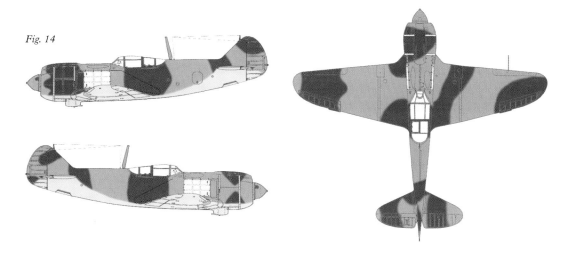

Left: *An excellent view of an La-5FN in a curious AMT-11/-12/-7 scheme in 1944. Note the very strange colour demarcation 'ramp' feature, and the application of a diamond 'FN' motor logo to the upper rudder (as per the La-7). (Photo: G.Petrov)*

Below: *La-5FNs of the 4 GIAPVVS KBF seen in 1944. Note the very large star and numeral on the fuselage of 'White 81'. (Photo: G.Petrov)*

Above: *A still taken from 16 mm film of the 159 IAP at Lavensaari in 1944. The colouration of the La-5FN in the foreground is dramatically different from the machine just behind it, causing some doubt as to the precise appearance of this shot – the numeral, star boarders, and rudder are all probably white. Such curiosities in appearance, changing with the field of focus, are not entirely uncommon on Soviet 16 mm film of the era. (Photo: G.Petrov)*

Left: *Another classic NKAP template of AMT-11/-12/-7 camouflage seen on this La-5FN during the winter of 1944-45. Most of the stencilling has been completed in white, but on the landing gear wheel cover, the bold stencil 'ne vstavat' ('do not stand') appears in red. (Photo: G.Petrov)*

Left: *An La-5FN of Hero of the Soviet Union Petr Likholetov of the 159 IAP in 1944. The inscription reads, 'Za Vas'ka i Zhoru' ('For Vaska and Zhoru'); a personal tribute to pilots he had probably known. The numeral '15' is outlined in red, and the inscription text has a very thin red border, just visible in certain parts of the photograph. (Photo: G.Petrov)*

Right: *An La-5FN and two La-5Fs moving for take-off at Lavensaari field on the Leningrad Front, 1944. The three machines were photographed in service with the 3 GIAPVVS KBF and 'White 45' is believed to have been the personal aircraft of Hero of the Soviet Union, Kpt. Ivan Tsapov. (Photo: G.Petrov)*

In Moscow, *Zavod* 381 was producing La-5FNs also finished with a standard camouflage scheme. The major difference in these patterns seems to have been along the forward fuselage, where the 'zigzag' feature was replaced by a large 'blob' of colour (see Fig. 15).

Fig. 15

Right: *The demise of this La-5FN following a landing mishap offers an opportunity to study the Zavod 381 camouflage scheme in detail. Note the La-5s and P-47Ds in the background. (Photo: G.Petrov)*

No further significant innovation in La-5 camouflage is known. During the winter of 1944-45 the last models to be completed were finished in the customary single upper colour scheme of AMT-11 (see Fig. 16).

Fig. 16

Typically, the upper/lower colour demarcation was soft and usually quite high – almost directly from the stabilizer to the wingroot. Also, AMT-7 colour running onto the rudder was not unusual in these late schemes, a fact which is quite interesting considering the pattern applications of the La-7.

Comes the La-7

The arrival of the La-7 in the summer of 1944 was not attended by the fanfare reserved in some Regiments for the Yak-3, and indeed passed somewhat quietly. The calm was deceptive; after only their first combats in the type, Soviet pilots were in an uproar over the La-7, and greatly coveted their machines. Indeed, it was not at all uncommon for pilots to travel to the factories to receive their La-7s *in person*, taking charge of their aircraft directly from the factory test pilot.

The first La-7 camouflage schemes at *Zavod* 21 were predictably based on the usual NKAP idea. The two-colour scheme on the upper surfaces was the standard AMT-12 over AMT-11; undersurfaces were AMT-7. The colour demarcation lines were semi-soft, in the modern fashion, and the rear fuselage 'ramp' feature quite elevated (see Fig. 17).

Fig. 17

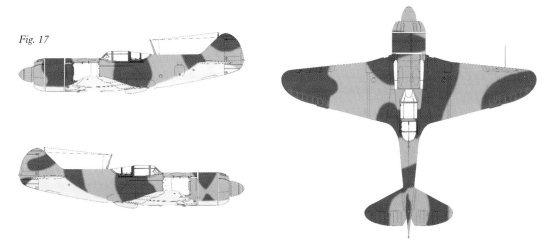

Above: *An La-7 of the 303 IAD during 1945. The oxygen system is being charged from tanks on the ground behind the pilots. (Photo: G.Petrov)*

Right: *An La-7 wearing a classic NKAP template AMT-11/-12/-7 scheme, 1945. The aircraft appears to be ready for its acceptance flight in Moscow. Note the hardstanding comprising hexagonal concrete sections, so typical of Soviet airbases. (Photo: G.Petrov)*

Curiously, on many La-7s the underside colour extends onto the rudder. This was not overly typical for the La-5's camouflage, and represents a minor change in practice. Camouflage applications at Ulan-Ude were virtually identical.

At *Zavod* 381, Moscow, there was a more simplified application typically in use. This application was in the usual AMT colours, but consisted of very simple bands of colour, both on the fuselage and uppersurfaces. The upper/lower colour demarcation line was fairly sharp, and the rear fuselage 'ramp' was quite unusual, harking back to practices some years out of date. The colour demarcations on the upper colours were semi-soft (see Fig. 18).

Fig. 18

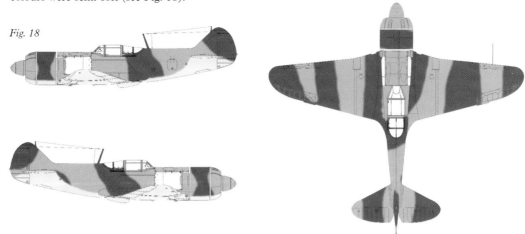

Again, the AMT-7 colour often extended onto the rudder, to some degree in this case.

During the winter of 1944-45, single-colour schemes were typically applied to all La-7s. However, as on the Yak-3 programme, the use of both AMT-11 and AMT-12 appeared to have been common. Presumably AMT-11 was the more usual colour, but photographs of the darker AMT-12 examples are quite numerous (see Fig. 19).

Fig. 19

Above: *A line-up of three La-7s with single-colour upper-surface camouflage in the Baltic region, 1945. This photograph shows clearly the two colour variations, the first two aircraft being finished in AMT-12, while the farthest machine wears the more common AMT-11 finish. The rear colour demarcation lines on the AMT-12-painted aircraft are low and sharply executed in a very 'old-fashioned' manner. 'Yellow 06', centre, is a three-gun Moscow-built aircraft. (Photo: G.Petrov)*

These single-colour schemes were applied well into the spring of 1945 – unusually late for these applications – for reasons unknown.

The very last of the wartime La-7s were the three-gun models manufactured at Moscow and Gor'ki. At *Zavod* 21, there seems to have been no change in camouflage pattern, but at *Zavod* 381 a new and quite interesting AMT scheme appeared (see Fig. 20).

Fig. 20

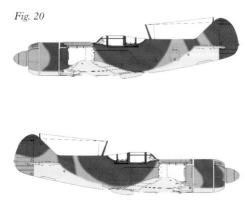

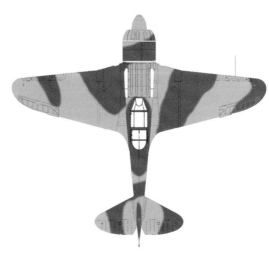

Above: *This La-7 wears a solid colour uppersurface scheme of AMT-11. The aircraft was photographed in service with the 111 GIAP during 1945 and is the personal machine of P.M.Baykov. In addition to the dragon head artwork on the nose, the port fuselage side bears the inscription, 's pobedi na rodinu' ('To the Victory for the People'). Note how the dragon's 'eye' has been made using the La-7 logo. (Photo: G.Petrov)*

This pattern seems to demonstrate a large disc-type feature over the cockpit area, and abbreviated applications over the upper surfaces. The colour demarcation lines were all semi-soft, and a more usual 'ramp' feature appeared on the rear fuselage. The underside colour did not usually extend onto the rudder, seemingly a reversal of current practice.

Internal Colouration

The interior colour of the La-7's cockpit was often a matter of unusual convention. The vast majority of surviving La-7s reveal an interior painted in a uniform application of ALG-5 metal primer. The practice was similar to that adopted at the same time in the Yak-3 programme, though any relationship between the two practices is a matter of speculation. The photographic record parallels these surviving examples, and thus it is most likely that most La-7s were so finished. It seems strange to paint a largely wooden cockpit with metal primer, though there were similar peculiarities in other fighter programmes of the same era. The reason for the use of ALG-5 in this way remains a mystery at the time of writing.

It is noteworthy, however, that the La-7 programme might have been influenced by certain recommendations from the NKAP, which during 1943 seemed to suggest the use of ALG-5 as a cockpit finish (along with other possibilities). Since La-7 production commenced first at *Zavod* 381 (Moscow), it is possible, given the known predilection for this factory to embody official recommendations closely, that this choice was deliberate, and that it was subsequently adopted at *Zavoda* 21 and 99 thereafter.

Right: *This interesting La-5F of the 2 GIAP was photographed in 1944. It appears to have been completely repainted on its uppersurfaces, and now wears a hand-applied AMT-11/-12 camouflage scheme. The unusual size and placement of the national markings are the result of this work, as is the numeral, which is trimmed below on the AMT-7 coloured portion (part of the original finish), and overpainted above. The inscription, in red, reads 'Mongol'skiy Arat' (Mongol Warrior). (Photo: G.Petrov)*

Left: *Pilot Alpatov of 3 GIAP VVS KBF poses in front of his shark-mouthed La-5 on the Leningrad Front in 1944. (Photo: G.Petrov)*

Right: *French pilots in front of an La-5FN of the 303 IAD during the winter of 1944-45. Note the Yak fighter (probably a Yak-9) in the background. (Photo: G.Petrov)*

1. Early difficulties with the type largely centred around cooling the relatively new and temperamental Shvetsov 14-cylinder radial – making for a fascinating comparison with the similarly-powered Fw 190. Temperature maintenance in the early M-82 series was critical, and it was not at all uncommon for engines to quite literally blow a cylinder head right off the engine if the pilot became inattentive. Happily, the M-82 was equally robust, and La-5s were indeed seen to return to base missing more than a couple of cylinders.

2. Performance figures for the La-5FN and –7 have been a source of unnecessary confusion, this resulting from the NII's inexplicable habit of issuing test results for the Lavochkin fighter on more than one occasion without the use of full engine power. Apparently, the attitude was that La-5 and –7 fighters were to be tested strictly 'as is', and any difficulties with the motor or supercharger reflected directly on the resulting reported figures. One has to wonder if this condition was not the direct result of tensions mounting from Lavochkin's perceived failings with regard to meeting the prototype machines' performance levels in production series aircraft.

Right: *A detail of a 254 IAP La-5FN with an eagle emblem and victory markings, seen in Poland in 1944. The drawing depicts an eagle grasping a wolf in its talons. The identity of the pilot remains unknown. (Photo: G.Petrov)*

Right: *The same aircraft featured in a still from 16 mm movie film. Note the polished metal spinner and white rudder. (Photo: G.Petrov)*

Below: *A handsome example of a La-7 three-gun model awaiting acceptance-testing in Moscow, 1945 and wearing a modified NKAP template AMT-11/-12/-7 scheme. (Photo: G.Petrov)*

Above: *Hero of the Soviet Union, Sultan Amet-Khan (left) poses in front of another pilot's La-7 (featuring a Hero of the Soviet Union emblem) in 1945. Amet-Khan was unquestionably one of the most outstanding, compelling, and fascinating figures of the entire GPW. (Photo: G.Petrov)*

Right: *Seen to the left is Hero of the Soviet Union, Sultan Amet-Khan's personal La-7 'White 24'. A common 9 GIAP unit badge, the 'mountain eagle' in a disc emblem, is clearly visible. Note the red front cowling and yellow spinner colours. Amet-Khan's '24' is often depicted wearing a lightning bolt emblem on the fuselage, but it is clear that no such marking was carried at the time of this photograph. Hero of the Soviet Union Pavel Golovachev's (also of the 9 GIAP) wingman, Lt. Chernik, flew an extremely similar La-7 '24' with a lightning bolt feature, and it is possible that the two have become confused. This photograph was taken in Germany in February 1945. (Photo: G.Petrov)*

Above: *This La-7 is an authentic GPW machine, but is pictured here in Czechoslovakia during 1968, awaiting the opening of the National Air Museum at Kbely. The aircraft has been repainted in a scheme resembling AII Dark Green over Green (and a tri-colour spinner) for the event – not a very authentic colouration. The aircraft can still be seen (albeit in different colours) in the Kbely collection.*

Right: *Kozhedub's famous La-7 as it now appears at Monino. (Photo: Author's collection)*

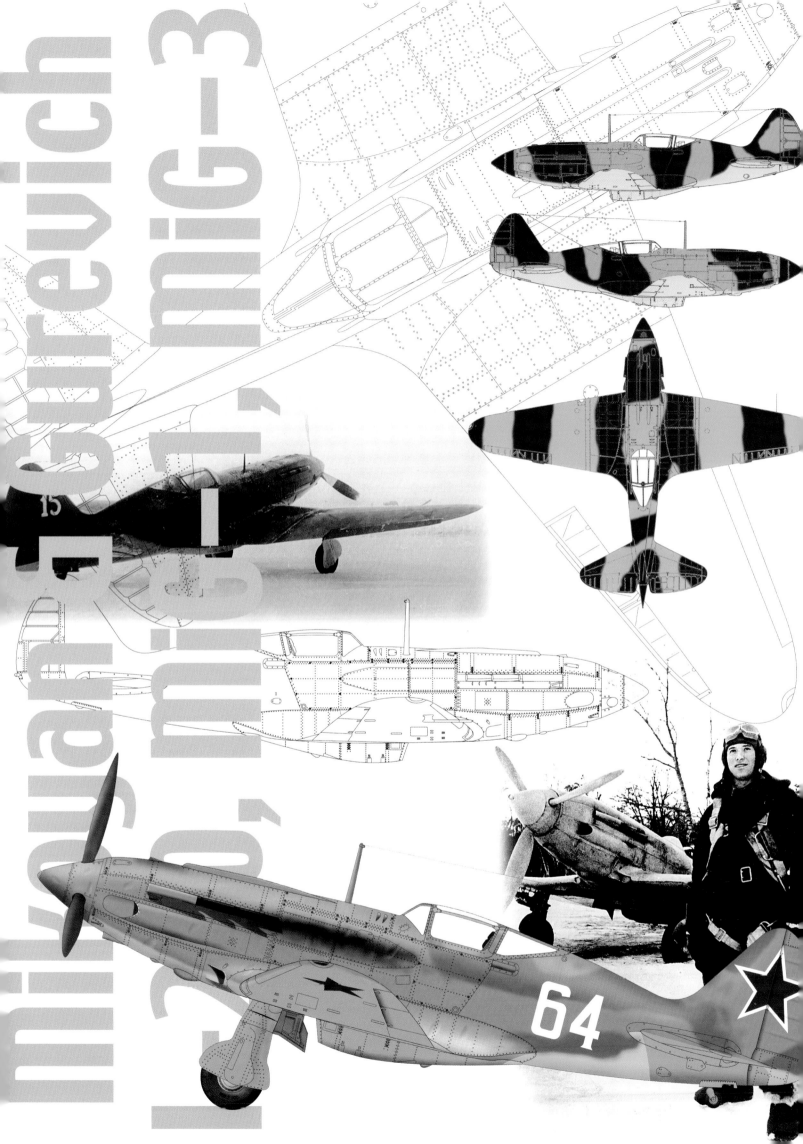

Mikoyan-Gurevich MiG-1, MiG-3

Chapter 3

Mikoyan and Gurevich I-200, MiG-1, MiG-3

'MiG' – the terse acronym formed by the combination of the initials of two Soviet aeronautical engineers Artem Mikoyan and Mikhail Gurevich (Mikoyan i Gurevich) has stood as a popular moniker for Soviet jet fighters for five decades and surviving as a household word to this day. Extraordinarily, the first of a long line of otherwise successful fighters emanating from their Design Bureau was designed by neither Mikoyan nor Gurevich, was not a particular success, and represented the sort of political machination, intrigue, and manoeuvring worthy of a modern investigative documentary. The small, rakish, long-nosed I-200 was remarkable not only for the speed of its development, but also for the speed of its withdrawal from manufacture and the consequent fall from grace of several leading figures in the Soviet Aviation Industry.

The concept of a small, fast, high-altitude interceptor had been festering in the mind of Nikolai Polikarpov throughout the 1930s. At this time, Polikarpov was the undisputed reigning prince of fighter aviation development in the USSR and within his enormous Bureau were not only several designers who would form the future elite of the industry, but also the almost unlimited resources of the State's premiere Aviation Factory, *Zavod* 1 in Moscow. With such industrial backing and supporting talent, Polikarpov's design submissions during the decade were profligate.

It was within this context that several related fighter prototypes emerged from the Polikarpov OKB between 1935-39 based on in-line engine layouts, beginning with the TsKB-17 and TsKB-19. These machines nearly entered production as the I-17, powered by the 12-cylinder upright 'Vee' M-100, and was followed by the TsKB-33 and TsKB-43. Development of this airframe then took a new course under the direction of Sergei Ilyushin, who wed a revised I-17 prototype featuring a rearward-positioned cockpit, with another V-12 motor, the Mikulin AM-34. For some time, the resulting TsKB-25 and TsKB-32 were mooted for production status as the I-21, and featured a ten metre wingspan, integrated fuselage/wing centre-section, and rearward-positioned cockpit; clearly, the Polikarpov Bureau pedigree was immensely evident in the I-21.

During the 1938 design specification competition, Polikarpov had submitted a proposal based on a fighter concept from OKB Designer Andrianov for an in-line fighter powered by the AM-37 engine then under development by Alexandr Mikulin. The proposal received no further comment from the Submissions Committee, but it was described as being similar to the I-21 in many respects, and the AM-37 was a direct development of the AM-34 motor of that prototype. However, in 1939 the Government realized that the development of the I-26 (and I-301) would take somewhat longer than was hoped, and that a third candidate fighter should be developed, this with the potential for earlier completion. Several proposals that had been submitted during the 1938 competition were reviewed in this vein, and the most promising of these was seen to be Polikarpov's Mikulin based design, in part because no other fighter prototype had planned to make use of these engines.

Polikarpov stepped in at this point and assured the NKAP that his OKB could quickly develop the new fighter prototype, and was thus ordered to assemble a development group for this purpose. But, while Polikarpov was out of the country negotiating various aviation licences, the Government decided to hand over the project to an entirely new Experimental Design Group (OKO) under the direction of Artem Mikoyan. Mikoyan at that point had been a Chief Designer within Polikarpov's OKB, but his rise to prominence during 1939 had been meteoric, due in no small part it seems to the influence of his brother

Anastas Mikoyan, Stalin's Commissar for Foreign Trade. The new prototype was given the designation I-200, and the Mikoyan OKO was established at *Zavod* 1 with full access and priority to the facility's resources. Under the young Mikoyan's direction were placed two very senior Engineers, Mikhail Gurevich and Viktor Romodin, serving as deputies to the vastly less experienced Bureau Chief. The remainder of the OKO was taken directly from the development team assembled by Polikarpov for the project, and simply transferred to Mikoyan's group along with all of its drawings, mock-ups, and other materials.

Construction of the I-200 prototype proceeded very rapidly under the dynamic leadership of Mikoyan, who was, of course, very eager to impress in his new elevated role. Drawings were finalized in January 1940, and by 30 March, the No.1 prototype of the I-200 had rolled off the Bureau workshop floor. The I-200 was essentially a slightly modified version of Polikarpov's 1938 AM-37 submission, but this time powered by the AM-35 engine of similar dimensions and configuration. The fuselage and wing centre section were a single unit of welded steel tubing with 3 mm dural sheet covering, while the fuselage and tail assembly were wooden monocoque structures skinned with spruce sheet which was covered with fabric and filler and sanded to a smooth finish. The wooden outer wing sections featured a single dural spar, attached to the centre section via a series of through-bolts, and were easily detachable. All control surfaces were dural-framed units with fabric covering, save for the split-flaps which were all-metal. Fuel was housed in two 200 ltr cells located in the wing centre-sections, these being easily accessible via panels on the wing undersurface. The 1,200 hp (1,350 hp for take-off and emergency) AM-35A engine was very tightly cowled in the I-200's long nose, the oil coolers being deployed in tunnels along the side of the cowling below the exhaust stacks. These tunnels were sophisticated aerodynamic structures with exhaust flaps for regulated cooling and were of thrust-giving energy transfer design, they had been developed during testing at TsAGI's T-101 wind tunnel during the previous winter. The radiator was placed well aft along the fuselage underside, directly below the cockpit.

The I-200 was fitted with its military equipment during April 1940, as drawings were prepared for these features. Much debate took place at *Zavod* 1 over the I-200's proposed armament, even Polikarpov himself joining in the discussions. The abandonment of the AM-37 motor by the Mikulin OKB had meant that the I-200 would instead be fitted with the AM-35 which, like the former, could not accommodate a weapon mounted between the cylinder banks to fire through the spinner. The very tight engine cowling of the prototype also complicated matters, and space was strictly limited for the deployment of various weapons. Indeed, the matter of suitable gun placement was debated yet again, some engineers opting for the solution of placing weapons in the wing roots, displacing the fuel cells. For numerous

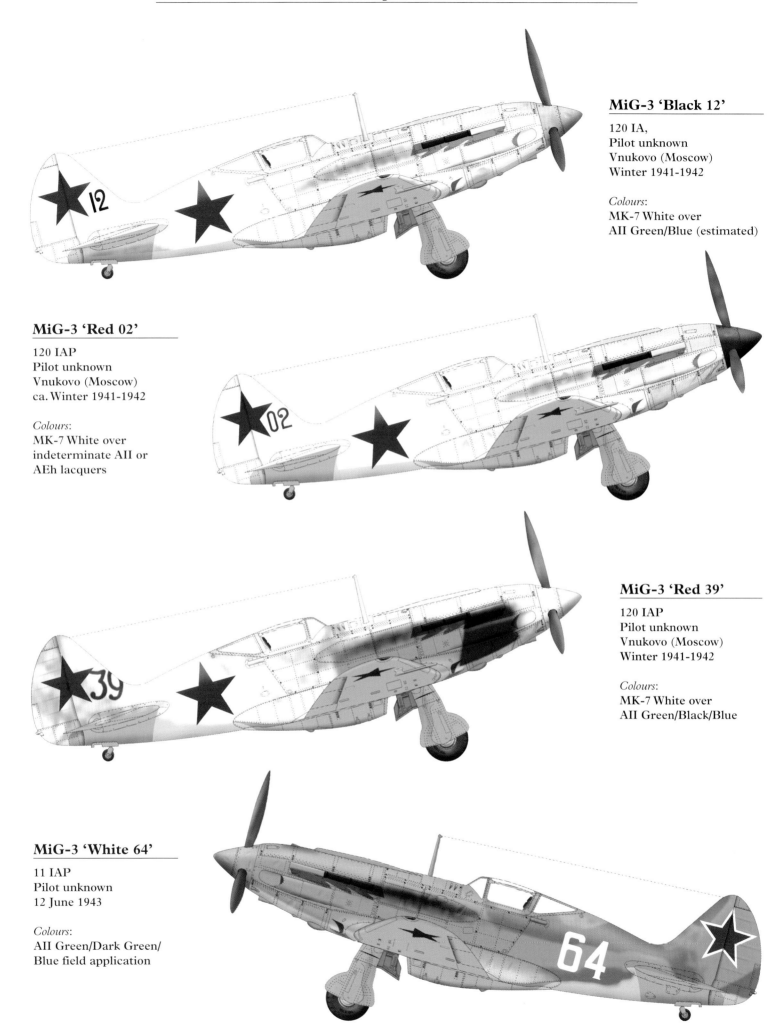

MiG-3 'Black 12'

120 IA,
Pilot unknown
Vnukovo (Moscow)
Winter 1941-1942

Colours:
MK-7 White over
AII Green/Blue (estimated)

MiG-3 'Red 02'

120 IAP
Pilot unknown
Vnukovo (Moscow)
ca. Winter 1941-1942

Colours:
MK-7 White over
indeterminate AII or
AEh lacquers

MiG-3 'Red 39'

120 IAP
Pilot unknown
Vnukovo (Moscow)
Winter 1941-1942

Colours:
MK-7 White over
AII Green/Black/Blue

MiG-3 'White 64'

11 IAP
Pilot unknown
12 June 1943

Colours:
AII Green/Dark Green/
Blue field application

reasons (relating to design time and function) these remedies were not taken in hand. It should be borne in mind that speed was of the highest importance and delays in the development programme would have been unacceptable. The I-200 was thus equipped with two 7.62 mm ShKAS guns above the engine, areas of which were faired over with several small blister fairings, and another 12.7 mm UBS was squeezed in just on the port side of the centre-line. An 8 mm sheet of armour plate was provided behind the pilot, and a PBP-1 gunsight installed.

The new prototype first took to the air on 5 April 1940 under the control of Senior Factory Test Pilot Ekatov, no weapons being installed in time for the flight. Significant engine over-heating problems arose at once, and all of the early test flights had to be abandoned due to such problems. Intensive testing continued during April with Ekatov finding the I-200 to be temperamental, the machine showing itself to be quite difficult to handle even in experienced hands. Control response was sloppy and ineffective at all heights, with directional stability being virtually non-existent under any high-speed conditions. The machine's stall under 'g' came without warning and with particular violence, a hopeless spin following automatically without the immediate and skilful application of rudder and a prompt reduction in power. Visibility during take-off and landing was very poor, and the wheel brake system failed repeatedly. Furthermore, the No.1 prototype was equipped with a hinged canopy – a feature detested by Soviet pilots – and this item drew intense criticism from Ekatov and other factory pilots.

However, despite all this, the new fighter did, in fact, do precisely what it was designed to do – namely to perform effectively at altitude. Indeed, during the month of May, Ekatov put on a splendid demonstration of the I-200's abilities, easily reaching 12,325 m on 22 May, and 650 km/h in level flight on the 24th. The prototype, with all military equipment installed, could reach 5,000 m in only 5.1 minutes, and climbed initially at the extremely impressive rate of 1,159 m/min. Throughout, the climb and speed performance characteristics of the I-200 prototype, at what were then considered to be extraordinary altitudes, were found to be entirely satisfactory. Moreover, these figures were obviously well in excess of those being obtained by other nations at the time, a fact which cannot be over-stated.

The I-200 was created at a time of heightened political tensions in Europe – especially between Germany and the USSR – and a possible eye was being cast towards developing any type of viable deterrent to German military aggression. Stalin was, as always, deeply interested in aircraft speed and height performance figures, notably because these could easily be incorporated into propaganda literature to enhance the appearance and technical reputation of the Red Army. As will become evident, the MiG-3 programme was driven almost entirely by these factors, and this aircraft's development history should be understood within this context alone.

As engineers gradually overcame the various cooling problems by fitting larger radiator units, Ekatov and other factory pilots continued to test the No.1 prototype energetically. It was Iosif Stalin, himself, who threw the project into such pandemonium shortly after the May Day celebrations in Moscow. Mikoyan was invited to demonstrate his new I-200 over the parade, and Ekatov duly flew the I-200 over Red Square at very high speed. The sleek prototype drew a very favourable reaction from Stalin, who later hearing of the machine's design performance (Ekatov's high speed trial run was still two weeks away) 'mentioned' that the I-200 should be placed into production. Taking its cue, the NKAP issued a Production Contract on 25 May, immediately after informing Stalin of the high speed trial the previous day; Stalin was delighted, and reportedly phoned Mikoyan to offer his congratulations.

Back at Mikoyan's OKO there was astonishment on the part of the Design Group. To order into production a prototype machine whose initial factory testing had not yet been completed successfully was unheard of – indeed, quite beyond belief. Chief Designer Romodin was horrified, and recorded in his papers that he feared the entire staff would be punished by Stalin when the project – under these conditions – failed

to result in a workable service fighter. On the 31 May, Commissar of Defence, Klim Voroshilov visited *Zavod* 1 with a delegation of military dignitaries, and paid particular attention and congratulation to Mikoyan over the I-200. The visit also confirmed Mikoyan's promotion to Head Designer at *Zavod* 1, Polikarpov and his Bureau having been reorganized as *Zavod* 51 in the meantime.

Testing of the I-200 prototype continued at an extraordinary pace during June and July, by which time the second and third prototypes had been completed. These prototypes received modifications and revisions of many kinds during their construction, many of which were applied at the very moment they were discovered, as the No.1 machine revealed them in testing. Even the AM-35A engine was poorly-built at this point, the motor having as yet failed to pass its 100 hour examination at TsIAM. During construction of the No.2 and No.3 aircraft, it seems that the second prototype received all of the minor engine and cooling modifications at once, while the No.3 aircraft was used to explore armament and control surface modifications, of which there were innumerable proposals. Factory-testing of both machines proceeded with remarkable speed, and by the early autumn, Mikoyan reported that the prototype's factory evaluation had been successfully completed.

On 28 August, the NKAP ordered the submission of the I-200 prototypes for State Evaluation Trials at the NII VVS. The No.2 I-200 was used for the flight evaluation, while the No.3 machine tested armament installation, maintenance features and airframe construction. Stepan Suprun, one of the Institute's most experienced pilots, was assigned the majority of the I-200's fight evaluation. At a take-off weight of 3,105 kg, the NII report found the I-200 No.2 prototype to reach 521 km/h at sea level and 629 km/h at 7,195 m with full boost, climb being 1,123m/min initially and reaching 5,000 m in 5.3 minutes. Suprun noted, however, that the machine was possessed of poor handling, and repeated Ekatov's observations about the prototype's behaviour, and even more interestingly, did not state his approval for the type in the NII VVS evaluation. The NII VVS staff also condemned the hinged canopy, but as the No.3 prototype was already fitted with a sliding unit, this matter was dropped from the report. However, the testing of the weapons systems and other maintenance features of the I-200 No.3 prototype were found to be entirely satisfactory, the sole reservation being that the total weight of fire from the three machine guns was seen to be too light for a modern fighter.

All things considered, the NKAP took the decision to go ahead with series manufacture at once, though simultaneously instructing aerodynamic testing and development to continue (using the huge, new wind tunnel completed by TsAGI, T-104), and the incorporation of the 112 recommended improvements listed in the NII VVS evaluation into the production version. These recommendations included the fitting of extra fuel cells to achieve a 1,000 km range, standardization on the No.3's armament arrangement, a small increase in fin area to improve lateral stability, and the inclusion of wing leading edge slats to improve stall and handling characteristics, in addition to others. Confidence was high that suitable refinements could be effected rapidly, and the initial series was authorized at last under the designation MiG-1.

Production at *Zavod* 1 commenced in late September 1940 with the manufacture of 25 pre-production MiG-1s. These aircraft were immediately distributed to the 146 IAP at Evpatoria for service trials, NII VVS Chief Test Pilot Suprun and Engineers Nikitchenko (airframe) and Karev (engine) accompanying the aircraft to assist the unit with the transition to the new fighter. These pre-series MiG-1s were essentially identical to the No.2 prototype, and did not incorporate any of the proposed modifications intended for series manufacture. As a result, pilot appraisal of the new fighter was very mixed. The obvious performance capabilities of the MiG-1 were lauded by the Regiment's pilots, but handling was still somewhat difficult, and not at all as similar to their former I-16s' characteristics as they had been led to believe. Mishaps in the new fighter were not uncommon, and sadly, two of the MiGs crashed during the 146 IAP's evaluation, one pilot losing his life.

In the meantime, series manufacture of the MiG-1 was underway at *Zavod* 1, but the various modifications specified in the NII report were not at all uniformly applied to these production examples. Indeed, all of the relevant changes were affected piecemeal on the lines as drawings and components were completed, and the resulting dissimilarity between individual examples was alarming. Additionally, sliding canopy units had not yet been delivered to the factory, and most of the initial MiG-1 fighters lacked any kind of closing canopy section, seriously affecting the aircraft's performance. None of the early MiGs incorporated leading edge slats on the wings, as drawings for this modification had not yet been completed, let alone the creation of jigs and tools for these parts on the lines. In November 1940, Ekatov examined the performance of production example No.53. The take-off weight of this machine was found to be 3,133 kg resulting in a greatly inferior rate of climb (6.3 minutes to 5,000 m) and handling, maximum speed with the open canopy dropping to 465 km/h at sea level and 608 km/h at 7,195 m; figures which can be regarded as typical for the production MiG-1.

The NKAP reacted quickly to the confusing conditions within the MiG programme, and instructed Mikoyan's OKO to submit plans and drawings for an updated production machine, due by 21 November. Working with great haste, the Mikoyan Bureau just managed to meet the deadline, and the NKAP immediately issued a revised Production Contract based on these papers. The improved model was to be known as the MiG-3, and 'standardized' manufacture was to commence no later than 1 December. However, despite these proclamations, the *Zavod* 1 production lines continued to apply improvements and corrections during production, and beginning with the 101st aircraft, the designation was simply changed arbitrarily to MiG-3, the new nomenclature having no relevance whatever to the specific nature of the machine manufactured.

Production of the MiG-3 accelerated during the early months of 1941, but success with the new fighter did not, and indeed the entire programme was quickly heading towards catastrophe. Serious trouble began on 12 January 1941, when test pilot Kuleshov was killed while testing spin recovery procedures in a MiG-3. Despite the fact that Kuleshov was a very experienced pilot (especially in spinning techniques), and literally fought the machine to the last second, the MiG simply would not recover from the spin; a property that was already being reported bitterly by service pilots converting to the new fighter. Engineers within the Mikoyan Bureau discovered that the centre of gravity on production machines was further aft than on the pre-production MiG-1s, resulting in even worse behaviour than before. Moreover, the AM-35A engine continued to give trouble, problems with faulty carburation, low oil pressure, and supercharger failure being common.

In the field, service regiments began to receive the MiG-3 in quantity, and pilots began to crash in them at an alarming pace. The fact that the more experienced pilots in each unit tended to acquire these new fighters seemed to do nothing to improve matters, and by early spring a full-blown mutiny was almost in force, VVS pilots in many cases refusing to pilot the MiG, and rejecting them for their trusted Polikarpov fighters. Regimental pilots also began to discover a number of unreported defects in the MiG, such as the inability of the sliding canopy to open at any but moderate air speeds, incessant over-revving of the supercharger, low-speed instability, and the lack of an inert-gas anti-fire system (as specified in the Production Contract). These disgruntlements were exacerbated by the general lack of very high altitude flight experience amongst Service pilots, resulting in poor operational performance under these conditions. Indeed, proper high-altitude flight in the MiG was not accomplished until May, following the outstanding efforts of Pilot-Engineer Kochetkov while working with the 31 IAP.

Noting these developments with discernible panic, the NKAP responded by issuing a flurry of directives to *Zavod* 1 regarding changes to the production model. The sheer number of these communications was bewildering, the factory's Production Diary once noting the arrival of 300 pages of corrections from the NKAP in a

single day. The result, perhaps inevitably, was confusion and disorder on the production lines, despite all efforts by the plant staff and Mikoyan's Bureau. Worse, the Government insisted categorically that the quantity of MiG production was not to be reduced under any circumstances, the MiG-3 forming the basis of its emergency modernization programme in the face of impending German hostility. Under these impossible conditions, MiG fighter production during the Spring of 1941 had reached nine aircraft per day, but virtually none of these machines represented any sort of uniform production standard, nor did they incorporate any of the requested design modifications issued by the NKAP.

By March, insurmountable difficulties beset the MiG fighter programme. Production aircraft reaching squadrons in the field were often of shockingly poor manufacture; leaking fuel and hydraulic systems, poor surface finish, ill-fitting panels, missing components, and even unharmonized weapons not uncommon. The Mikoyan OKO and *Zavod* 1 staff worked with great endeavour to redress the situation, dispatching repair 'brigades' out to the various regiments to correct the worst of the manufacturing problems. Then, on the 13th, Senior Factory Test Pilot Ekatov was tragically killed while completing factory testing on a MiG-3 when the supercharger apparently exploded. Crashes and accidents involving the MiG-3 in VVS Regiments also reached an all-time high during March 1941, the situation rapidly getting out of hand. When the true extent of these difficulties became clear to the NKAP, tempers were lost, and *Zavod* 1 was immediately ordered to provide two MiG production examples to the NII VVS for testing and evaluation.

When the two requested MiG fighters arrived at Kubinka Field at the beginning of April, however, the Institute pilots of the NII VVS scarcely recognized them. These MiG-3s were beautifully turned out, with high standards of manufacture and superb surface finishes. Indeed, despite being some 250 kg heavier than the factory test machines, these aircraft were able to reach 495 km/h at sea level and 642 km/h at 7,775 m – better performance even than the I-200 prototypes. When the pilots of the 34 IAP left their poorly-built, ill-performing MiG-3s and crossed the field to examine the two evaluation machines, it was the final straw.

Shocked, and incredulous that aircraft of this standard could be supplied for examination when the production examples were unfit for operation, the Government stepped in and declared that its MiG-3 rearmament programme had failed. The implications of this failure were far broader in scope than merely the MiG-3 fighter programme effort, for Moscow had been hard at work during the Spring of 1941 to dissuade German plans for hostilities against the USSR by means of military intimidation. In April, a German delegation was received via invitation from the Soviets following the crash in Russian territory of a *Luftwaffe* Ju 86 P 'spy' aircraft. The intent was to impress the German military staff with the power of Soviet arms and war preparations, and one of the major venues of the delegation's tour was the *Zavod* 1 facility and the MiG productions lines. The German delegation was treated to a spectacular demonstration flight by Stepan Suprun (piloting one of the two NII evaluation aircraft), and the presentation included speed and altitude measurement calculations to drive home the MiG's performance. Tours of various airfields around Moscow were undertaken, all the while stressing that the MiG fighters were in widespread VVS service. The German General Staff was indeed impressed, and it was upon hearing of the MiG-3's performance that Hitler was said to have issued his famous invocation to attack at once [1]. The resulting embarrassment to the Soviet government caused by the failure of this high profile programme was intolerable.

The almost inevitable result of this was a criminal investigation, but in the irrational world of Stalinist oppression, Artem Mikoyan – politically untouchable through the good offices of his popularity with Stalin – was not held responsible, and an immediate need for scapegoats quickly seized the Government. In this absurd atmosphere, the Air Force's Scientific Testing Institute was accused of improperly testing the MiG prototypes, leading to erroneous decisions on the part of the NKAP. This preposterous notion was in part based on an earlier incident involving the MiG-3's operational radius and Mikoyan's own complaints that the NII's evaluation was improperly conducted. To his condemnation Mikoyan must be criticized here for his various testimonies against NII VVS Director Aleksandr Filin. Nikolai Polikarpov also came under investigation at this time, it being noted with great conspicuousness by the *Zavod* 1 directorate staff that the I-200 was originally based on Polikarpov's design.

The result of the investigation was predictably disastrous. Several of the NII VVS's most able and accomplished pilots and engineers were dismissed, including A. Voevodin, N. Maksimov and P. Nikitchenko. Most tragically Filin, the NII's outstanding Director – a brilliant early Soviet pilot and Hero of the Soviet Union, and the first man to qualify for the title of Pilot-Engineer – was condemned as being ultimately responsible for the failure and was subsequently shot by the NKVD. The incident was the final nail in the professional coffin of Polikarpov, who, though avoiding criminal prosecution, was essentially banished from Moscow and sent to Novosibirsk, from where his designs would play no further mentionable part in Soviet fighter development until his death in 1944. Chief Designer Viktor Romodin – a long time associate of Polikarpov – also escaped criminal prosecution, but his career was similarly destroyed, and he joined his old boss in obscurity in Novosibirsk.

In the wake of these investigations, however, the staff at both *Zavod* 1 and Mikoyan's OKO received the clear message that matters were to improve, and immediately. During May a number of equipment changes and improvements materialized on the production lines. The RSI-4 radio became standard equipment, and this addition was characterized by the appearance of a large radio mast forward of the cockpit, well offset to starboard. Wing leading edge slats were at last a standard feature, and some of these models also included an inert gas anti-fire system in either or both main fuel cells. Aircraft armament was improved with a variant featuring underwing pods housing a 12.7 mm UBS. The increase in the MiG-3's modest hitting power with the five gun arrangement was very popular, but performance in these models suffered under the additional weight and drag. A typical five gun MiG of early summer weighed 3,382 kg at take-off and could reach only 455 km/h at sea level, 547 km/h at 5,000 m, and 589 km/h at 7,775 m, climbing initially at 884m/min and requiring 7.1 minutes to achieve 5,000 m. Meanwhile, most of the serious defects were at last resolved on the production lines, and by the time of the invasion, *Zavod* 1 was turning out a MiG-3 that at the least could be considered acceptable from a serviceability point of view. During the summer, many MiG-3s had their extra guns removed by their service regiments and in this form, a typical MiG could reach figures of 463 km/h at sea level and 603 km/h at 7,775 m, climbing at 915m/min initially, and having a service ceiling of 10,855 m.

When the German war machine rolled across the Soviet border on 22 June 1941, the MiG-3 was one of the most numerically significant fighters available to stem the invasion in the Western Military Districts. Despite the loss of the majority of these aircraft on the ground, MiGs were ever-present in aerial engagements against the *Luftwaffe* all the way to Moscow, and from the start, the performance of the MiG-3 against its German rivals was mixed. Compared to the Messerschmitt Bf 109, the MiG-3 did not rate particularly well. The MiG was superior to the E model and even slightly better than the F model at very high altitudes (above 6,100 m), but combat on the Russian Front took place at such heights so infrequently so as to render this advantage irrelevant. At medium and low altitudes, the Soviet machine was not only slower, but also heavier, and with its higher wing-loading, could not turn with its *Luftwaffe* rivals in the horizontal plane. This problem was exacerbated by the poor climb performance of the MiG, and by its instability at high speeds. Worse, the combination of three machine guns – two of which being mere rifle calibre – was completely inadequate in modern aerial combat. The overall effect was to leave the MiG-3 with no significant advantages over its enemies, and thus success in combat could come only from tactical acumen and initiative, and from the skills of the pilot.

Despite all these difficulties, many pilots did surprisingly well in the MiG during the early *Barbarossa* period. Pilots from the 55 IAP discovered that the MiG-3 had very much better control surfaces than the Messerschmitt, and specialized in high-speed attacks against German aircraft from height, and also at low airspeeds. A young Aleksandr Pokrishkin was one of the successful fliers from this period, destroying no fewer than five Bf 109s in one month. Under great pressure, the 16, 27, and 34 IAPs were all notable for their successful employment of the MiG-3, and despite the difficult conditions, it must also be noted that the aircraft maintained a very high rate of serviceability and combat readiness under dreadful conditions.

By mid-summer, as the German onslaught swept across the Belorussian and eastern Ukrainian countryside, a new MiG-3 began to leave the production lines at *Zavod* 1. The new model, which was, as usual, undistinguished by any change in designation, featured a repositioned engine, this being mounted some 10 cm forward (with a consequent lengthening of the fuselage) to counteract the overly rearward centre of gravity problem. The AM-35A's gearing ratio was adjusted from 0.902 to 0.732, and a new ViSH-22K constant speed propeller was fitted, though this failed to improve take-off run or fuel economy. Two long and narrow one-piece blister fairings now covered the ShKAS guns over the engine, giving a distinctive appearance. Leading edge slats, an anti-fire system, the newer PBP-1b gunsight, and an improved sliding canopy section all became standard, while fuel capacity and armament remained unchanged. Quality control measures at the Moscow assembly lines had now been fully developed and production machines now sported improved surface finishes, and indeed no further examples of unusable MiG fighters appear to have left the factory from this time. The new summer model typically weighed 3,305 kg at take-off, it could achieve 466 km/h at sea level and 616 km/h at 7,775 m, climbing at 945m/min initially and requiring 7.1 minutes to reach 5,000 m with a service ceiling of 12,045 m.

Two of the first units to fly the new variants in battle were the 401 and 402 IAPs, both staffed by test pilots drawn from the NII VVS and the LII. These elite units were intended to set an example to other VVS regiments, and to develop effective tactics and procedures for the operation of the MiG fighter. Unfortunately, however, conditions prevailing at the Front did not allow the attainment of either goal, and although these units did score well (as might be expected with such experienced aviators), the performance of the MiG-3 was disappointing in virtually every respect. Indeed, on 4 July 1941, Stepan Suprun, one of the most accomplished and experienced pilots in the entire Soviet Union, and Commander of the 401 IAP, lost his life in combat with enemy machines at low-altitude, having been accredited with four victories in as many days. By the end of the month, LII pilots Belov, Sorbkin, and Vasiliev, in addition to NII pilots Tsilovev and Kaminski, had been killed as well.

As the German advance pushed ever closer towards Moscow, production at *Zavod* 1 reached a frenzied tempo. In August 1941, the Factory delivered 562 MiG-3 fighters – a figure never again even approached in Soviet aero production. Indeed, from July-September 1941 no fewer than 1,508 MiGs were completed, but despite the superb manufacturing effort underway in Moscow, the future of the MiG-3 had fallen into grave uncertainty. The aircraft's inauspicious performance at the front, in addition to the NKAP's persistent irritation that production examples simply refused to match the capabilities of the prototype examples, led to a negative impression of the programme on the part of the Government. Indeed, even Stalin – once a vocal supporter of the project – now cast a frosty glance at Mikoyan and his OKO group. On 20 August, during a meeting of the GKO, the NII VVS, and the People's Commissariat of the Aviation Industry, the relocation of the aviation factories was discussed for the first time in detail, and with regard to the re-establishment of manufacture of various aircraft at the new proposed locations, the MiG-3 was not even mentioned.

With the die cast firmly against his Bureau's single production aircraft, Mikoyan struggled with great energy to improve matters on the MiG lines. Before the evacuation of *Zavod* 1 in September, several new MiG-3 modifications appeared, including a variant with six underwing rails for the RS-82 rocket. Similar installations had been accomplished hitherto in the field, but almost 200 such MiGs left the factory in August. Over Moscow, the 6th Guards IAK-PVO successfully employed these weapons, which have long been derided in Western literature. Taking note of the experience gained in the air battles over Mongolia, the highly trained pilots of this experienced PVO unit fired RS-82 rockets from their MiGs against German bombers with impressive results. The best position was found to be slightly above and behind the target, and close range was required for accurate placement of the missiles. However, the strike of even a single rocket was sufficient to cause catastrophic damage to the target, which was inevitably destroyed. A number of later MiG-3s had their 7.62 mm ShKAS guns removed and replaced by two 12.7mm UBS weapons, resulting in very much improved striking power with three UBS guns closely grouped in the nose. Underwing supplemental fuel tanks of 100 litres apiece were introduced on the last models, and a few machines were fitted with the ViSH-105KCh broad-chord airscrew, at last improving climb and take-off performance.

However, the most significant work in August at Mikoyan's OKO in Moscow was the search for a new aircraft powerplant. As early as 2 August, the decision had been taken by the Government that production of the AM-35 motor would not continue after the evacuation of *Zavod* 24. Simultaneously, Mikhail Gudkov, also at Moscow in the OKB 301 workshops, was hard at work fitting various airframes experimentally with the Shvetsov M-82 radial. Already he had successfully fitted the big radial on a LaGG-3 airframe, this resulting in the very promising Gu-82, and was just then at work on a radial-powered Yak-7 fighter. As early as July, Gurevich had approached Gudkov about the possibility of assisting with the project to fit an M-82 to a MiG-3 airframe, and Gudkov enthusiastically agreed. By early August Gudkov's work was complete, and the resulting MiG-3 M-82 demonstrated once again his skill in such engine matters, the cowling being faired very elegantly into the MiG's fuselage. Gurevich added armament to the new prototype in the form of three 12.7 mm BS guns disposed around the cowling, and in this form, the machine was flown experimentally by the LII on 17 August.

Found to be acceptable, the MiG-3 M-82 was dispatched to the NII VVS on 20 August, and three days of intensive testing ensued. The NII VVS recorded a maximum speed for the MiG-3 M-82 of 476 km/h at sea level and 566 km/h at 5,000 m at normal power only, the failure of the supercharger preventing any test data to be accumulated at maximum boost. Handling was said to be satisfactory, and indeed the radial-powered MiG did not demonstrate the severe torque effects found in the Gu-82 with the same power plant. Generally satisfied, the NII VVS granted its approval of the MiG-3 M-82 on 23 August. The NKAP immediately drew up a request for five pre-production machines, and reserved the designation 'MiG-9' for the aircraft should it enter series manufacture. However, the resulting evacuation of *Zavod* 1 to Kuibishev meant that none of these pre-production models was completed in Moscow, and after the inevitable delays experienced during the resulting confusion of the move, these five machines were not completed until the end of 1941. In the event, production of the MiG-3 M-82 did not reach fruition, and development of the radial-engined MiG fighter continued with the revised I-211 series.

At the same time, yet another MiG-3 airframe was fitted with the Mikulin AM-38 engine, this a slightly larger and more powerful cousin of the AM-35. The choice was an obvious one, and no significant difficulties were experienced in the conversion process.

However, with the heavier engine the machine's weight rose to 3,382 kg, and though maximum speed increased at sea level, performance was reduced at altitude (the figures being 547 km/h and 594 km/h, respectively). Moreover, climb performance was severely affected in the MiG-3 AM-38, the machine now requiring 7.3 minutes to reach 5,000 m. Test Pilot Kochetkov piloted the AM-38 prototype during August 1941, and found the aircraft to possess poor handling, and experienced unending cooling problems with the AM-38 motor. With the variant clearly in need of extended development work to reach production status, and the generally poor performance of the type, the MiG-3 AM-38 was abandoned as the factory evacuated to the south.

Ironically, it was just at the time when production of the MiG-3 teetered on the brink of cancellation that the MiG fighter experienced its most glorious performance. As German forces pushed towards Moscow, the PVO forces disposed in and around the city – many equipped with the MiG-3 – began to exact a frightening toll on the *Luftwaffe* machines venturing over the capital. In the ensuing Battle of Moscow, MiG units, spearheaded by the 6th Guards IAK-PVO, gave a magnificent account of themselves. Serviceability remained extremely high throughout the battle, despite the exhausting number of sorties flown, and interceptions were made not only at low and medium altitudes in daytime *and* at night, but high-level raiders and reconnaissance aircraft were destroyed as well. In fact, so furious was the defence of the skies over Moscow that of 8,278 German bomber sorties launched against the city, a mere 207 enemy machines were effective in delivering their bomb load. MiG fighters played a key role in this astonishing success, one which has no other equal – not remotely – in the annals of aviation history.

When *Zavod* 1 finally resumed some manner of aircraft production in December 1941, some 100 MiG-3 fighters were assembled from components evacuated to Kuibishev. Additionally, five pre-production MiG-3 M-82 aircraft were completed as per the NKAP request, but these were to be the swansong of the aircraft's development. On 23 December, the factory received written orders from the NKAP that all production capacity at *Zavod* 1 was to be devoted to the manufacture of the Il-2 *Shturmovik*; the orders were sealed and codified by the highest authority, the all-too-familiar (and dreaded) scratchy blue pencil: '*Confirmed – Stalin.*' The MiG-3 programme was over.

In all, some 3,100 MiG fighters were manufactured over the extraordinarily short interval of 14 months, from October 1940 to December 1941. The unnerving speed with which the MiG had been rushed into service had everything to do with the subsequent difficulties experienced in the programme, and here the only culprit in fact worthy of blame was the Government, itself. Despite the hardships, it must be mentioned that the MiG-3 acquitted itself admirably in combat, many examples soldiering on well into 1943. Mikoyan and Gurevich would continue their work on fighter aircraft during the GPW, but their rise to prominence and fame would arrive later with the introduction of jet-powered fighters and the Cold War.

---

1. *Oberst* Heinrich Aschenbrenner was the Technical Chief Investigator of the delegation, and described the MiG-3 and the manufacturing lines in the delegation's report to the *Generalstab*, which was shown to Hitler. He stressed that the measurements had been made in their presence by the Russians, and were scientifically verifiable. Upon hearing that the VVS had a 645 km/h fighter in service in large numbers, Hitler exclaimed to the assembled Generals: 'Well, you can see how far they have already progressed. We must begin [Operation Barbarossa] at once!'

	MiG-1 1940	MiG-3 1941 Early	MiG-3 1941 Standard	MiG-3 1941 5-gun Variant	MiG-3 1941 Lengthened Version	MiG-3 Final Variant
Weights						
Empty:	2692 kg	2775 kg	2768 kg	2785 kg	2683 kg	2701 kg
Loaded:	3313 kg	3382 kg	3318 kg	3357 kg	3305 kg	3314 kg
Wing Area:	17.44 sq.m	17.44 sq.m	17.44 sq.m	17.44 sq.m	17.44 sq.m	17.44 sq.m
Engine:	AM-35A 1200 (1350) hp	AM-35A 1200 (1350) hp	AM-35A 1200 (1350) hp	AM-35A 1200 (1350) hp	AM-35A 1200 (1350) hp	AM-35A 1200 (1350) hp
Maximum Speed						
At Altitude:	608 km/h at 7180 m	598 km/h at 7180 m	603 km/h at 7180 m	587 km/h at 7180 m	616 km/h at 7620 m	640 km/h at 7620 m
Sea Level:	465 km/h	452 km/h	463 km/h	450 km/h	466 km/h	476 km/h
Climb						
Initial:	976 m/min	915 m/min	915 m/min	884 m/min	945 m/min	983 m/min
Time to Height:	6.3 min to 5000 m	7.2 min to 5000 m	7.2 min to 5000 m	7.5 min to 5000 m	7.1 min to 5000 m	6.5 min to 5000 m
Service Ceiling:	11130 m	11130 m	11130 m	10670 m	12050 m	12050 m
Armament:	2 x ShKAS 1 x UBS	2 x ShKAS 1 x UBS	2 x ShKAS 1 x UBS	2 x ShKAS 1 x UBS 2 x UBS	2 x ShKAS 1 x UBS 6 x RS-82	3 x UBS 6 x RS-82

MiG-3
typical production
('long-nosed')

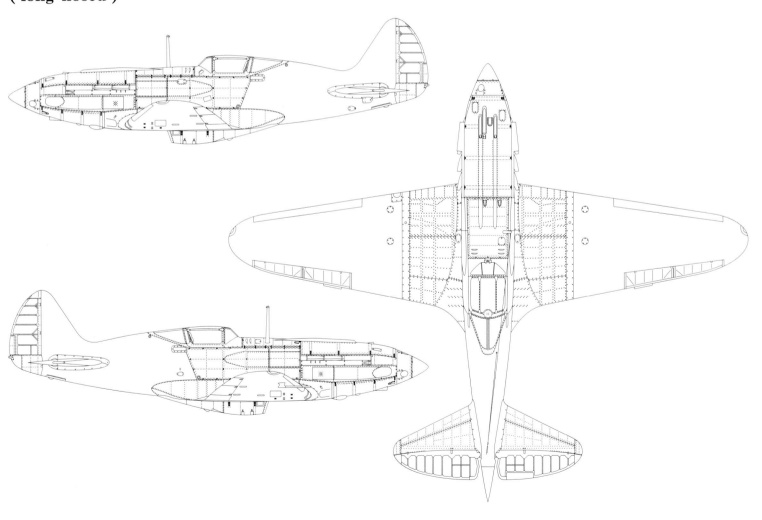

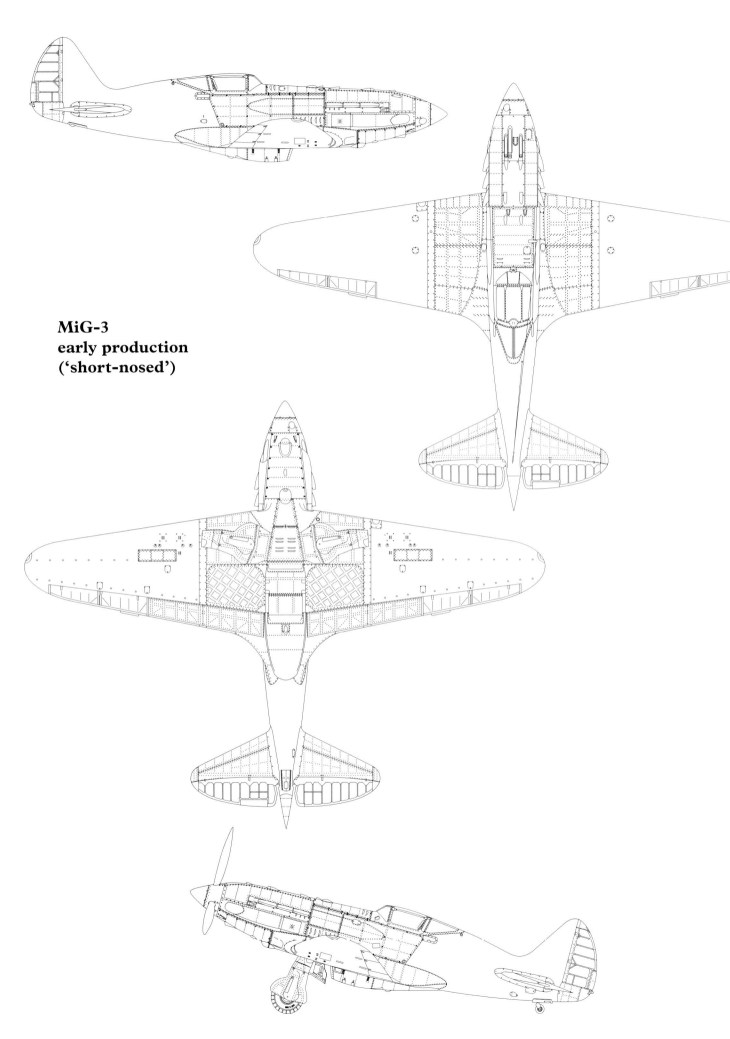

**MiG-3
early production
('short-nosed')**

THE DEVELOPMENT OF CAMOUFLAGE ON
THE MiG-1 AND MiG-3 FIGHTERS

The Curious Way

Unlike all other VVS camouflage application practices, the colouration of the MiG fighter enjoyed no development at all. That is not to say that there were not different schemes available and in use, but these do not follow each other in any recognizable pattern. Rather, there are examples of virtually all of the identified factory applied schemes appearing throughout the MiG programme.

This fact is all the more curious in that some of these applications were decidedly obsolete. Indeed, the 1940 Camouflage Directive specifically stated that fighters were to be finished in a two-tone livery at the factories. Inexplicably, this was not often done to the MiG, and even to the end of MiG-3 manufacture it is possible to find single-colour schemes, albeit they became increasingly rare. Unfortunately, there is no information available to explain any of these odd curiosities.

The first and most easily recognized schemes are the single-colour applications. The use of AII Green on the upper surfaces with AII Blue undersurfaces was a relic of pre-1940 manufacture at *Zavod* 1, and MiGs can be seen in this livery as well (see Fig. 1).

Fig. 1

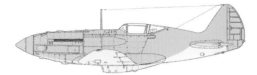

Of all the known MiG-3 schemes, this single-colour application theme was the only such to have been applied with any significant consistency, although it had largely disappeared by the summer of 1941 following the NKAP's camouflage directives. The pre-war sharp demarcation was evident between upper and lower colours, and national insignia were common on the upper wing surfaces.

Zavod 1, however, also made use of a lacquer unique to that enterprise. 'Factory Green' was seen nowhere else in Soviet manufacture, and it is thought that this might have been some older AE series lacquer from the 1930s (AE-5 has been suggested) (see Fig. 2).

Fig. 2

The colour demarcations with Factory Green schemes vary widely from sharp to soft. The underside colour was AII Blue, and this type of finish was seen all the way to the end of the programme in September 1941.

In several photographs taken by the Germans of captured MiGs of early manufacture, there are a number of curiosities. Many of these machines show signs of significant repainting (certainly the work of the *Zavod* 1 field repair teams). The colour used in much of this work is quite dark, and in photographs, resembles the *Zavod* 1 lacquer Factory Green. It is improbable that units in the field would have had quantities of this proprietary varnish on hand, and so if the two finishes are indeed the same, it is very much more likely that this paint is one of the pre-war aviation lacquers such as AEh-5. AEh-15 lacquer has been suggested as the actual shade. Be that as it may, the appearance of these early MiGs is unusual.

The first recognizable two-colour application was seen from the outset of manufacture. The upper surfaces were finished in AII Black over AII Green, and again in AII Blue undersurfaces (see Fig. 3).

Fig. 3

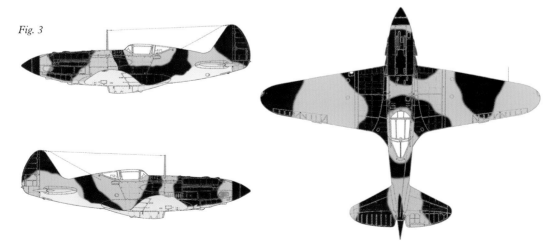

The colour demarcations in all locations tended to be hard, or semi-hard. The rear fuselage upper/lower colour demarcation was irregular, but sharp-edged, giving an odd appearance.

A somewhat similar scheme evolved on the MiG programme, this again in AII colours (Black/Green/Blue). This application features its characteristic 'V' shape on the port side nose (see Fig. 4).

Fig. 4

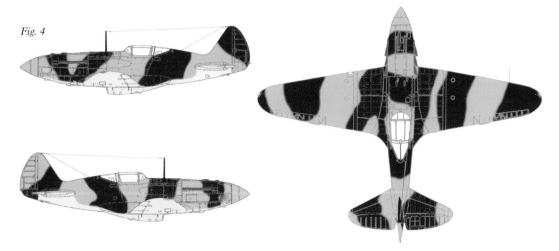

The colour demarcations tended to be softer than on the previous scheme, semi-hard to semi-soft being common. The rear fuselage colour demarcation 'ramp' was also more traditional in appearance.

Only one pattern application is known on the MiG-3 that includes the two green colours. This scheme, executed in AII Dark Green over AII Green, seems to have been used infrequently, and is known from just a few photographs (see Fig. 5).

Fig. 5

Right: *This dark and indistinct photograph is believed to show one of the original MiG-1 examples in evaluation testing during the winter of 1940-41.*
(Photo: G.Petrov)

Despite being unusual, the pattern was extremely striking. The uppersurface colour demarcations appear to have been semi-soft, and the upper/lower rear fuselage demarcation 'ramp' was quite 'modern' in appearance.

As with most camouflage practices, the MiG-3 sported a simplified version as well. This pattern was completed in AII Black over AII Green, as was usual for this aircraft (see Fig. 6).

Fig. 6

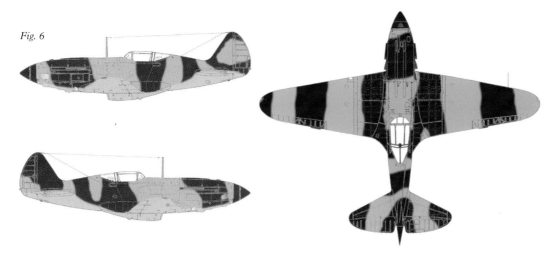

Above: *Two later manufacture (or 'long-nosed') MiG-3s of the 7 IAP VVS ChF, Kuban, 1943. These aircraft appear to be wearing the simple 'banded' camouflage pattern. (Photo: G.Petrov)*

Right: *Another photograph from the same series; a line-up of MiG-3s of the 7 IAP VVS ChF in the Kuban, 1943. The fourth MiG is somewhat darker than the previous three, and might be finished in Factory Green. Note the P-40 Warhawks lined up after the furthest MiG. All of these aircraft appear to have white spinners. (Photo: G.Petrov)*

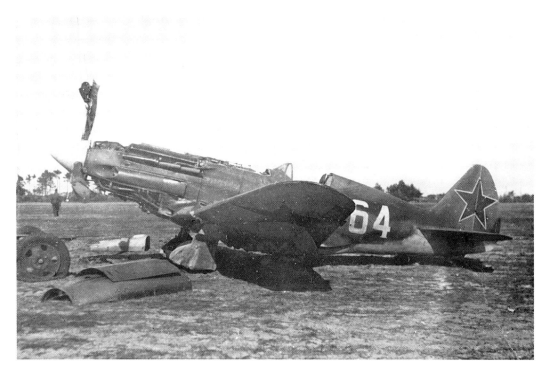

The colour demarcations on this pattern tended to be semi-hard, including the upper/lower colour 'ramp'.

Winter Schemes

During the Winter of 1941-42 most MiGs were given a white camouflage application. The usual treatment was a coat of MK-7 white, this applied by various units in the field. Around Moscow, however, many MiG-3s served on various airfields, including the factory field behind the old *Zavod* 1 workshops. Despite the evacuation of the factory, some of the personnel remained at the workshops, and a number of MiGs seem to have been very professionally camouflaged by them with MK-7 white over their temperate scheme (see Fig. 7).

Fig. 7

Occasionally, areas of the undersurface were painted white. In some cases, the outer wing panel unders and even the entire forward fuselage were white.

Interior Colours

MiG fighters, no doubt due to the transitional and confused nature of their manufacture, wore a perplexing mix of internal finishes. Many pre-war cockpit colour schemes existed, including AII Blue and AII Aluminium uniformly painted cockpit surfaces. Uniform Wood Finish cockpits were common, and completely unfinished cockpits were very typical of manufacture during the late summer of 1941.

Unusual MiG Schemes

During the defence of Moscow, many MiG-3s serving in the capital demonstrated large areas of red colour painted about the aircraft. Red noses, wings and stripes, etc, were common.

A handful of unusual appliqué camouflage schemes occurred on MiG fighters. These were probably the result of colour being applied in the field over AII Green solid colour, so as to comply with the 1940 Directives. One famous photograph shows a wrecked MiG (early variant) with the number '8' in a very elongated font. The colours appear to be a mottle of AII Dark Green over AII Green.

Above: *A classic photograph of MiG-3s lined up at Vnukovo field, Moscow in late 1941. These machines are thought to belong to the 120 IAP, part of the 6 GIAK-PVO protecting the capital. Some of these MiGs sport coloured outer wings on the uppersurfaces, and colourful spinners. The suggestion has been made that the wings are green, and are replacement units of some kind. While this interpretation is indeed possible, a careful analysis of the photographic negative suggests that the best matching colour, by far, is in fact red (as with the national marking). The winter coat of MK-7 white is wearing away at the wingroots, and especially over the engine cowling, where the underlying colour is showing through rather badly (especially on the leading aircraft, 'Red 02'). Several machines are still finished in temperate colouration, and the under-exposed photograph leaves one in doubt as to whether these show two-colour applications, or a single-colour uppersurface scheme of Factory Green.*

Above: *MiG-3s of the 120 IAP lined up at Vnukovo field, Moscow in 1941. (Photo: A. Kraft collection)*

Polikarpov I-15, I-15², I-153

Chapter 4

Polikarpov I-15, I-152, I-153

One of the many classic fighter designs emanating from the prodigious Polikarpov design staff, the I-15 family of machines were of a class of aircraft regarded by some as fundamentally obsolete throughout their flying career. Nevertheless, these diminutive little biplanes remained in production into January 1941, and were one of the last of their type in use anywhere in the world. The story of these little fighters was a metaphor of a larger sense of turmoil within the world-wide aviation community, and their fate would chronicle the development and the resolution of this controversy over the history of their service life.

In the summer of 1931, Polikarpov, then working at the Central Design Bureau (TsKB), began work on a successor to his earlier I-5 biplane fighter. Though related by family to the I-5, the new machine was of an entirely later generation in design. Polikarpov intended to make use of an engine of no less than 700 hp, and although the machine was of biplane design (in contrast – perhaps intentionally – to his radical new monoplane) it would incorporate many innovative features. The most notable arrangement was a dramatically dipped upper gull wing featuring a Gettingen-436 airfoil cross-section (similar to the classic Clark Y section), designed to reduce drag, improve forward visibility and simplify production. By 1933, the primary drawings had more or less solidified, and GUAP authorized the development of a prototype under the designation TsKB-3.

The new fighter was of highly mixed construction (a Polikarpov trademark), with wooden twin-spar wings and a metal-framed fuselage, all covered in fabric. The upper wing was decidedly gull-shaped and carried very large ailerons, whilst the lower wing was a single-piece unit that transversed the fuselage, forming part of the cockpit floor. A single streamlined brace was provided between the mainplanes well outboard. The fuselage was constructed of KhMA chrome-steel alloy tubing, with light dural stringers forming the contour shape aft. The entire forward part of the fuselage was covered in dural sheet, while all tail and control surfaces were metal-framed with fabric covering. Large spat-type fairings covered both main wheels. Power was provided by the nine-cylinder Wright 1820-F3 Cyclone motor of 720 hp, and armament was to include two 7.62 mm PV-1 machine guns mounted along the fuselage sides and synchronized to fire through the propeller.

In October 1933, two of the initial prototypes were evaluated by a State Commission, which received them with considerable scepticism. The somewhat short fuselage, combined with the type's relatively powerful engine and unusual wing, drew considerable pre-flight comment from the assembled pilots, including some from the NII VVS and LII. After some debate it was decided that Valeriy Chkalov – one of the most experienced pilots in the entire USSR – would make the initial flight. In the event, however, any concerns proved completely unfounded, for the TsKB-3 was possessed of the most superior handling. Indeed, during the prototype's twelfth test-flight Pilot-Engineer Filin (future director of the NII VVS) looped the aircraft from 200 m altitude, performed acrobatics, and later Senior Test Pilot V. Stepanchenok deliberately induced the machine into a spin. During flight trials the TsKB-3 demonstrated what was then regarded as adequate performance (both level speed and rate-of-climb proving somewhat lower than had been predicted), reaching 369 km/h at 3,000 m and climbing at nearly 610 m/min.

Testing proceeded well and by early December 1933, TsAGI was ready to submit the TsKB-3 for State Evaluations by the NII VVS. Once again, no difficulties were encountered by the Institute during testing of the prototype. The performance recorded by the State Commission was confirmed, and some detailed recommendations were made with regard to the aircraft's systems. During the second month of NII VVS testing, Engineer Polotkin had determined that two more

PV-1 guns could be mounted easily just ahead of the pilot astride each wing-root fairing, giving the little fighter the relatively heavy armament of four machineguns. The TsKB-3 was also tested by the Institute with the 480 hp M-22 engine, which recognized that supplies of the licence-built Wright Cyclone – the M-25 – would not be ready in time, and that original Cyclones might not be forthcoming.

In this form the TsKB-3 passed its State examinations and GUAP authorized production of the new fighter at two Moscow factories as the I-15. *Zavoda* 1 and 39 both tooled up for series manufacture, and by November and December 1934 the first completed models were being tested at the factories. However, production of the M-25 motor had yet to materialize, and the M-22 was selected to power the initial versions as a stopgap, at least until supplies of the more powerful engine became available. As a result, the production I-15 was to be powered by the nine cylinder M-22 engine, giving 480 hp. Provision was made for an RA-1 radio set (though the unit was rarely fitted) and allowance was made for a sheet of 8 mm armour plate to be installed behind the pilot's head and shoulders. Both factories seemed to have manufactured I-15s both with *and* without their wheel spats (fairings), but these items were often removed under service conditions. Armament was held to just the two upper PV-1 guns (the M-22 being seen to offer too little flying horsepower to accommodate the extra weight of four), and these were supplied with 1,500 rounds of ammunition. Powered by the M-22, the production I-15 was capable of 347 km/h at 3,000 m and climbed at the somewhat unimpressive initial rate of 421 m/min. with a ceiling of 7,515 m.

The first operational machines reached units in the field during the spring of 1935, the 71 IAP being the first to convert entirely to the type. In direct contrast to the I-16 – which appeared almost simultaneously – pilots were thrilled with their new gull-winged mounts, handling and flight behaviour being extremely safe, reliable, and predictable (as opposed to the I-16 which was seen to be dangerous and radical). Certainly it was an easy aircraft for pilots to appreciate, as it handled magnificently, manoeuvrability being quite exceptional under any conditions. Indeed, it was at this time that the aircraft received its famous sobriquet, 'Chaika', meaning 'gull', after the deep bend in the wing centre-section.

A few difficulties were noted in the initial production examples. Both factories produced aircraft that were slightly heavier than the prototype TsKB-3, and performance suffered accordingly. At higher airspeeds pilots began to notice a distinct warping of the lower wing surface, and calls were made to stiffen these units at the earliest opportunity. Furthermore, no examples of armour plate for the pilot had been fitted to date, and this type of protection was certainly expected by the UVVS staff.

Almost at once, the tiny new fighter became embroiled in the considerable politics which surrounded Soviet military aviation of the time. Argument blew up over the necessary attributes that a fighter of the 1930's should possess. On the one hand, there were the more traditional pilots and theoreticians who maintained that manoeuvrability, handling, and turning-circle were the prerequisite of successful combat flying, the close-in dog-fight being the standard and preferred method of engaging the enemy. In the other camp were a 'new'[1] breed of fighter pilots who believed that speed and altitude, employed in the slashing and surprise attack, would obviate the need for such 'acrobatics', and protect the flier from the hazards associated with co-ordinated formation tactics.

In the USSR, these differences in fighter theory were alarmingly exacerbated by the flying characteristics of the two new Polikarpov designs. Though the accident rate for the new I-15 was by no means non-existent, it was dwarfed by what was fast becoming an unworkable situation with the tricky I-16, which at the time were crashing almost continuously. 'Old school' pilots leapt on the fact and insisted that the new design parameters were dangerous and incompetent, a claim which they politicized with great zeal both within the Army command structure and even on the floor of the Supreme Soviet. Soon, investigations were called for on the I-16 design, whose reputation had deteriorated so badly that many pilots with regular VVS squadrons in the field refused – almost to the point of mutiny – to fly it. In time, of course, these difficulties were overcome and the I-16 vindicated as an excellent design, but the rivalry between the two camps persisted.

Throughout 1935, numerous development and experimental flights were carried out with the basic I-15 airframe. The No.2 pre-series example first flew with an M-25A motor on 15 July, achieving 379 km/h at 2,530 m, even better than in the Cyclone-powered prototype. Manoeuvrability in the M-25 variant was also improved, and the initial climb rose to 640 m/min, well ahead of world standards for biplane fighters at that time. In November, Test Pilot Vladimir Kokkinaki flew a modified I-15 which had been stripped down for the attempt on a world altitude record of 14,575 m. Later, in July 1936, an I-15 was tested with two of the new 12.7 mm UBS gun prototypes at *Zavod* 1, whilst another machine featured underwing bomb racks and conducted various dive-bombing trials.

It was also during 1935 that the TsKB-3 prototype was rebuilt at *Zavod* 39. Traditionalists within the Army Air Force regarded the gull centreplane feature as being too 'radical', and noted that some forward visibility was lost on take-off and landing. As a result, engineers at *Zavod* 39 rebuilt the prototype with an unbroken 'normal' upper wing centre-section. The rebuilt machine was powered by a Wright 1820 'Cyclone' radial and included an armament of four PV-1 machine guns.

Beginning in May 1935, this machine was handed over to the NII VVS for extended testing trials. However, the evaluation was interrupted for some months to carry out extensive wind-tunnel analyses at TsAGI when it was discovered that the modified aircraft demonstrated markedly reduced performance compared to the anticipated performance calculations made on the type. The rebuilt machine reached only 360 km/h, and required 7.1 minutes to reach 5,000 m. It was soon shown that the adoption of a conventional wing centre-section resulted in dramatically increased drag, as per Polikarpov's warnings, and that the aircraft's manoeuvrability and handling were seriously impaired. The pilot's forward view problems on take-off largely disappeared, however, and the traditionalists leapt on the fact to try to force a change in design. Despite much politicking, the NII VVS was unmoved, and with performance already a disappointment, the new configuration was deemed to be completely unacceptable by the Institute pilots, and the prototype was rejected for further development at that time.

It was just at this point, however, that developments in Spain would bring the ongoing monoplane versus biplane fighter debate to a head. On 18 July 1936, an open revolt by Falangist and Fascist military forces ushered in the brutally-contested Spanish Civil War. Nations around the world scrambled to take up sides, issue proclamations, and find new ways to profit from the disaster. Opposing the Germans and Italians, the USSR became the primary weapons supplier for the Republican Government. But more than just political and economic factors were at work, for the various military establishments throughout Europe viewed the event as being the perfect environment in which to evaluate their latest military equipment. This was the case in the Soviet Union, where the UVVS staff at Moscow was seriously divided by arguments

as to the direction of fighter aviation; this, in spite of the fact that the I-15 had fallen into increasing disfavour throughout the VVS due to its modest performance and the burgeoning pilot confidence in the I-16. Indeed by 1936, manufacture of the biplane had halted while various improved versions were debated and designed, and no further machines were planned for that year. In the event, Stalin himself authorized the sale of both the I-15 and I-16 to Spain, initial batches of each arriving by ship almost simultaneously.

In the VVS, great excitement followed these developments, various officers and staff joining the machines near Madrid. Amongst them were included not only a healthy proportion of ideologically motivated foes of Fascism, but also advocates of each fighter type – and its attendant school of thought – and for the biplane fighter faithful it seemed a last gasping chance to prove their ideas and tactics. In combat over Spain, the I-15 proved initially formidable as more than a match for the Nationalist Fiat CR-32 and especially the Heinkel He-51 over which it dominated. Many of the later I-15s destined for Spain were modified at *Zavod* 1 to mount four PV-1 guns, as per the original specification, when it was found that two rifle-calibre weapons were insufficient for modern aerial combat. These I-15s were referred to by the factory staff as '*Ispanskiy*' (Spanish) models, and many also at last featured the 8 mm sheet of armour protection for the pilot. With the extra weight of these additions, performance undoubtedly suffered.

The later appearance of newer monoplane fighters like the Italian G.50 and the German Bf 109 did show the obsolescence of biplane fighters of all types, but the VVS traditionalists pointed to the confusion of the later Civil War period within the Republic as the real cause for the shortcomings of the I-15. Such a claim was not entirely without merit – there was certainly a catastrophic breakdown in operations during 1938 – and so, while the I-16 was clearly the shining star over Spain, the tiny I-15 had acquitted itself well enough for its advocates to ply considerable leverage within the GUAP Directorate and the UVVS. Though the UVVS was delighted, if somewhat surprised, the view began to form that, perhaps, there *was* still a place in a modern inventory for biplane fighters.

Meanwhile, back in Moscow, work had continued unabated on improving the I-15 throughout 1936. Polikarpov's staff had hoped to begin production of an M-25-powered version by the end of 1935 at the latest, but so low was the priority accorded the biplane that no engines of that type had yet been released for the programme (indeed, so low was the I-15's production priority that it was left to make use of the already superseded PV-1 machine guns). In December 1935, Polikarpov left the TsKB and was placed at the head of his own Design Bureau at *Zavod* 21, Gor'ki, with a staff also at the small *Zavod* 84 facility in Moscow. Neither factory possessed a proper development workshop nor testing apparatus, and all of 1936 was devoted to building such structures at Gor'ki.

As a result, development of the I-15 also continued within the workshops of *Zavod* 1, Moscow, the State's premier aviation facility. The priority assigned to this project was small and in competition with other designs and as a result the pace of development was modest. Finally installed at Gor'ki, Polikarpov's Bureau built another revised variant of the I-15, again constructed featuring a 'normal' upper wing. The new prototype, bearing the unusual designation TsKB-3*bis*[2], featured a traditional unbroken upper plane of 10.2 m span. The new wing incorporated a revised and considerably more efficient Clark-YH airfoil section, supported by two outwardly-splayed N-struts bracing the central section. The machine was designed from the outset around the 750 hp M-25V motor contained in a new broad-chord NACA cowling (similar to that on the I-16 Type 4). Following developments within the Polikarpov OKB at *Zavod* 84, the fuselage framing was strengthened, and various sundry equipment was added (such as an electric generator, cabin heater, etc.). A two-pitch 2.8 m metal airscrew replaced the earlier unit of the I-15, and the new prototype featured improved aerodynamic details such as revised wheel spats.

The first prototype was received by the NII VVS during July 1937 following factory evaluations at *Zavod* 21. Though from a safety standpoint the I-15*bis* did not represent a problem, the Institute pilots roundly disliked the prototype. The new I-15*bis* was much heavier on the controls that the I-15, and greatly inferior to its predecessor in manoeuvrability. The tremendous increase in weight of 300 kg was certainly evident, as it was with the *bis'* unimproved performance despite an increase of 220 hp. The Institute's final report gave a fair account of the machine, regarding it as a safe, plodding aircraft of poor performance, certainly uncharacteristic of a fighter. Production was not recommended.

But, at *Zavod* 1 in Moscow, events moved on dramatically. Polikarpov's lobbying in Moscow may well have been taking effect, and Stalin himself, was calling for a dramatic increase in aircraft production. Moreover, due to the unanticipated failure of several prototype designs, the State's premier aviation factory – *Zavod* 1 in Moscow – was looking at the prospect for 1937 of having *no* major aircraft manufacturing programme. Such a condition was intolerable, of course, and with really no other design at hand, and production facilities already in place for Polikarpov's biplane, GUAP took the decision to reinstate manufacture of an improved I-15 variant powered by the 725 hp M-25A radial. This work was to be carried out with a view to manufacturing the newer I-15*bis* prototype with the conventional upper wing as soon as tooling and preparations could be made ready.

Manufacture of the I-15 M-25A began at *Zavod* 1 at once. The new variant was powered by the M-25A radial (some of the latter machines also with the M-25V), and now included the improved armament option of four PV-1 machine guns, these supplied with 1,800 rounds in total. Most of the 1937 production I-15s appear to have been completed with armour plate at the factory, and the majority without wheel spats. The production I-15 M-25A weighed 1,563 kg at take-off and could reach 374 km/h at 3,000 m, climbing to 5,000 m in seven minutes. All of the structural modifications embodied in the No. 6019 prototype were incorporated into manufacture, and no further significant difficulties were experienced with wing flutter.

Meanwhile, tooling for production of the I-15*bis*, to be known as the I-152, progressed in Moscow. It is ironic that while Polikarpov's Bureau worked quite diligently on preparing and designing the I-15*bis*, Polikarpov himself complained continually during this period that removing the 'gull' feature of the central wing section would be disastrous in terms of increasing drag. Wind tunnel testing by TsAGI during 1936 and 1937 had proved Polikarpov correct, but conservative forces within the UVVS, in particular, were determined to have their way, and despite being twice rejected by the NII VVS in this configuration, the I-152 was ordered into series manufacture.

The production series I-152 was powered by the 750 hp M-25V engine driving a VISh-6A propeller, and fitted with a conical spinner similar to that on the I-16 Type 10, but with the addition of sliding shutter-type cooling louvres displayed along the front of the cowl face, a modification which changed the appearance of the aircraft quite dramatically. The armament remained unchanged with four PV-1 guns in the fuselage, except that the ammunition store for the lower guns was reduced to 300 rounds to make room for a fuel cell of increased capacity (310 litres). Wheel spats were occasionally seen, and the proportion leaving the factory with such spats is unknown, but the sheet of 8 mm armour aft of the pilot was standard. The new fighter could reach 370 km/h at 2,900 m and could climb initially at 2,535 ft./min., with a service ceiling of 9,100 m.

The pilots in front line VVS squadrons were only just cutting their teeth on the type, when a number of the new I-152s were dispatched to China to engage in operations against the Japanese. On 21 August, the USSR and Chinese Central Government signed a formal Non-Aggression Pact, with the Soviets agreeing secretly to re-equip and reform the Chinese Air Force. For this purpose, a group of Soviet fighters was supplied to China consisting of I-16 and I-152 fighters, these arriving in the Nanking and Hangkow areas in December 1937. Soviet Air Force advisors also accompanied the fighters under the experienced leadership of NII VVS test pilot *May.* Stepan Suprun. Although charged with the primary responsibility of training their Chinese colleagues, the Soviet aviators routinely engaged in combat operations against official policy. In contrast to the inexperienced Chinese airmen, when Soviet pilots engaged the Imperial Army and Navy units they quickly established control of the local air space. Deeply frustrated, the Japanese responded by introducing quantities of the superbly manoeuvrable A5M2 monoplane, this Naval fighter being more than a match for the I-152. In the expert hands of *May.* Suprun's advisors, however, the result was something of a draw – the I-152s finding it difficult to catch the speedy and fast-climbing Mitsubishi, whilst the latter found it nearly impossible to down the robust and well-protected I-152-*bis* with their two 7.7 mm guns. But the writing was clearly on the wall, and Suprun reported to the UVVS that the I-152 was useless and should be withdrawn, much to the consternation of the Air Force Command.

In January 1939 another NII VVS pilot, *May.* Konstantin Kokkinaki, arrived in China to relieve *May.* Suprun. He was greatly disturbed to find that the I-152 was still in use in significant numbers, despite Suprun's strongly worded warning that the type was increasingly obsolete. But, once again, the biplane – in Russian hands – had done just well enough for its traditionalist proponents in the UVVS to forestall the I–152's elimination. Indeed, in January 1939 small quantities of the I-152 also reached Spain (where they were dubbed '*Super-Chatos*'), and served there briefly under conditions of extreme confusion and dislocation.

Although development of the I-152 continued throughout 1937 and 1938 at *Zavod* 1, nothing further was to come of it. An experimental enclosed cabin was developed by A. Sherbakov, and although this was of excellent design and construction, it was not adopted on the I-152. A two-seat training model had been mooted in late 1938, and prototypes of this machine, designated DIT, were evaluated at the NII VVS in July 1939. They were found to have unacceptable spinning characteristics, and plans to produce the type in quantity were dropped. By 1939, the I-152 was acknowledged to be hopelessly obsolete, and only as a test-bed vehicle would the *bis* continue to feature in any future development. As such, a number of experimental flights were conducted making use of these airframes, including the I-152TK with two TK-3 turbo-supercharger units, the I-152GK with pressurized cabin, and the I-152DM with two under-wing DM-2 ramjets. Despite the novelty of these experiments, the development of the I-152 as a fighter aircraft was over.

Back at Polikarpov's Design Bureau in Gor'ki, the Head Designer had not been idle. Throughout 1937, Polikarpov's OKB had continued work on the original TsKB-3 with its characteristic gull wing, as intended by its designers. The NACA cowling and the various detail improvements of the I-152 had been taken from these efforts, and Polikarpov fumed because development work on his fighter had been partly removed from his hands. Moreover, the work at *Zavod* 1 was clearly sponsored by traditionalists within the Army and Government, and Polikarpov was adamant that they had "ruined" his TsKB-3 with "... useless, infernal wing(s)." Indeed, he regarded the entire effort at Moscow to be completely off course.

With the mock-up building facilities at Gor'ki largely absorbed by work on the I-16, however, Polikarpov's OKB was forced to turn to pen and paper. Herculean efforts were made to draft and re-draft various design proposals and features, many of which could only be evaluated on the blueprints. Polikarpov was convinced that improved streamlining along with a retractable undercarriage would boost the performance of the TsKB-3 to much more modern levels, and also looked to the greater horsepower that might become available with the M-62 radial. Keeping this in mind, several sets of landing gear were built at *Zavod* 21, and these units had to be tested on their existing TsKB-3 prototype. After much work and re-tooling, the adopted units featured an ingenious retractable unit similar to that on the I-16, with the wheels rotating through 90 degrees to lie flush in wells on the lower fuselage undersurface. A new cowling patterned on the I-16's unit was designed, featuring individual exhaust stacks and a large cut-out on the bottom left trailing edge for the oil cooler exhaust port.

With the drawings complete and approved by the end of 1937, these were then transferred to the *Zavod* 1 workshops in February 1938. Work on the new prototype began in May and proceeded without major difficulty and the Polikarpov OKB's drawings must be credited here as having been outstandingly complete and well prepared. Inspired by personal visits by Polikarpov and his team to the workshops, the *Zavod* 1 staff completed the new I-153 prototype on 5 August 1938. The aircraft's structure, though quite similar externally to the original I-15, had in fact been considerably re-stressed once again, with particular attention paid to the upper plane, which was also of the improved Clark YH section. The gull joint of this unit was refined and strengthened, and the wing's internal structure was almost completely new, being much stronger in terms of torsional rigidity. As a result of all of these changes, the upper wing was some 25 cm longer in span than the TsKB-3 reaching exactly 10.0 m, and featured very subtly modified wingtips. The M-25V motor and VISh-6A propeller of the I-152 were retained (including spinner), but the NACA cowling was replaced by a tapered unit with individual exhaust ports and shortened chord. On the first I-153 prototype, no cooling grille was fitted along the forward cowl face. The obsolete PV-1 guns were at last replaced by four of the vastly superior 7.62 mm ShKAS weapons, each with the extraordinary total of 650 rounds.

Factory testing of the first I-153 prototype began in Moscow in September 1938. With the onset of winter, it was decided to dispatch the prototype to Azerbaizhan, to the NII VVS facility at Baku, for evaluation testing. Pilot-Engineer Fedrovi (later of the Yakovlev OKB fame) was immediately impressed by the I-153 prototype's handling, and it was clear that the new I-153 was a considerable advance over the current I-152. Handling and manoeuvrability in the new type had recaptured all of the I-15's attributes, and control harmony was judged to be near-perfect. Some need for additional wing torsional stiffening was noted, and some minor defects in the tailplane and rigging were reported, but overall the revised airframe seems to have been satisfactory. The stalling characteristics were again lauded and all spinning trials were passed (though, it was noted that the spinning behaviour was inferior to that of the I-15 M-25A), and indeed, the final report was favourable save for the power plant. In the matter of engine horsepower, the M-25V radial was seen to be completely inadequate, and the NII staff damned the prototype as grossly under-powered. Fedrovi flew the M-25V-powered No.1 prototype to 424 km/h at a take-off weight of 1,650 kg, and the initial climb reached the mediocre figure of 731 m/min.

Polikarpov and his design staff were vindicated, at least to a degree, in that the gull wing layout was superior to the more conventional planform of the I-152. At the NKAP however, there was still considerable scepticism about the need for yet another biplane fighter variant, and tremendous discussion passed on the point. In the end, it was clear that a few traditionalist die-hards had persisted within the UVVS, and indeed Polikarpov's standing was such that any attempt to forestall the programme would result in extended political conflict. Moreover, the I-153's handling was outstanding, and the Acceptance Report by the NII VVS was quite favourable save for the lack of engine power. With these highly political considerations in mind, the NKAP authorized production of several evaluation machines under the designation I-153, to be powered by the M-25V but with a view to locating a suitable motor for replacement.

At *Zavod* 1 production commenced immediately based on the No.1 prototype and the M-25V engine. The I-153 M-25V weighed 1,685 kg at take-off and could reach 371 km/h at sea level and 434 km/h at 3,659 m. The initial climb figure was 701 m/min., and 5,000 m could be attained in 6.9 minutes. The I-153 M-25V's armament comprised four 7.62 mm ShKAS guns with 650 rounds each. Provision was made for an RSI-1 radio set and the initial versions were fitted with a telescopic OP-1 sight.

In all, about 12 M-25-powered I-153 models left the Moscow factory by the end of 1938, and nine more followed in the spring of 1939. Some of these machines were dispatched to Baku for evaluation (including No.6005, with improved wing and structural

modifications), whilst others were examined operationally by pilots of the 16 IAP near Moscow. Both the NII VVS and service pilots who examined the new aircraft reached the same conclusions as regards the new fighter. They found it to be extremely manoeuvrable and well behaved, with characteristics similar to the I-15 which they knew very well. But it was seriously under-powered, and performance on the M-25V was simply inadequate for inclusion into the VVS inventory.

At the same time, early in 1939, airframe No.6019 was completed with the M-62 radial. The Shvetsov M-62 was a thorough redesign of the nine-cylinder M-25 series and could produce 800 hp (920 hp for take-off and emergency), with a two-stage supercharger. Modifications to the horizontal stabilizers were made, and a strengthened undercarriage fitted, and I-153 No.6019 was sent for evaluations on 16 June 1939 with the NII VVS. The handling characteristics of the I-153 were confirmed again, the small increase in weight having no effect on manoeuvrability. Ominously however, a dramatic worsening in the I-153's spinning behaviour was noted, and although it was still considered to be acceptable, it must have been marginally so; the report ended with a recommendation to examine spinning in detail. With greater power, No.6019 performed better still, reaching 462 km/h with a two-pitch VISh propeller. The initial climb was similarly improved, and the rate exceeded 823 m/min., while 5,000 m could be reached in 6.1 minutes, numbers which, for a biplane, were reasonably high.

Despite the improved performance on the M-62, however, the NKAP was still not convinced of the need for serial production of the I-153 fighter. Sensing this, Polikarpov set about at once concocting various political machinations throughout Moscow. By the summer the matter was even debated on the floor of the Supreme Soviet. Polikarpov's reputation was then under a cloud (following the death of Chkalov in the I-180), and now he sought to 'rectify' matters with a new production programme for his I-153. It was at this very moment of intense politicking that fighting flared up along the Manchurian border with Japan across the Khalkin-Gol river.

For Polikarpov this was a chance not to be missed, and under considerable pressure the NKAP authorized the manufacture and dispatch of a series of I-153 M-62s to the zone of conflict. The speed of manufacture and distribution of the initial batches of I-153 M-62s has always been a source of wonderment and confusion, and it seems likely that, in fact, *Zavod* 1 in Moscow was probably engaged in the production of I-153 fighters (at least on a minimal scale) *before* the summer of 1939 on Polikarpov's initiative alone, and entirely without a State Contract. Be that as it may, the first 20 I-153s were in Mongolia by the end of June, serving with a special operational evaluation group led by Sergei Gritsevets under the 70 IAP.

These early I-153 M-62s could be identified by the shorter chord engine cowling and propeller spinner for the fixed pitch unit. The structure was thought to be similar to No.6019's (i.e. with the strengthening improvements), and most appeared to have been completed with the full landing gear cover fairing assembly from the factory. The armament is usually reported as the intended standard of four ShKAS guns, but at least one machine in Manchuria featured the revised configuration of two UBS guns in their place. Performance is thought to have been similar to No.6019, but as there was no contract to produce them there was also no official evaluation, and thus no proper data for comparison.

On 7 July 1939, the I-153 was in action on a large scale for the first time. *May.* Gritsevets led nine I-153s and some I-16s from the 22 IAP against the Japanese, and in a now famous manoeuvre, they lowered their undercarriages to convince a group of Ki-27 fighters that they were facing old I-15s by adopting external similarities. Turning and appearing to flee, the Soviet pilots then retracted their gear and turned again into the face of the Japanese formation with complete surprise, destroying four Nakajima fighters without loss. Indeed, despite the overall superiority of the more modern Japanese monoplane designs, the I-153s performed well in combat operations throughout the theatre. In the 22 IAP, 13 *Chaikas* were in ceaseless action during August, sometimes completing five to six sorties each per day. Despite the frantic pace of operations only two of these were lost, and the reliability of the type in action was entirely laudable.

Production of the I-153 under these conditions grew rapidly. By the end of September 1939, when the fighting in Khalkin-Gol finally came to an end, no fewer than 70 I-153s had reached the battlefront, and more still were delivered to the regiments within the sector. However, despite the obvious tempo of *Chaika* production at *Zavod* 1, there still had not been any Production Contract awarded to Polikarpov. This most peculiar situation was punctuated, when during the height of the fighting in Manchuria during August and September, the NKAP decided to commence State Testing of the I-153 M-62, which was then involved in combat operations against the Japanese!

An improved I-153 prototype with all of the structural modifications proposed to date (possibly aircraft No.6019) was examined by the NII VVS at Moscow. This machine was equipped with an M-62 engine, driving a variable-pitch VV-1 propeller. Some of the *Chaikas* in Mongolia had been so-equipped, and while take-off and climbing performance had improved, maximum speed and fuel economy were inferior with this unit. The I-153 in this configuration reached 431 km/h and could climb to 5,000 m in 5.5 minutes. With the fixed-pitch airscrew the improved structure I-153 M-62 could achieve 446 km/h but required fully 6.7 minutes to reach 5,000 m. In the event, such performance was deemed to be inadequate for a modern fighter aircraft, and once again the NII VVS refused to pass the I-153 M-62 through its State Trials on the grounds that it was still under-powered.

At the same time, several examples of the I-153 were being completed in Moscow with the more powerful M-63 radial. This engine was somewhat heavier than the M-62, but it could produce 900 hp (1,100 hp for take-off and emergency) with the same two-stage supercharger. I-153 Nos.6012 and 6039 were completed with M-63 motors driving a constant-speed ViSh propeller (as on the M-62 variant) by the autumn, and testing at *Zavod* 1 in Moscow commenced at once. Aircraft no.6039 was further refined, and sported a lengthened engine cowling which was extended some 50 mm rearwards, giving improved aerodynamic streamlining. With the M-63, the oil cooler exhaust was repositioned to exit through the bottom of the fuselage at the edge of the cowling.

Considerable factory-testing ensued, both of the M-63-powered *Chaika* and also the improved M-62 variant with the VV-1 propeller. During these examinations, the *Zavod* 1 staff reached several conclusions regarding the I-153 programme. First, the lengthened engine cowling was seen to offer superior aerodynamic streamlining in all cases, and this unit was immediately adopted for all I-153 manufacture from that point onward, regardless of engine type. Second, the performance of the variable-pitch airscrew was beyond doubt, and all aircraft were to be fitted with units of this type. The VV-1, however, was substituted with the ViSH AV-1 propeller in series manufacture, this unit offering improved function and performance.

Production of the I-152 had at last been abandoned by October 1939, and all of the Polikarpov manufacturing impetus at Moscow shifted to the I-153 programme. The new M-62-powered models began to appear during the autumn, these identified by the lack of a propeller spinner and the lengthened engine cowling. The oil cooler exhaust was positioned as before, but now just at the rear edge of the cowling on the lower port side, projecting through a cut-out in that unit. The new M-62-powered I-153 was typically armed with four ShKAS machine guns disposed around the engine, each with 650 rounds of ammunition, and with a PAK-1 reflector sight. The 8 mm armour sheet behind the pilot was standard. Performance in the new production model was mostly unchanged, 366 km/h attainable at sea level and 426 km/h at 2,920 m, while the initial climb rose to 915 m/min and 5,000 m could be reached in the impressive time of five minutes.

During December, manufacture of an M-63-powered I-153 variant also got underway. The very first M-63-powered models were virtually identical to their M-62 counterparts, save that the oil cooler exhaust was located at the bottom of the cowling, as usual with the M-63 motor. The AV-1 propeller and lengthened cowling were both used, and

the armament appears to have been the typical quartet of ShKAS guns. No official data exists for these *Chaikas*, but from Factory documents it seems that the maximum speed rose to 373 km/h at sea level and 440 km/h at 3,650 m, and that 5,000 m could be attained in five minutes.

The most remarkable aspect of both I-153 variants, however, is that neither of them was authorized by any State Production Contract. It is extraordinary to think that the State's premier aviation factory in Moscow, at the hub of the State bureaucracy, could be producing very significant numbers of aircraft without any official instructions to do so – but so it was. Indeed, during the fourth quarter of 1939 no fewer than 657 I-153s were completed at *Zavod* 1, bringing the total for the year to 1,011 (including 13 with the M-63). Production at this pace continued into the new year of 1940. In fact, it was in January 1940 when the only known Production Contract for the I-153 was ever received, this for the manufacture of 200 M-63-powered aircraft with ski-type landing gear. These units simply replaced the standard wheels and were designed to lie flush along the bottom of the fuselage when retracted. The tail wheel was also replaced with a ski unit.

Starting with the 76th M-63 example (No.8076), manufacture of these ski-equipped models started sometime during February-March. Unfortunately, it is not known how many were completed in this way (perhaps all 200), since the ski gear could be replaced with normal wheeled items by any field unit, the matter is quite unclear. However, most if not all, of these ski-gear models did seem to sport the revised propeller hub of 1940 M-63 variant manufacture. Although the propeller type did not change, a 2.7 m model replaced the usual 2.8 m airscrew used with the M-62. A new and diminutive spinner covered the hub and pitch boss assembly, this item probably relating to the 2.7 m unit, and most M-63 I-153s from 1940 production appear to have it. Predictably, with the extra weight and drag of the ski units, performance in the type fell. The standard ski-type M-63 model weighed 1,887 kg at take-off and could reach 370 km/h at sea level and 431 km/h at 3,650 m, climbing to 5,000 m in 5.1 minutes at the initial rate of 915 m/min.

VVS pilots in the various regiments receiving the I-153 began to notice that the stalling and spinning characteristics of the type were not at all as pleasant as the earlier models of the *Chaika*, and much inferior to those of either the I-15 M-25 or the I-152. The last NII VVS evaluation of the I-153 recommended a full examination of spinning behaviour in the type, and this testing commenced at the end of February 1940. M-62 production model No.6566 was examined by pilots from both the NII VVS and the LII during March. Although the M-62 *Chaika* was seen to have acceptable spinning behaviour for experienced pilots, the report (signed by pilots A.G.Kubishkin and *Kapitan* Proshakov) recommended that student pilots be taught to recover the I-153 during the first two revolutions of the spin, "... lest the machine escape from [their] control." During June-July of 1940, a production M-63-powered *Chaika* (No.8019) was delivered for similar testing, this aircraft apparently being fitted also with the 2.7m AV-1 propeller. The spinning characteristics of the I-153 with the heavier M-63, however, were suddenly found to be extremely unpleasant. The forward shift in the aircraft's centre of gravity had resulted in very difficult spinning behaviour, so bad in fact that monitoring instruments were attached to the elevators and rudder. The final report concluded that in the M-63 *Chaika*, student pilots should not attempt to practise spins at an altitude "... less than 5000 metres." The service pilots' observations were indeed vindicated.

Meanwhile at *Zavod* 1, full-scale production of the I-153 continued apace. A number of specific permutations and variants were produced during 1940, and experiments with different armament and equipment profiles continued. Most of the 1940 manufacture *Chaikas* were completed with the standard quartet of 7.62 mm ShKAS guns, but 148 examples of M-62-powered machines were armed with a pair of 12.7 mm UBS guns instead. Eight *pushechniy* (cannon) models were constructed, these armed with two ShVAK cannon, and 20 examples of the TK supercharger driven M-62TK were completed (mostly for testing of the supercharger). About half of the total 1,238 I-153s produced were equipped with radio sets – mostly RSI-3 units – but these were not distinguishable externally, as the RSI-1 and the initial

	I-15	I-15 M-25A	I-152	I-153 M-25V	I-153 M-62 early Series 1939	I-153 M-62 standard Series 1940
Weights						
Empty:	1108 kg	1220 kg	1375 kg	1340 kg	1448 kg	1459 kg
Loaded:	1418 kg	1564 kg	1703 kg	1683 kg	1765 kg	1796 kg
Wing Area:	23.51 sq.m	23.51 sq.m	22.49 sq.m	24.26 sq.m	24.26 sq.m	24.26 sq.m
Engine	M-22	M-25A	M-25V	M-25V	M-62	M-62
	480 hp	725 hp	750 hp	750 hp	800 (920) hp	800 (920) hp
Maximum Speed						
At Altitude:	345 km/h at 3000 m	373 km/h at 2880 m	368 km/h at 2900 m	432 km/h at 3660 m	435 km/h at 3000 m	424 km/h at 2800 m
Sea Level:	285 km/h	334 km/h	326 km/h	369 km/h	373 km/h	364 km/h
Climb						
Initial:	420 m/min	656 m/min	468 m/min	701 m/min	823 m/min	915 m/min
Time to Height:	11.0 min to 5000 m	7.0 min to 5000 m	7.3 min to 5000 m	6.9 min to 5000 m	6.1 min to 5000 m	5.0 min to 5000 m
Service Ceiling	7529 m	8687 m	9083 m	8687 m	9784 m	7528 m
Armament	2 x PV-1	4 x PV-1	4 x PV-1 2 x FAB-50 2 x AO-25	4 x ShKAS	4 x ShKAS	4 x ShKAS or 2 x UBS

series RSI–3 did not require the fitting of external aerial leads. Many of the aircraft constructed from the summer of 1940 onwards were fitted with sheet metal plates on the lower wing undersurfaces to accommodate eight RO82 rocket rails, and at least 240 *Chaikas* left the factory with these installed (they could also be added in the field). Underwing fittings were also provided for four bombs, often the FAB-50 or AO-25 type, or for external fuel tanks of 50 (in pairs), 150 or 200 litre capacity. Whatever the intentions of *Zavod* 1, supplies of the M-63 motor were largely consumed by I-16 manufacture at Gor'ki, and thus only 332 M-63 powered *Chaikas* of all types were completed during 1940, the majority being completed with the M-62.

For the I-153, however, the writing had been on the wall during the whole of 1940. Nearly all of the *Zavod* 1 design facilities were now at the disposal of a new Experimental Design Group (OKO) led by Artem Mikoyan, whose I-200 prototype was the subject of furious development at the behest of the Government. Despite the persistent lobbying of Polikarpov at the factory, little development work was completed on the *Chaika* during 1940. An I-153B variant was proposed (and complete drawings provided by Polikarpov), featuring drastically revised swept-forward wing planforms for both surfaces, but construction was not attempted by the factory staff. A single example of the I-153UD was manufactured, however. This prototype was an otherwise standard M-62-powered I-153 with a cloth-covered wooden monocoque rear fuselage, just as in the I-200 programme (see 'MiG 3'). Testing during the autumn of 1940 revealed no unusual behaviour, but the I-153 was simply no longer a candidate for development, and nothing further came of the model. The *Chaika* also served as a test-bed for the DM-2 and DM-4 ramjet engines, and flights with these mounted under the lower wings were made during 1940. With the close of 1940 came also the end of I-153 manufacture, the last 64 examples of which rolled off the factory floor during January 1941. For the staff at *Zavod* 1, it was the penultimate chapter of their lengthy association with Polikarpov's biplanes (see 'I-190').

When the *Wehrmacht* struck on 22 June 1941, the I-152, and I-153 families made up the second largest part of the front line VVS squadrons facing the enemy, and large numbers of these were either destroyed on the ground or abandoned in the ensuing weeks of *Barbarossa*. Still, many of these diminutive fighters fought on, and although truly outclassed by the best *Luftwaffe* machines, they enjoyed a fair number of successes. Indeed, in expert hands, the extreme manoeuvrability of the *Chaika* made it a frustratingly elusive target – a number of German fighter pilots were dispatched, when on the verge of what appeared to be an almost certain kill, the little biplane suddenly wheeled around a full 180 degrees to fire into their faces.

	I-153 M-63 with skis	I-153 M-63 1940 Series
Weights		
Empty:	1552 kg	1495 kg
Loaded:	1906 kg	1853 kg
Wing Area:	24.26 sq.m	24.26 sq.m
Engine	M-63 950 (1100) hp	M-63 950 (1100) hp
Maximum Speed		
At Altitude:	429 km/h at 3500 m	439 km/h at 3500 m
Sea Level:	368 km/h	371 km/h
Climb		
Initial:	915 m/min	945 m/min
Time to Height:	5.1 min to 5000 m	5.0 min to 5000 m
Service Ceiling	9083 m	8687 m
Armament	4 x ShKAS 2 x FAB-50 2 x AO-25	4 x ShKAS 8 x RS82

Generally, however, as with similar fighters everywhere, the time of the biplane had indeed been eclipsed by monoplanes of superior performance. As a result, both the I-152 and I-153 were increasingly employed in the ground-attack role, and here they performed very well (just as the German Hs 123 biplane did), affording on-the-spot assistance to Red Army units in battle. Many field units fitted RO rocket rails for this work, and in this fashion the *Chaika* in particular contributed much useful work throughout 1941 and 1942.

The I-153 (and to a lesser extent, the I-152) laboured on in service, particularly with the Baltic Fleet air arm, until well into 1942, though increasingly in reserve and coastal patrol-type roles. The final few such machines were in service in 1943, after which the type faded from front line use.

Though a beautiful aircraft, and with quite unmatched manoeuvrability, handling and aerobatic prowess, the age of the biplane had simply passed. If the I-153 had been the best of the line – and, indeed, it may have been – it was still no protection from the advance of the monoplane fighter.

**I-153
early manufacture
1939**

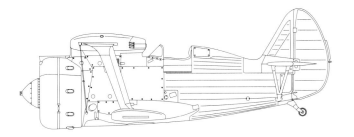

**I-153 M-62
standard production**

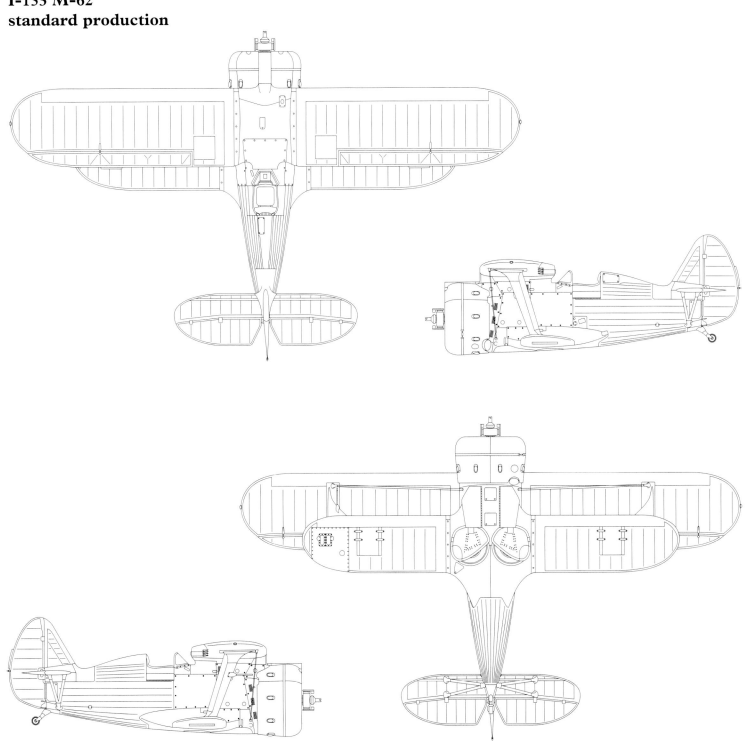

**I-153 M-63
with ski gear**

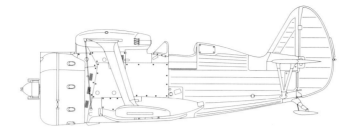

**I-153 M-63
typical production**

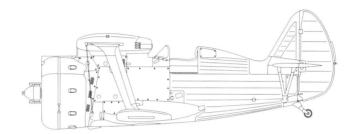

THE DEVELOPMENT OF CAMOUFLAGE
ON THE I-153 FIGHTER

Pre-War Aircraft

The matter of camouflage for the I-15 and I-152 fighters is really a subject which falls somewhat beyond the scope of this volume. Both machines' production programmes were terminated before the GPW, and indeed even before the 1940 Camouflage Directive. As such, it is likely that all I-15s and I-152s were completed in the factories according to pre-war standards. For the I-152 one can estimate that solid-colour AII Green uppersurfaces were common, along with AII Blue undersurfaces. The same colouration seems to be common on the I-15, though AII lacquers came into general use after the entry of this fighter into the VVS inventory, and so it is likely that older AEh lacquers were used.

A few I-15s did fly in the opening days of *Barbarossa*, but no more than that. However, I-152s remained active in the ground-attack role into 1942. A few of these machines seem to have received appliqué camouflages in the field, these probably including Black over Green in some manner. However, generally, most I-152s soldiered on with their pre-war colours (see Fig. 1).

Below: *An I-152 seen in the Kiev area in 1940. Note the pre-war 'circle-star' national marking on the fuselage. The tiny, 'miniaturized' star on the fin was not at all uncommon during the 1940 period on the I-152 and I-153. (Photo: G.Petrov)*

Fig. 1

Below: *A winter-camouflaged I-152 near Leningrad during the winter of 1941-42. 'Red 52' is mounted on ski gear, and the cockpit seems to be painted a darkish colour, very likely Wood Aerolak or A-14. (Photo: G.Petrov)*

During the winter of 1941-42, many surviving I-152s were covered with a coat of MK-7 white distemper, as was then common, but certainly one can expect that there would have been little in the way of camouflage innovation thereafter.

Right: *A contemporary photograph of a restored I-152. The colours and finish of this restoration are outstanding, and involved many hours of colour analysis from the surviving painted surfaces. (Photo: Author's collection)*

Below: *A superb aerial photograph of an AII Aluminium-finished I-153 over Moscow in 1940. This colouration seems to have been preferred on the I-153 programme before the GPW. Note the very bright and reflective lacquer. (Photo: G. Petrov)*

The Chaika

The I-153 also began its history in the time before the GPW. I-153s manufactured at *Zavod* 1 in 1939 seem to have been finished in a common 1930s VVS scheme, but one *not* involving the use of the ubiquitous AII Green. This alternate livery was a simple overall application of AII(Al) aluminium dope. AII Aluminium was a very striking aviation dope with bright reflective properties, and was applied over all surfaces, regardless of construction. Occasionally, examples appear in which the forward dural-skinned areas of the aircraft are not painted with AII(Al) being left in their natural state, but these are unusual (see Fig. 2).

Fig. 2

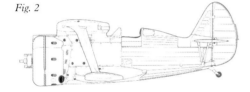

Typically, the stainless steel cowl band was left unpainted. The internal finish of these early machines was probably in agreement with the pre-war application of a solid overall coat of A-14 Steel or AII Aluminium.

Chaikas of this era often wore the pre-1940 national star markings with black circles in the centre, and usually had them applied in eight locations (including the upper wing's uppersurfaces), rather than the customary six positions of the GPW.

The use of overall AEh-9 Grey on the I-153 is documented at the factories as well. The colouration is mostly seen in early manufacture, notably during the winter months of 1940-41.

An alternative form of finish making use of AEh-9 was also seen at this time, where the forward dural panels were covered with this grey lacquer, whilst the rear fabric portions of the aircraft seem to have worn a coat of AII Aluminium. The reason for the apparent 'dullness' of this otherwise usually bright finish is not understood, but it is possible that a layer of clear AII lacquer had been applied over it (see Fig. 3).

Below: *A pre-war scheme I-153 photographed in late 1940. Despite the ski gear, this aircraft appears to be powered by the M-62 engine. (Photo: G. Petrov)*

Fig. 3

A similar winter application was seen during the following season. However, during 1940-41 the colouration was somewhat reversed, and the forward metal areas and cowling were covered in MK-7 white, while the remainder of the machine was left in AII Aluminium.

It is remarkable and curious that an AII Green and Blue camouflage was not employed in the I-153 programme. Given that this scheme was so very typical on many aircraft of the immediate pre-war period, the specific practices of the I-153 are somewhat strange.

1940 – The Camouflage Directive

During 1940, instructions were issued from the NKAP and the UVVS that all military aircraft should be camouflaged, and if possible with a two-colour disruptive livery on their upper surfaces. Many aircraft serving in regiments in the field were never repainted, and continued to serve in their pre-war colours. However, many more aircraft were camouflaged according to these instructions, most in the field by the operating unit. Not surprisingly, many of these schemes are *quite* remarkable, and run the full gambit from those applied with great care and artistry, to those demonstrating neither attribute. On the I-153, the most common approach was simply to paint over the existing AII Aluminium uppersurfaces with AII Green (see Fig. 4).

Fig. 4

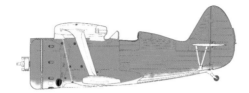

This was usually accomplished fairly neatly, and the upper/lower colour demarcation could vary from soft to sharp. In other cases, great complexity was exercised to produce a scheme of complicated lines or dappling (see Fig. 5).

Fig. 5

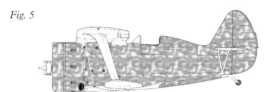

Above: An archetypal sight in June 1941; derelict and abandoned VVS fighters of outdated pedigree. Visible are several I-153s in a dapple-over-green camouflage, some I-153s in a rare AEh-9 overall livery, an I-16 Type 5, and a few I-152s. (Photo: M.Biskun collection)

The last category of these repainting practices are seen on the rather strange machines at some forward units. Some of these are quite informal in appearance, and a few are just shabby. Others still, are admirably exercised with great imagination.

1941

On I-153s which left the factory during and after the summer of 1940, two-tone camouflage schemes appear to have been standard. At the time of writing, the author is not aware of any convincing photograph showing an I-153 of this period of manufacture in a single-colour scheme. The first of the identifiable patterns was quite common, and features in many photographs from the early part of the GPW. The scheme was usually completed in AII

Above: This hand-applied two-tone camouflage was utilised whilst the aircraft was in service with the 7 IAK on the Leningrad Front in 1941. The scheme started as an AII Aluminium application, and was then refinished with a two-colour scheme of AII Black over AII Green covering the upper surfaces. The skill with which this scheme was applied, alas, leaves much to be desired, and it is not representative of the better work of this type. Despite the lack of the usual miniature spinner, this aircraft featured the shorter 2.7 m propeller and was powered by the M-63 motor. (Photo: G.Petrov)

Fig. 6

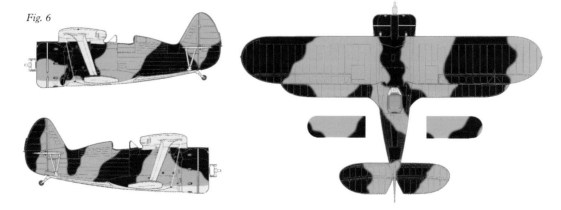

Black over AII Green, and with AII Blue undersurfaces. The colour demarcation lines in all locations were typically hard. Curiously, it seemed to be the standard practice to paint over the cowling band on the uppersurfaces, while not doing so on the lower. In the odd cases where this pattern is seen in AII Dark Green over AII Green, the bands are usually not painted over (see Figs. 6 and 7).

Fig. 7

A second Black over Green scheme is usually associated with late 1940 production. Again using AII colours above and below, this pattern application was unusual in having semi-soft colour demarcations, but unpainted cowl bands (see Fig. 8).

Fig. 8

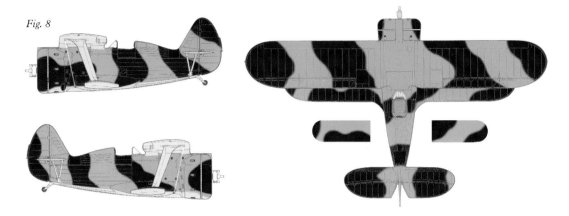

As was typical on the I-153, the upper/lower colour demarcation was quite low, and sharply painted.

Only one I-153 application theme was usually seen in the AII Dark Green over Green livery. The pattern is highly simplified in appearance, with all manner of uppersurface colour demarcation lines, from hard to soft (see Fig. 9).

Fig. 9

Left: *Pilot Kucheryaviy preparing for a sortie from the Kronstadt (Leningrad) naval base, in 1941. 'White 45' is thought to wear the AII Dark Green and Green scheme. (Photo: G.Petrov)*

The final known I-153 pattern seems to have come about late in the programme, and typically appears to have been applied to the M-63-powered version. The pattern was executed in AII Black over AII Green, and featured semi-soft colour demarcation lines on the uppersurface (see Fig. 10).

Fig. 10

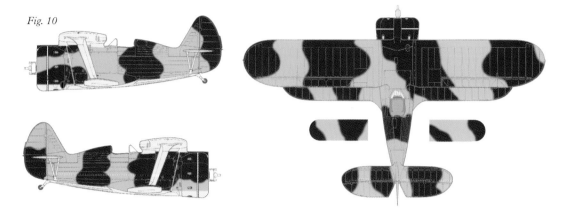

Again it was common for the cowl bands to be painted over on the uppersurfaces, and not on the lower.

Interior Colouration

The interior finish of the I-153 seems to have been somewhat 'old fashioned' throughout the programme. There are surviving examples of A-14 and AII Aluminium-coated cockpits, and also one demonstrating an overall coat of AII Blue. It is possible that there were other internal finishing procedures, especially noting that *Zavod* 1 is the relevant production facility, and an overall coat of Wood *Aerolak* (or other wood finishes) was quite likely. Furthermore, unfinished examples were undoubtedly seen from time to time.

Unusual I-153 Schemes

There exist a few photographs that appear to show I-153s wearing a two-segment camouflage scheme comprising AII Dark Green and Tractor Green. After considerable analysis of these photographs, I have reached the conclusion that the base colour is in fact most probably a very new shade of AII Green, somewhat masked by strange lighting and/or photographic reproduction conditions, or even Army 4B0. The use of Tractor Green remains to be verified at any factory other than at *Zavoda* 153 and 18.

Many authors continue to insist that some I-153s were finished at Moscow in a single-colour Factory Green over AII Blue livery. This supposition is both logical and compelling, and the photograph leading to those suppositions has been located. The I-153 below was photographed in Moscow in 1940, the picture being taken on 'journalistic'-type 35 mm film. However, this photograph rules out the colouration of VIAM-B3 maroon, and the most likely candidate is, in fact, Factory Green, but applied *overall*, with no blue undersurfaces. The cowling looks to have been left in natural metal.

Right: *I-153 'White 93' of the 4 GIAP VVS KBF takes off from a Leningrad area base, 1942. The aircraft appears to be carrying RS-82 rockets. (Photo: G.Petrov)*

1. In fact, these ideas had already received considerable attention during the First World War, when the performance of machines such as the SE5, SPAD and Albatros had caused some pilots to call into question the usual tactics of the classic turning dog-fight. Remarkably, all of the lessons learned in 1914-18 had apparently been forgotten, as had the resulting performance and tactical parameters required for aircraft of differing design philosophies.
2. To this day, it is unknown why the Soviets occasionally employed this rather Latinesque naming system (one which was flatly rejected by *Narkomaviaprom*, which insisted on using the -152 and -153 designations) for the I-15. While it was – and is – quite common in French, Italian, or Spanish aircraft to use the *-bis* and *-ter* designation for sub-variants, they have absolutely no equivalent in Russian.

Right: *An I-153 of unknown colouration, on the Kalinin Front in 1941. The wear along the wing leading edge and the appearance of the lower cowling indicates that this aircraft was perhaps originally finished in AII Aluminium lacquer. Note that the negative has been 'reversed' and that the numeral '2' is backwards on the print. (Photo: G.Petrov)*

Left: *This ski-equipped I-153 was photographed in 1940 with some of the infamous 'journalist'-type 35 mm film. As a result, the red areas of the national markings appear washed out. The camouflage colour is quite dark, and might well be Zavod 1's Factory Green. The cowl is possibly unfinished metal, but noting the film type, it is more likely to be red (note the cowl band, which is painted). None of these colourations seem overly appropriate for winter. (Photo: G.Petrov)*

Right: *An I-153 of the 72 IAPVVS SF at 'Vaenga-1' airbase, summer 1941. The white fin and rudder constitute a personal marking, and the numeral '6' is rendered in red. (Photo: G.Petrov)*

Polikarpov I-16

11

Chapter 5

Polikarpov I-16

At the time it entered service in 1934, the stubby little I-16 was the most advanced fighter in the world and remained so until well into the latter part of the decade. Though none of its innovative design features were by themselves revolutionary, their introduction into a single package comprising a tiny high-speed fighter was shattering, and marked a significant leap forward in the history of aerodynamics. But, as with any design so ahead of its time, the Ishak's ('mule') history was rife with early difficulties, and indeed, it was not until the type demonstrated its full potential during the Spanish Civil War that it was fully accepted by its pilots.

The Polikarpov fighter's origins reached back to early in 1932, when the concept for a radical new monoplane fighter was mooted during discussions held between TsAGI, Tupolev, and the NII VVS. The resulting ANT-31 (I-14), largely the product of the young and upcoming Pavel Sukhoi, was technically impressive and incorporated many of the features found on the later TsKB-12. But it was by no means a pilot's aircraft, and was virtually damned by the NII VVS testing staff. It was at this time, that another designer who had contributed much to the ANT-31, Nikolai Polikarpov, had achieved prominence within the Central Design Bureau (TsKB). Polikarpov was fully convinced that he and his team could produce a lighter, more advanced fighter to the same specifications.

For his new machine, given the designation TsKB-12, Polikarpov employed a mixed structure featuring a wooden monocoque fuselage covered with bakelite-ply wooden skinning (*shpon*), and chrome-molybdenum alloy twin-spar wings. The inner wing panels and leading edges were skinned in duralumin sheet, while the outer panels aft of the forward spar were fabric covered. All control surfaces were of alloy steel tube construction with fabric covering, as was the tail unit. The large ailerons were designed to droop 15 degrees during landing, acting as flaps as well. The design had planned to incorporate the new 710 hp M-25 (a Russian licence-built Wright-Cyclone 1820), but as difficulties in obtaining a manufacturing permit continued, the much less powerful M-22 (licence-built Jupiter) of 480 hp was installed. The nine-cylinder radial was cowled in a neat NACA cowling with internal exhaust collector ring and drove a two metre fixed-pitched two-blade metal propeller. The cockpit was enclosed by a forward-sliding single-piece canopy, actuated by rubber shock-cord. The new fighter featured fully retractable landing gear, being hand-operated by means of a crank located in the cockpit, though the first prototype lacked gear door covers on the main oleo legs. A standard armament scheme of two 7.62 mm ShKAS guns was mounted in the wings, each with 900 rounds.

The initial TsBK-12 prototype first took to the air on 31 December 1933 with Valeriy Chkalov at the controls. Handling in the new TsKB-12 prototype was mixed. Chkalov found the control response to be immediate and extremely sensitive about all three axes, a condition which was delightful for an experienced aviator such as himself, but challenging for a novice pilot. The aircraft also demonstrated a curious tendency to change its pitch at different power settings, and the landing speed was extremely high. Stability was judged to be marginal, but the TsKB-3 recovered from a spin positively, and its stall was prefaced by a comfortable aileron buffet and shuddering. All manner of acrobatics could be performed with precision. Powered by the M-22, the No.1 prototype reached 301 km/h at sea level, and 283 km/h at 5,000 m fitted with ski landing gear (due to the winter conditions in Moscow).

In order to test the normal flight conditions of the prototype, the TsKB-12 was shipped south to the Crimea for testing by *May.* Kokkinaki of the NII VVS. With wheeled gear installed, the M-22 prototype reached 361 km/h at sea level and 326 km/h at 5,000 m. With a motor of only 480 hp these figures were remarkable, and whilst in the Crimea, several service pilots examined and flew the type, largely with positive results.

The M-22-powered No.1 prototype was followed immediately thereafter by a second prototype, dubbed TsKB-12*bis*. The No.2 machine was completed on 18 February 1934, and was powered by an imported Wright Cyclone F-2 engine driving a Hamilton Standard 2.8 m three-bladed propeller. Though handling was largely unchanged, performance with the Cyclone jumped to 384 km/h at sea level, and 439 km/h at 3,000 m, with an initial climb of 851 m/min. The latter figures were – by the standards of the day – sensational in the extreme, and generated considerable enthusiasm throughout the NII VVS and the Central Design Bureau. Moved to the Crimea for testing under Kokkinaki as the No.1 had been, service pilots flew the No.2 TsKB-12 and were thrilled by its performance.

Although much of the initial testing had been successfully completed, many doubts remained about the new TsKB-12. The tiny new prototype was radical – *very* radical – and with all such new designs there is always resistance and doubt on the part of those not open to change. Pilot-Engineer N. Pishnov of the NII VVS and Prof. A. Zhuravchenko of TsAGI, both involved in aircraft spinning theory and aerodynamics, claimed that the TsKB-12 would have insufficient vertical surface area to recover from a spin. TsKB test pilot Chkalov, however, had *already* successfully completed spin trials, and publicly denounced their objections most vociferously. Criticism over the retractable gear was put forward by the UVVS, and so worrisome did it become that NII VVS Director Konart was put in charge of the matter.

Ultimately, the sheer performance of the new TsKB-12 put paid to such misgivings, and GUAP was forced to act. Production would centre around the M-25-powered aircraft, but since quantities of the motor were not yet available for series manufacture the M-22 prototype was recommended as being suitable for pilot familiarization, training, and development in the interim. Manufacture of the TsKB-12 was to commence at *Zavod* 39 in Moscow under designation I-16, 50 such aircraft being authorized. Meanwhile, preparations were put in hand for large-scale production of the I-16 at Gor'ki (*Zavod* 21), which would serve as the nucleus of the programme.

The first I-16 examples were completed at *Zavod* 39, and all 50 machines were delivered during the course of 1934. These examples carried no 'type' designation, and were simply known as I-16s, representing serial numbers 123901-123950 (meaning TsKB-'12', *Zavod* '39', example No. X). Powered by the 480 hp M-22, these machines had performance that was similar to the No.1 prototype upon which their manufacture was based. No armour was fitted, and the fuel cell was not self-sealing, as the aircraft were intended strictly for familiarization and were not built to military specifications. During 1935, a further eight examples were completed, these numbered 123951-58.

At *Zavod* 21, there was much difficulty in launching the new I-16 programme, since three other fighters were in production there already. Polikarpov's I-5 biplane fighter was the factory's main product, but the I-14 and KhAI-1 were also manufactured, and the staff were not pleased to be assigned yet another aircraft type. However, by June all difficulties had been met, and manufacture of the new Polikarpov fighter at last got underway. As the fourth product of the factory, the staff at *Zavod* 21 referred to the I-16 as the 'Type

I-16 Type 5 'White 11'

13 OIAE, 61 Aviation Brigade
Finland Front
pilot unknown
early 1940

Colours:
AII Green/Blue application
from *Zavod* 21

I-16 Type 24 'White 13'

7 IAP
Leningrad Front
pilot unknown
autumn 1941

Colours:
AII Green/Black/Blue
application from *Zavod* 21
or 153

I-16 Type 24 'White 71'

13 IAP VVS-KBF
Podpolk. Romanenko
autumn 1941

Colours:
AII Green/Blue
application from
Zavod 21 or 153 with
supplementary field
applications of AII Dark
Green and AEh-9(probable)

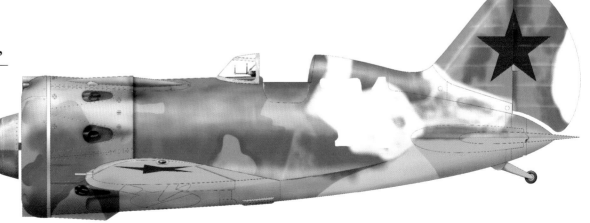

Number 4'. Somehow this designation stuck, and the curious naming convention (of 'type' numbers) would follow the aircraft for the remainder of its existence.

From the outset the Gor'ki Type 4s were powered by the M-22 radial. Although the aircraft produced at *Zavod* 21 were manufactured according to the improved TsKB-12*bis* standard, including all local strength reinforcements and improvements, no M-25 engines were as yet available. Externally the M-22 Type 4s were indistinguishable from the Cyclone-powered prototype, and were fitted with the same long-chord NACA cowling and two-pitch two-bladed airscrew of the latter. The production Type 4 M-22 weighed 1,354 kg at take-off, the all-up weight including an 8 mm armoured sheet aft of the pilot and a 7.62 mm ShKAS gun in each wing with 650 rounds. Maximum speed at sea level was 362 km/h and 346 km/h at 3,000 m, with an initial climb of 396 m/min. and reaching 5,000 m in 9.9 minutes.

I-16s began to reach service regiments by the late summer and autumn of 1934, where they were not received warmly. Almost from the first deliveries, front line VVS pilots were virtually unanimous in condemning the radical machine, its vicious landing behaviour and poor visibility coming as a particularly rude shock in comparison to the delightfully well-behaved I-5 and I-15 biplanes to which they had become accustomed. Accidents occurred not infrequently when pilots forgot to lower the landing gear (being unaccustomed to such a feature), and selecting the improper propeller pitch on landing intensified the I-16's pitching misbehaviour. Moreover, the type's handling characteristics were far from docile – indeed, it was clear immediately that the tiny Polikarpov was not a machine for novices. While the flight controls were crisp and light in full flight, at low speeds the machine's handling became increasingly difficult. The flow of air over the elevators was badly disturbed by the wings during the landing approach, this 'blanking' effect having the very unfortunate tendency to cause the nose to rise unexpectedly, resulting in a potentially catastrophic stall. This was exacerbated by the considerable porpoising induced by lowering the landing gear, and the distraction of the pilot's attention while cranking the gear to the down position. The latter procedure also resulted in a rather sloppy climb-out, though this was not nearly so dangerous a situation as during the landing approach. The aircraft's landing speed of nearly 120 km/h – an unheard of approach velocity in 1934 – was incompatible with nearly every military airfield in the USSR, and caused much difficulty when combined with the I-16's poor forward visibility. Indeed, if all this were not enough, the new fighter showed a tendency to drop its port wing very sharply in any stall, entering a spin almost as a matter of course, and due to its rather pronounced positive static stability it was difficult to hold the nose down during any significant dive.

Crashes and injuries became endemic throughout the latter half of 1934 and into the new year. By the spring of 1935 some VVS pilots were *flatly* refusing to fly the I-16, even to the point of insubordination. By March, the situation was virtually out of control with pilots literally dreading the day that their unit was due to convert to the new type, and the UVVS was in a state of unrestrained panic, issuing absurd proclamations in every direction. At this dire moment, the salvation of the entire programme materialized at the Gor'ki factory in the form of five of the most experienced aviators in the NII VVS – Kokkinaki, Shevchenko, Suprun, Evseev, and Preman. Collecting five Type 4s directly from the production lines and painting them bright red, the five Institute test-pilots toured the front like circus barnstormers, putting on a tremendous exhibition. Flying in formation with the aircraft connected by a short ribbon, they performed extraordinary aerobatics, and generally highlighted the machine's more positive aspects. In particular, they demonstrated that the machine was very manoeuvrable, with a superb rate of roll. Aerobatics could be performed with high precision given the machine's excellent high speed characteristics, and the zoom climb was completely unmatched by any other fighter of its day – or for years to come. Further, its unusual sensitivity on the controls was a bonus in the hands of an experienced pilot, who could then exploit the I-16's marginal stability

to produce extraordinary nimbleness and response. The effect was to restore morale in the front line units considerably, even though a high accident rate persisted for some months.

Almost simultaneously, during the late spring of 1935, quantities of the M-25 engine at last became available. Of the last batch of eight I-16s manufactured in Moscow, many were experimental prototypes featuring various aerodynamic refinements, and aircraft No.123954 of this series was rebuilt in March with a 700 hp M-25 motor and incorporated an entirely new engine cowling developed as a result of wind tunnel testing at TsAGI. The new cowling – which would impart upon the I-16 its distinctive profile – was highly tapered towards the trailing edge. Eight individual exhaust stack cut-outs replaced the earlier collector ring arrangement, these protruding through teardrop-shaped openings in the cowl sides. This new unit served not only to improve the machine's aerodynamic profile, but also resulted in better cooling for the power plant and improved forward visibility. Armament remained at two ShKAS guns, each with 600 rounds, in the outer wings, and the pilot's armoured headrest was increased to 9 mm thickness. In addition, the landing gear tyres were increased in size to 750 x 150 mm units, giving better handling on rough surfaces.

The new prototype was tested during November-December 1935 by the NII VVS. The flight behaviour characteristics were virtually unchanged, but with the additional power of the M-25, performance was much improved. Maximum speed in the new 'Type 5' reached 390 km/h at sea level and 445 km/h at 3,000 m, climbing initially at 716 m/min. and reaching 5,000 m in 7.8 minutes. By the standards of the day, such figures were remarkable, placing the new prototype very far ahead of the rest of the world in these aspects.

GUAP authorized an immediate series of the new I-16, and once again *Zavod* 39 (Moscow) played a leading role. With retooling and engine deliveries coming on line at Gor'ki, *Zavod* 39 produced the first aircraft, now dubbed 'I-16 Type 5' (to conform to the odd *Zavod* 21 nomenclature), as a pattern machine for *Zavod* 21. By January 1936, Type 5s had replaced the Type 4 on the lines at Gor'ki, and to their credit the production examples matched the prototype's performance very well.

At the same time, manufacture of a training version of the I-16 got underway. With a view towards mitigating the conversion difficulties being experienced, a two-seat instructional model of the Type 5 was developed at Gor'ki. The cockpit was moved aft and a second, pupil's cockpit installed ahead of that. The fuel cell was recontoured to make legroom for the student, all primary flight controls were installed in the forward position, and the armament was removed. The initial version of the training machine, dubbed the UTI-2 (UTI= *uchebno-trenirovanniy istrebitel*', or 'student-training fighter'), was powered by the M-22 engine and featured the broad-chord NACA cowling of the Type 4. Some 100 UTI-2s were manufactured before production switched to the UTI-4, this based on the I-16 Type 5. Many UTI-4s featured fixed landing gear, and this training machine remained in production until the beginning of the GPW, notably at *Zavod* 458 (Rostov-on-Don) during 1941.

With pilots in VVS regiments at last mastering the I-16, developments elsewhere were about to affect the aircraft tremendously. The I-16 was destined to be a major participant in the Spanish Civil War. In October 1936, two squadrons of I-16 Type 5s were delivered to the Republican forces at Camposoto and Alcalá de Henares, forming the 1a and 2a *Esquadrillia*. These machines became the first of the I-16 family to fire their guns in anger when, on 15 November, two machines of the 2a *Esquadrillia* encountered three CR.32s over Muón.

In Spanish service, the I-16 Type 5 proved itself more than a match for the various machines of the Nationalist forces, and quickly earned itself numerous epitaphs on both sides of the front. To the Republican pilots, the I-16 became the *Mosca* ('flea'), but it was from the victorious Nationalists that the West acquired its nickname for the type, the *Rata* ('rat'). Despite the derisive nickname, there was no doubt that Franco's air forces were completely dumbfounded by the tiny Polikarpov. Though the Fiat CR.32 was more manoeuvrable, the *Mosca* was superior in every other respect, and could attack and break-off combat at will. Certainly, however, the Soviet and Republican pilots were forced to rethink considerably their operational and combat tactics. For the first time, they had to learn the unfamiliar art of the high-speed pass and climb away; no longer could they afford to dogfight their opponents. But in the main, the I-16's pilots were confident in the type, and indeed, the arrival of the *Esquadrillias de Moscas* resulted in at least functional aerial mastery wherever it was encountered.

In the course of operations over Spain, and also in VVS front line service, a number of deficiencies were noted in the I-16. First, the machine's firepower was considered to be insufficient despite the performance of the ShKAS gun, a pair of 7.62 mm weapons were unable to deal with such targets as modern twin-engined bombers and the like. Torsional stiffness to the wing outer sections was found to be inadequate, and strengthening was required. The engine mounts were far too rigid and of poor design, resulting in considerable vibration at full RPMs, and having a deleterious effect on gunnery. In addition, there were repeated complaints concerning the lack of a radio set. Lastly, the enclosed canopy was a subject of continuing dissatisfaction, some examples of early Soviet-made Perspex being of very mixed quality; some units were nearly opaque, and optically distorted as well. A few squadrons simply fixed the sliding canopy in the open position, and some Spanish units were known to have removed them altogether.

During their service in the early phases of the Spanish Civil War, the firepower of the Type 5 (with only two rifle-calibre guns) was seen to be inadequate by most Republican pilots. A somewhat ad-hoc solution was put forward by the staff at *Zavod* 21 (Gor'ki), who modified some 30 aircraft at the factory to mount an additional 7.62 mm ShKAS gun in the lower engine cowling, synchronized to fire through the propeller arc. Unfortunately, the factory records do not specify the location where the weapon was mounted, but it is thought it might have occupied the space at the bottom centre of the cowling, as was done later on the Type 29. The resulting aircraft were known to the Gor'ki staff as *Ispanskiy* (Spanish) models, and were not reported in any other way. The designation Type 6 is known only from records from the NKVD, and from a shipping manifest in its archival collection. If this designation was used (and it seems it may have been), then it would be known, presumably, only to the Soviet pilots in Spain, and not in 'general' VVS service.

Back at *Zavod* 21, the Polikarpov OKB staff realized that there would be room to mount two such weapons above the engine if the fuel cell was slightly modified in shape with 'slots' cut out to accommodate the gun breaches. Such modifications were made, and the new fuel tank was examined and cleared for manufacture by VIAM.

At the same time, improvements were made to the wing outer sections. To improve torsional stiffness, the number of stringers in the outer section were doubled, and the leading edge sheet of duralumin was increased in depth, largely eliminating the scalloped appearance on the wing's upper side. Modified wings of this type were tested at the LII, and although moderately heavier, offered much improved high-speed stiffness and redressed the wing warping problem. By the time GUAP had given their official approval for the modification, production Type 5's were already being completed with the new wing, a number of these going to Spain. Under service conditions, the improved wing was a great success, and manufacture of the original wing was terminated at *Zavod* 21.

The improvements resulting from these considerations – based largely on combat experience in Spain – were embodied in a new production series, the Type 10. Based around the improved M-25V motor of 750 hp, the first Type 10s joined the Type 5 on the production lines in March 1938. The production Type 10 was identical to the improved manufacture Type 5, save for the upper engine cowling which now sported two long, squarish fairings. These covered two new ShKAS guns mounted above the engine, each with 450 rounds, and with the fuel tank thus decreased slightly in capacity. The sliding canopy unit was replaced with an all-glass framed windscreen – as on some later Type 5s – and the Aldus type OP-1 telescopic sight

replaced by the PAK-1 reflector mechanism. The M-25V incorporated improved engine mounts, and vibration at higher throttle settings was considerably reduced. The Type 10 was characterized by a slightly modified profile to the cowling leading edge, with the two ShKAS gun barrel openings protruding along the upper lip. Lastly, cockpit instrumentation and outfit were demonstrably improved, and provision was made for a three-channel RSI-1 radio.

The first 31 examples of the Type 10 were despatched directly to Spain. Both Russian and Spanish pilots were thrilled with the increased firepower of the Type 10, and the considerable improvement with regard to vibration. As a result, the new model largely dispelled the I-16's reputation as a poor gun platform, the first batch of Type 10s reaching the Republican forces on 18 March 1938, and being immediately dubbed 'Super-Moscas'. Indeed, the Type 10 arrived just in time to counter two new and more dangerous adversaries in the Nationalist inventory, the Fiat G.50 and the Messerschmitt Bf 109 B and C. There was little to choose between the G.50 and the Type 10 in turning circle; while the former possessed slightly greater power and speed, and the I-16 was more rugged, more heavily armed, and far more responsive in handling. The same was largely true of the early Messerschmitt 109s, which had demonstrated a certain ascendancy over the Type 5 and 6, but with the Type 10 parity was restored. Later in the conflict the pendulum again swung towards the German machine with the introduction of the Bf 109 D and early E models, but no newer models of the I-16 managed to reach Spain.

The I-16 Type 10 was also active in the Far East by this time. By late 1937, two groups of I-16 Type 5s were working up in the Nanking and Hangkow areas under the direction of *May*. Suprun. By the late summer of 1938, a number of new Type 10s joined them, and with similar results to those achieved in Spain. With Soviet crews in the fore, the Type 10 gave a very good account of itself, though in Chinese hands the I-16 was less effective due to limited experience on the part of Chinese pilots.

Back at Gor'ki, numerous experimental options were being explored in an effort to further boost the type's firepower. Considerable interest evolved around the new 20 mm ShVAK aircraft cannon which was just then ready to enter mass-production. As early as 1936, a modified Type 5 was fitted with one of the ShVAK prototypes, and an I-16P (*pushechny* – 'cannon') variant was mooted. Difficulties with the early gun however, prevented rapid development, but by early 1937 an I-16 Type 12 machine was authorized for limited manufacture based on the Type 5 with two of these weapons replacing the ShKAS guns in the wings. Only some 24 examples were completed, but GUAP was most enthusiastic about the trials results, and decided that a cannon-armed variant should be put forward as soon as possible.

During 1938 development of a cannon-armed I-16 refocused on the Type 10. Two of the 20 mm ShVAK cannon replaced the wing-mounted ShKAS, as before, and with improved mounting braces. The installation was entirely successful and soon, other improvements began to join the cannon on the new prototype. The exhaust stacks were rearranged to exit through six openings in the cowling rather than eight, thereby reducing drag, and also making room for two troughs along the lower cowling. These trough cut-outs were intended to receive ski type landing gear when fitted, allowing them to lie flush with the lower surface.

The new I-16 version, the Type 17, was placed into series production at Gor'ki alongside the Type 5 and Type 10 during October 1938. The production Type 17 weighed 1,810 kg at take-off, was powered by the 750 hp M-25V radial, and was armed with two ShKAS guns above the engine and a 20mm ShVAK in each wing with 120 rounds. With the extra all-up weight, performance fell to 385 km/h at sea level and 425 km/h at 2,700 m, climbing initially at 549 m/min. and reaching 5,000 m in nine minutes. Wing-loading was equally adversely affected, and consequently the turning circle was fully 10 per cent larger than in the Type 10.

However, despite the adverse effects on performance, Soviet pilots were thrilled with the increased firepower of the Type 17. A number were deployed to Manchuria during the Khalkin-Gol conflict of 1939, much to the consternation of the Japanese. The ShVAK gun wrought havoc amongst lightly-protected Japanese aircraft, a single strike often being sufficient to down a twin-engined bomber. On the debit side, the aircraft was quite heavy, and the nimble Japanese fighters proved to be a difficult target for the I-16 'gunships'.

A number of experimental I-16 developments were mooted leading up to 1938. Type 4 airframe No.8211 was modified with a long, enclosed 'greenhouse'-type canopy, and was proposed as the training version UTI-3. During 1937 the I-163 prototype was built with the M-25E motor. Based on the Type 5, the I-163 was intended as a super-lightweight I-16 variant; no production was undertaken. Several *shturmovik* I-16 prototypes were developed, the most significant of which was airframe No.9211. This machine was tested on ski landing gear which was faired neatly into the wing undersurface. Three ShKAS guns were mounted in each wing, and provision was made for two FAB-100 bombs. Though several other attack machines resulted from this work, no series production was attempted.

By early 1939 it had become apparent that the I-16 was now woefully under-powered. In just four years, flying horsepower had increased only 5.5 per cent while all-up loaded weight had soared nearly 50 per cent. Fortuitously, the Shvetsov OKB's latest radial developments were in hand, two new nine-cylinder engines developed from the basic M-25; the M-62 was available, was designed to operate on common 86 octane fuel, and gave 800 hp (920 hp for take-off and emergency); the M-63 was a further development, still underway, intended to operate with 94 octane fuel at a higher compression ratio (7.2:1) and greater RPMs (2,300 max.), and deliver 930 hp (1,100 hp for take-off and emergency). With the European political situation deteriorating rapidly, the NKAP decided to move ahead with an M-62-based model at the earliest possible moment.

The resulting I-16 Type 18 was a progressive development of the Type 10 airframe mounting the M-62 engine. The new prototype incorporated minor local strengthening and equipment revisions to accommodate the increased power, including heavier engine mounts. A new, self-sealing fuel cell material was developed by VIAM, and this was included in the Type 18's tank (indeed, many of the earlier I-16 models still in production in 1939 received these self-sealing tanks). The new variant could be identified externally by a slightly modified cowling face, having a somewhat 'square-ish' face and featuring a new intake scoop along the top forward edge. A larger spinner was fitted, changing the I-16's profile dramatically. The armament remained as on the Type 10 – two 7.62 mm ShKAS in the wings with 650 rounds each, and two similar weapons mounted above the engine with 450 rounds each. Provision was made for six RS-82 rockets under the outer wing sections.

Testing of the new Type 18 by the NII VVS was completed during September-October 1938. Despite the increase in both weight and power over the preceding models, handling in the new version was essentially unchanged. The new I-16's landing speed rose to 130 km/h, and turning circle suffered similarly with the increase in wing-loading. Powered by the M-62 driving an AV-1 or VISh-6A two-bladed variable-pitch propeller, the production Type 18's performance jumped to 461 km/h at 4,400 m, and the initial climb increased to 1,037 m/min and reaching 5,000 m in 5.4 minutes.

Production of the new variant commenced during January 1939, joining a number of other older versions on the lines. During that year, the I-16 programme became a confusing morass of concurrent older and newer variants simultaneously in production. As far back as late 1937, manufacture of the Type 5 I-16 had begun at *Zavod* 153, Novosibirsk. During 1938, the Type 5 made up a large portion of I-16 production, both at Novosibirsk and Gor'ki. The Type 10 joined the earlier variant during the year, and at *Zavod* 21 these were joined by the Type 17. Even into 1939, *Zavod* 153 was still manufacturing Type 5s, in addition to Type 10s, but *Zavod* 21 was by then manufacturing the Type 10 and 18 – not to mention the Types 24, 27, and 28 – and a very large number of UTI-4s.

During the summer of 1939 another crop of I-16 variants began to emerge. Interest in ShVAK-armed fighters featured in NKAP planning at this time, and as the Type 17 phased out of production during the first half of the year, it was replaced by the Type 27. The new machine was simply a Type 17 airframe upgraded with an M-62 radial of 800 hp; all equipment and armament features were the same as on the Type 17. The Type 27 was manufactured in strictly limited numbers – 59 were completed at Gor'ki before being supplanted by the Type 28. The Type 28 was a re-engined version of the Type 27, powered by the M-63 and entered production at the end of 1939. Many models designated 'Type 28' were manufactured using components from incomplete Type 24s, and featured some or all of the improvements made to the new airframe. A number of these were simply Type 24s with two ShVAK mounted in the wings, and it is not uncommon to find Type 28s in the photographic record with underwing fuel tanks, tailwheels, starboard cockpit and radio doors, gun-camera mounts, and other Type 24 refinements. At least 293 Type 28s were completed, and a number of the later models appear to have had revised supercharger gearing, these aircraft demonstrating a dramatic change in performance during testing.

The most significant update during 1939, however, was to the Type 18. Re-engined with the more powerful M-63 radial of 930 hp, the I-16 became the Type 24. A number of improvements attended the new version in addition to the engine, including a second crew access door on the right-hand side of the cockpit. A castoring tailwheel was installed to replace the tail skid, facilitating ground taxiing on prepared airbases. An internal RI inertia-type starter was installed, and the PAK-1 gave way to the newer PBP-1 gunsight. The improved ViSH AV-1 propeller was standard on the Type 24, driven by a new R-2 constant speed regulator. A large radio access hatch was added to the fuselage starboard side, and provision was made for a PAU-22 gun-camera to be mounted above and behind the pilot on the fuselage combing.

Entering production in the final quarter of 1939, the Type 24's performance suffered from its heavier engine. At an all-up weight of 1,882 kg the Type 24 could achieve 410 km/h at sea level and 462 km/h at 4,700 m. The initial climb figure fell to 991 m/min, and the time to 5,000 m was six minutes. Handling and manoeuvrability were virtually the same as the Type 18, and with the added power of the M-63 the I-16's legendary zoom-climb capability was restored.

Numerous variants of the I-16 participated in the Winter War of November 1939 to March 1940 against Finland, the Types-5, -10, -17, -18, -24, -27, and -28 operating in VVS service. Their performance, as with the VVS as a whole, was reasonably good, but these accomplishments were masked by the catastrophic incompetence of the Stalinist cronies who were in command of operations from the start of the battle.

During 1940, the I-16 programme had clearly reached maturity, and with war clouds gathering in the West, all efforts were made to 'stretch' the effective life of the little fighter. First, the operational range of the I-16 had fallen from already modest figures with the advent of the thirsty M-63 motor, and an increase in flight time was deemed essential. Polikarpov was also asked to improve the performance of the I-16 if possible, and at the same time to make provision for improved communications with the RSI-3 radio.

With the seemingly contradictory requirements at hand to both increase performance and the amount and types of equipment carried by I-16, the Polikarpov OKB responded at once. The new Type 29 was based on the prevailing Type-24 airframe, but with a number of modifications. To save weight, the outer wing ShKAS guns were removed, and in their place a 12.7mm UBS was installed in the central lower engine cowling. This placement caused the oil cooler intake to move to port, where it was improved in shape for better effect. The pair of ShKAS guns above the engine were retained, and two attachment points were added to the wing undersurface for two underwing 100 litre fuel tanks. Two different tanks were developed, the first being a typical VVS teardrop-shaped unit. The second type was specific to the I-16, these units being constructed of light-gauge dural sheet and of the 'slipper' type, resembling quite notably an underwing gun pod. Additionally, the RSI-3 single-channel radio became standard and an external aerial mast was mounted ahead of the pilot to starboard, angled to the right.

Though the all-up weight of the Type-29 was slightly higher than the Type-24, performance in both level speed and climb improved. The production Type 29 weighed 1,914 kg at take-off and could reach 419 km/h at sea level and 470 km/h at 4,480 m. The initial climb figure rose to 1,044 m/min. and 5,000 m could be attained in 5.8 minutes. With external fuel tanks the Type-29's range increased to 700 km at a gross weight of 2,115 kg.

A number of later manufacture Type-29s were further modified to reduce drag, and in these machines the oil cooler intake was omitted altogether. The intake ducting for the oil cooler was re-routed through the engine bay, and air taken in through two oval-shaped cut-outs in the cooling louvres on the cowl's forward face. No specific performance data is known to be available on these machines, but VVS pilots were well aware of the new modification, suggesting that it did indeed result in some improvement.

Polikarpov I-16s fought heroically during the first years of the German invasion. In fact, the *Ishak* was the backbone of the Soviet aerial defence, and was still the most frequently encountered Soviet fighter on some fronts well into 1942. The capabilities of the I-16 have long been underestimated in the West, where it is often viewed as obsolete. The combat history of the I-16, however, demonstrates clearly that it was not as outdated as we have been led to believe. The history of the VVS fighter arm during the early months of Barbarossa is replete with the success of I-16-equipped regiments, not to mention individual pilots who scored very well in the type. The M-62 and M-63 powered models were in no way inferior to their *Luftwaffe* rivals in vertical capabilities nor rate of climb, while they vastly exceeded them in horizontal manoeuvrability and turning circle. The inferiority of the I-16 was evident only in regards to level speed, though admittedly the discrepancy was significant (in the order of 80-110 km/h).

Success in the I-16 was very much a matter of experience. Inexperienced pilots, and units demonstrating poor tactics or overly rigid control, suffered heavily. It was the same for all slow, manoeuvrable types – a pilot had to be skilled in dogfighting to prevail; novice pilots unable to evoke these properties would fall to the faster and higher-climbing enemy. The experienced pilots – able to make the maximum use of the type's superb manoeuvrability – scored well in the fighter, confounding their *Luftwaffe* opponents with the ability to slip from their gun-sights at the last moment and fling themselves around in a viciously tight turn to attack head-on. In addition, the I-16 made an ideal platform from which to carry-out the dreaded *Taran* ramming attacks of 1941-42, most of which – contrary to the commonly held perception in the West – were carried out with success and saw the safe return of the attacking Soviet pilot.

In action from the start, some I-16 pilots were successful even under the most appalling conditions. During numerous sorties on 23 and 24 June 1941, *Lts* Vershinin and Fomin of the 67 IAP each destroyed a pair of Ju 88s and a Bf 109. *St.Lt.* Moklyak of the same Regiment dispatched two SM.79 bombers on 22 June, whereupon he rammed a

third bomber to destruction, losing his life. *Lt* Anatoli Rudenko of the 28 IAP scored doubles on the 22 and 24 June in his I-16 Type 27, all of them Bf 109s. Other notable aces scored very heavily in the I-16, including *Lt* A.Golubev, M.S.Baranov, and the immortal Naval pilot *Kapitan* Boris Safonov.

One final development of the I-16 fighter family that deserves mention is the unusual and innovative 'Parasite Fighter' concept of 1931. Initially making use of the Tupolev I-4Z and Polikarpov I-5 biplanes, the *Aviamatka* ('mother-ship') concept blossomed in 1935 with the utilization of the I-16. A special unit, known simply as *Zveno* 6 (Flight 6), was formed using the TB-3 heavy bomber as the carrier aircraft. Two I-16 Type 1s were attached via tubular-steel rigs underneath the wings' outboard section, test pilots Suprun and Evseev making the first successful airborne launch with I-16s on 1 July 1935. This success was followed in November by the even more spectacular *Zveno* 7 demonstration, with two I-16 Type 5s hung underneath and two I-5s mounted above the wings (with the I-16s running their engines full-out to help lift the contraption off the ground). After take-off, the unit was joined by an I-4Z fighter which hooked onto a trapeze lowered from the fuselage. With no fewer than *five* other aircraft attached to it, the TB-3 nevertheless managed to display a considerable degree of air-worthiness, making several turns and other typical flight manoeuvres during the exercise. Following this, all of the 'parasite' machines successfully separated from the *Aviamatka*, and landed in formation with their lumbering host.

Under the direction of Engineer Vladimir Vahkmistrov, the experience gained during these extraordinary operations was further developed in line with *Zveno* 6 methods as a long-range dive-bomber concept. A pair of I-16 Type 24-SPBs, each carrying two 500 kg bombs were deployed under the wings of a 'mother' TB-3. The idea was for the *Aviamatka* to deliver the fighter-bombers to within 50 km of their target, whence they would detach, make their attacks, and then return to base using their own fuel. In this way it was possible to almost double the range at which the I-16 dive-bombers could operate, and in an emergency it was intended that the I-16s could launch and jettison their bombs to defend the mother ship. Service trials proceeded smoothly throughout 1938, and several units formed-up on the aircraft in VMF service under the designation '*Zveno* 6 SPB'. By the time of *Barbarossa*, however, only one such unit remained fully operational, this being *May*. Pavlov's regiment stationed at Evpatoria in the Crimea. This unit made numerous successful attacks on Constanza harbour and Chernovodsky Bridge in Rumania, and continued operations for over a year, flying its last operational sortie in September 1942. Though often spectacular, the unit's success was regarded as something of a novelty and of largely nuisance value, and no further development was attempted.

Amazingly, the I-16 was still in service *10 years* after the first TsKB-12 cut across the sky near Moscow. Though its career had been long and rife with difficulty, the I-16 marked one of the most important milestones in aviation history, leading by many years those other Western designs that have traditionally been awarded such epithets. The I-16 is, indeed, worthy of this level of attention, and its place in history cannot merely be brushed aside by the exigencies of Cold War politics.

	I-16 Type 4	I-16 Type 5	I-16 Type 10	I-16 Type 12	I-16 Type 17	I-16 Type 18
Weights						
Empty:	1070 kg	1147 kg	1339 kg	1265 kg	1428 kg	1413 kg
Loaded:	1354 kg	1533 kg	1730 kg	1699 kg	1814 kg	1850 kg
Wing Area:	14.54 m.sq	14.54 m.sq	14.54 m.sq	14.54 m.sq	14.54 m.sq	14.54 m.sq
Engine	M-22 480 hp	M-25A 725 hp	M-25V 750 hp	M-25A 725 hp	M-25V 750 hp 800 (920) hp	M-62
Maximum Speed						
At Altitude:	360 km/h	390 km/h	398 km/h	394 km/h	385 km/h	411 km/h
Sea Level:	345 km/h at 3000 m	445 km/h at 2745 m	448 km/h at 3200 m	432 km/h at 2500 m	426 km/h at 2500 m	460 km/h at 3200 m
Climb						
Initial:	396 m/min	716 m/min	640 m/min	623 m/min	549 m/min	1037 m/min
Time to Height:	9.9 min to 5000 m	7.8 min to 5000 m	8.2 min to 5000 m	8.3 min to 5000 m	9.0 min to 5000 m	5.4 min to 5000 m
Service Ceiling	7440 m	8250 m	8250 m	8350 m	8250 m	9450 m
Armament	2 x ShKAS	2 x ShKAS	4 x ShKAS	2 x ShVAK	2 x ShKAS 2 x ShVAK	4 x ShKAS 6 x RS-82

	I-16 Type 27	I-16 Type 28 with revised supercharger	I-16 Type 24	I-16 Type 29
Weights				
Empty:	1491 kg	1529 kg	1440 kg	1548 kg
Loaded:	1957 kg	2085 kg	1882 kg	1914 kg
Wing Area:	14.54 m.sq	14.54 m.sq	14.54 m.sq	14.54 m.sq
Engine	M-62 800 (920) hp	M-63 930 (1100) hp	M-63 930 (1100) hp	M-63 930 (1100) hp
Maximum Speed				
At Altitude:	439 km/h at 3200 m	463 km/h at 2000 m	460 km/h at 4700 m	468 km/h at 4480 m
Sea Level:	405 km/h	427 km/h	408 km/h	418 km/h
Climb				
Initial:	915 m/min	768 m/min	991 m/min	1044 m/min
Time to Height:	6.9 min to 5000 m	7.3 min to 5000 m	6.0 min to 5000 m	5.8 min to 5000 m
Service Ceiling	9000 m	9300 m	9700 m	9800 m
Armament	2 x ShKAS 2 x ShVAK	2 x ShKAS 2 x ShVAK 6 x RS-82	4 x ShKAS 6 x RS-82	2 x ShKAS 1 x UBS 6 x RS-82

I-16 Type 5

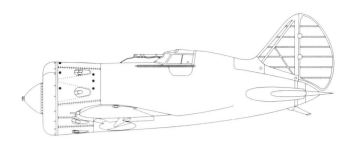

I-16 Type 10

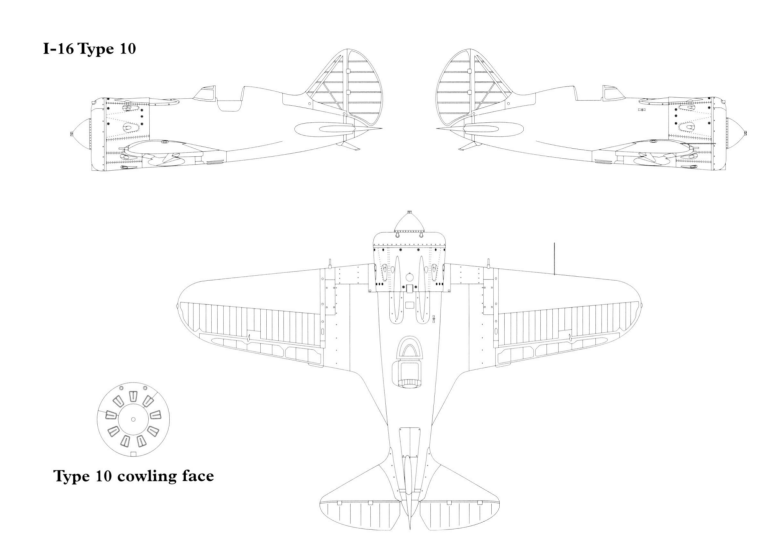

Type 10 cowling face

I-16 Type 17

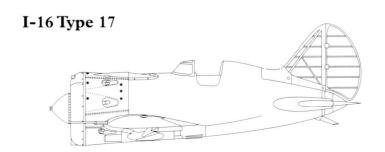
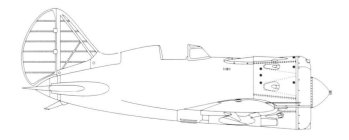

I-16 Type 18

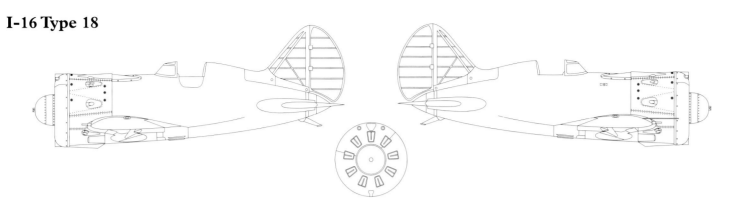

Type 18 cowling face

I-16 Type 24

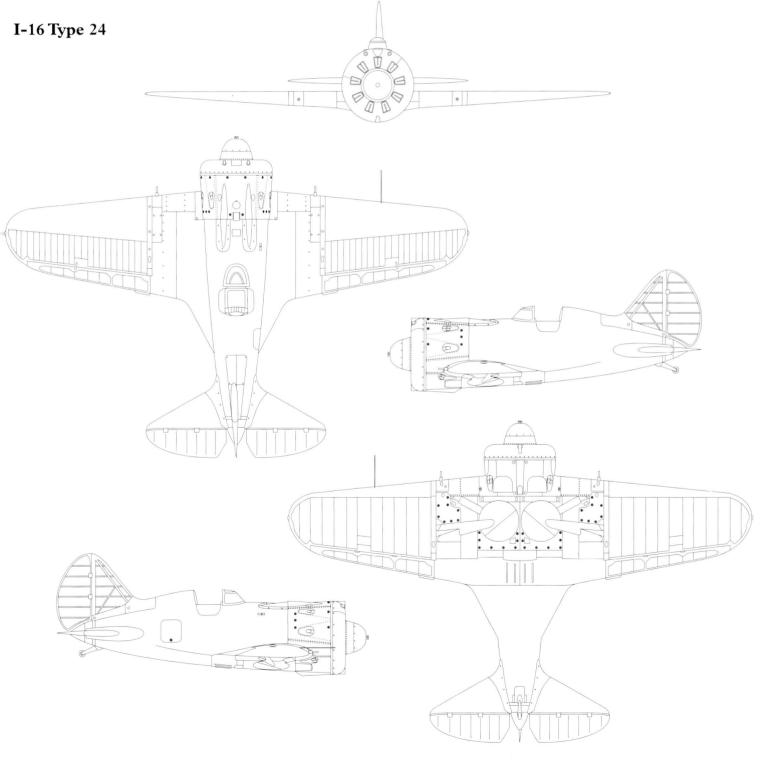

I-16 Type 29

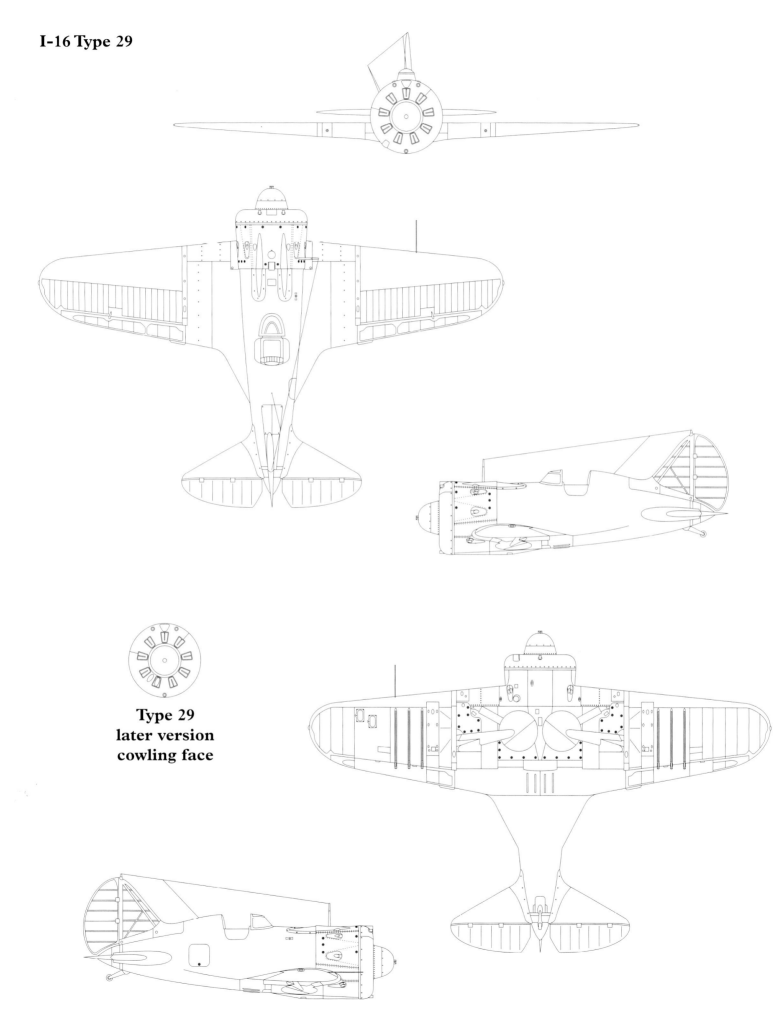

**Type 29
later version
cowling face**

THE DEVELOPMENT OF CAMOUFLAGE ON THE I-16 FIGHTER

Pre-War Camouflage

The greatest portion of the manufacturing programme of the I-16 occurred before the onset of the GPW. As such, the camouflage employed on those machines falls somewhat outside of the scope of this volume. However, some of the common pre-war schemes can be identified with certainty, and those patterns are presented here.

The first easily identifiable pre-war scheme is shown here on an I-16 Type 10, but would be similar on other types of the same period. The scheme is an overall (upper and lower surfaces) application of AEh-9 Light Grey with a Black AEh-11 cowling (see Fig. 1).

Fig. 1

The spinners on these machines were often painted white, or sometimes AEh-9, but less often appear to have been black.

The second common application was a classic livery of AII Green uppersurfaces over AII Blue lowersurfaces. At the time these finishes were new, and this scheme was quite modern in the 1936-37 period (see Fig. 2).

Below: I-16s of various types wearing an overall green finish. 'White 96', at least, appears to be a Type 28. The padded engine covers were typical for winter operations, and number '85' is about to be connected to the Hucks starter truck. These machines were photographed with the Baltic Fleet in the autumn of 1941. (Photo: G.Petrov)

Fig. 2

Similar to this scheme there was another concurrent Green over Blue application, but here the colours are unknown (see Fig. 3).

Fig. 3

Above: An abandoned I-16 Type 5 (1938 manufacture) photographed in the Kiev area in 1941. The scheme is a classic AII Green/ Blue application. The apparent dark colour of the rudder is probably just the result of shadow. The condition of these aircraft (including the I-152 behind) is very typical of VVS aircraft that were 'captured' by the Germans; they are clearly derelicts, have not been operational for some time, and have been abandoned in an un-airworthy state. (Photo: G.Petrov)

The paints are thought to be AEh lacquers (there is written evidence to suggest this), but are as yet unidentified (AEh-5 and AEh-15 have been suggested). The green colour is quite dark on K-16/39 film, and appears very much like *Zavod 1* Factory Green; it is not known if the two aerolacquers are related. Similarly, the underside blue colour also looks like AII *goluboi* (blue), but may well be some kind of AEh shade. The spinners on both green livery aircraft were usually painted in the underside blue colour.

Slightly later on, here shown on the Type 17, some colour changes were seen. Both greens were still employed widely, but now the spinners were being painted according to the uppersurfaces. Furthermore, the upper/lower colour demarcation at the cowling face changed, and it was common for the entire cowl to wear the upper colour (see Figs. 4 and 5).

Fig. 4

Fig. 5

Above: An I-16 Type 27 (or perhaps a Type 17) seen in flight in 1940. This aircraft is finished in AII Green and Blue with the 'newer' cowling demarcation in view. (Photo: G.Petrov)

Maskirovka

The first identifiable two-colour camouflage pattern application appears to have been applied at Gor'ki to the Type-17 and Type-27 during 1939. AII Black was applied over AII Green, and the undersurfaces were AII Blue, all colour demarcation lines being quite sharp (see Fig. 6).

Fig. 6

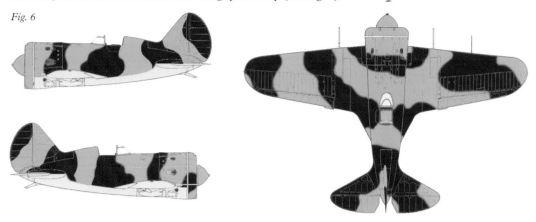

By 1940, a new identifiable scheme appeared, here shown on the Type 24. The new colouration was often (not exclusively) AII Dark Green over AII Green, with AII Blue undersurfaces (see Fig. 7).

Fig. 7

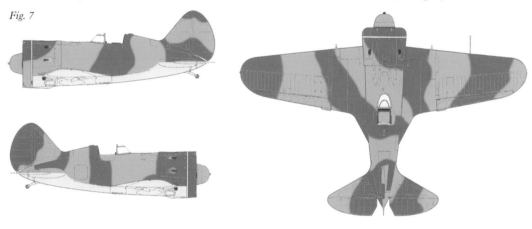

Right: *An exceptional view of an AII Black and Green application on a Type 24. This machine was photographed in service with the 7 IAP on the Leningrad Front during 1941. Note the six RS rockets under the wing. (Photo: G. Petrov)*

The colour demarcation lines were typically sharp, though semi-hard examples are known, as well. The propensity of Soviet camouflage to follow panel lines scrupulously was seen on this application quite commonly.

The last widely-recognized scheme known on the I-16 occurred somewhat later in the programme. During 1940 and 1941 this new AII Black over AII Green application appeared. Again with sharp colour demarcation lines, the pattern was, unusually, somewhat symmetrical (see Fig. 8).

Fig. 8

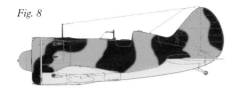

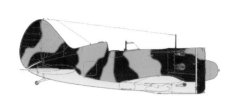

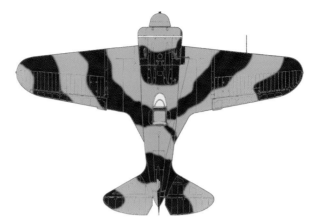

Here shown on the Type-29, this application was commonly seen on that variant.

Winter camouflage practices were fairly typical, and MK-7 white distemper was seen throughout 1941-42.

Internal Finish

The cockpit colouration of the I-16 was somewhat different from its 'cousin', the I-153. At Gor'ki, interiors were usually completed in A-14 in the pre-war era. Examples of I-16s with AII Blue interiors are not at all uncommon and, in fact, might have been the most popular option during 1940-41. A large number of I-16s also show unpainted interiors. Two surviving I-16s demonstrate Wood Finish interiors, again uniformly applied, and it is possible that a large number were also completed in the more usual manner, in which various items were left in their primed state.

Above: *I-16 Type 29 'White 75' was the personal mount of V.P. Segalaev of the 71 IAP VVS KBF in 1942. This aircraft wears the last of the recognized AII Black/Green schemes and is armed with four RS-132 rockets. The absence of any national markings on the fuselage and/or fin is unusual. Many details are evident in this photograph, and the machine appears to be undergoing gun harmonization testing. Note that the landing gear door covers have been removed. (Photo: G.Petrov)*

The Mystery of Camouflage Mysteries

Given that the I-16 programme resulted in excess of 10,000 fighters, the preceding camouflage information seems quite anaemic. The I-16 represents the greatest mystery in colouration during the GPW. Many factors contribute to this, including the extreme dislocation of the aviation industry during the early months of the War, the fact that many machines were completed prior to the new 1940 Camouflage Directive, and the fact that the I-16 became a canvas for the expression of individual and regimental ideas in colouration.

The sheer number of I-16s wearing adhoc and individual camouflage applications is staggering. Even as early as 1940, Naval units were modifying their own I-16s' paint styles to match their own preferences. In the Army Regiments, unit schemes became fashionable on the I-16 (but not, strangely, on other aircraft) during 1940-41, and other experimental patterns were also common.

The result of all these endeavours is confusion on the part of researchers trying to understand VVS camouflage. Innumerable single views exist of patterns which *seem* to have been factory-applied, but with no corroborating views from other angles they cannot be confirmed. Furthermore, some of the field-applied

Left: *Type 24s of the 4 GIAP VVS KBF displaying a very professionally-applied MK-7 white distemper winter livery at Novaya Ladoga airfield during the winter of 1941-42. The machine in the foreground, 'Red 21', is thought to be the personal aircraft of G.Tsokolaev. It is likely that this winter finish was applied at the factory, as the aircraft's Production Number (No. 2423321) is still visible on the fin and rudder. (Photo: G.Petrov)*

schemes were completed with such skill and professional touch that they simply cannot be distinguished from factory applied camouflage, and these applications cloud the colour question for this aircraft still further. A final and significant difficulty arises in that apparently, no photographs were taken of I-16 manufacture at *Zavod* 21 during the relevant 1940-42 period.

On the positive side, these field applications are often highly noteworthy, and represent some of the most innovative camouflage of the entire GPW.

Left: *This I-16 Type 17 wears one of the innumerable appliqué schemes utilized during 1940-41. In this case, it appears that AII Black was applied over an original single-colour AII Green/Blue scheme. It is possible that a third colour was applied as an outline to the black areas as well, or that this might be the remains of some removed MK-7 white distemper. 'White 28' was the personal machine of Hero of the Soviet Union Mikhail Vasil'ev of the 4 GIAP in 1942.*

Right: *A Type 10 of the 728 IAP in 1942. Its remarkable scheme shows many field- and unit-applied colouration features. First, a non-standard application of AII Dark Green has been made over the wing and fuselage (on a base of AII Green), and this was then supplemented by white MK-7 distemper over the wing and tail surfaces. The colour is quite worn over the wing, but fresh over the rear fuselage, suggesting that it was not executed at the same time. The tactical number '91' has clearly been applied by hand. (Photo: G.Petrov)*

Below: *The I-16 Type 24 of the famous Naval ace Alexei Denisov (left), of the 13 IAP VVS KBF (the 4 GIAP from January 1942). The date is unknown, but the photograph was probably taken during 1941. This machine is numbered '70' in white on the tail, which, like the cowling and wing outer sections, is painted red. This striking scheme was expertly completed on '70', and is thought to have been applied as the subject of a propaganda film. (Photo: G.Petrov)*

Right: *A superb example of the extraordinary camouflage practices of the VMF (Naval Aviation) during the early war period. Over a base of AII Green, the unit has applied AII Dark Green in patches, and then a light colour, such as AEh-9 Grey, over the rear fuselage. These colours are also evident on the wing uppersurface. Type 24 'White 71' is thought to be the personal aircraft of the 13 IAP VVS KBF's commander, Podpolk. Romanenko in 1941. (Photo: H.Seidl)*

Below: *The incomparable Hero of the Soviet Union, Boris Safonov, of the 72 SAP VVS SF. His famous I-16 Type 24 'White 11', production No.2489121, is behind him. The inscription on the port side fuselage reads 'Za Stalina!' ('For Stalin!'); an inscription to starboard (not in view) exclaimed 'Smert' Fashistam!' ('Death to Fascists!'). (Photo: G.Petrov)*

Above: *A I-16 Type 5 with ski landing gear of the 13 OIAE, 61 Aviation Brigade. This machine was one of several aircraft in this unit bearing large slogans, and was photographed in Finland during the Winter War in early 1940. The colour is quite dark, and might be the pre-war Dark Green AEh lacquer. The tactical number is rendered in red with white trim, and the inscription (in white) reads 'Za Konstitutsiyu SSSR!' ('For the Constitution of the USSR!'). (Photo: G.Petrov)*

Below: *Another ski-equipped I-16 Type 5 in Finland during early 1940, also from the 13 OIAE. The inscription in white proclaims 'Za Kommunizm!' ('For Communism!'). (Photo: G.Petrov)*

Right: *The port view of 'White 11' reveals the inscription (probably in white, noting the discolouration of the print), 'Za VKP(b)' ('For the VKP(b)'). The term 'VKP(b)' refers to the All-Union Communist Party (Bol'shevik). This aircraft has been updated with a later version of the RSI-3 radio, the aerial of which can be seen running to the starboard wing tip. The sliding canopy has been replaced by the later, fixed unit, but the telescopic sight was retained. (Photo: G.Petrov)*

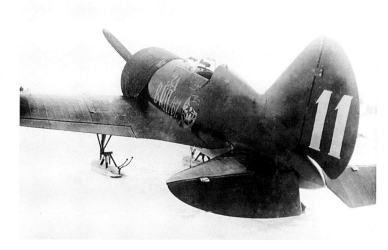

Below: *Another view of another example of the 13 OIAE's I-16 Type 5s in Finland, early 1940. The inscription on the starboard side reads 'Svobodu Ugnetennim!' ('Freedom to the Oppressed!'). (Photo: G.Petrov)*

Right: *Another I-16 (probably a Type 10) 'captured' in 1941. The colours are thought to be AII Green dapple over AEh-9 Grey. Note the interesting winged badge on the tail. (Photo: Author's collection)*

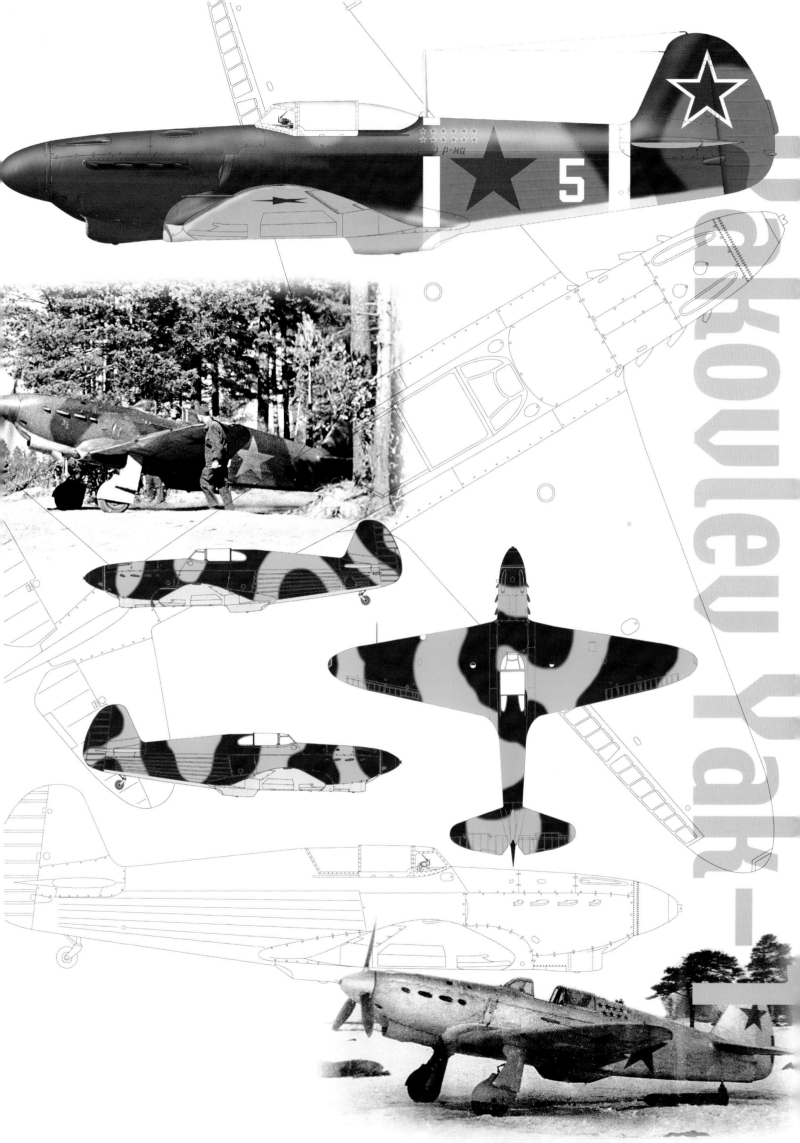

Chapter 6

Yakovlev Yak-1

When, on 13 January 1940, the shiny, maroon-coloured I-26 prototype first climbed into the air under the control of test pilot Yulian Piontkovski, few people could have guessed that the machine would stand at the head of a whole family of fighters, which taken together, marked the most extensive manufacturing and development programme in the history of such aircraft. With the production of nearly 37,000 units, constructed from the first day of Barbarossa to the final hours of the War and well beyond, the Yakovlev fighter passed through an extraordinary genealogical progression. Always, however, the basic lay-out and design of the I-26 family remained clear and unpolluted. Indeed, it was precisely this cleanliness of procession that made the series so formidable, never losing – as was the wont of nearly every other design of the period that was so developed – the essential characteristics that made it great: robust and reliable simplicity, beautiful handling, and superb manoeuvrability.

The I-26 can be said to have been derived from a series of light sport and trainer aircraft originating from Aleksandr Sergeievich Yakovlev. Yakovlev, working in Moscow, designed a series of elegant high-wing sport and utility monoplanes throughout the 1930s, the AIR - 1, -2, -3, -4, -5, and -6. These successful machines were followed by the AIR-14 low-wing monoplane trainer of 1936, which entered VVS service as the UT-1 trainer, followed by a two-seat development of the AIR-9 as the UT-2. The UT-1 was exceedingly popular throughout Soviet aviation, its handling qualities were superlative, while its manoeuvrability was equally impressive, and the type was flown as an aerobatic demonstration machine well into the 1950s.

Work on the AIR-14 project was formative and critical for Yakovlev, and elements of this fine machine could be seen in many of his OKB's later designs. The type's twin-spar, wooden wing and steel tube fabric-covered fuselage were Yakovlev trademarks, as was the extreme attention paid to excess weight in the design. Certainly, it was based upon his success with the UT-1 that Yakovlev fielded no fewer than four submissions to the 1938 Design Specification competition, more than any other entrant. In light of the fact that Yakovlev had no previous experience in fighter aircraft design – and indeed not even in combat aircraft design of any type – the selection of Yakovlev's I-26 proposal seems unusual. Moreover, no proper engineering documents or drawings were turned in by Yakovlev for the competition, and neither was any mock-up available for testing by TsAGI, inevitably giving rise to accusations of political influence and favouritism.

Whatever the truth, the reasons behind the selection of the I-26 as one of the winners of the competition were certainly more than these superficial considerations describe. Yakovlev was always possessed of a certain industrial genius; a capacity to understand how aircraft were produced, how factories operated, and how to navigate the Ministerial bureaucracy in Moscow. Probably better than any other Soviet designer, he understood the need to present to the NKAP a plan in which it could have the utmost confidence. The I-26 proposal fitted this need precisely, because all of the fundamental manufacturing methods and practices required were entirely conventional and well proven in prior Yakovlev designs. There would be no radical materials employed, as with the new wood-plastics in the LaGG programme, nor was the design contrived for unusual performance characteristics, as was the I-200. The I-26, rather, was a clever combination of proven technologies whose performance characteristics would depend on traditional design factors such as the need to keep weight and drag to a minimum, factors seen already to be a Yakovlev speciality.

With these factors in mind, the NKAP authorized the installation of the Yakovlev OKB team at the tiny *Zavod* 115 facility in Moscow in May 1939. Yakovlev was free to utilize the local factory staff in his development work, but as this numbered fewer than 200 employees the task of creating the first I-26 prototype within the allotted 12 months seemed unlikely. However, Yakovlev had drawn around himself a team of senior engineers of the very highest order – the likes of Senior Engineer K.V. Sinel'shikov, Senior Engineer E.G. Adler and Assistant Head Designer K.A. Vigant, to name just a few – and he was confident that not only could his Bureau meet the one year deadline, but in fact better it. In the industrialist's lively autobiography *Life Target*, the impression is given quite strongly that Yakovlev was pressed by Stalin to complete his I-26 prototype early, by the new year, and that he was forced to agree only begrudgingly, with the consequent difficulties faced by the staff in delivering the I-26 No.1. In fact, this view is completely inaccurate, and indeed, the truth is the opposite – it was Yakovlev, himself, who constantly promoted his fighter prototype and assured all comers that he would be finished by the beginning of 1940, ahead of his competition. The manifestations of this haste were soon to become evident.

With work on the new fighter already under way in Moscow, the UVVS determined that the I-26 was the most advanced of the 1938 design submission winners, and that as a result it would involve itself in crafting the specifications for the new fighter. The figures drawn up by the UVVS were remarkable, and quite challenging: based on the Klimov M-106 motor the aircraft was to attain 620 km/h at 5,640 m, have a ceiling over 10,670 m, and possess a range of 1,000 km. In addition, the second prototype (not yet even mentioned in the NKAP development contract) was to have revised supercharger gearing for improved high-altitude performance. These meddling influences weighed heavily on the OKB design staff, and were exacerbated by the Bureau Chief's incessantly optimistic claims about the speed of the project. To achieve such performance, the I-26 would have to be very light, and the matter of weight obsessed Sinel'shikov and Adler throughout the autumn.

However, by September 1939 it had become clear to all parties that Viktor Klimov's 12-cylinder upright Vee M-106 engine would never be ready for regular manufacture by 1940. As a result, the less advanced and less powerful M-105P (*pushenniy* or 'cannon') was selected for the prototype, this motor featured a hollow propeller hub to accept a weapon mounted between the cylinder banks. At this juncture one might conclude that the development programme would have had to drastically change direction, necessitating a considerable design revision of the I-26; but, such a course was expressly *not* in the plans of Aleksandr Yakovlev. Despite the considerable reduction in flying horsepower resulting from the switch to the M-105, Yakovlev still wanted to meet the challenging UVVS specifications to the fullest extent, while at the same time completing the prototype in the advertised time frame; i.e. three months early. To accomplish the impossible, as it were, Yakovlev seems to have convinced his staff to build two *different* prototypes. Although no documentation exists to confirm this, no other theory manages to explain the behaviour of the Yakovlev OKB staff during the following months – essentially, the first prototype was to be deliberately lightly-built, thus providing high-performance and serving as something of a promotional effort, while the No.2 machine would be finished to military strength and loading parameters.

The I-26 No.1 prototype was a classic Yakovlev OKB design. The wings were twin-spar dual-box structures with wooden spars and members of ten metre span, and featuring classic Clark Y-H section. The large ailerons were placed well outboard and were constructed of metal tubing with fabric covering, while the wing was covered with *shpon* laminate sheet, save for the split-type flaps which were of all dural manufacture. The first wing (for the No.1 prototype) was lightly built with 2.5 mm thick longerons, 8 mm *shpon* skinning over the wing leading edge section and 5 mm sheet aft, while simultaneously a second wing was constructed with 3 mm longerons and skinning increased to 9 mm and 8mm thickness, respectively. The Klimov engine was very tightly cowled, giving an extremely aerodynamic profile, while the forward fuselage and engine cowling panels were covered in dural sheet. The rear fuselage was a standard steel tube frame structure with wooden formers, fabric covering and a laminate turtledeck. The stabilizers and vertical fin were also wooden units covered in *shpon* sheeting, and, interestingly, the latter was not part of the fuselage structure, but rather bolted onto the fuselage tubing and flared in with a large fillet. Power was provided by the 1,050 hp (1,100 hp for take-off and emergency) M-105P driving a 2.8 m ViSH-52P airscrew, and the very small oil cooler was mounted under the engine just at the wing leading edge. The radiator bath was of the 'energy-transfer' (through-flow) type, and placed well aft, below the rear of the cockpit. Proposed armament for the I-26 No.1 was to have included a 20 mm ShVAK cannon firing through the spinner and four 7.62 mm ShKAS machine guns disposed around the nose. However, when the prototype was dispatched to the Moscow Central Aerodrome only the ShVAK cannon appears to have been installed, all other guns presumably being omitted due to weight concerns.

One intriguing aspect of the I-26's design development which has received scant attention hitherto, concerned the considerable attention to detail that was directed at the wing, the flying and control surfaces, and to the rudder, in order to produce a machine with excellent handling characteristics. Reams of documents exist within Yakovlev's surviving papers that refer to the extensive debates conducted between Yakovlev, Sinel'shikov, Vigant and Adler on these points during 1939. The rudder, in particular, was boldly inclined *forward* some 10 degrees, a feature considered unusual, and even radical, for its day. The AIR-14 (UTI-1) was fitted with a similar rudder design over the objections of much of the Yakovlev OKB staff, but which in the event, turned out to offer outstanding control characteristics, and as a result the I-26 was built similarly. An even more lengthy series of debates took place on the concept of fitting the wing leading edge with automatic slats (as the LaGG-3 and MiG-3 would later adopt), and the issue was not fully resolved when the prototype finally left the workshop floor. Indeed, Yakovlev's other 1938 design submissions (the I-28, and I-30) did include leading edge slats, and there is no evidence that these were omitted on the I-26 due to weight concerns.

With considerable haste the I-26 No.1 prototype was completed ahead of schedule – as Yakovlev advertised – on 27 December 1939. After roll-out the prototype was finished with a maroon-coloured lacquer known as VIAM-B3 which featured a very glossy finish. On the 30th, the machine was transported to the Moscow Central Aerodrome for factory evaluation. Static testing confirmed that the wing was very lightly-built, and indeed its loading capacity was determined to be 40 per cent less than required for the design weight of 2,300 kg, while the prototype in fact weighed in at 2,613 kg. Despite these concerns, Pilot-Engineer Yulian Piontkovsky took the machine up for the first time on 13 January 1940, the flight lasting some 15 min. Though experiencing difficulty with high engine temperatures (the temperature in the cockpit routinely exceeded 110 deg F), and some trouble on the second flight with raising and lowering of the landing gear, he was, nonetheless, most enthusiastic about the machine's flight and handling properties which were extremely pleasing. The No.1 prototype's lightly-built wing structure precluded some high-g testing,

but within the first month, Piontkovsky had already completed the majority of the aircraft's flight control evaluation. Predictably, performance in the No.1 prototype was breathtaking. Despite unending problems with the ViSH-52P propeller, the I-26 No.1 could reach 595 km/h at 5,000 m before the oil temperature became too great to continue acceleration, but climb performance was restricted by the same over-heating difficulties and this height could not be reached in less than 6.5 minutes.

Yakovlev, naturally, touted the flight performance of the new I-26 far and wide, claiming that his design had essentially met the UVVS requirements despite the introduction of the less powerful M-105 engine, and even *before* the I-200 prototype which had been initiated as something of a crash-programme to produce an immediate fighter. The Party apparatus and Bureaucracy took immediate notice of these successes, and Yakolev's personal stock in Moscow rose to an all-time high. Simultaneously, testing of the second prototype began with test flights commencing on 23 March, primarily under the control of Pilot-Engineer S.A. Korzinshchikov. The No.2 machine was completed with a number of improvements as suggested by testing of the first prototype. The wing structure was more robust, but still it did not meet the required loading specification for the design. More important were the changes made to the oil cooler and radiator bath, it being especially noted that the No.1 prototype's cooling properties were woefully inadequate. Various revisions were conducted on a trial-and-error basis, none being particularly effective. By the third week of testing the No.2 machine was fitted with an entirely new oil cooler of larger proportions, this moved ahead to a position below the spinner, and conferred on the aircraft its classic profile.

As tested on 11 April 1940, the No.2 prototype with the revised cooling structure weighed just over 2,700 kg. The VISh-52P propeller was discarded in favour of a more reliable VISh-61P unit, and it is not known if the No.2 carried any of the four ShKAS guns intended in the specification. The performance of the second machine is a source of some confusion, as Yakovlev refused to make any differentiation in his reports between figures taken from both prototypes, presumably to mask the fact that the machines were different in detail, and perhaps to chose the better of the scores for the test results. On 11 April, Korzinshchikov reached approximately 585 km/h in the No.2 prototype, and achieved 5,000 m in the excellent time of 5.2 minutes. Severe overheating continued to be a problem, and the motor had to be replaced in the second machine after Korzinshchikov's speed trials.

However, disaster struck the I-26 programme on 27 April when Piontkovsky crashed fatally in the No.1 prototype. The machine was seen to enter a flat spin mysteriously at low-altitude while banking and turning, before slamming immediately to the ground. Such disasters had not been experienced in either prototype thus far – on the contrary, the handling characteristics in a turn were extremely safe and forgiving – and considerable bewilderment beset the Yakovlev OKB. A not-so-minor crisis might have developed, centring around the need for leading-edge slats and the disposition of the rudder, had not Piontkovski's earlier and quite brilliant work proved beyond doubt that the aircraft's stalling characteristics were entirely laudable. As a result, the ensuing investigation concentrated on a potential mechanical failure as the cause, and soon the various failures of the landing gear were examined. Ultimately, the crash report determined that – unknown to the pilot – the gear might have lowered asymmetrically (as had happened more than once before), and precipitated a violent stall. During the crash investigation of the first prototype, the No.2 machine was returned to the factory workshop and refitted. A revised armament package was installed, this comprising only two ShKAS guns mounted above the engine, and retaining the 20 mm ShVAK firing through the cylinder banks. The oil cooler was revised internally with new ducting, and various minor changes were made to the hydraulic and fuel systems.

Meanwhile, and despite the crash of the I-26 No.1, the NKAP organized a committee to determine if mass production of the I-26 should commence at no less than three State Aviation Factories –

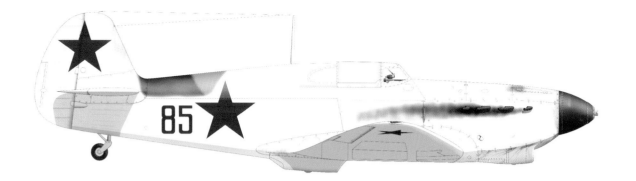

Yak-1 'Red 85'

158 IAP
Pilot unknown
Leningrad Front
Spring 1942

Colours:
MK-7 White over
AII Green/Black/Blue

Yak-1 'White 1'

183 IAP
Mikhail Baranov
1942

Colours:
AII Green/Black/Blue
application from *Zavod* 292

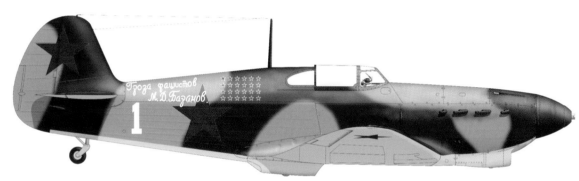

Yak-1 'Yellow 44'

586 IAP
Lidiya Litvyak
circa Summer 1942

Colours:
AII Green/Black/Blue
application from *Zavod* 292

Yak-1b 'White 5'

1 AE 'Mcch' Detachment
P.M. Ulvilev
August 1943

Colours:
AMT-4/-6/-7 unknown
application

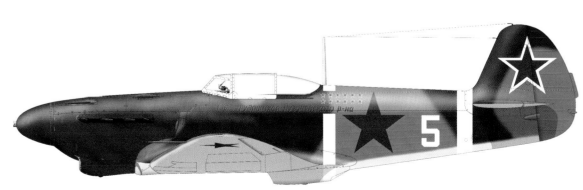

Moscow, Leningrad, and Saratov. Curiously, this NKAP Committee was led by none other than Yakovlev, who had been promoted to Deputy rank within the organization following his political ascent in January, 1940. Perhaps not surprisingly, the I-26 No.2 prototype was ordered to be handed over to the NII VVS for evaluation testing on 1 June 1940, following another month of factory-testing to iron out any remaining difficulties.

The I-26 revised No.2 prototype reached the NII VVS and commenced testing on the same day, the series continuing for two weeks until the 15th. Senior Pilot-Engineer Maksimov was assigned to the evaluation and performed most of the 52 test flights, most of which were conducted in a somewhat 'generous' light. Since engine cooling remained a major problem, the aircraft was taxied to its take-off position on most flights and then allowed to sit with the engine switched off to cool the oil and glycol temperatures, whereupon take-off would ensue (interestingly this type of 'pampering' of the engine was strictly not permitted on the I-301 prototype which was tested during the same month). Testing of the No.2 prototype did not reveal any unexpected performance characteristics. Handling and manoeuvrability were excellent, and Maksimov's report indicated that the I-26 would be comfortable for any VVS pilot of average flying abilities. Maximum speed was measured at 490 km/h at sea level and 585 km/h at 4,800 m, with the ceiling reaching 10,200 m. Control harmony was superlative throughout the speed range, and stick forces remained light and effective, while the initial climb figure was equally impressive at 1,055 m/min. and required only 5.6 minutes to reach 5,000 m. The test weight of the No.2 was given as 2,700 kg at take-off.

On the debit side, Maksimov did not conduct any of the high-g testing in the I-26 No.2 as planned, due to concerns with the structural strength of the wing. Yakovlev brushed aside these concerns, noting that the No.3 prototype was in the midst of construction, and that its wing had already been tested in excess of the design strength parameter. Furthermore, cooling problems with the M-105P continued to be a significant problem, and innumerable smaller difficulties were also listed, including failures of the hydraulic system, landing gear retraction mechanism and canopy framing, to name a few. Moreover, there was a complete absence of several pieces of equipment as specified in the NKAP submission documents, such as the radio, electric generator, and even certain flight instruments. As a result of these deficiencies, and despite the otherwise favourable report by Maksimov, NII Director Filin ruled that the I-26 had not successfully passed its State trials, much to the exception and discomfort of Yakovlev.

Despite this moderate setback, the charismatic Bureau Chief was not deterred. With the support and blessings of the Commissar of the Aircraft Industry A. Shakhurin, Yakovlev's three-man Committee had issued instructions for the manufacture of 25 pre-production I-26 fighters at the *Zavod* 301 facility in Moscow as early as May 1940. Despite the fact that these pre-series machines (eleven had been completed) were based on drawings of the No.1 prototype – complete with its lightly-built wings – Yakovlev moved the NKAP to accept all machines immediately and order them to Regimental service for field evaluations. The Yakovlev OKB staff was thrown into considerable panic over this order, and Engineers Sinel'shikov and Skrzhinskiy led a 'repair team' out to the *Zavod* 301 workshop to rebuild all of the aircraft's wings. Other sundry detail changes were undertaken, including installation of the updated No.2 type's oil cooler and radiator bath, landing gear arrangement, and armament. All 11 aircraft were test-flown and updated, the entire project running from July until August to complete.

At the same time the No.2 prototype was being rebuilt extensively, Yakovlev developed yet another design based on the I-26 airframe. Noting the type's outstanding flight characteristics, and Yakovlev's own experience in building flight-training aircraft, he sought to develop a version of the I-26 as an advanced trainer, particularly with a view to conversion-training for pilots moving from fixed-gear biplanes. The *Zavod* 115 workshops thus modified one of the semi-complete No.2 airframes as the UTI-26 trainer prototype. The cockpit was enlarged

aft to accommodate a second pilot, the entire compartment being covered in a long, attractive 'greenhouse'-type canopy with two sliding sections. The rear cockpit position was completed with a full set of flight and engine controls, and all armament was removed.

The UTI-26 took to the air on 23 July 1940, and it was immediately obvious that the handling of the machine was excellent. However, the NKAP had not requested a trainer variant of the I-26 from Yakovlev, and the results of the flight evaluation were reviewed with some surprise and scepticism. Despite this, Yakovlev lobbied for the type throughout Moscow, and soon the Government began to express an interest in the type. Development of the UTI concept thereafter, would take an interesting and complicated course and lead eventually to the Yak-7 programme.

Meanwhile, the heavily redesigned No.3 prototype had rolled off the workshop floor and entered factory-testing under the skilful leadership of Pilot-Engineer Korzinshchikov. The No.3 machine featured improved front and rear spars and introduced a new bonding compound for the laminate skin, all of the improvements adding a mere 7 kg to the total weight. These changes resulted in a wing that surpassed its strength design parameters, and even added superior torsional stiffness to that which had been calculated by Senior Engineer Adler. Many of the sundry systems had been updated, and improvements made to virtually every component on the I-26 No.3 airframe. Armament settled on the twin ShKAS and single ShVAK arrangement of the later No.2 prototype, but in the No.3 the ammunition complement for the 7.62 mm guns was increased to 650 rpg while the 20 mm magazine was expanded to contain 120 cartridges. A sheet of 8 mm steel plate was fitted behind the pilot's chair for protection, and an inert gas anti-fire system installed in the main fuel cells (as on the LaGG-3). Power was again provided by the Klimov M-105P driving a 3.0 m VISh-61P airscrew, but the radiator bath and oil cooler were of improved design, these the result of wind tunnel testing under the direction of Prof. Polinovski of the T-101 facility.

Factory-testing of the I-26 No.3 was eminently successful, and the prototype passed very quickly into the hands of the NII VVS on 13 October. The evaluation team was headed this time by no less a figure than Petr Stefanovski, and flights were completed by a pantheon of experienced pilots, including A.Kubyshkin, A.Proshakov, K.Gruzdev and A.Nikolaev. Stefanovski, in particular, flew the No.3 very hard, performing both positive and negative high-g manoeuvres, spins, and other aerobatics. All pilots reported that the flight and handling characteristics of the I-26 were outstanding, the machine almost refusing to enter a spin except under deliberate action. Performance in the No.3 was largely unchanged. Weighing 2,805 kg at take-off the third prototype could reach 492 km/h at sea level and 583 km/h at 4,800 m, with the ceiling reaching 10,200 m. Initial climb suffered under the extra weight – 1,007m/min was achieved – and the time to 5,000 m required 5.8 minutes. However, with the improved wing stiffness manoeuvrability at high speed was dramatically enhanced even over the satisfactory results in the No.2, and the extreme enthusiasm of the Institute pilots for the I-26 could hardly be concealed. Despite concerns on the part of Director Filin that the No.3 prototype still lacked a radio set, the machine passed its State trials with flying colours, and the evaluation ended successfully on the 27th.

With success in hand, the NKAP issued a sweeping Production Contract on 30 September 1940 for the I-26, to be produced under the designation Yak-1 in keeping with the new naming convention. Three factories were involved in the ambitious order, *Zavod* 301 at Moscow, *Zavod* 292 at Saratov, and *Zavod* 126 at Komsomol'sk. Of these, the Saratov plant was to be the primary facility for Yak-1 production, and Yakovlev was ordered to prepare to move his Bureau there upon notification from the NKAP. Indeed, parts and jigs from *Zavod* 301 had already arrived in Saratov, and the first three Yak-1s were assembled there as early as 3 October. At this juncture, however, Iosif Stalin decided to intervene personally in the matter and threw – as was his customary way – the entire aviation industry into confusion and disarray. In a baffling series of directives issued between October 1940 and January 1941, Stalin ordered *Zavod* 126 to undertake production of the DB-3 bomber to the exclusion of all else; *Zavod* 81 was instructed to produce Yak fighters instead. Then, in January, *Zavoda* 448 and 131 (Tbilisi and Kitais') were ordered to manufacture the new Yak-1, despite the fact that neither facility possessed the tools nor personnel necessary to even contemplate production of such an advanced design.

By January 1941, only *Zavod* 292 at Saratov was producing the Yak-1. Instructions to begin manufacture at *Zavod* 448 and *Zavod* 131 were pure fantasy and came to nothing. *Zavod* 301 in Moscow had become completely absorbed in the production of the LaGG-3 fighter, and under no circumstances could the staff there continue with the I-26 programme. Distraught, Yakovlev was ordered to move his Bureau to *Zavod* 292 during February, and during the same month *Zavod* 301 assembled the last of its Yak-1 components and manufacture of the type ceased at that facility. However, once installed at Saratov, Yakovlev regained his old form. He immediately set about a reorganization of the production lines with the assistance of the plant staff and Directorate, and exercised his good name far and wide to ensure the prompt supply of parts and sub-assemblies from the various suppliers and contractors. Within three months, *Zavod* 292 was bristling with activity, Yak-1 production rising from one aircraft per day to three per day by June 1941.

Just over 300 Yak-1s had been received into the inventory of the VVS before the fateful day of 22 June 1941. Many of these machines had been delivered to the 11 IAP from whence they were distributed to other units, the Regiment acted as a make-shift familiarization centre for the new fighter. A mere 61 Yak-1s were available on-hand for the invasion in the Western Districts, most of these operating with the 20 IAP at Karachev. The production Yak-1 of early 1941 was very similar to the I-26 No.3 prototype, both in detail and performance. Aircraft No. 04-06, was completed in February 1941, weighed 2,858 kg for take-off, could reach 480 km/h at sea level and 577 km/h at 4,950 m, climbed initially at 1,000 m/min and reached 5,000 m in 5.7 minutes. Some of the last Yak-1s assembled at *Zavod* 301 were fitted with new 130 round ammunition tanks for the 20 mm ShVAK.

From the outset of the invasion, though available in only limited numbers for operations against the *Luftwaffe*, the Yak-1 proved to be an outstanding dogfighter, capable of out-turning the Messerschmitt Bf 109; its rate of roll was superior, its stalling speed considerably lower, and, with a much lower wing loading, its sustained turning ability was vastly superior. Pilots found the control harmony to be excellent, and the Yak exhibited very docile stalling characteristics, inviting even an average pilot to push the fighter to its limits. On the debit side, however, it was slower than the Bf 109 F (especially the F-4), increasingly so at altitude. The German fighter could also outclimb the Yak, and possessed far better performance above 5,000 m. Once again, as a result, the tactical initiative lay most often with the German pilots, who could attack from height, and who could escape more readily. Furthermore, a number of pilots complained about the armament, which was seen to be too light. In particular, the 7.62 mm ShKAS was seen to be outdated and outgunned; though useful against lightly-built aircraft like the Bf 109, the rifle calibre rounds were no longer effective against the *Luftwaffe's* medium bombers that made up a significant element of the VVS's important targets.

A useful account of the performance of the early Yak-1 is demonstrated by the actions of the 158 IAP around Leningrad. On three separate occasions during the last week of June 1941, *Lt*. Valeriy Chirkov met small formations of He 111 bombers and in each case fired on two aircraft. Despite Chirkov's excellent marksmanship only a single bomber could be downed each time, leaving but a few rounds with which to damage the second Heinkel. David Dzhabidze was able to down several Bf 109s with his Yak during June-August, but required the assistance of *Sr.Lt* Pokrishev to down a single Junkers Ju 88. In each case, the pilots spoke highly of the Yak-1's manoeuvrability, handling, and aiming capabilities – not to mention the armour plating that saved Chirkov's life – but criticized the armament as "insufficient" and recommended the immediate abandonment of the ShKAS guns.

As production of the Yak-1 began to acquire momentum throughout the latter half of 1941, so did the importance of the type grow amongst front line units facing the German onslaught. Indeed, just when many of the other fighter production programmes were facing dislocation and turmoil due to the evacuation of their respective factories, halting deliveries of fighters, *Zavod* 292 was already safely to the rear at Saratov and no evacuation was necessary. As a result of these conditions, the proportion of Yak-1 fighters in the VVS inventory rose from a mere two per cent of the operational fighter strength in July 1941 to eight per cent by December, and 12 per cent by the following February.

The Army had been demanding a version armed with the RS-82 rocket from the outset, though the NKAP did not include this specification in any of the initial contracts. At last, during the autumn of 1941, manufacture of a Yak-1 with six RO82 rails got into stride. At one point, the Saratov factory was ordered to produce all Yak fighters with six rocket rails, but the *Zavod* 292 production records indicate that it did not, and versions with and without rails were manufactured. However, so unpopular was this installation with many front line pilots, that the Yakovlev Bureau issued kits to field units to enable the rails to be removed easily. Judging by the photographic record, these kits must have been used to great effect as the number of Yak-1s operating with rocket rails attached during this period was very much less than the number of such variants produced. Complaints resulted from the weight and drag penalties caused by the RO82 rails and the six rockets. A typical Yak-1 from the winter of 1941 with six rocket rails could achieve only 444 km/h at sea level and 533 km/h at 4,950 m, climbing initially at 846 m/min and required 6.8 minutes to reach 5000 m.

Not being forced to evacuate to the east, development at Saratov was able to continue during the latter months of 1941, and a suitably winterized Yak-1 was able to reach series manufacture during the winter of 1941-42. As early as August, instructions were issued for a Yak-1 variant with ski undercarriage. Airframe No.38-55 was rebuilt in the *Zavod* 292 workshop primarily under the direction of Senior Engineer Grigorev, ski units very similar to those originally mounted on the I-26-1 prototype being utilized. The main units were 1.65 m long and 0.65 m wide and were attached to the oleo struts via a simple V-shaped strut. When retracted the ski units fitted semi-flush with the bottom wing surface, though the rear tailwheel-mounted ski could not retract. Other winterizations were also added to this variant, including a petrol oil dilution mechanism, new coolant, and other sundry changes. Testing with the ski undercarriage commenced at both the LII and NII VVS during November, the entire apparatus found to be satisfactory even for novice pilots, no mentionable change occurring to the Yak's handling characteristics. Naturally, there was a consequent loss in performance, the NII VVS recorded the figures of 441 km/h at sea level and 533 km/h at 4,950 m, and a time to 5,000 m of 6.3 minutes. Furthermore, some of the winterized Yak-1s were also completed with six RO82 rocket rails; performance in these versions is not recorded, but must have suffered accordingly.

By the start of 1942, Yak-1 production at Saratov was in full gear, and models with standardized features and performance were pouring out of the factory at a rate of 8-9 per day. The standard Yak-1 for the new year (known at the factory as the '*massoviy*', or 'standard') featured a new look. In order to reduce the demands on Soviet Perspex production, the clear canopy section aft of the sliding main unit was replaced by extending the fuselage turtledecking up to the rear of the sliding unit. Two roughly half-round windows were installed on either side of the turtledeck just behind the sliding canopy for rearward visibility. At the same time the extended 8 mm armoured seat headrest (as on the LaGG-3) was replaced by a normal pilot seat, rearward armour protection being provided by a sheet of 55 mm armoured glass behind the pilot's head. This arrangement was far more popular with Soviet pilots, and was said to improve visibility rearward even despite the new turtledecking. Other smaller improvements were incorporated, including an engine oil drainage tray, a rudder trim tab, improved landing light, and provision for an RSI-4 radio.

Meanwhile within the Yakovlev OKB, development of the Yak-1 fighter continued. Much attention was given to a thorough review of the airframe with an eye to reducing the Yak-1s overall weight. The superb trio of Senior Engineers Sinel'shikov, Adler and Vigant were to toil remorselessly over the next two years on the problems of improving the aircraft's aerodynamic profile and simultaneously introducing weight savings. By 1942 the improved M-105PA motor had become standard in series production, and the matter of aircraft armament was being studied at length by Engineers Barsukov and Sidel'nikov. The new year promised much at the Saratov factory.

The standard production Yak-1 for the first half of 1942 demonstrated much improved quality-control uniformity and fit. A typical Yak-1 of this period weighed 2,883 kg at take-off, was armed with two 7.62 mm ShKAS above the engine and a 20 mm ShVAK cannon through the spinner, and had provision for two bomb racks under the wings to accommodate up to two 100 kg bombs. Maximum speed reached 478 km/h at sea level and 563 km/h at 4,850 m, it could climb initially at the useful rate of 1,037m/min. and achieve 5,000 m in 5.9 minutes, with the service ceiling also being improved to 10,625 m.

The summer of 1942 brought an explosion of improvements in the Yak-1 programme. The first of these were carefully executed weight savings masterminded by Sinel'shikov and Adler. After an excruciating analysis of the Yak's structure, several airframes from the 60th production series were rebuilt to a lightened standard. Some of these aircraft were completed especially for the PVO forces at Moscow, and many of these examples had their armament reduced to a single ShVAK firing through the spinner with 150 rounds to save weight. However, No. 33-60 was a completely re-built example, this incorporating the standard armament and equipment fit, but with all of the weight-savings developed by the OKB. The wing main spars had been reduced in weight, as had the rear empennage (in addition to several small and sundry items), all without any reduction in structural strength, resulting in savings of 162 kg in all.

At the very same moment, however, supplies of Klimov's new and improved M-105PF ('Boosted') motor began to arrive at Saratov. The M-105PF engine featured higher compression than the earlier M-105s and revised supercharger gearing, and could produce 1,180 hp (1,260 hp for take-off and emergency). The supercharger engagement altitudes were lowered for both stages to 700 m and 2700 m respectively, it being acknowledged at last that for the Yak-1 low- and medium-altitude performance was paramount. NII VVS testing of the M-105PF-powered Yak-1 was deemed unnecessary, and the NKAP ordered Yakovlev to produce M-105PF powered versions of the Yak-1 as engines of the type became available, with an eye to phasing out the use of the –PA motor by late summer. The first –PF Yaks left the *Zavod* 292 lines in June 1942, and their performance was significantly improved. With the standard 1942 airframe, the Yak-1 M-105PF could reach 510 km/h at sea level and 571 km/h at 3650 m, and could attain 5,000 m in six minutes, but climbing initially at the much improved rate of 1,072 m/min.

As production of the M-105PF-powered Yak-1 got into stride, the weight-savings developed by Sinel'shikov and Adler were now ordered to be incorporated into production as well. Based on the work done with aircraft No. 33-60, drawings were prepared for all of the new spar and fuselage pieces, and modified jigs deployed on some of the production lines. Starting with example No. 45-96 the lightened airframe entered production with the M-105PF motor, this variant having a finished all-up weight of 2,780 kg at take-off (i.e. 137 kg less than the standard M-105PF model). Powered by the same M-105PF motor, the new *Oblegchenniy* ('lightened') model was formidable. Maximum speed in the Yak-1(*Obl.*) shot upwards to 526 km/h at sea level and 592 km/h at 3,800 m, with the initial climb reaching 1,133 m/min. and attaining 5,000 m in the astonishing time of 4.7 minutes. The equipment and armament fit remained unchanged.

VVS front line pilots were thrilled by the new M-105PF-powered Yak-1s, and especially by the *Oblegchenniy*. By September 1941, the Yak-1 PF models began to appear in strength on the Stalingrad Front, and played a major role in the defeat of the *Luftwaffe* over that sector. The Yak-1 was now equal or superior to its *Luftwaffe* rivals in the climb below 4,268 m, and demonstrated even better manoeuvrability. In

addition, the –PF motor had done much to redress the speed imbalance between the Yak and its adversaries at low-medium altitude where the majority of combat was taking place, though at higher levels it was still slower. The result was a rude shock to German pilots on the Eastern Front, who found themselves out-flown by a far more nimble opponent, having to rely on speed and altitude to effect any sort of advantage whatsoever. Worse still, the Germans could not distinguish between different versions of the Yak-1, and so they were never certain what kind of performance to expect when they engaged these machines in combat; a situation similar to differentiating between the Spitfire Mark V and Mark IX.

Even more dramatically, the Yak-1(*Obl.*) began to reach the Stalingrad Front during November in service with the 512 IAP of *May*. Gerasimov. At once the Regiment met with resounding success in the *Oblegchenniy*; indeed, pilots *Lt.* V.Makarov and *Kpt.* I.Motorniy even destroyed a Messerschmitt apiece during their ferry flights to the unit's airfield. By the start of 1943, the 512 IAP success rate had risen from one loss for every 2.5 victories (1:2.5) to a ratio of 1:6.5, and victories accrued at three times the rate seen previously, all while engaged in some of the most vicious aerial fighting of the War, and against some of the most battle-hardened *Luftwaffe* fighter units. The crowning achievement of the 512 IAP's struggle over Stalingrad occurred on 17 January 1943 when eight Yak-1s led by Makarov encountered 21 Bf 109 G-2s over Pitomnik airfield. The Soviet pilots in their *Oblegchenniy* Yaks flew rings around the German fighters, destroying nine without loss, Makarov claiming two. The Bf 109 G and F were outperformed on all counts by the lightened Yak-1 below 5,000 m, even in vertical manoeuvres, which had hitherto been a staple of the Messerschmitt's combat repertoire. The *Jagdwaffe's* willingness to engage in combat at lower altitudes after Stalingrad would ebb continuously for the remainder of the War.

Innovations in the Yak-1 programme over the second half of 1942, however, were still not exhausted. Even as the M-105PF and *Oblegchenniy* variants were entering production, the work of Adler, Sinel'shikov, and Vigant was reaching new ground. Aircraft No.35-60 was rebuilt in the Saratov workshops at first with improvements suggested by TsAGI, but subsequently revised again by removing the turtledecking aft of the cockpit and installing a rounded clear canopy rear section. The origin of this modification is the stuff of many colourful stories throughout Soviet aviation history, many of which are apocryphal indeed. The modification is often attributed to the work of *May*. Shinkarenko and his 42 IAP, who performed similar modifications on his initiative to their Yak-7B fighters, but this claim does stand up to examination. In fact, Yakovlev's OKB had already examined the idea of a cut-down rear fuselage, not only on one variant of the I-30 submission of 1938, but also Yak-1 No.10-47 had been built with exactly this type of modification before the end of 1941, and was subsequently tested by TsAGI under the direction of Prof. Polinovski.

But Polinovski's typically inspired testing had resulted in many more aerodynamic improvements on No. 10-47. The radiator bath's interior structure was completely redesigned, resulting not only in improved cooling but also in greatly reduced drag. The oil cooler intake was similarly modified, and all manner of local airflow disturbances were rectified under wind tunnel test. In addition, the supercharger's air intake was relocated to a position in the port wingroot, improving its function and allowing for a shallowing of the oil cooler housing. These improvements were all built into No. 35-60, in addition to the lightening modifications of the *Oblegchenniy* Yak-1.

After completion and factory testing No. 35-60, known to the Yak OKB staff as the 'Yak-1 *s uluchshennoy aerodinamikoy* ('with improved aerodynamics'), was returned to the Moscow PVO for evaluation in June 1942. Despite being powered by the M-105PA motor, performance in the redesigned Yak proved exhilarating, and a maximum speed of 606 km/h was routinely achieved. All aspects of the fighter's characteristics were improved, including a smaller turning circle and higher rate of climb. PVO pilots were literally queuing to fly the machine, and Yakovlev returned to Moscow in July to bathe in these glowing reports. Back at Saratov, further detailed improvements were being worked out, some 70 minor changes in all, including a plan to improve aileron response by increasing the gap between the wing and the control surface from 6 mm to 7 mm. Furthermore, a new armament scheme had at last been agreed along the lines of the emerging Yak-9 fighter, this comprising a single 12.7 mm UBS gun above the engine to port with 200 cartridges and retaining the ShVAK firing through the spinner with 120 rounds.

Back in Moscow, Yakovlev's three-man NKAP Committee ordered *Zavod* 292 at Saratov to immediately construct 10 pre-production machines 'based on the 35-60 aircraft', and on 11 August the NKAP issued a Production Contract for the new Yak-1 incorporating all of the recommendations of TsAGI and the OKB staff and powered by the M-105PF motor. All aerodynamic modifications were to be finalized by the 99th Series (though many of the preceding machines from September and October were similar to the new specification), while all of the sundry internal and external modifications were to be standard by the 110th Series (from December). The new standard received no special nomenclature in the Production Contract, simply being referred to as the 'Yak-1 *s uluchshenniy obzorom, bronirovaniem i voorzheniem*' ('with improved vision, armour and armament'). The reference to improved armour resulted from the installation of a wider armoured seat back and a slightly repositioned armoured glass installation aft, now angled directly behind the pilot's head, in addition to a flat panel of 55 mm armoured glass in front of the pilot.

The new Yak-1 variant began to leave the facility at the end of November from at least one of the production lines, the remainder following suit quickly. The new fighter weighed 2,884 kg at take-off and could reach 531 km/h at sea level and 592 km/h at 4,100 m. The initial climb was outstanding at 1,113 m/min., but the time to reach 5,000 m rose to 5.2 minutes as a result of the increase in overall weight (mainly due to the extra armour protection). Aileron response was improved over the 'lightened' models, and directional stability remained outstanding despite the loss of vertical surface area to the cut-down fuselage. The bomb storage racks under the wings were modified to allow the fitting of 100 litre drop tanks and provision was made for an installation kit for six RO82 rocket rails.

So numerous were the changes to the new variant that field units and maintenance personnel quickly adopted the designation 'Yak-1B' to distinguish the improved fighter. The name came into widespread use in these circles, but the aircraft's official designation never changed, and factory staff never referred to the new Yak in this way. Despite the disagreement on a naming convention, however, all parties were united in their belief that the new Yak-1 fighter represented a major advance over previous models. The new Yak-1s were received in the field with great enthusiasm, the first of these entering combat with the 32 GIAP on the Kalininskiy Front, and with the 176 IAP at Stalingrad in early January 1943. During January alone, the 58 Yak-1Bs of the 176 IAP completed 669 sorties and destroyed 38 enemy aircraft confirmed for the loss of six Yaks and one pilot.

As the number of new Yak-1s swelled over the various Fronts, so too did Soviet mastery of the skies. Yak-1Bs were instrumental in the defeat of the *Luftwaffe* over the Kuban bridgehead with the 812 and 236 IAPs, in particular. The actions of 7 May 1943 were particularly noteworthy for the 236 IAP, during which day of furious combats a total of 22 Yak-1s faced no fewer than 122 enemy aircraft, destroying 13 without loss. The 812 IAP recorded 78 confirmed victories (including 56 Bf 109s, mostly from JG 52) during April-June in 462 encounters, losing 25 Yaks and 18 pilots. On the Baltic Front, the 3 GIAP-KBF began to rout the Finnish air units in their sector with their new Yak-1s so badly, that enemy aerial activity came to a halt in their area for months. Finishing the War with a mix of La-5 and Yak-1 fighters, the unit ended as the top-scoring Naval IAP of the entire conflict.

At the Battle of Kursk in July 1943, the new Yak-1 was prevalent throughout the VVS frontal units. Stories of Yak-1 triumphs over this monumental theatre are legion, and only a few will suffice to deliver the flavour of the impact of the new fighter. On 9 July 14 Yak-1s of the

270 IAP under the leadership of *May*. Merkushev were escorting Il-2s over the battlefield when they were intercepted by at least 16 enemy fighters, both Fw 190s and Bf 109s. Leaving four Yaks to defend the *Shturmoviki*, Merkushev led ten of his fighters into the midst of the attacking Germans, destroying four and routing the survivors without loss. Two days later, nine Yak-1Bs led by *Kpt*. Chuvalev attacked two huge formations of Ju 88s plus their escort of more than 30 Fw 190s and Bf 109s, destroying seven Ju 88s and two Bf 109s for the loss of one aircraft. Finally, on 15 August eight Yak-1s of the 236 IAP intercepted 60 bombers and their escort of 20 Messerschmitts above Akhtirka. Diving from the sun with complete surprise, the pilots of the 236 IAP destroyed nine aircraft (five Ju 88s and four Bf 109s) and routed the entire formation, *M.Lt* Tikhonov scoring a 'triple'.

Throughout 1942 there had been numerous experimental versions of the Yak-1 fitted with increasingly powerful Klimov engine prototypes. Amongst these were successive versions of the M-106, which, ironically, was to have been the intended power plant for the I-26 some three years before. By the end of 1942 the M-106 was *still* not sufficiently developed for mass production, but despite this the promise of its increased power output and compression caused the Yak OKB to build yet another M-106 powered prototype. The new machine was based on the improved 'Yak-1b' type airframe (No. 32-99), and the virtually unaltered external dimensions of the M-106P allowed the motor to fit within a standard cowling arrangement, though the armament above the engine was removed to make room for various sundry items.

The first flight of No.32-99 M-106 prototype took place on 12 December, and at once the unfortunate engine gave trouble. Overheating was endemic, and sometimes catastrophic, and virtually every test flight had to be cut short due to the imminent failure of the motor. However, as predicted, performance with the more powerful engine, 610 km/h being achieved at 3,750 m and the initial climb figure rose to the outstanding mark of 1,142 m/min. Noting that the Yak-1's radiator was clearly inadequate to cool the M-106, the prototype was shipped by rail to Novosibirsk to be fitted with a Yak-7-type radiator for further evaluation. Once at Novosibirsk, the plant staff decided upon a more ambitious re-design of the M-106 prototype making use of ideas emerging on the new Yak-9 fighter. The wing spars on No.35-99 were replaced by metal units as on the Yak-9, though the ten metre span and rounded wingtips were not changed. A Yak-9-type radiator was fitted beneath the cockpit as with that fighter's usual placement, and a Yak-7 type metal fin and stabilizer were installed in place of the wooden units. A single UBS gun was also added above the engine, whose installation was improved and rationalized.

Highly re-built, the Yak-1 M-106P was completed during January 1943. Pilot-Engineer A.Kokin led the flight evaluation series, with several pilots from the LII joining later in the month. At last, the larger radiator tamed the cooling problems which had dogged the machine hitherto, but the all-up increased weight of the rebuilt prototype erased many of the performance gains that had been realized in the earlier version. Maximum speed remained unchanged, however, 608 km/h still being possible in the new example, and perhaps as a result of this figure some considerable enthusiasm was shown for the project. Yakovlev's three-man NKAP Committee ordered 47 pre-series machines to be completed at Saratov based on the re-built example, and work began on these machines in February.

However, all such enthusiasm was misplaced, for the M-106 motor very quickly revealed itself a lost cause. Many defects and failures beset the engine, and never did it manage to pass even a 25 hr. static test course, let alone the required 100 hr. examination that was mandatory for any service motor. By April, Yakovlev had at last abandoned the idea of a Yak-1 M-106 series, and many of the pre-series machines ordered by the NKAP committee were, in fact, completed as specialized high-altitude aircraft for use by the PVO around Moscow, a good portion of which were powered by the M-105PF.

With the search for more flying horsepower seemingly at an impasse, attention at the OKB turned to an aerodynamic solution for increased performance. During October and November 1942, Senior Engineer Grigor'ev and Assistant Head Designer Vigant released a joint theoretical paper on various matters relating to the Yak-1's wing. In particular, they cited the data from a series of tests conducted at the T-103 wind-tunnel facility in Moscow under the guidance of Prof. Polinovski of Moscow State University. With a view to provide for heavier armament and other stores, the Bureau had been contemplating larger, metal spar and even all-metal wings (as with the I-28 and I-30) for the programme, but in the joint thesis Grigor'ev suggested – on the basis of these data – that a *smaller* wing might provide for both decreased weight and improved payload. The idea was extremely radical, but the wind-tunnel data seemed irrefutable, and after a great deal of debate Yakovlev authorized work in this direction.

What followed was one of the most thorough and remarkable structural analyses ever conducted in military aviation, the results of which could not possibly have been imagined at the time. The resulting design was the diminutive Yak-1M prototype, which, along with its cousin the Yak-1M *dubler*, led to the creation of the legendary

Yak-3 fighter within a single year. The transformation was extraordinary, and it marked the end of development of the trusty Yak-1; all efforts at Saratov now would concentrate on the Yak-3.

Production of the Yak-1 continued virtually unchanged until July 1944, when the last machine of this type rolled off the Saratov floor. In all, some 8,670 Yak-1s of all types were manufactured over four years of endeavour, comprising 192 series and seven major Production Contracts. Yak-1s served in frontal units from the first day of the War until the last, acquitting themselves wonderfully over a long and difficult passage. Always a pilot's aircraft, the Yak-1 was a classic dog-fighter in the traditional sense, besting its opponents by virtue of its superb handling and manoeuvrability. It was rugged and forgiving, especially of a novice's heavy hand, and well protected. And above all, it is interesting (and the highest tribute of all to the design) that in an environment where its opponents were powered by engines of 1,700 or even 2,000 horsepower that the Yak-1 remained competitive even with its old and reliable 1,180 hp Klimov V-12. It was superior design, and not raw power, that highlighted the family of the I-26 fighter of the Yakovlev OKB.

	Yak-1 1940-41	Yak-1 1941	Yak-1 1941 with rocket rails	Yak-1 1941 with skis	Yak-1 1942 *massoviy*	Yak-1 1942 M-105PF
Weights						
Empty:	2370 kg	2400 kg	2434 kg	2409 kg	2399 kg	2400 kg
Loaded:	2864 kg	2882 kg	2923 kg	2921 kg	2889 kg	2906 kg
Wing Area:	17.16 m.sq.	17.16 m.sq	17.16 m.sq	17.16 m.sq	17.16 m.sq	17.16 m.sq
Engine	M-105P	M-105PA	M-105PA	M-105PA	M-105PA	M-105PF
	1050 (1100) hp	1050 (1100) hp	1050 (1150) hp	1050 (1150) hp	1050 (1150) hp	1180 (1260) hp
Maximum Speed						
At Altitude:	577 km/h at 4950 m	561 km/h at 4800 m	534 km/h at 4950 m	534 km/h at 4950 m	565 km/h at 4850 m	573 km/h at 3800 m
Sea Level:	481 km/h	469 km/h	445 km/h	442 km/h	479 km/h	511 km/h
Climb						
Initial:	1000 m/min	918 m/min	881 m/min	915 m/min	1037 m/min	1072 m/min
Time to Height:	5.7 min to 5000 m	6.3 min to 5000 m	6.8 min to 5000 m	6.3 min to 5000 m	5.9 min to 5000 m	6.0 min to 5000 m
Service Ceiling	9300 m	9900 m	9900 m	9900 m	10635 m	11000 m
Armament	2 x ShKAS	2 x ShKAS	2 x ShKAS	2 x ShKAS	2 x ShKAS	2 x ShKAS
	1 x ShVAK	1 x ShVAK	1 x ShVAK	1 x ShVAK	1 x ShVAK	1 x ShVAK
			6 x RS-82			

	Yak-1(*Obl.*) 1942 M-105PF	Yak-1 1943 ('Yak-1b')
Weights		
Empty:	2355 kg	2361 kg
Loaded:	2785 kg	2890 kg
Wing Area:	17.16 m.sq	17.16 m.sq
Engine	M-105PF	M-105PF
	1,180 (1260) hp	1,180 (1260) hp
Maximum Speed		
At Altitude:	594 km/h at 3800 m	593 km/h at 3800 m
Sea Level:	527 km/h	532 km/h
Climb		
Initial:	1133 m/min	1113 m/min
Time to Height:	4.7 min to 5000 m	5.2 min to 5000 m
Service Ceiling	11400 m	11000 m
Armament	2 x ShKAS	1 x UBS
	1 x ShVAK	1 x ShVAK

**Yak-1
early manufacture
(Saratov)**

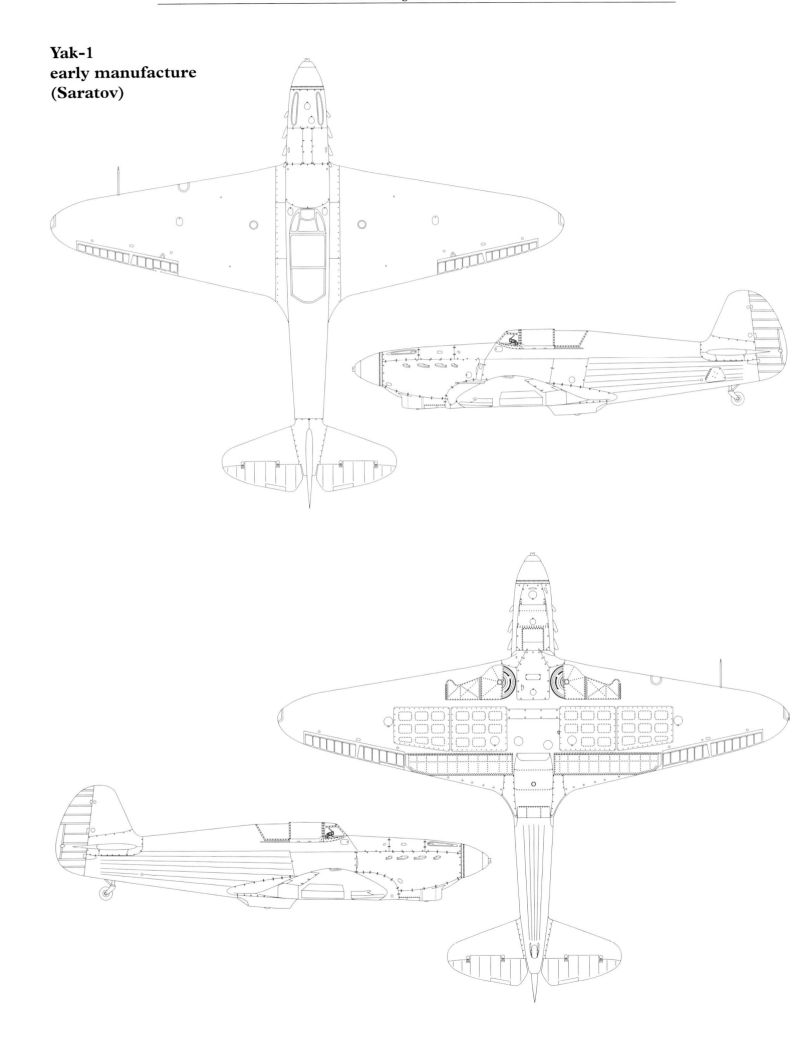

**Yak-1
standard production**

**Yak-1
1943 production
("Yak-1B")**

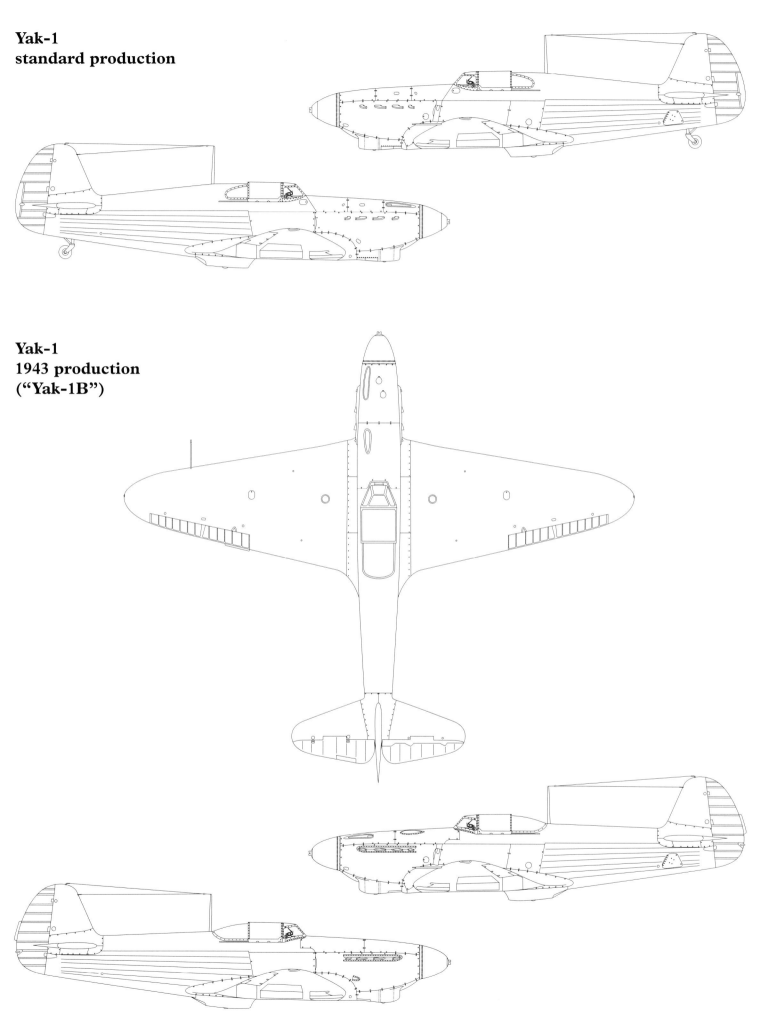

THE DEVELOPMENT OF CAMOUFLAGE ON
THE Yak-1 FIGHTER

The Early Series

The instigation of series production of the Yak-1 fighter at *Zavod* 301, Moscow, in October 1940 was not at first attended by large quantities of aircraft. This fact was somewhat by design, in fact, as the Production Contract for the programme had intended to centralize Yak-1 production at the large Saratov factory – *Zavod* 292 – which was soon to be the new home of the Yakovlev Design Bureau. Only small quantities, for example, the Series 1 comprised only 19 examples, began to roll off the lines at Moscow, these serving as patterns for series manufacture at Saratov, which got under way properly in October/November. Aircraft manufactured at *Zavod* 301 were distinctive – in reality they were pre-production examples – featuring different forward cowling details from Saratov-built examples, but both were largely similar in colour finish. These early aircraft demonstrated a unique 'angular' camouflage pattern somewhat out of character for Soviet finish. The scheme consisted of AII Black applied over AII Green with AII Blue undersurfaces, the colour demarcation lines in all cases tending to be quite sharp (see Fig. 1).

Fig. 1

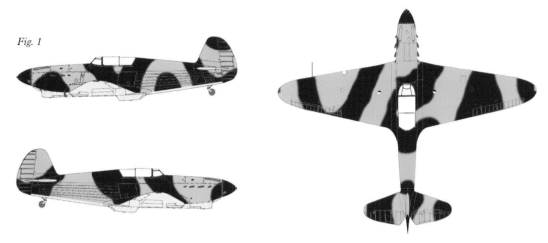

The interior colour application on all early manufacture Yaks appeared to vary considerably. Metal Use Primer (of the earlier 'bright' variety) was commonly found over all of the metal or steel interior surfaces, such as tubular framing, armour plate, etc., while the internal fabric surfaces were not typically painted over, but rather coated with clear 17-A dope. The wooden areas in the cockpit appear to have been variously unpainted or covered in Wood Finishes. Interiors covered in either finish entirely were not uncommon, as were examples that were not painted at all.

The interior wheel well structure was often finished in underside AII Blue, as were the struts, wheels, and oleo scissors. Examples are known that seem to have these bays painted black, but this was certainly not the usual treatment. The spinner was often finished in AII Black at this time, as were, usually, the propeller blades; polished and unpainted examples of both, however, were not unknown.

Mass-Production Begins

During the first days of 1941, production of the Yak-1 in Moscow came to a halt as large-scale manufacture of the type at last got into its stride at Saratov. Some of the very earliest examples from the *Zavod* 292 were completed in an extremely abbreviated scheme which presented a mystery for many years. Several photos of the type have emerged, and what they show is odd, to say the least (see Fig. 2).

Fig. 2

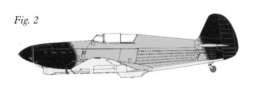

The finish was usual in consisting of AII Black over Green, but the colour demarcations were very loose indeed, as if the Black areas were applied as an afterthought. Similarly, the upper surfaces were sprayed as two simple wide bands, essentially with no significant attempt at a pattern.

During the Spring of 1941, a new and more 'typical' irregular-type pattern emerged on the Yak-1, still completed in AII Black over Green, even though examples of the earlier, angular pattern persisted into the late autumn (see Fig. 3).

Fig. 3

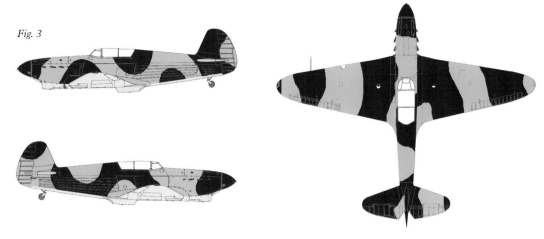

Left: *The Yak-1 of Naval ace Hero of the Soviet Union Mikhail Avdeev of the 8 IAP VVS ChF in 1942. His Yak wears the 'Great Meander' scheme in AII Black/Green and was numbered '5'. The photograph shows clearly the details of an early manufacture Yak-1 (note the rear canopy section and lack of a radio aerial). (Photo: G.Petrov)*

Above: *These Yak-1s are of a much later Series than Avdeev's machine, but nonetheless wear the 'Great Meander' scheme. The fact that this pattern was still in use by the time of these aircraft testifies to the application's popularity. (Photo: G.Petrov)*

Variations of this application were common, but most of these were obviously related to the master 'theme'. Furthermore, though the colour demarcation lines on the uppersurfaces tended to remain sharp, some semi-soft demarcation schemes of this type can be found in the photographic record, and the author has seen one photographic example that was very 'loosely' sprayed. This scheme has become known as the 'Great Meander' pattern. At *Zavod* 292 a variant of this application was developed, known as the 'Symmetrical Meander', wherein the fuselage pattern was not 'continued' across the top of the spine, but rather applied to each fuselage half (mostly) symmetrically. The Symmetrical Meander would go on to become one of the most significant camouflage applications of the GPW.

New Patterns

Beginning in the autumn of 1941, an entirely new pattern application began to join the earlier schemes, though by no means was it the most common Yak-1 camouflage. I have come to call this famous pattern the 'Snake' theme (on account of the meandering, wavy, port-side features), though undoubtedly it is well-known to some by other nicknames (see Fig. 4).

Fig. 4

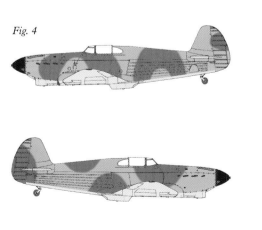

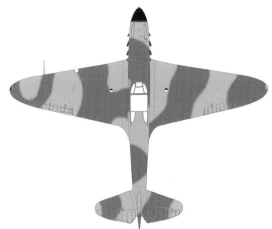

Above: A classic AII Dark Green/Green 'Snake' theme adorns this Naval Yak-1 of the 21 IAP VVS KBF from 1942. This machine, 'White 3', is thought to belong to Pavel Pavlov. (Photo: G.Petrov)

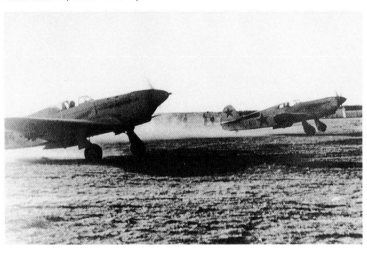

Above:
These Yak-1s were photographed during the spring of 1942 and have been variously identified as belonging to both the 42 IAP and 158 IAP. The background terrain seems to support the latter claim, as it does look like the Leningrad Front. Of interest is the unusual manner in which part of the underlying temperate camouflage has been deliberately exposed on the fuselage spine of 'Red 85'. (Photo: G.Petrov)

There are a number of very familiar characteristics in this 'theme' when compared to earlier patterns, though a good deal of refinement is also evident. This application was somewhat popular at *Zavod* 292, not simply for its visual appeal, but in that it was claimed to be easier to apply than previous schemes, and represented time-saving as a result. The 'Snake' application was often finished in AII Black and Green, though later examples using both AII Greens were also known (as illustrated).

Throughout the Winter of 1941-42 the standard winter camouflage scheme was a water-based distemper of MK-7 White applied over the summer scheme. Considerable weathering was often seen on this coating within a very short time, and various areas of the White finish were deliberately removed to form an adhoc camouflage (see Fig. 5).

Fig. 5

Above:
A very professionally winter-camouflaged Yak-1 on the Leningrad Front during the winter of 1941-42. Some authors have identified this aircraft as belonging to the 247 IAP, but no definitive evidence is yet available. Note the nine victory markings on the fuselage side. (Photo: G.Petrov)

New Yak-1 Variants

By the end of 1941, several new Yak-1 variants began to emerge from *Zavod* 292 at Saratov. These were clearly identifiable externally by the replacement of the rear canopy green-house section with a built-up turtledeck housing featuring two half-round windows. Initially, many of these machines continued to carry the 'Snake' theme, but a modification of this pattern quickly emerged by the New Year sporting some interesting features (see Fig. 6).

Fig. 6

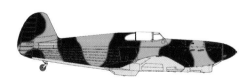

The most immediate differences aside from the more 'open' pattern, were the new common semi-soft colour demarcation lines for all upper surfaces. Indeed, hard-edged demarcations became increasingly rare, and would disappear for the most part during 1942. This theme appears to have been a clear development of the 'Great Meander' pattern in some respects, though it is highly refined and rationalized in application. In fact, because of this continuity of Yak-1 themes, many of these patterns are commonly confused when assessing wartime photographs (for example, M.D. Baranov's famous 'White 1' has been depicted in many drawings and illustrations hitherto as both a Meander and a Snake application; it is in fact neither, being one of the new 1942 schemes – with some individual variation, of course).

"That Camouflage Woman"

In the annals of Soviet wartime aircraft manufacture, there is one woman whose name comes immediately to the fore. Nadiya Ivanovna Bukhanova was a native of Novosibirsk, and as with many other notables from that city in Siberia (such as Aleksandr Pokrishkin), she developed a strong and uncompromising personality from an early age. Shortly before the outbreak of the GPW, Nadiya obtained employment at *Zavod* 153 in Novosibirsk. She was said to have started her career as a sheet metal fitter, but quickly took up her true vocation in aircraft painting and finish.

Often recalled in various factory papers as "...that camouflage woman", Nadiya was responsible for many innovations in Soviet aircraft finish. She moved to Saratov, *Zavod* 292 early in 1942, and from the middle of that year onwards all Yakovlev OKB prototypes were camouflaged personally by her. She travelled widely with the Yakovlev OKB, and was ever-present in Novosibirsk and Omsk, where Yak fighters were also manufactured.

Nadiya was also instrumental in the integration of women into the wartime workforce. Her efforts in this regard were the source of much consternation to the directorates of several aviation factories, and the effect of these activities stretched across the nation in manufacture of every description. Nadiya was later active in improving health and safety measures in the workplace, and in the introduction of superior work clothing and equipment.

As with so many other Soviet women, the extraordinary accomplishments of Nadiya Bukhanova were unfortunately not recognized in her lifetime. When the USSR was dissolved, a petition was still pending to recognize this remarkable woman as a Heroine of Socialist Labour, a title that was fully warranted. Beloved by all who knew her, or knew of her efforts, Nadiya tragically contracted cancer of the stomach after the War, and passed away in Rostov-on-Don in 1961. She was in her 44th year.

Mid-1942

During the spring of 1942 yet another Yak-1 camouflage innovation appeared, involving the wide-spread use of AII Dark Green. To date, most Yak-1s seem to have been completed in a Black/Green AII livery – except on the 'Snake' application – but *Zavod* 292 also began to utilize Dark Green (it is now widely thought at the behest of Ms. Bukhanova) as an alternative colour choice in most of its camouflage themes for a time. It appears from the photographic record that nearly all Dark Green/Green schemes were finished with semi-soft demarcation lines for the uppersurface colours, and some show a revised upper/lower colour demarcation, as well. Many of the known examples seem to show a 'Snake' scheme application, though some shots of the new '1942' pattern also exist in these colours (see Fig. 7).

Fig. 7

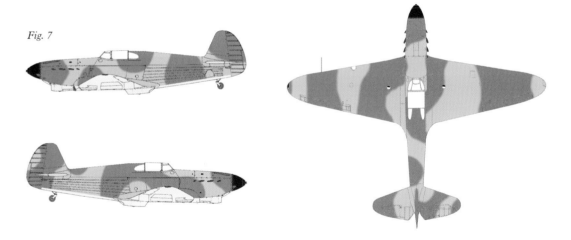

One final scheme was developed during the Spring and Summer of 1942, this being a hard and soft demarcation pattern usually shown in Black/Green. Though it was by no means a wide-spread camouflage theme, it has gained considerable notoriety, having appeared on Lidya Litvyak's beloved Yak-1 'Yellow 44' (see Fig. 8).

Fig. 8

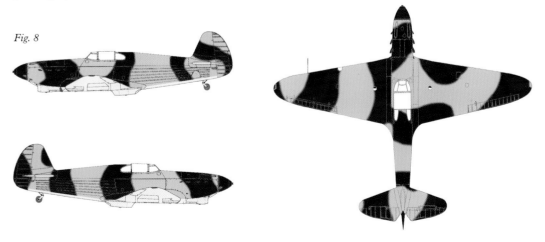

Right: *Lidiya
Litvyak's famous
Yak-1 'Yellow 44',
of the 586 IAP
(or possibly from
the 437 IAP). This
photograph was
taken in the
Kharkov area,
1942. Very much a
contemporary of
Nadiya
Bukhanova, who
performed similar
work in the
industrial sector,
Litvyak was not
only a superb fighter
pilot, but also
crucial in the
integration and
appropriate
treatment of women
serving in the
Red Army.
(Photo: G.Petrov)*

The year 1942 was critical for VVS camouflage, and specifically for the Yak-1 programme. The new AMT aerolacquers were at last widely distributed by this time, and these were in use at Saratov sometime during the late summer or autumn of that year. At the same time, another well-known application theme appeared, this usually seen in AII paint, but some examples of AMT coloured machines have also been recognised (see Fig. 9).

Fig. 9

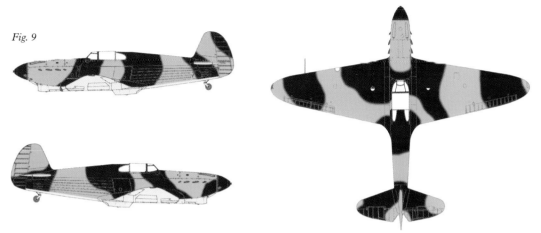

This interesting application appears to be somewhat simplified along the fuselage sides, while at the same time is more complicated in pattern along the uppersurfaces. In cases where AMT finishes were used, the colours would be AMT-6 over AMT-4, presumably with AMT-7 undersurfaces.

Unusual Early Yak-1 Schemes

Very unusually, there existed a reverse colour pattern application of the Snake scheme from early 1942 in Dark Green/Green, something which does not appear to have been executed using Black.

Many of the Yak fighter prototypes, whether manufactured at Saratov or Novosibirsk, carried striking and individualized camouflage applications rendered by no other than Nadia Bukhanova. Indeed, it seems to have been the standard procedure for her to paint these prototypes personally and by hand, presumably as an experimental application. These schemes are legion, and often influenced the development of later series camouflage.

The Oblegchenniy

The new Yak-1s tended to be finished in AMT colours in Green/Black schemes, while the use of AII lacquers persisted in cases where Dark Green/Green were used. Indeed, it should be noted here that it was not at all unknown for older patterns to be applied at this time, but in the main these gradually gave way to the newer application themes.

The first significant scheme appearing primarily on the *Oblegchenniy* was the pattern known often as the 'Starboard Theme' (noting the large quantities of black colour on the right side) (see Fig. 10).

Fig. 10

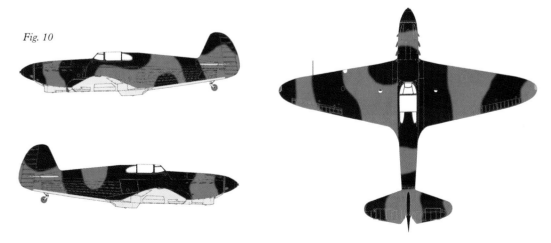

The lower colour demarcation remained quite low still, somewhat in character with camouflage on the contemporary Yak-7. The application along the fuselage starboard side could vary quite substantially, and often small 'blobs' of the underlying green colour could be seen below the cockpit.

With the shift to AMT lacquers, there is sadly, scant evidence of interior colouration and the only surviving example of such a machine exhibits interior painting in line with earlier practices. Certainly, clear doping remained standard for the interior fabric surfaces, and the ratio of painted to unpainted examples seems to be the same.

The use of the new paints, however, did not at all displace the use of earlier finishes, as seems to be true with most cases in Soviet wartime manufacture. In fact, one common application on the Yak-1(*obl.*) was the pattern using AII Dark Green and Green (see Fig. 11).

Fig. 11

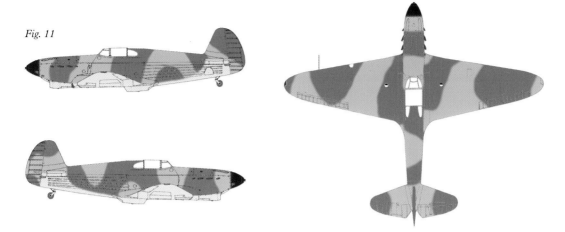

This theme was significant in many respects, not least in appearing to be the first-known 'loops'-type application on the Yak-1 for the uppersurfaces. The fuselage pattern is reminiscent of earlier 'Snake' and 'Meander' schemes, and was certainly influenced by them, but at the same time demonstrates another camouflage innovation in VVS use. The revised upper/lower colour demarcation over the rear fuselage prefaced the development of all later applications, replacing the lower colour line with a revised pattern where the underside colour rose via a 'ramp' feature to meet the bottom of the horizontal stabilizer. The spinner continued to be finished in Black (it could be either AII or AMT), as were the propeller blades.

Interior Colour Choices

At some point in early 1943, the practice of overcoating all cockpit surfaces with Wood Finishes (or occasionally in A-14) came into sporadic fashion. This practice may be related to events then underway at *Zavod* 153 (for the Yak-9), or might have come about through some local idea. In any case, this behaviour persisted - though only on occasion - throughout the year, and appears to have vanished as mysteriously as it arrived during 1944. No explanation for this colour practice exists.

The New Yak-1

By October/November of 1942, the appearance of the Yak-1 changed dramatically for the last time with the introduction of a cut-down rear fuselage and all-round vision canopy.

Along with the new design came a host of new camouflage applications. The most striking of these undoubtedly is a pattern that saw only infrequent application to service fighters. This pattern, widely thought to be based upon the work of Nadia Bukhanova, has gained conspicuous status by appearing on many famous photographs of the various Yak-1 development prototypes from the Summer and Autumn of 1942. It is most often seen in AII Dark Green/Green, but versions with AMT-6 Black over AMT-4 Green are known (see Fig. 12).

This pattern introduced another new camouflage

Fig. 12

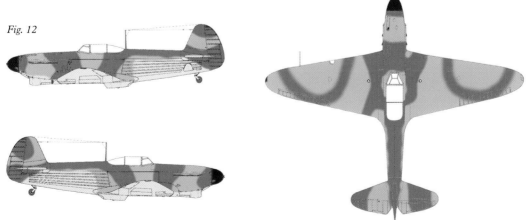

variation to the Yak-1 programme in the appearance of the very high upper/lower colour demarcation, which would return later on. Indeed, so popular and beloved was this camouflage by service personnel that photographs exist of units in the field – even *after* the GPW – replicating this scheme, sometimes using their own colours or innovations.

Through the winter of 1942-43 it was not common for Yak-1 aircraft at Saratov to be completed at the factory in a winter MK-7 White over-wash finish. Rather, it seems that most machines were completed and delivered to service units in their temperate camouflage, requiring those units in the field to apply a winter coat if desired. This resulted in some very haphazard winter schemes, and photographs of Yak-1s from this time sporting a professionally applied white finish are rare (see Fig. 13).

Fig. 13

Many of the new Yak-1s manufactured into early 1943 were finished in a theme very similar to the scheme that had become popular on the last 'razorback' models, but featured a highly revised upper surface pattern application (see Fig. 14 and 15).

Below: *Hero of the Soviet Union Yakov Shishkin's Yak-1B of the 32 GIAP, 1943. The white lightning bolt was replicated on both sides of the fuselage, but the inscription is thought to appear to starboard, only. Note the lack of the starboard gear door. The appearance of this aircraft seems consistent with AII lacquers, Black/Green/Blue. (Photo: G.Petrov)*

Fig. 14

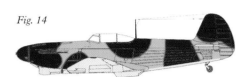

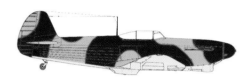

Fig. 15

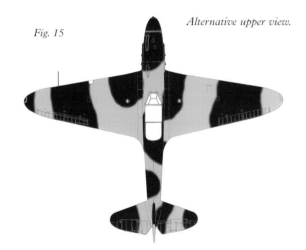

Alternative upper view.

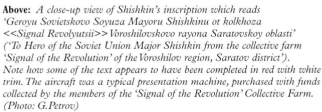

Above: *A close-up view of Shishkin's inscription which reads 'Geroyu Sovietskovo Soyuza Mayoru Shishkinu ot kolkhoza <<Signal Revolyutsii>> Voroshilovskovo rayona Saratovskoy oblasti' ('To Hero of the Soviet Union Major Shishkin from the collective farm 'Signal of the Revolution' of the Voroshilov region, Saratov district'). Note how some of the text appears to have been completed in red with white trim. The aircraft was a typical presentation machine, purchased with funds collected by the members of the 'Signal of the Revolution' Collective Farm. (Photo: G.Petrov)*

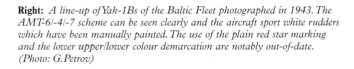

Right: *A line-up of Yak-1Bs of the Baltic Fleet photographed in 1943. The AMT-6/-4/-7 scheme can be seen clearly and the aircraft sport white rudders which have been manually painted. The use of the plain red star marking and the lower upper/lower colour demarcation are notably out-of-date. (Photo: G.Petrov)*

Not only did the upper/lower colour demarcation return to its earlier appearance, but there was a standard alternative uppersurface pattern. Another distinctive development of this theme was the seemingly complete lack of hard-edged colour demarcations. The use of Black also seemed to have returned to popularity, this probably indicating a switch in emphasis from the use of AII to AMT aerolacquers on the uppersurfaces (though still shown here in AII). As 1943 dragged on into the summer, two new AMT-only applications became increasingly popular.

1943-44

A somewhat retroactive scheme began to appear on some Yak-1 machines leaving *Zavod* 292 during the Spring and early summer of 1943, just as had happened on the Yak-9 programme at Novosibirsk. Suddenly, aircraft were being completed in an extremely simplified – almost minimalist – application with very sharp colour demarcations. These simplified schemes seem to have been completed almost exclusively in AMT-6 over AMT-4 (see Fig. 16).

Fig. 16

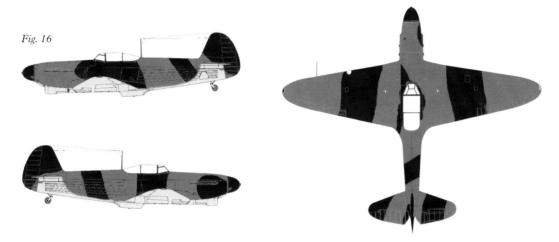

Left: *One of Major Boris Eremin's, (Hero of the Soviet Union post-war), famous dedication Yak-1Bs, this one photographed just after the war while being displayed in Saratov. Despite the date, the machine had essentially the same appearance while in service during 1943-44, as confirmed by the heavily worn finish. (Photo: G.Petrov)*

Apparently these camouflage applications were a little too minimalist, for they were replaced on the production lines by two new themes which demonstrated all the complexity and complication of the earliest patterns. These new schemes were completed entirely in AMT-6/-4/-7 (see Fig. 17).

Fig. 17

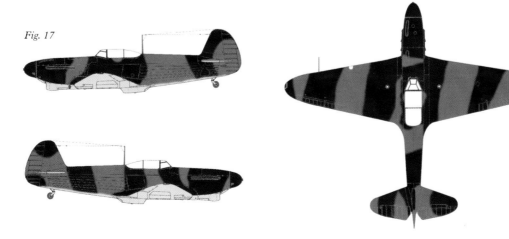

Curiously, the 'old-fashioned' lower upper/lower surface colour demarcation returned on this pattern.

The second application showed again the classic raised and curved upper/lower colour demarcation that would hallmark Soviet camouflage practices throughout the rest of the GPW. Soft-edged upper/lower colour demarcations were also not unknown, particularly along the forward fuselage (see Fig. 18).

Fig. 18

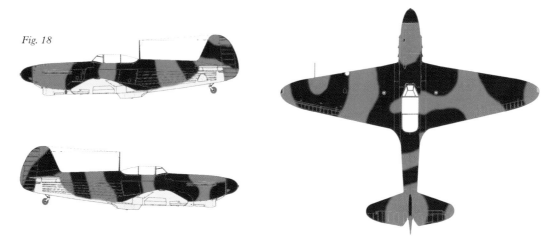

In this form the Yak-1 carried on in production until the Winter of 1943, when an entirely new set of colours and camouflage applications would sweep away all of the old practices. The new camouflage was based on an instruction from the NKAP dating from summer 1943 to begin painting Soviet fighters with two new colours, AMT-11 Grey-Blue and AMT-12 Dark Grey. As previously mentioned, the exact date of introduction of the new colours continues to be a source of some mystery, but at *Zavod* 292 the vast majority of available photographs show aircraft manufactured at the factory leaving the plant in black/green colours well up to the end of the year.

During the winter of 1943-44, Yak-1s seem to have been finished in a number of different ways. Some white colour schemes were seen at Saratov, these presumably wearing MK-7. More common were single-colour uppersurface applications using what seems to be both Wood *Aerolak* and AMT-11. The usual practice seems to have been that Wood *Aerolak* coloured machines featured an old fashioned lower upper/lower colour demarcation, as was in use years before (see Fig. 19).

Fig. 19

AMT-11-painted examples seemed to carry a more usual upper/lower demarcation, one that was often quite soft in application (see Fig. 20).

Fig. 20

These same variations were repeated at *Zavod* 153 on the Yak-7 and Yak-9 programmes.

When the new two-tone temperate grey application did emerge – probably in early 1944 – the pattern was a classic. Somewhat simplified in appearance, it featured easily-applied forms on both upper and fuselage surfaces, and was popular with personnel in both factory and field (see Fig. 21).

Fig. 21

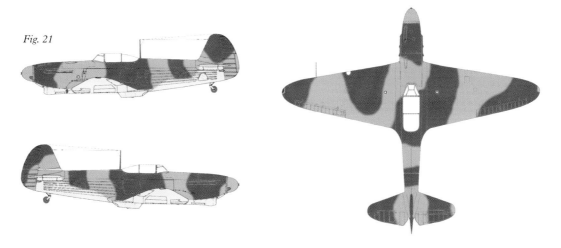

Some new features are evident. On schemes using the new grey lacquers, the usual practice was to paint the spinner with AMT-11; that is to say, no longer was it painted black. Furthermore, the upper/lower colour demarcation now featured a 'double ramp' format which would be increasingly popular to the end of the GPW. Indeed, so popular was this camouflage that freshly-applied examples of this pattern application can be seen in the photographic record to the end of Yak-1 production.

By the late spring of 1944 two more pattern applications were to be seen at Saratov; along with the previous pattern, these would close the book on manufacture of this fighter. The first permutation was seemingly influenced by the immediately preceding scheme, and was relatively straightforward in appearance (see Fig. 22).

Fig. 22

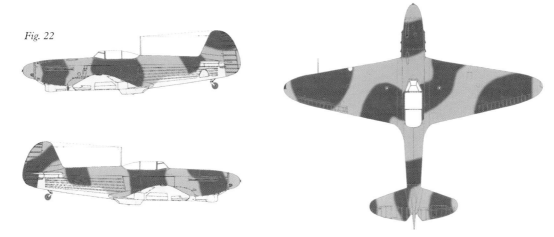

The latter scheme, however, was much less symmetrical in application, as well as being more complex. Moreover, the upper/lower colour demarcation reverted to a much earlier format – not only was the 'ramp' feature singular and of curved execution, but the underside blue colour extended onto the bottom of the rudder as well (see Fig. 23).

Below: *An AMT-11/-12/-7-camouflaged Yak-1B of the 1 Polish IAP 'Warszawa' (Warsaw) in 1944. The scheme appears to be an NKAP Template and features an interesting rear fuselage colour demarcation 'ramp'. (Photo: G.Petrov)*

Fig. 23

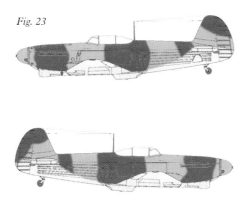

Fig. 24

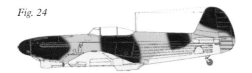

This pattern certainly gives the impression that the last of the Yak-1s were increasingly finished in a manner similar to the Yak-3s, which were then replacing the Yak-1 in production.

Unusual Yak-1B Schemes

In July of 1943, a large portion of one production block was finished in a South Front scheme application of AII Black over AII Light Brown for use with the 6th GIAP ChF (amongst other units), then at Kacha. Though I know of only one photograph of this group of aircraft, I believe all were finished in the same general pattern, with loose demarcations and a raised upper/lower colour separation (see Fig. 24).

Certain early Yak-1s can be seen in very sophisticated field-applied camouflage schemes. These appear on first glance to be unknown factory schemes, but on analysis one can determine that the paint has been applied *by hand*. The reason for this significant effort on the part of some units – especially during the difficult days of 1941 and 1942 – remains unknown.

Left: *This remarkable scheme serves as a good illustration of the lengths to which some units would go to apply camouflage of their own design. 'White 21' of Lt. Kozlov suffered an engine mishap and crashed along the Leningrad Front during 1943. Given the date, and the appearance of this aircraft, it is certainly possible that AMT varnishes were used; indeed, the aircraft has been completely repainted on the upper surfaces. (Photo: G.Petrov)*

Below: *A port view of 'White 21'. From this photograph it can be seen that the scheme has been applied by hand. The very low upper/lower colour demarcation and the hard edges are certainly out of line with existing factory practices. Such unit-specific camouflage is by no means unknown, but it is more common on aircraft such as the Il-2 and less common on Yak fighters. (Photo: G.Petrov)*

Below: *The Yak-1 of Hero of the Soviet Union Mikhail Baranov of the 183 IAP seen in 1942. The inscription on both sides of the fuselage reads, 'Groza Fashistov M.D. Baranov' ('Threat to Fascists, M.D. Baranov'). Tragically, Baranov was killed in a flying accident in 1943 having been accredited with 24 personal and 28 shared confirmed victories. (Photo: G.Petrov)*

Below: *A Yak-1B has its engine serviced during the Kharkov battles of 1942. The T-34 rumbling past indicates that the Front is nearby. (Photo: G.Petrov)*

Above: *A presentation Yak-1B in winter camouflage at Stalingrad during the winter of 1942-43. The inscription – in red – reads, 'Zaschitnikam Stalingradskovo Fronta ot kolkhoznikov kolkhoza 'Bol'shevik' Khsilinskovo rayona Saratovskoy oblasti' ('To the Defenders of Stalingad from the collective farm workers of the 'Bolshevik' collective from the Khsilinski region of the Saratov district'). The presentation was made in person from representatives – seen here – of the Bolshevik Collective Farm. (Photo: G.Petrov)*

Above: *Kpt. Korobov of the 34 IAP-PVO standing proudly in front of his Yak-1 in Moscow, 1942. The colouration of the national insignia on Korobov's Yak are a matter of heated debate. The use of 'journalist'-type 35mm film has greatly clouded the issue. It is argued that if the victory markings are in red, then the national stars (which seem to have a black border) must be a lighter colour. However, if the victory markings are in yellow, then the lightness of the national markings are definitely explained by the 'journalist'-type film and are therefore the usual red (this is a known characteristic of the film). The latter hypothesis is almost certainly the correct one. (Photo: G.Petrov)*

Yakovlev Yak-7

Chapter 7

Yakovlev Yak-7, UTI-26

In the development and life of many great aircraft, serendipity often plays a significant role. In this respect, stories about the Mustang or the La-5 might be legion, but so it was with the Yak-7. Born of a project initiated by Alexander Yakovlev to corner the Advanced Trainer specification in the USSR, the unexpected result was a heavy fighter very much in the tradition of the Red Army's air-ground operational theory, and one whose handling was so good that it excelled in its aerial duties equally. The movement from Fighter to Trainer to Fighter (and, indeed, to Trainer again) is unparalleled in aviation history, and it is the fascinating story of the Yak-7.

Training aircraft were always in Yakovlev's mind. In the years before the GPW, Yakovlev rose to some fame for producing outstanding primary training machines for the VVS, and indeed even years afterwards – in the age of jet fighters – his Bureau would continue to develop and manufacture such aircraft. Yakovlev began to consider a training variant of his emerging I-26 fighter late in 1940. The I-26 prototypes had already demonstrated excellent handling characteristics, behaviour that would suit student pilots well in the advanced training role, or for experienced pilots as a conversion trainer for those re-equipping from biplanes to newer high-speed monoplanes.

Yakovlev foresaw a significant role for such machines in the coming few years. It was clear to him that the other emerging fighter prototypes, the I-301 (see LaGG-3) and I-200 (see MiG-1/-3), were not possessed of such laudable flight capability, and pilots being trained for the types would require an advanced trainer of higher performance and more similar configuration than a UT-1. Furthermore, many pilots in the VVS were still flying I-15, I-152, and I-153 biplanes operationally, and these were planned to be phased out of the inventory over the next two to three years. As a result, a conversion trainer to assist with the transition to high speeds, retractable landing gear and monoplane configuration would be invaluable. In this light, the importance placed on the trainer prototype effort by Yakovlev becomes more understandable.

During December 1939, Yakovlev directed the OKB staff to begin work on a training version of the I-26, known as the UTI-26 (UTI= *uchebno-trenirovanniy istrebitel'*, or 'student-training fighter'). The UTI was to be based on the I-26 No.2 prototype, and for this work a partially-completed I-26-2 example was selected from the *Zavod* 115 workshop. An analysis was made of the existing structure, and calculations were prepared using the wing of the I-26 No.3. The initial calculations were complete just after the New Year, and construction of the UTI-26 began in January 1940.

Changes in the distribution of weight in the UTI, along with the centre of gravity, called for structural modifications of the I-26-2 airframe. The No.3 prototype wing was mounted aft some 100 mm, while the radiator was repositioned forward. The aircraft featured a standard cockpit forward and an instructor's cockpit aft, this fitted with all primary flight instruments and controls. Provision was made in the forward cockpit to mount a movie camera for flight evaluation purposes, and communication between the instructor and student was via a speaking tube. The canopy was neatly extended to the rear via two additional square sections giving it a 'greenhouse' appearance, the first being fixed and the second sliding back to provide access to the rear cockpit. Power was provided by the 1,050 hp M-105P engine driving a ViSH-61 propeller. The UTI's armament was reduced to a single ShKAS gun mounted above the engine to port.

Late in February, with construction of the UTI-26 well underway, Yakovlev announced his new trainer prototype to the NKAP. The Government response, however, was rather less enthusiastic than the Bureau Head had envisioned, and in fact bordered on acrimony. Debate broke out publicly on Yakovlev's "dissolution of effort", and Yakovlev was reminded sharply that the Government had not requested such an aircraft, and certainly not from his Bureau. Regardless of this initial setback, Yakovlev worked his charm and debating prowess to reverse the situation, and by March he was being commended for his initiative and "...positive understanding of the current production requirements." As debate circulated throughout Moscow, the situation became increasingly confused, much in the way a humorous anecdote circulates at a party to become something rather different from how it began. By 10 March, Yakovlev's three-man NKAP committee was able to send instructions back to his Design Bureau to continue work on the UTI, but this was accompanied by a resolution adopted by the GKO that Yakovlev should develop this training machine into a series of possible combat aircraft. Indeed, not at all related to the UTI, some of the development machines listed in the resolution include assault machines, high-altitude interceptors and even a bomber with a rear-firing gun.

Assembly of the UTI-26 was complete by June 1940. Factory-testing of the new prototype commenced on 23 July and lasted just over a month, the course ending on 25 August. Pilot-Engineer P.Fedrovi led the evaluation, and it was immediately clear that handling and even performance of the UTI-26 was virtually identical to that of the I-26 fighter prototype. Fedrovi was well satisfied with progress of the UTI, but in his remarks some question was brought over the use of the smaller 2.8 m ViSH-61 propeller, and accordingly a second 3.0 m unit was secured as well.

With factory-testing complete, the UTI-26 was handed over to the NII VVS on 28 August for State evaluations. The NII VVS examination team included such notables as P. Stefanovskiy and N. Maksimov, and progressed with two series including the 2.8 m and 3.0 m propellers, respectively. The flight behaviour of the UTI-26 was confirmed as outstanding, and no difficulties were foreseen for student pilots of virtually any skill level. The instructor's cockpit was judged to be satisfactory, both in visibility and function, and flights were made from the rear cockpit as a matter of course. However, there were serious difficulties with overheating in the M-105 engine, as on the current I-26 prototypes. Worse, the landing gear at the greater all-up weight of the UTI was grossly inadequate, both in dampening during landing and in structural strength. During testing the starboard gear failed while taxiing, causing minimal damage to the wing. Improvements in both engine and landing gear were urgently required.

Back at *Zavod* 115, the Yakovlev OKB continued work on a second UTI prototype, this to incorporate both the evaluation testing data and also the concurrent work from the I-26 programme. The No.2 machine's radiator was increased in size, and featured revised and enlarged ducting from the engine. New and more robust landing gear was installed, these being similar to the units fitted to the I-28 prototype. The revised gear members could be identified by their more acute, forward-facing angle (which also helped to mitigate a nose-over tendency while braking hard), and single-piece gear door cover. Larger tyres were installed, and the tailwheel was modified to rotate through 215 degrees. Also, and more significantly, the vertical stabilizer was increased slightly in area, as was the rudder, which now took on a more rounded look, especially in the 'heel'. The larger fin area was made at

Yak-7 'Red 03'

Unit uncertain
Pilot unknown
Kharbovsk region
Autumn 1942

Colours:
AII Green/Black/Blue
application from
Zavod 153

Yak-7B 'Red 41'

Location and assignment
uncertain
1943

Colours:
AMT-4/-6/-7 application
from *Zavod* 153

Yak-7 'Red 65'

434 IAP
Pilot unknown
Stalingrad
December 1942

Colours:
MK-7 White over
unknown lacquers

Yak-7B 'Red 8'

42 IAP,
Nikolai Tikhonov
November 1942

Colours:
AII Green/Dark Green
over AMT-7 field
application

the suggestion of Senior Engineer K.V. Sinel'shikov to counter the greater torque of the larger 3.0 m propeller, and the revised stabilizer unit was of all-metal construction to prevent any increase in weight.

The UTI-26 No.2 prototype – begun earlier in the summer – was complete by September 1940, and factory flight-testing commenced on the 16th of that month. Once again Fedrovi led the examinations, and this time there was no doubt whatever that the UTI-26-2 was quite exceptional. Fedrovi tested all aspects of the machine's behaviour, including ground handling and routine maintenance procedures, and even tested the ShKAS armament. Virtually the only minor difficulty, involving a rise in the temperature of the forward cockpit, was solved over the course of a single afternoon by experimenting with re-arranged firewall insulation pieces. By December, the UTI No.2 prototype had been put through an exhaustive factory analysis, and was ready for its State Acceptance Trials.

Successful NII VVS testing of the UTI-26-2 began on 1 January 1941. The Institute pilots were almost queuing to fly the UTI No.2, and indeed the NII VVS report on the type is signed – in what must be a record – by virtually every pilot at the Institute. Test Pilot Petr Stefanovskiy recorded that the UTI-26-2 was the most pleasing machine he had tested at the NII VVS, being approached only by the I-153 (Kokkinaki had described the I-153's behaviour as "perfect"). NII VVS Director Filin, took the trouble to compose the Institute's final report on the UTI No.2 prototype, and even in his critical eyes the machine had passed its acceptance evaluation with flying colours.

With great satisfaction and personal pride, Yakovlev signed the NKAP Production Contract for manufacture of the UTI-26 at *Zavod* 301, on 4 March 1941. The nomenclature was changed to Yak-7UTI to conform to the new convention, and production was to be based on the UTI-26 No.2 prototype. With manufacture of the Yak-1 fighter already in hand, *Zavod* 301 had no difficulties launching the Yak-7UTI programme, and the first example was tested by Yakovlev OKB Pilot-Engineer Fedrovi as early as 18 May.

By August, Factory Engineer Sharapov at *Zavod* 301 recommended that the Yak-7UTI's landing gear be fixed. The intention was both to simplify production, and also to extend the service life of the training machines, landing gear being one of the components most likely to suffer wear in such a role. After a short debate, and some test-flights by Fedrovi, Sharapov's modifications were accepted and a new Production Contract was issued on 5 September for another 99 machines. However, also during the month of August, one of the key Senior Design Engineers from the Yakovlev Design Bureau, K. Sinel'shikov, left Saratov – at the height of the German invasion and with maximum pressure on the OKB staff to deal with problems on the Yak-1 programme – and materialized at *Zavod* 301 in Moscow. Nowhere in Yakovlev's surviving papers is there an explanation for this move, nor is there any hint in the papers preceding this time as to its reasons. Once in Moscow, Sinel'shikov immediately set about the conversion of the Yak-7UTI trainer *back* into a fighter. No specific request was made by the Government to undertake work of this type, and the *Zavod* 301 plant staff were less than delighted to have Sinel'shikov 'overrunning' the workshops.

At the same time it is curious to note that numerous specifications were being issued by the NKAP to *Zavoda* 301, 153, and 21. These directives primarily included instructions to engage in the production of Yak-1 fighters, though most unusually *no* Production Contracts to this effect were ever seen. Hitherto, it has been widely assumed that these instructions were issued in error, and that the directives were really intended to refer to the Yak-7 (fighter), mentioning the Yak-1 by mistake. However, it is critical to recall that at this moment – August 1941 – the fighter version of the Yak-7 did not yet exist. The author is convinced that the reference to Yak-1 fighters is no mistake at all.

It seems increasingly clear, that in his position as a Deputy Minister at the NKAP, Yakovlev was issuing instructions *on his own account*, and without the official approval of the Ministry itself, to these factories for the manufacture of his fighter (the Yak-1). It should be recalled, that at this time Yakovlev was engaged in a heated contest with Semen

Lavochkin for the primacy of their respective fighter programmes, the Yak-1 and LaGG-3. In retrospect, it is evident that Yakovlev was victorious in this contest, and that by the early months of 1942, only *Zavod* 31 was engaged in the production of Lavochkin's LaGG fighter, while the Yak-1 and now -7 were in place at *Zavoda* 21, 301, 292, and 153. Thus, it is easy to understand the confusion at Novosibirsk (*Zavod* 153) when, in late 1941, manufacture of the Yak fighter got under way and the factory reported itself to be engaged in production of the "...Yak-1 fighter of the Yak-7 type". This mis-reporting continued until a Production Contract was issued on 11 February 1942, (this time from the NKAP); the Contract clearly referred to the Yak-7.

Back at *Zavod* 301, Sinel'shikov was at work on a fighter variant of the Yak-7, making use of airframe No.04-11 for this purpose. In fact, so satisfactory was the Yak-7UTI that only the most straightforward modifications needed be made to produce an operational combat machine. An armoured seat, as on the Yak-1 fighter, was mounted in the forward cockpit, while all controls and instrumentation were removed from the aft compartment. The camera apparatus was removed, and self-sealing fuel cells replaced the trainer's unprotected tanks. The usual fuel tank anti-fire pressurization system was installed, but in the case of the early Yak-7 no ducting from the engine exhaust manifold was possible, and so a carbon dioxide bottle replaced the back-up nitrogen bottle of the Yak-1, and was the primary system. Armament "...equal to the Yak-1 fighter" was requested by Yakovlev, and two ShKAS guns were duly mounted above the engine with 750 rounds each, in addition to the usual 20 mm ShVAK intended to fire through the spinner (with 120 rounds). Six underwing RO82 rails were installed to accommodate a similar number of RS-82 rockets. Power was provided – as in the Yak-7UTI – by the 1,050 hp M-105PA driving a 3.0 m ViSH-61P propeller.

Conversion of the UTI airframe was very straightforward, and Sinel'shikov encountered no significant difficulties (undoubtedly, it must also have helped that Sinel'shikov was one of the finest Design Engineers in the entire Soviet Union). Indeed, so well did the work proceed that the Yak-7 pre-production machine (it was never regarded as a prototype) was completed within 30 days. Upon hearing of this miraculous timing, Yakovlev was quite alarmed and travelled to inspect the machine in Moscow. In the event any anxieties were groundless, and the Yak-7 was a complete success. Machine No.04-11 was so good that it was immediately turned over to the NII VVS on 19 September for State Acceptance testing, where it was received very warmly.

The Yakovlev OKB Evaluation Brigade at the NII VVS (led by A. Stepanets) tested the Yak-7 most thoroughly over the following two weeks, and, as the UTI before it, the Yak-7 fighter passed its acceptance evaluation admirably and was officially accepted on 2 October 1941. The Yak-7 weighed 2,960 kg at take-off, could attain 471 km/h at sea level and 560 km/h at 5,000 m, reaching that height in 6.8 minutes with an initial climb rate of 884 m/min. Control harmony was outstanding, and in particular, directional control – by virtue of the Yak-7's increased fin and rudder area – was exhilarating, while stick forces remained light and effective up to very high airspeeds. In total, the Yak-7's performance was nearly identical to that of the Yak-1, save for the lower rate of climb and larger turning circle (by virtue of its higher weight), and the improved directional control. Ground-handling was vastly improved with the modified and strengthened landing gear members, and hard braking over rough terrain offered no difficulties.

Again basking in the glow of success, Yakovlev conveyed personally the Government's instructions to produce the Yak-7 at Gor'ki, Novosibirsk, and at Moscow. Without even having received a Production Contract, manufacture of the Yak-7 commenced at *Zavod* 301 immediately, 51 being completed before the evacuation of the facility to Novosibirsk. *Zavod* 153, already at Novosibirsk, managed to launch production of the Yak-7 during December 1941, and at Gor'ki (*Zavod* 21), lines for the Yak-7 were just about to commence operation in the New Year. However, with the evacuation of *Zavod* 301 to

Novosibirsk, all of the tooling, forms, and other manufacturing apparatus for Yak-7 production, in addition to the technicians and staff related to that project, were absorbed into *Zavod* 153's Yak-7 programme, making that factory the central and premiere focus for production of the type. This was in order, for in February 1942 production of the Yak-7 at Gor'ki was suddenly terminated (in favour of the new M-82-powered Lavochkin LaGG) after only five examples had been completed, and all tools and jigs were relocated to Novosibirsk once again. By early 1942, *Zavod* 153 was the sole centre for Yak-7 manufacture, and the NKAP duly issued a Production Contract to that enterprise only, on 11 February.

Meanwhile back at Saratov, the Yakovlev OKB was at work on an improved Yak-7 variant known as the Yak-7M (*modifitsirovanniy*, or 'modified'). Yak-7UTI airframe No.05-12 was extensively rebuilt for the project, starting with the wings. The fuselage was mated to a 9.74 m wing taken from the I-30 programme. This wing was somewhat similar in planform to the later 'Yak-9' wing, but featured inner and outer wing sections, the outer having a dihedral of three degrees, and carrying large Handley-Page-type leading edge slats. As on the I-30, a 20 mm ShVAK cannon was mounted in each wing just outboard of the wing section joint, and the ShVAK mounted to fire through the spinner was retained; the twin ShKAS above the engine were discarded. The engine and propeller were unchanged from the UTI airframe, and an additional fuel cell was mounted just aft of the pilot's seat.

The Yak-7M prototype was evaluated by the NII VVS from late October 1941. Technically, the Yak-7M was a fine machine, and the review signed by Stepanets about the new variant was very positive. The Yak-7M reached 469 km/h at sea level and 556 km/h at 5,000 m, but required fully 7.5 minutes to climb to that height. Excessive weight was the telling problem with the Yak-7M, and at take-off the prototype tipped the scales at virtually 3,160 kg. Though technically sound, and possessed of excellent firepower, the pilots of the NII VVS did not like the machine. Virtually every pilot report described the Yak-7M as "sluggish", "unresponsive", and possessed of poor control harmony and excessive stick forces. These claims were indeed true, and the turning circle of the Yak-7M was poor, largely caused by the steep increase in wing loading to 3.84 kg/m2. While the evaluation's claim that the stall in the Yak-7M came on gently and was easily recovered was correct, these characteristics were already true in the Yak-7; slats were simply not required in this case, and the Institute pilots saw no advantage in having them.

However, with the positive results of the report in hand, some contemplation of production for the Yak-7M did ensue. Yakovlev was concerned with a number of production issues surrounding the type, mostly connected with the greater cost and complexity of manufacturing the new variant. Moreover, a major reorganization of the production lines at *Zavod* 153 at the height of the crisis involving the German advance on Moscow was quite unthinkable. In December, the OKB's Senior Pilot-Engineer Fedrovi flew the Yak-7M, and confirmed the findings of the report – including the negative impressions of the Institute pilots concerning the aircraft's 'feel'. This seemed to be the final straw, and the Yak-7M prototype was abandoned shortly thereafter.

The rearrangement of the fuselage was not the only significant development idea applied to the Yak-7 at this juncture. Aircraft engine specialist and Head Designer Mikhail Gudkov, still at the *Zavod* 301 facility in Moscow, began work on fitting various fighters powered by the M-105 with the 14 cylinder Shvetsov M-82 radial during the autumn of 1941. Amongst the machines so modified, the Yak-7 was one of Gudkov's major projects. The physical installation of the M-82 presented Gudkov with no significant difficulties, and the prototype was completed by December. However, the ground clearance of the Yak-7 necessitated the used of a smaller radius propeller than had been suggested by Shvetsov's Bureau, and thus a specialized 2.8 m AV-5L-127 unit was installed on the Yak-7 M-82A. Gudkov provided two ShVAK cannon mounted at the wing/fuselage joint and firing along the side of the motor for armament.

The most extraordinary aspect of the new M-82-powered Yak-7, however, was the fuselage. Gudkov, always forward-looking, modified the airframe supplied to him with a cut-down rear fuselage. As a former employee of TsAGI, Gudkov was in close contact with that organization, and he must have been aware of the T-101 wind tunnel unit examinations on Yak-1 airframe No.10-47 then underway just next door to his workshop. This airframe had been rebuilt by the Saratov workshops with a cut-down rear fuselage and clear rear canopy section, and this appears to have been identical to the modifications fitted to the Yak-7 M-82A.

In the end, however, performance in the Yak-7 M-82A did not meet expectations. Despite the dramatic increase in horsepower, the smaller airscrew was simply inadequate to translate the added power into thrust, and performance on all counts suffered. When the prototype was flown by the OKB 301 staff pilot in early December, just before the final evacuations to Novosibirsk, 505 km/h was said to be achieved at sea level and 615 km/h at 5,000 m. However, when Yakovlev OKB Pilot-Engineer Fedrovi examined the Yak-7 M-82A at Novosibirsk in January 1942, he concluded that the figures achieved were some 24-32 km/h slower than those put forward by Gudkov. He also noted that the centre of gravity had moved forward yet again, and that the climbing performance was not improved over the new 1942 standard Yak-7 M-105PA proposal. However technically sound and well-constructed – the M-82 prototype was, Fedrovi concluded that there was no basis for manufacture of the radial-powered Yak-7; Yakovlev concurred.

Development of the M-82-powered Yak-7 did continue at a low-priority level in 1942. By May of that year the prototype had been rebuilt once again, now sporting improved aerodynamics and new, more powerful armament. The cowling was vastly more streamlined and longer in shape, and looked to have been similar to the unit designed by Prof. Polinovski for the La-5 at TsAGI. Armament was revised to incorporate two 12.7 mm UBS guns in the lower fuselage, replacing the original cannon, while two 20 mm guns were now moved to the wings just outboard of the landing gear attachment points. The canopy was more streamlined, and incorporated a flat armoured glass panel ahead of the pilot. Lastly, a VISh-105 3.0 m propeller was fitted, a modest lengthening of the undercarriage legs permitting the required ground clearance. Despite all improvements, however, performance of the improved M-82-powered prototype was still not sufficient to warrant production, and development of the radial Yak-7 was abandoned in June 1942.

At the same time, the UVVS discovered that its need for advanced and conversion trainers was greater than had been anticipated. The staff at *Zavod* 301 had already modified the Yak-7UTI with fixed landing gear, as per the final batch of the original Production Contract. This model was proposed for further manufacture, and some sundry improvements were applied to the new run. Provision was made to accept a 20mm ShVAK if so desired, though the number completed with the cannon were modest; the single ShKAS gun was retained. Provision was also made for an RSI-3 radio, but no mast was installed (it was reasoned that the trainer would not stray far from its base of operations, and communication to other aircraft was not a priority). Other detail changes and improvements were made to the instructor's cockpit, the tyres, and the oleo strut calibration.

Placed back into production by the NKAP, the improved trainer was designated the Yak-7V (*vivoznoy*, or 'advanced trainer'). The Yak-7V was deemed by the UVVS to have been rugged, reliable and eminently satisfactory in service, the variant subsequently manufactured without modification until December 1943 at *Zavod* 153, 597 examples in all being completed.

During the winter months of 1941-42, preparations were made to outfit the production Yak-7 with ski landing gear. Units were taken from the Yak-1 programme and mounted on Yak-7 airframe No.14-13, which also received a factory coat of MK-7 white distemper. As expected, performance was adversely affected by these modifications and these results were confirmed by NII VVS testing during December 1941. Limited production of 'winterized' Yak-7s commenced immediately, and continued until March 1942.

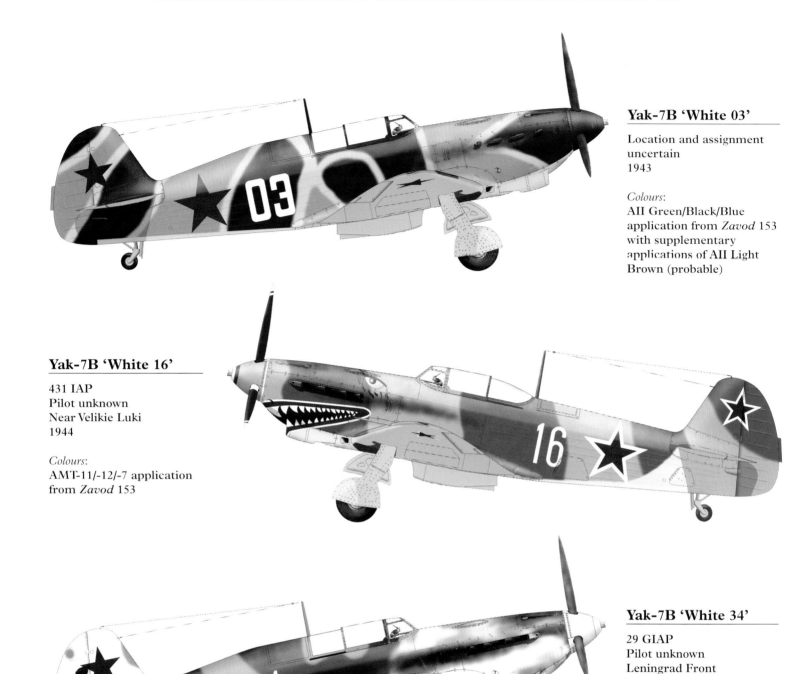

Yak-7B 'White 03'

Location and assignment
uncertain
1943

Colours:
AII Green/Black/Blue
application from *Zavod* 153
with supplementary
applications of AII Light
Brown (probable)

Yak-7B 'White 16'

431 IAP
Pilot unknown
Near Velikie Luki
1944

Colours:
AMT-11/-12/-7 application
from *Zavod* 153

Yak-7B 'White 34'

29 GIAP
Pilot unknown
Leningrad Front
Winter 1942-1943

Colours:
MK-7 White over
AII/Green/Black/Blue
application from
Zavod 153

Work on aircraft No.14-13 was far from completed, however. While at the NII VVS, the Institute's Yakovlev Evaluation Brigade worked closely with both the OKB staff and TsAGI to improve the Yak-7 fighter. Following extensive testing and flight evaluation, a number of detail modifications were made to No.14-13. The rear sliding canopy was replaced by a hinged plywood unit, thus being able to fit flush with the canopy and thereby reducing drag. Additional wheel well covers were fitted, these covering the tyre, so that the entire bay was sealed when the gear was retracted. Provision was made for an RSI-3 or -4 radio, and a radio mast was installed just aft of the hinged canopy. The tailwheel was made semi-retractable, and there were minor modifications to the instrument layout, oxygen system, and other sundry details, including the reduction of the ammunition supply to the ShKAS guns to 500 rounds apiece.

The resulting aerodynamic improvements to No.14-13 were exceptional. In this condition the new, modified Yak-7 could reach 495 km/h at sea level and 571 km/h at 5,000 m, climbing to that height in the improved time of 6.4 minutes with an initial climb of 3,000 ft./min. All other aspects of handling and flight behaviour were unchanged, and the Institute pilots were delighted with the enhancements. Based on the No.14-13 airframe, these modifications were ordered into production immediately at *Zavod* 153, and began to leave the production lines as soon as the 1 January 1942, and it was upon this standard that the 11 February Production Contract was written; aircraft of this standard later acquiring the designation Yak-7A.

Yak-7 fighters began to reach service units in the field during the final days of 1941 around Moscow. The 172 IAP was first into action with the new fighter, in addition to its Yak-1 and LaGG-3 fighters, and the unit effectively became a test unit, allowing each machine to be compared in combat to the others. In the 172 IAP, success in the Yak-1 and Yak-7 was comparable, and much superior to the *Eskadrilya* operating the LaGG-3. Pilot reaction to the Yak-7 was very favourable, and requests to replace the other aircraft in the Regiment were soon legion.

Batches of the improved Yak-7A fighter were distributed widely over the Western and Volkhov Fronts, the 283 IAP being the first Regiment to equip entirely with the type. Pilots discovered at once that the key to achieving success in aerial combat lay in manoeuvring with enemy fighters in the horizontal plane. The Yak-7's climbing ability was very much inferior to all of its German opponents, and its advantage lay in its turning and dogfighting characteristics. On the plus side, the Yak-7 was a superlative gun platform as a result of its excellent directional stability and rudder control; indeed, it was universally regarded as the most accurate weapons platform in the entire VVS. Pilots with a shooting eye soon discovered that they could hit anything in the Yak-7, and that the machine's controls allowed them the chance to bring their guns to bear.

In battle from May 1942, the 283 IAP began to show what the Yak-7A was made of. On the 29th, Regimental Commander *May.* Morozov led 11 Yak-7A fighters into enemy airspace, whence they were attacked by more than 20 Bf 109s. A swirling dogfight ensued, Morozov claiming a 'double' in the encounter along with pilots Shipanov and Kuzinskiy. No Yaks were lost in the action. On 16 June Morozov was in action again, but this time he was able only to seriously damage a Ju 88, which was subsequently dispatched by his wingman *Lt.* Pavlov, despite the accuracy of his fire. In a report to Alexander Yakovlev, Morozov, while generally praising the Yak-7, complained (as had Yak-1 pilots) that the ShKAS guns were ineffective, and thus the firepower too weak. In addition, he noted that all German fighter types could out-climb the Yak-7, which he regarded therefore as being underpowered. He implored Yakovlev to rectify the situation "...at the earliest possible moment, (in order) to save lives."

At Yakovlev's OKB, such requests from the front were heeded. By spring 1942, work was underway on a new version of the Yak-7, once again making use of aircraft No.14-13. Following requests received from pilots, the two ShKAS guns above the engine were replaced by two of the popular 12.7 mm UBS weapons, each with 150 cartridges. The M-105PA engine was retained, but modifications to the ViSH-61P propeller allowed normal operating revolutions to increase up to 2,700 rpm. RO82 rocket rails were at first standard, but from 10 May these were discarded in production, though they could still be added in the field by means of a kit. Even with the rocket rails omitted, however, weight in the new Yak-7 variant rose inevitably. The aircraft's centre of gravity also moved forward, once again introducing the type's nose-over problem during taxiing, much to the irritation of service pilots. In an effort to mitigate the centre of gravity problem, an additional 80 litre fuel cell was mounted aft of the pilot's seat.

Testing by the NII VVS centred around the weight problem to a large degree, and continued well after production of the new variant commenced. The Yakovlev OKB and *Zavod* 153 staffs, however, reasoned that the Yak-7 was already heavier than the Yak-1 and its climb performance was thus inferior; the increase in weight of 220 kg was acceptable in view of the vast improvement in firepower. Additionally, they noted with relief that the change in centre of gravity had no effect on the aircraft's handling in flight, and drafted a report to the GKO to this effect. As a result, the GKO instructed *Zavod* 153 to begin immediate manufacture of the Yak-7B (as the type would be designated in the June Production Contract), which commenced as early as the end of April 1942.

The Yak-7B M-105PA, as completed without rocket rails from 10 May, demonstrated mixed performance. The new Yak-7B weighed 3,136 kg at take-off and could reach 500 km/h at sea level and 580 km/h at 4,850 m as a result of the decreased drag from the removed underwing rails. However, with the increased all-up weight, climb performance suffered, the initial rate dropping to 869 m/min. and requiring 6.5 minutes to achieve 5,000 m. All other flight and handling aspects were unchanged.

The appearance of the Yak-7B coincided with the establishment of a new production facility for the fighter. *Zavod* 82 in Moscow was reconstituted making use of the old *Zavod* 115 workshops, in addition to the empty space that once housed *Zavod* 301, specifically to manufacture the Yak-7. Some technicians from Novosibirsk were relocated, and on 25 May production of the Yak-7B commenced with the M-105PA motor. The NKAP issued a specific Production Contract for all *Zavod* 82 manufacture and so machines leaving the Moscow facility were numbered starting with Series 1 (thus a *Zavod* 82-built Yak-7 Series 1 equated roughly to a *Zavod* 153-built Series 22 machine).

VVS fighter regiments reacted immediately to the increased firepower of the Yak-7B. Pilots of the 434 IAP, including several women, flew an impressive 827 missions in the Yak-7B between 13 June and 3 August 1942. A total of 55 German fighters was destroyed during this period, the most by any VVS Regiment for the time, for the loss of three Yaks. However, pilots detested the extra fuel cell, regarding it as a fire hazard and more useless weight, and most units removed it immediately upon receipt of their machines. Nose-over accidents during ground-taxiing also increased in the new fighter, but happily none of these led to serious injury.

Another Yak-7 development was underway simultaneously to address pilots' complaints of insufficient firepower. In April 1942, the new Yak-7-37 prototype was completed mounting the huge Shpitalniy 37 mm MPSh-37 gun firing through the spinner. To counteract the great weight of this weapon, the prototype's cockpit was moved aft 400 mm. A box containing 20 shells for the big gun was installed into the vacated space, and two 12.7mm UBS weapons replaced the ShKAS guns above the engine for good measure. Thus equipped, the firepower of the Yak-7-37 was fearsome, and was rightly judged to be the heaviest of any fighter then in existence anywhere in the world.

Factory-testing of the Yak-7-37 during April and May revealed no difficulties of any kind. Though heavy, and with obviously reduced performance, the Yak-7's superlative handling and aiming properties were ideally suited to the operation of such a devastating weapon. Testing of the MPSh-37 cannon on various derelict airframes revealed that even an indirect strike was liable to blow the target to pieces, rip off a wing, or cause a catastrophic explosion. Moreover, Shpitalniy's OKB had developed a lethal incendiary/fragmentation round (in addition to armour-piercing ammunition) for use specifically against enemy aircraft; the shrapnel effect of this round alone was sufficient to bring down virtually any target.

Limited manufacture of a brief series of 22 aircraft was completed at *Zavod* 153 during August 1942. These machines were delivered to *May.* Shinkarenko's 42 IAP for combat evaluation, a unit specializing in the testing of fighters mounting big guns. Whilst the Yak-7-37 was by no means invulnerable to German fighters, largely due to its formidable weight, it was equally successful in destroying enemy aircraft with its awesome firepower. Shinkarenko concluded that series manufacture of the Yak-7-37 was not warranted, and that improvements would have to be made to the machine's performance before a service fighter could be introduced along these lines. However, he simultaneously acknowledged the formidable striking power of the 37 mm gun, and encouraged Yakovlev's OKB to continue to develop fighters based on this weapon.

Meanwhile at the NII VVS, it was patently clear that the M-105PA motor was simply no longer sufficiently powerful for the Yak-7 fighter. The NKAP reacted positively to the situation, and placed the Yak-7 programme first in the list of priority to receive the improved Klimov M-105PF engine as mass production began. As a result, Yak-7B No. 22-41 was rebuilt with a new M-105PF motor straight from the Klimov lines at *Zavod* 26 on 11 May. In Yakovlev's surviving papers there are many documents referring to the grave concerns of the OKB staff as to potential problems with cooling of the M-105PF motor on the Yak-7 (it is worth recalling the concurrent difficulties with engine cooling on the Yak-1). The discussion was intense, and many possible solutions were offered. However, Yakovlev countered that the Yak-7 already possessed a radiator capacity in excess of the Yak-1 and better ducting from the engine. Over the objections from both his own staff and the NII VVS, Yakovlev took the decision to complete airframe No.22-41 without any modifications to the cooling system, and ordered the machine to be finished and handed over for State evaluations immediately. Certainly, Yakovlev knew that what he was doing must have been risky, and that his reputation was in grave jeopardy.

Yak-7B No.22-41 was duly handed over to the NII VVS for evaluations on 30 May. Over the next two weeks the aircraft was flown intensively by pilots from the NII VVS (Puzanov, Aronov), LII (Limar), the Novosibirsk factory staff (Lazarev), and also by OKB Pilot-Engineer Fedrovi. In the event, the old Yakovlev magic was still alive and well. During intensive testing, the temperatures in the cockpit did occasionally rise to 35 deg C during fully-boosted operation, but never to an intolerable degree, and never to the point of damage to the motor. The risk had paid off – performance in the Yak-7B was dramatically improved, and all doubts and misgivings of the Institute's test staff were laid to rest. At full boost, the new prototype could reach 514 km/h at sea level and 570 km/h at 3,650 m, initial climb rocketing to 1,043 m/min. and attaining 5,000 m in only 5.8 minutes. All aspects of the Yak-7's first-class handling remained unchanged.

The NKAP, upon receipt of the NII VVS data, reacted at once. On 10 June 1942, a letter was sent from the NKAP Directorate showering Yakovlev with praise. The same day, a new Production Contract was issued by the NKAP to *Zavod* 153 for the Yak-7B powered by the M-105PF engine. Provision was made in the document to continue manufacture with the M-105PA as the need arose, until supplies of the new boosted motor could be assured. In the event, regular supplies of the M-105PF motor from *Zavod* 26 did not materialize until late June, and continuous manufacture of the Yak-7B M-105PF began with the 23rd production series in June-July 1942. *Zavod* 82, Moscow, followed suit in the same month with its own Series 2 production, but various delays and an incessant shortage of engines and materials kept manufacture of the Yak-7 at this facility to a snail's pace until the end of the year.

Examples of the new Yak-7B began to reach units in the field during the summer. Although much appreciated by the Regiments which received the new machines, it was clear that they did not meet the performance specifications of the M-105PF prototype as tested by the NII VVS. The matter came to a head in September 1942 during the fighting around Stalingrad. The entire 288 IAD was equipped with the Yak-7B M-105PF, and *Podpolk.* Sergey Konovalov, commander of the Division, complained directly to Stalin that the performance listed in the NII VVS report could not be achieved under service conditions. Somewhat taken aback by these allegations, the NII VVS and the LII sent a joint commission at the behest of the NKAP to the field to examine the situation.

The results of its investigations were quite revealing, and pointed to two major areas of concern. Firstly, pilots routinely flew the fighter with the canopy open in combat, largely because they had heard a number of spurious rumours about the failure of the canopy locking system (thus trapping the pilot in an emergency). Also, they routinely operated the engine at less than maximum rpms because of the elevated cockpit temperatures during fully-boosted engine operation. In the Yak-1, this condition often presaged damage to the motor in the M-105PF-powered versions; this was simply not the case in the Yak-7, however. These problems were largely solved when the NII VVS and LII pilots proved to their colleagues that both allegations were nonsense. Secondly, there were defects and irregularities found in the finish and workmanship of the Yak-7Bs being operated by the 288 IAD, especially those manufactured at *Zavod* 82 (but not exclusively). The commission's report listed the condition of every Yak-7 machine in the entire Division, and noted any problems on any of the affected aircraft in great detail.

One machine that was in a particularly sorry condition was retrieved by the NII VVS and repaired. The modifications were undertaken locally using the facilities of the nearest PARM, specifically to show the Division that improvements could be carried out by themselves in the field. The results of this work were exceptional. The NII VVS engineers not only repaired the machine in question and helped the Division restore its remaining Yak-7Bs to proper performance, but also developed several new finishing techniques that were recommended for production. These recommendations were forwarded at once to the NKAP, and by November had been officially accepted. Production of the Yak-7B M-105PF with the improved finishing techniques was ordered to begin at once, and models with these features were leaving Novosibirsk during that same month.

The new Yak-7 with all improvements became standard beginning with the 31st production series at Novosibirsk. *Zavod* 82 at Moscow lagged behind, but by early 1943 it was also producing machines to this standard. The improved Yak-7B M-105PF could once again match the performance of the original M-105PF prototype, 514 km/h being achieved at sea level and 582 km/h at 3,650 m. Initial climb with the finishing improvements rose again to 1,009 m/min, attaining 5,000 m in only 5.7 minutes. Enthusiasm for the improved production models amongst service pilots rose to an all-time high.

During the late spring and summer of 1942, the Yak-7 programme took another significant direction. The NKAP was, as usual, issuing requests for fighters of vastly improved range. Yakovlev's OKB responded with the Yak-7D (*dal'niy*, literally 'distant' for 'long-range') fighter in May, featuring a new 9.74 m wing full of extra fuel cells, and a revised rear fuselage. This aircraft devolved into the Yak-7DI (*dal'niy istebitel'*, or 'distant'/long-range fighter) of June-July, the ultimate result of which being the new Yak-9 fighter.

The Yak-7DI was significant for the Yak-7 programme for other reasons, however. Most Yak-7 prototypes during 1942 were demonstrating cut-down rear fuselages, and the Yak-7DI demonstrated a particularly satisfactory version of this modification. The shift towards cut-down rear fuselages throughout the Yakovlev Bureau at this time was manifestly evident and a number of units in the field (notably Shinkarenko's 42 IAP) were undertaking modifications of this type to their Yak-7s on their own initiative during the summer and autumn of 1942.

No detailed information on this exists either in Yakovlev's own papers nor his various works, nor in A.T. Stepanets' book on the Yak fighters. The NKAP instructions of November 1942 covering the improved finishing methods proposed by the NII VVS say nothing on the matter at all, neither do the factory records of *Zavod* 153. Judging by the photographic record, it is thought that *limited* manufacture of Yak-7Bs with cut-down fuselages began sometime around October or November 1942. To date it has proved impossible to locate a photograph pre-dating April 1943 in which a Yak-7-equipped unit features only cut-down fuselage models; there is always a mix of these and 'razorback' models in each case. These mixed situations were common well after this date, but increasingly from this time, the cut-down fuselage Yak-7B was ever more common.

Performance in the 1943 model Yak-7 with cut-down fuselage was thought to be similar in most respects to the contemporary 'razorback' models produced earlier. In January 1944, the NII VVS examined Yak-7B No.258201 (Series 25, *Zavod* 82, unit No.01) and recorded performance figures that seem to confirm the belief: 516 km/h at sea level, 579 m/h at 3,650 m; initial climb was measured at 1,095 m/min. and 5,000 m was attained in 5.7 minutes.

The Yak-7B M-105PF was, essentially, the definitive model of the Yak-7 family, though there were a number of developments (proposed and otherwise) which stemmed from it. Various examples of the basic Yak-7B 'razorback' were adapted to carry a passenger in the space behind the cockpit, where the instructor's position had once been, and these were known as *Kurierskiy* (courier). There was a proposed development featuring the M-105PF motor and two DM-4S ramjets under the wings, but this resulted in just two prototypes. The very last series of Yak-7s at Novosibirsk was examined with an eye to producing a Yak-7P (*pushechniy*, or cannon) version of the fighter, this to mount three 20 mm B-20 cannon. However, no manufacture of this type was realized.

The final significant member of the Yak-7 family were the *Razvedchik* (scout) reconnaissance variants. No suffix was attached to the Yak-7 designation to identify these machines, but limited manufacture of Yak-7s with the AFA-IM tactical camera installed was carried out as early as 1941 as a kind of 'emergency', or stopgap. During 1943, the type was highly desirable, and *Zavod* 82 was issued instructions by the NKAP to manufacture a Yak-7B *Razvedchik* in series. The *Razvedchik* was armed with a single 20 mm ShVAK to fire through the spinner and performance was slightly improved over a standard Yak-7B fighter. Some 315 *Razvedchik* Yak-7s were manufactured during 1943-44 by this enterprise, and later in the run, kits were produced that allowed the installation of the reconnaissance package in any Yak-7B in the field.

If it can be said that the Yak-7 was something of a fortunate 'accident' of development, it cannot be said that its transformation into a premier dogfighter was anything but due to the indefatigable work of the Yakovlev OKB. Always possessed of handling "...too beautiful for a weapon of war, and too gentle for a killing machine," the Yak-7 was *the* pilot's aircraft. Indeed, this very handling instilled in its pilots the confidence to push the Yak-7 to the very limit; a characteristic that went a long way to compensating for its slightly inferior performance. Always rugged and reliable, the Yak-7 was the proud progenitor to its eminently successful successor and the most-produced Yak fighter of the GPW – the Yak-9.

	Yak-7	Yak-7A	Yak-7B	Yak-7-37	Yak-7B M-105PF 1942	Yak-7B M-105PF 1943
Weights						
Empty:	2482 kg	2455 kg	2586 kg	2700 kg	2495 kg	2461 kg
Loaded:	2566 kg	2941 kg	3135 kg	3241 kg	3016 kg	2995 kg
Wing Area:	17.16 m.sq.	17.16 m.sq	17.16 m.sq	17.16 m.sq	17.16 m.sq	17.16 m.sq
Engine	M-105PA 1,050 (1150) hp	M-105PA 1,050 (1150) hp	M-105PA 1,050 (1150) hp	M-105PA 1,050 (1150) hp	M-105PF 1,180 (1260) hp	M-105PF 1,180 (1260) hp
Maximum Speed						
At Altitude:	560 km/h at 5000 m	573 km/h at 5000 m	577 km/h at 3890 m	565 km/h at 4725 m	565 km/h at 4725 m	582 km/h at 3650 m
Sea Level:	471 km/h	497 km/h	498 km/h	485 km/h	489 km/h	515 km/h
Climb						
Initial:	884 m/min	915 m/min	867 m/min	793 m/min	976 m/min	1009 m/min
Time to Height:	6.8 min to 5000 m	6.4 min to 5000 m	6.5 min to 5000 m	7.2 min to 5000 m	5.8 min to 5000 m	5.7 min to 5000 m
Service Ceiling	9225 m	9450 m	9900 m	9230 m	9900 m	10185 m
Armament	2 x ShKAS 1 x ShVAK	2 x ShKAS 1 x ShVAK 6 x RS-82	2 x UBS 1 x ShVAK 6 x RS-82	2 x UBS 1 x MPSh-37	2 x UBS 1 x ShVAK	2 x UBS 1 x ShVAK

	Yak-7 *razvedchik*
Weights	
Empty:	2495 kg
Loaded:	2948 kg
Wing Area:	17.16 m.sq
Engine	M-105PA 1,050 (1150) hp
Maximum Speed	
At Altitude:	574 km/h at 4725 m
Sea Level:	506 km/h
Climb	
Initial:	930 m./min
Time to Height:	5.9 min to 5000 m
Service Ceiling	9900 m
Armament	1 x ShVAK

Yak-7A

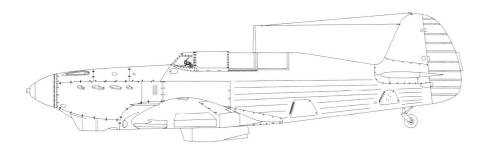

Yak-7UTI

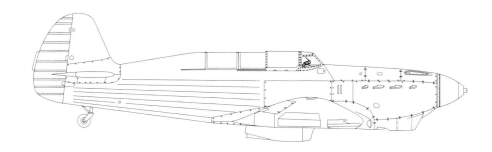

**Yak-7B
with cut-down
rear fuselage**

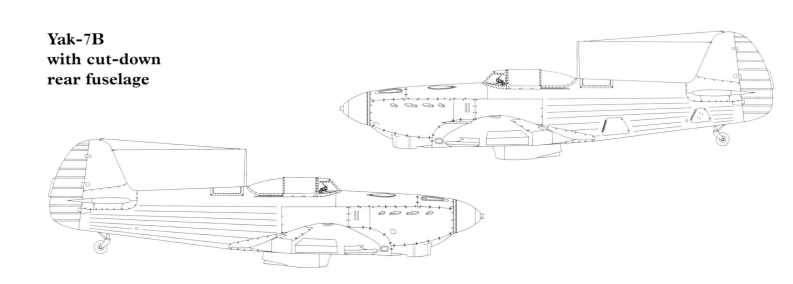

Yak-7-37

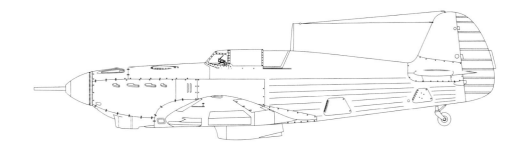

Yak-7B

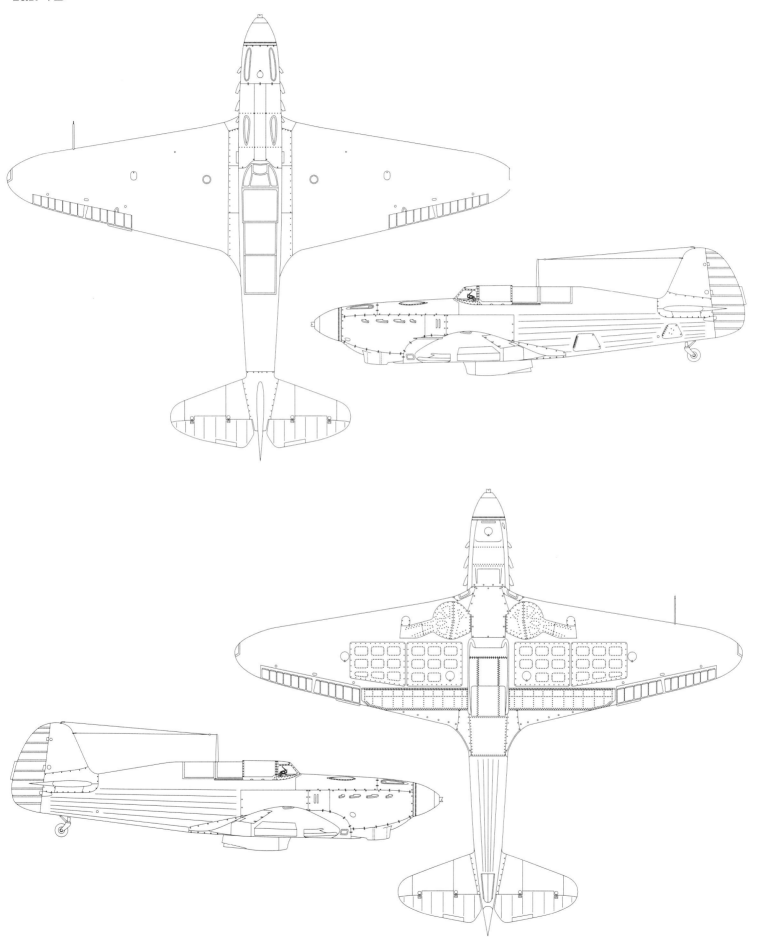

THE DEVELOPMENT OF CAMOUFLAGE ON
THE YAK-7 FIGHTER

The Trainer

In the Spring of 1941, manufacture began on a training variant of the I-26 prototype, this being known as the Yak-7UTI. The Yak-7UTI was usually camouflaged in a curious early-War application that was extremely angular, and unlike most other VVS patterns. AII Black was applied over AII Green, and the undersides were the usual AII Blue (see Fig. 1).

Fig. 1

Below: *The Yak-7 prototype at the Zavod 115 workshops in Moscow. This excellent view shows the early, angular camouflage pattern of the time. See early Yak-1. (Photo: G.Petrov)*

When a second series of Yak-7UTI trainers was ordered back into production in 1943 as the Yak-7V, these were camouflaged as per the prevailing Yak-7 and Yak-9 practices at *Zavod* 153 where they were built. A few Yak-7Vs, however, appeared in the older AII Greens, and the exact nature of this loosely-applied scheme is still under investigation at the time of writing.

Yak-7 Fighters Emerge

At the beginning of 1942 no fewer than three factories began manufacture of the Yak-7 – *Zavod* 301, Moscow; *Zavod* 153, Novosibirsk; *Zavod* 21, Gor'ki. At Moscow, *Zavod* 301 applied a scheme in AII Black over AII Green that was typical of its usual practices. The lower surfaces were finished in the usual AII blue livery. This application pattern was organic in shape, but reminiscent of *Zavod* 301's angular work on the UTI; it appears in some parts to be a rounded version of this pattern (see Fig. 2).

However, manufacture of the Yak-7 at Moscow came to an end after the evacuation of the plant to

Fig. 2

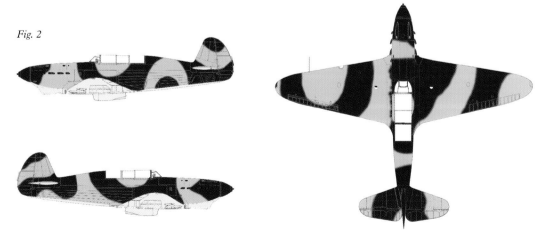

Novosibirsk (to join *Zavod* 153), only a single series (51 machines) ever being completed. At Gor'ki, manufacture of the type had just got underway when the entire factory was switched to production of the La-5. A mere five Yak-7s were delivered by *Zavod* 21, and there is no known photograph which shows their appearance.

At the Novosibirsk facility, production was gearing up to vast output. The first recognizable pattern emerging here became a Yak-7 'classic', and endured throughout the programme even up to the arrival of the Yak-7B (see below) (see Fig. 3).

Fig. 3

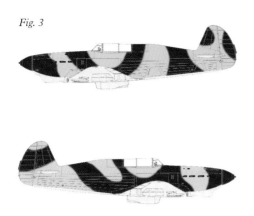

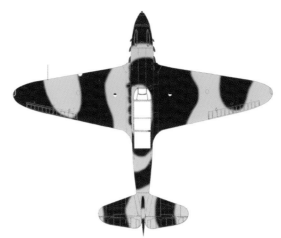

This scheme comprised a two-colour application of AII Black over AII Green, and with AII Blue undersurfaces. The demarcations between all of the colours ranged from very sharp to semi-sharp, though in the very last of these patterns, semi-soft lines can be seen. The upper/lower colour demarcation line was very low and tidy, as was then traditional on VVS fighters.

Internal Colouration

In all early Yak-7s, the interior colour practice was typical for the 1941-42 period. There were many cases of unpainted interiors in Yak-7 manufacture, and indeed of the surviving airframes of this type the majority were not finished. The early Novosibirsk examples seem especially prone to non-painted cockpit interiors, and finished examples from this factory until the late spring of 1942 would have to be considered the exception to the rule. Thereafter, the typical *Zavod* 153 method was to finish the cockpit, but not in a single, uniform colour. Metal Use Primer was common on metal and steel surfaces, and Wood Finishes on the wooden panels and structural members. All fabric areas were doped with clear 17-A lacquer on the interior surfaces.

Above: *Andrey Chirkov of the 29 GIAP is pictured here on the Leningrad Front on 16 May 1943 with his Yak-7B. Note the Guard's emblem which has been applied at a curious angle and which does not have a white background. (Photo: G.Petrov)*

"That Hideous Soup"

The great dislocation of production that followed the frantic evacuation of much of the aviation industry over the winter of 1941-42 had a profound impact on factories everywhere. Nowhere was this more evident – *visually* evident – than at *Zavod* 153, Novosibirsk. This giant complex had been in the business of manufacturing farm machinery before the war, which had been finished in a very bright green paint that was something of a factory trademark. Today, in rural Russia, one still encounters this green colour on old pieces of equipment, and it is just as bright and extraordinary now as it was some 60 years ago. To the eternal discomfort of many VVS pilots, alas, the factory – faced with a shortage of aero paints – decided to employ this shade for manufacture on the Yak-7 (see Fig. 4).

Supplies of AII Black seem to have been well in hand, and so a two-colour pattern using this and the 'substitute' Tractor Green colour was invented.

Fig. 4

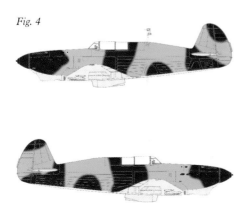

The pattern was very straightforward, being a symmetrical fuselage application with more typical upper surface shapes. The colour demarcation lines were usually semi-soft on the uppersurfaces. Aesthetically, however, the colours were ghastly, and a noted Russian historian, upon examining the surviving example of this work, uttered in disgust that it resembled "... that hideous [pea] soup!"

Examples in this colouration were sporadic. It seems that manufacture with these colours was undertaken only when required as a result of shortages. However, such colour applications are known in the photographic record only during 1942, probably occurring as far as late summer of the year. One last feature of these schemes is that the interiors are invariably not painted; one wonders if the factory staff preferred to avoid working around such aircraft.

Transition to the Yak-7B

The last scheme to appear on the early Yak-7 and -7A models was a striking pattern with many new upper surface features. Sometimes referred to as the 'Doughnut Application' (due to the circular feature around the cockpit), this pattern theme was dominated by round shapes on the upper view. The wings, in particular, demonstrated features that could be said to form nascent 'loops' – a feature that would soon dominate much of the Yak-7 programme (see Fig. 5).

Fig. 5

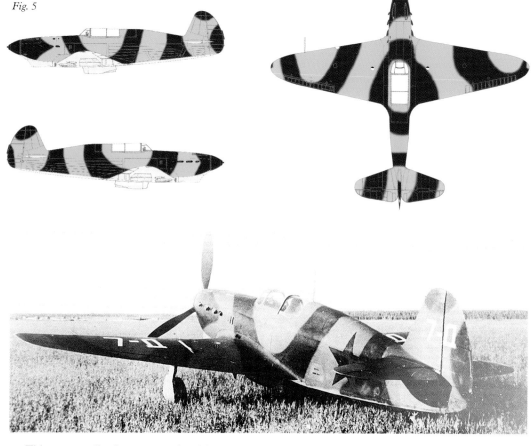

Right: *The Yak-7D prototype demonstrates a common camouflage pattern of mid-1942, in this case finished in AMT lacquers. The white letters '7-D' indicate the prototype's identity. (Photo: G.Petrov)*

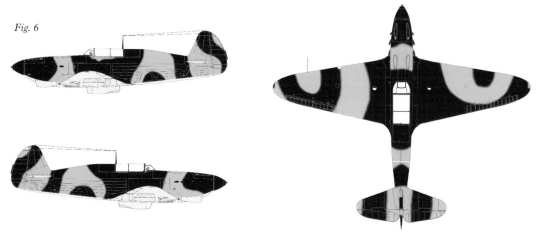

This new application was rendered in AII Black over Green, and continued well into the period of Yak-7B manufacture.

Along with the improved Yak-7B came a new camouflage application that was certainly a precursor to the 'loops' pattern. Clearly building from the previous 'Doughnut' theme, the new scheme was usually rendered in the new AMT paints, AMT-6 Black over AMT-4 Green with AMT-7 Blue undersurfaces, but many examples with AII lacquers were known, as illustrated (see Fig. 6).

Fig. 6

It is suspected that the early Yak-7 products manufactured at *Zavod* 82 all wore pattern applications very similar to that shown in the illustrations.

The following camouflage scheme, perhaps a culmination of all previous work, was a 'classic', and is thought to have been developed personally by Bukhanova (certainly it bears her influences). Indeed, this application has come to be associated with the Yak-7 programme, and any generically illustrated example of the type usually wears this extremely handsome theme. AMT-6 over AMT-4 were the usual colour choices, but early versions wore AII colours as illustrated here (see Fig. 7).

Above: *A fine line-up view of Yak-7Bs directly off the production line at Zavod 153, Novosibirsk. These aircraft appear to be wearing AMT lacquers. (Photo: M.Biskun collection)*

Fig. 7

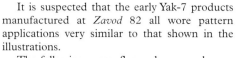

Above: *'White 29', the personal Yak-7B of the commander of the 29 GIAP, Podpolk. Aleksandr Mateev seen in the autumn of 1943. Note the white spinner common to this Regiment. (Photo: G.Petrov)*

Interestingly, there were two possible uppersurface applications, and they seem to have been applied equally, and simultaneously; several photographs exist of adjacent Yak-7s on the lines at Novosibirsk wearing either upper pattern. The first uppersurface version is sometimes called the 'W-Wing Pattern', for obvious reasons. The alternative uppersurface pattern is the original complete 'Loops' application, one of the classic VVS camouflage patterns of the GPW (see Fig. 8).

The upper surface colour demarcation lines in both cases are usually semi-soft, marking a trend away from harder-edged lines.

The Bukhanova scheme prevailed into the winter of 1942. During the winter, *Zavod* 153 adopted the usual practice of applying a coat of MK-7F white distemper over the temperate camouflage scheme (see Fig. 9).

Fig. 8

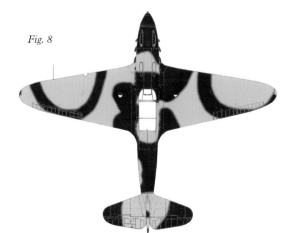

Fig. 9

Above: *A line-up of Yak-7Bs of the 3 IAK donated by collective farm workers of the Bashkortostan Autonomous Socialist Republic in the Kuban sector, 1943. The flash on the fin/rudder is white, and the spinners appear to have red tips. The spinner colour is less certain and might be polished bare metal. (Photo: G.Petrov)*

Right: *A fine winter-camouflaged Yak-7B of an unknown unit seen sometime during the winter of 1942-43. (Photo: G.Petrov)*

As winter gave way to spring it was not uncommon for the *factory* to apply only a partial coat of MK-7F, leaving part of the aircraft in temperate camouflage (it was certainly common for field units to do this, but this is one of the rare cases of a factory doing so) (see Fig. 10).

Fig. 10

Full-gear production

With the arrival of 1943, the goal in the Yak-7 programme turned away from development towards production efficiency. The older 'razorback' models were just starting to give way to versions of the Yak-7B with cut-down rear fuselages, and the Yak-9 was also being produced in series in the same factory complex. *Zavod 82* in Moscow had joined the Yak-7 programme in the late spring of 1942, but output had been anaemic so far. Entering 1943, the Moscow factory at last got into stride, and Yak-7s began to emerge from this facility in serious quantities.

With the goal of increasing production in mind, new camouflage applications appeared at both Yak-7 factories. *Zavod 153* led the way by largely discontinuing the beloved Bukhanova pattern for a simplified – and no doubt more efficient – camouflage scheme again using AMT-6 and AMT-4 over AMT-7 undersurfaces (see Fig. 11).

Below: *The famous Yak-7B of twice Hero of the Soviet Union Petr Porkrishev of the 29 GIAP (ex-154 IAP). The aircraft is shown here preserved in the Defence of Leningrad Museum in 1945, but it appears as he had last flown it during the late spring of 1943. The finish appears to be AMT lacquers AMT-6 over AMT-4. Note that the top two and bottom rows of 'kill' markings are in red, and the Guard's emblem has been applied in the 'ground angle' manner. (Photo: G.Petrov)*

Fig. 11

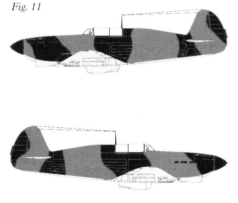

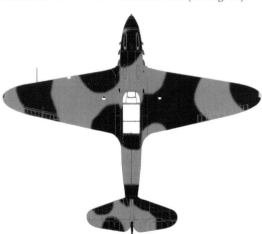

The old-fashioned lower and restrained upper/lower colour demarcation line persisted, but the demarcation lines on the uppersurfaces were semi-soft, in keeping with new preferences. It is just possible that a few AII lacquer examples of this scheme were completed, but none yet have emerged in the pictorial record.

At *Zavod 82* a new scheme appeared almost on the stroke of 1943. The new pattern was curious in that it featured relatively simple upper surface features along with a more complicated fuselage application. The use of AII Black over Green was still common here, but as the year progressed, the finish was completed increasingly with the new AMT paints. AII finish is shown here (see Fig. 12).

Fig. 12

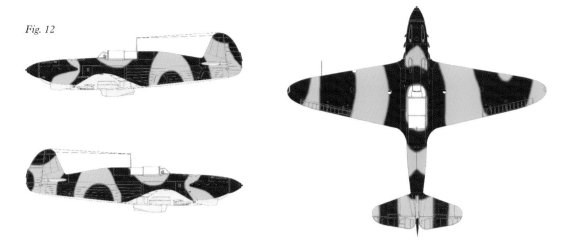

The most remarkable feature of this pattern application is its extreme symmetry. No other known VVS scheme of the War period was so symmetrical on each side of the fuselage, and clearly the principle seems to have been to introduce time-saving. Indeed, a small swipe with the air gun and even the upper pattern could have been symmetrical; a very strange example of Soviet camouflage.

Internal Colours – 1943

An important development occurred during 1943 at the Novosibirsk factory regarding interior cockpit colouration. A Lithuanian named F. Rimenich became a Line Supervisor during this time, and apparently forbade the appearance of Metal Use Primer on the interior surfaces of the cockpit, complaining that the colour was so bright that it jeopardized the aircraft's camouflage scheme; some of his written complaints form part of the factory records. Although Rimenich worked on the Yak-9 programme, it is possible that his influence might have been felt on the Yak-7 lines during 1943. Some photographs appear to show that this might be the case, but many more demonstrate the more usual approach – as before – to the finish of Yak-7 cockpits during this year. There is still speculation surrounding this.

The Last Yak-7s

The final versions of the Yak-7B with cut-down rear fuselages were usually attended by their own camouflage application. Some did, in fact, wear patterns of earlier styles, but in the main, the change in appearance of the airframe seemed to call for a revised colouration. At *Zavod* 153 this idea was taken up with gusto. Perhaps regretting their rather dour 'efficiency' scheme, the staff at Novosibirsk launched a handsome 'loops' application pattern on the last Yak-7s and early Yak-9s (see Fig. 13).

Fig. 13

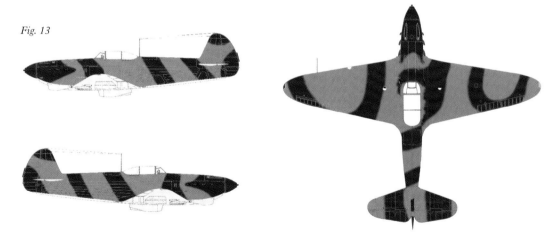

Left: *A line-up of AMT-6/-4/-7-finished Yak-7Bs seen during the summer of 1943. Three different and known camouflage applications can be seen on the first three aircraft – not at all unusual for a VVS Regiment. The first two Yak-7Bs carry cut-down rear fuselages, and are both numbered '09'. The machine in the foreground features small white figures on the rudder, which might be the numbers '76'. (Photo: G. Petrov)*

AMT lacquers (-6,-4,-7) were standard, as illustrated, but a few AII examples are known. The new PARMs and other field units took up the new 'loops' scheme with enthusiasm when conducting repairs and other work.

At *Zavod* 82, meanwhile, Yak-7B manufacture carried on well into 1944. During 1943, a common scheme appeared on its own cut-down fuselage models, this being a clear development of the earlier simplified symmetrical pattern (see Fig. 14).

Fig. 14

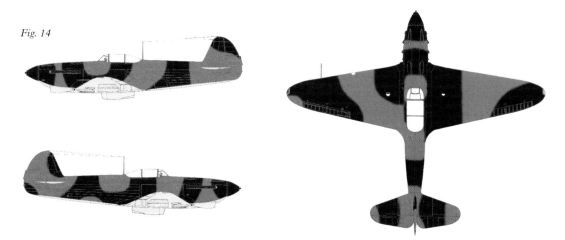

Once again, the pattern showed complicated fuselage areas and simplified uppersurfaces. Clearly derivative, the demarcation lines were all semi-soft, and AMT lacquers were entirely standard.

The final run of Yak-7s at Moscow stretched well into 1944, and as a result the new camouflage colours of AMT-11 and AMT-12 were seen on this programme. Starting early in the year, the new camouflage application was somewhat generic, and was not based on the new NKAP recommendations to any useful degree (see Fig. 15).

Fig. 15

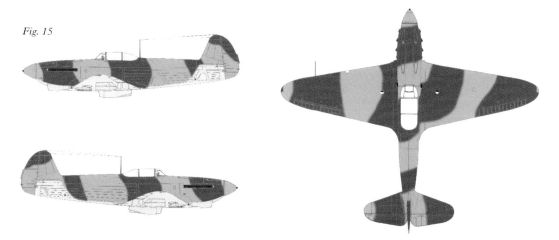

The pattern was simple, and apparently well received by field units (who often copied it). Interestingly, some of Yak-7 manufacture during the winter of 1943-44 seem to be wearing this two-colour scheme as completed with the old Medium Grey and Wood *Aerolak* paints. Photographs of this appearance are rare, and it is thought that the number of aircraft so completed was small (see Fig. 16).

Fig. 16

Unusual Yak-7 Schemes

Similar to earlier examples found on I-16s, a few photographs exist depicting both Il-2s and Yak-7s with the VMF-SF (Naval Northern Fleet) during the winter of 1941-42 finished in a very odd experimental Black and White disruptive scheme, presumably AII Black and MK-7.

A number of Yak-7Bs serving on the South Front during 1943 were modified by the receiving units to bear unique three-colour applications. The traced border type scheme seen in the photograph opposite centre, right, is typical of these.

Above: *A colourful Yak-7 of the 434 IAP at Stalingrad in December 1942. The inscription and trim on the fin/rudder are in red, as is the text, which reads 'k-z Politotdelets Zashchitnikam Stalingrada' ('From the Politotdelets Collective Farm to the Defenders of Stalingrad'). (Photo: G.Petrov)*

Above: *This Yak-7B is the recipient of some of the very finest field camouflage work of the GPW, pictured here during 1943. Though this aircraft is not serving in the South Front region, its scheme is entirely reminiscent of those applications, and also of similar three-colour schemes found on bomber aircraft. This Yak is thought to wear a basic AII Black and Green 'loops' scheme supplemented by lines of AII Light Brown. 'Red 41', behind, wears another known camouflage scheme in AMT-6/-4/-7. (Photo: G.Petrov)*

Above: *This spectacular Yak-7B is thought to be the personal mount of Nikolai Tikhonov, and was photographed during November 1942. Tikhonov was a pilot in May. Shinkarenko's illustrious 42 IAP, and several pilots of this Regiment carried a 'score card' scroll motif, including Legchakov, Kondakov and German. The aircraft is wearing a Bukhanova 'loops' application in AII Dark Green and Green, but oddly over what appears to be AMT-7 undersurfaces. It is almost certain that this machine was refinished outside the factory (where it was probably finished in AMT lacquers), and with its raised upper/lower colour demarcations and superb flowing lines, this aircraft represents the epitome of Bukhanova-style camouflage during the GPW. (Photo: G.Petrov)*

Right: *Another line-up of several Yak-7s and a MiG-3 (foreground). All of these fighters belong to the famous 'Komsomol' squadron, allegedly from the 1st and 3rd eskadrilya of the 12 GIAP. The MiG-3 and Yak-7B in the immediate foreground are both Razvedchik reconnaissance models. Most of the Yak-7s (As and Bs) are wearing various 'loops' applications in AII Black/Green lacquers, and feature white or red trim. Novosibirskiy Komsomol ('Red 03') is visible behind '27', which is wearing a Bukhanova-style raised colour 'ramp' feature on the fuselage. (Photo: G.Petrov)*

Left: *A colourful Yak-7B of the 438 IAP (212 GIAP), spring, 1943. The pilot seated left, playing black, is thought to be Anatoli Kozhevnikov (later Hero of the Soviet Union), but it is not known if 'White 22', behind, might have belonged to the 27-victory ace. (Photo: G.Petrov)*

Below: *Another view of Yak-7B 'White 22', of the 438 IAP (212 GIAP), spring 1943. The inscription reads 'Latvian Gunner'. (Photo: V. Romanenko)*

Below: *Another 438 IAP Yak-7B photographed at the same time as 'White 22'. This aircraft sports an illegible inscription just above the pilots' heads, and also carries the white lightning bolt. (Photo: G.Petrov)*

Right: *A close-up of one of the 'Komsomol' Yak-7Bs seen in 1943. This machine is 'Komsomol Kuzbassa' ('Communist Youth League of the Kuzbass region'). (Photo: G.Petrov)*

Below: *A Yak-7A, 'White 23', wearing an as yet unidentified camouflage application pattern completed in AII Black over Green. (Photo: M.Biskun collection)*

Above: *This rather worn Yak-7B was photographed on the Baltic Front during the autumn of 1944. The inscription is in Lithuanian, and states 'Soviet Lithuania'. These machines were presented to the 146 IAP on 20 February 1943, the money for them having been collected by Lithuanians in Russia. Originally a Yak-7B fighter, this machine was subsequently converted into a UTI trainer (probably via a kit offered by Zavod 153 for this purpose), and repainted. The aircraft seems to have begun life as a Zavod 153 Black over Tractor Green specimen, some of the original and ungainly scheme still being visible. (Photo: G.Petrov)*

Right: *This aircraft (on evidence, probably a Yak-7B rather than a Yak-9) is believed to be wearing an AII Dark Green/Green scheme, and was photographed in the summer of 1943. The inscription reads, 'Kievskiy Zheleznodorozhnik' ('Kiev Railway-Worker'). This photograph also demonstrates another VVS painting peculiarity: Russians of the time seemed to have possessed an aversion to using standard fonts. In this case, 'Black 44' (visible behind) has two different fonts on the same aircraft – both of them '4's! Though bewildering, it was not at all unusual! (Photo: G.Petrov)*

Left: *A Yak-7B of the 29 GIAP, spring 1943. This aircraft is thought to demonstrate an example of the partially-applied winter white scheme from Zavod 153. The forward fuselage had originally been finished very sharply at the factory but has faded with wear, while the MK-7 white over the rear fuselage looks to be of a more recent application. The photograph shows several details quite clearly, such as the ejection slot for the UBS gun along the wing fillet, and the later pattern 'Yak-9'-style exhaust stacks. (Photo: G.Petrov)*

163

Yakovlev Yak-9

Chapter 8

Yakovlev Yak-9

Another type to make its debut over Stalingrad – at the very end of 1942 – was the Yak-9. The Yak-9 represented the culmination of all the various type-improvements introduced on the Yak-7 programme up to that time. In June 1942, Yakovlev finally accepted the inevitable division that had grown in the development of his fighter aircraft, essentially along two lines. On the one hand, the Yak-7 had to a degree become a 'Frontal' fighter – in line with the original 1938 specification – heavier and more heavily-armed than the Yak-1, and on the other, the Yak-1 was increasingly evolving into a 'light' air-superiority machine. The Yak-9 was certainly conceived as a Frontal fighter – a direct development of the Yak-7 – but in time would fill both roles, Frontal and air superiority, and with equal success.

During the spring and summer of 1942, work had been underway on the Yak-7 programme to develop a long-range tactical fighter for the VVS. Stalin had been agitating throughout 1942 for fighters with increased range, and a report appeared on his desk describing several foreign aircraft. With his usual ineptitude for all things technical, the *Generalissimo* confused the range reported for the British Photo Reconnaissance Spitfire as being that of the standard Mk.V fighter, and decided that Soviet fighters should also have such a range lest they fall behind technologically. No amount of explanation could pry him from his belief and so the NKAP issued a specification for fighters from both Lavochkin and Yakovlev with a range of more than 1,500 km.

In his usual no-nonsense manner, and with a polite, yet firm tone, Lavochkin refused. Having the wherewithal to rebuff Stalin to his face must have been remarkable, but Lavochkin knew that the La-5 simply could not be made to meet this specification, and rightly so. A.S Yakovlev's reaction, however, was the opposite – he immediately saw the NKAP request as a challenge, and he knew that his fighters were well disposed to meet the requirements. The Yak-7 was the obvious platform for this type of development, and he ordered his Bureau to work. Extra fuel cells had been installed in Yak-7 fighters hitherto, but these were no more than adhoc arrangements. Yakovlev and his OKB knew that a fundamentally new machine must be developed specifically for long-range capabilities.

The basis of the new Yak-7 long-range variant was to be an entirely new wing. Following an exhaustive evaluation of possible configurations, Senior Designers Sinel'shikov and Adler hit upon the idea of burying four large fuel cells into the structure of the wing. By using dural spars and longerons of very advanced design, the wing structure could be made light enough to permit the large quantities of fuel necessary without degrading performance, but also strong enough to bear the increased loads that would result from the extra weight. The I-28 prototype's wing was an obvious source of inspiration for the new design, both because it was constructed with a dural spar and therefore had already solved many of the major issues associated with fitting wooden members to it, and also due to its shape.

The I-28's wing employed an ingenious wing tip shape, one that was variously seen on Soviet fighter prototypes during the last part of the 1930s. This wing-tip was of a quarter-round wedge shape, with the blunt edge pointing forward. Bisnovat had used this wing-tip on his early SK fighters, as had other designers, and the I-28 and I-30 both sported it. In the case of the latter, the reasoning was that this shape lent itself well to the installation of leading edge wing slats. However, engineers at the Yakovlev OKB noticed that this wing tip shape also gave a similar wing area for less span, being more efficient in area squared than a rounded tip (as on the I-26). The effect, they realized, on a wing of similar area would be a saving of nearly 0.3 of a metre of span, and this would confer a superior rate of roll on the machine.

The new long-range Yak-7 prototype's metal spar wing was duly completed with this blunt tip planform. This may have seemed a trivial point, but by summer 1942, the VVS was encountering for the first time a new and formidable German fighter, the Focke-Wulf Fw 190 A. This machine was fast, well-armed, and well protected, but above all it came as a shock to the Soviets because of its superb controls, particularly the ailerons, since they had become accustomed to facing stiff and clumsy 'energy' fighters like the Bf 109. Typically, VVS fighters relied on turning dogfight techniques to engage the enemy successfully, and having a significantly inferior aileron response was intolerable in the prosecution of these tactics. Pilots at the front were screaming for something to be done.

At the *Zavod* 153 workshops, Yakovlev had placed Senior Engineer Skrzhinskiy in charge of extending the range of the Yak-7. Upon the completion of Adler and Sinel'shikov's work, the new wing and latter gifted designer were transported to Novosibirsk to pool all the considerable talents working on the matter. The new wing was mated to a Yak-7 airframe already modified by Skrzhinskiy's team. This new fuselage contained no fewer than five small petrol tanks with a total capacity of 95 litres, all carefully distributed to avoid inordinate changes in the fighter's centre of gravity. To operate such a complex arrangement, Skrzhinskiy had designed a simple and very effective valve-regulator to equalize the usage of fuel through the various tanks. After attaching the new wing to the modified fuselage, which also featured a rounded rear section of improved aerodynamic shape, two additional tanks were added outboard in each wing, raising the number of fuel cells in the wing to six. The wing fuel tanks were fitted with the valve-regulator system, and now carried 883 litres; total capacity was 925 litres.

In this form the prototype was dubbed Yak-7D (*dal'niy*, or 'distant' for long-range) and rolled out of the workshop floors on 3 June 1942. The proposed armament for the Yak-7D had been reduced to a single heavy Shpitalniy MPSh-20 cannon, but photographs of the Yak-7D prototype show it mounting at least one machine gun above the engine. With a flying weight of 3,135 kg, and powered by the standard M-105PA motor, performance was understandably reduced. Pilot-Engineer Fedrovi could achieve only 495 km/h at sea level, and 5,000 m could not be reached in under seven minutes. Nevertheless, the goal of extending the Yak-7's range was reached and far exceeded, and Fedrovi flew the Yak-7D 2,285 km in 6.5 hours. He reported that all flight behaviour and conditions were normal, and that the prototype handled well.

However, even as the Yak-7D was being completed and rolled out for testing, a standard Yak-7B fighter, No.23-26, was removed from the production lines and modified along the same lines as the *dal'niy*. As a Series 23 Novosibirsk machine, this Yak-7 had the M-105PF motor and the higher RPM VISh-61P propeller combination, giving much better power and thrust. A new wing was built as on the Yak-7D, and provision was made for all six tanks. A supplementary oil tank was installed under the pilot, this containing an additional 6 litres of engine oil. A large 78 litre fuel tank behind the pilot replaced the five smaller units, though the outstanding valve-gauge system was

Yak-9D 'Berezans'kiy Kolgospnik'

Unit and pilot unknown
Ukraine, 1944

Colours:
AMT-11/-12/-7 application
from *Zavod* 153 or 166

Yak-9 'White 17'

4 IAP
Ivan Stepanenko
near Kursk
Summer 1943

Colours:
AMT-4/-6/-7 application
from *Zavod* 153

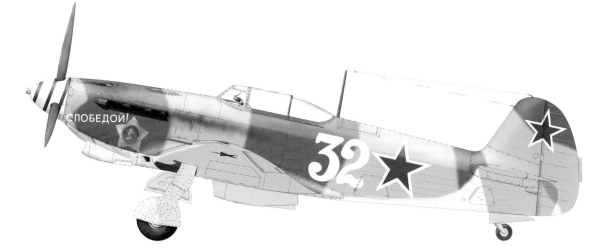

Yak-9 'White 32'

Unit and pilot unknown
Poland
1944

Colours:
AMT-11/-12/-7 application
from *Zavod* 153

Yak-9B 'Mali Teatr Frontu'

130 IAD
Location uncertain
1944

Colours:
AMT-11/-12/-7 application
from *Zavod* 153

retained. To keep weight down, and also to avoid a forward shift in the centre of gravity, the armament was reduced to a single 12.7 mm UBS above the engine and the ShVAK firing through the spinner. Most obviously, however, the fuselage's rear section aft of the cockpit was cut down, as was then coming into wide-spread use in the Yakovlev OKB, and a clear, rounded canopy section fitted to the rear. For pilot protection a 55 mm sheet of armoured glass was installed behind the pilot's head, as was a Yak-1-type pilot seat, and a similar panel was placed in the front windscreen.

For various technical and engineering reasons, much of the internal ducting of the Yak-7 was discarded in favour of the Yak-1 type arrangement. This arrangement was more efficient in terms of used space, but inferior in engine cooling and radiator supply. As a result, a radiator of increased capacity was installed, this having a similar frontal aspect to the previous unit, but a more 'squarish'-looking aft section, thus imparting the classic 'Yak-9' look. The Yak-7 type carbon dioxide bottle anti-fire system was replaced by the standard inert exhaust gas ducting, and a supplementary nitrogen tank was installed.

In this form, the 'normal' (*normalniy*) Yak-7DI (*dal'niy istrebitel'*, or distant fighter) was completed on 25 June 1942. Though considerable effort had been expended to reduce weight, at take-off the Yak-7DI was only 100 kg lighter than the Yak-7D prototype, and consequently performance suffered similarly. Fedrovi flew the Yak-7DI in this form extensively, and concluded that the speed and climbing performance were similar to that of the current Yak-7B M-105PF. He also recorded however that the new wing had imparted a significantly better rate of roll and aileron response over the older design, and maintained that the Yak-7DI could best any another Yakovlev fighter variant.

After a week of examination, the Yak-7DI prototype was then modified to its *oblegchenniy* (lightened) form. In this permutation, the outermost four wing fuel tanks were discarded along with the fuselage tank, reducing overall capacity to 440 litres. The supplementary oil tank was removed, and the ammunition supply was reduced to 120 rounds of 2mm and 140 rounds for the UBS. Having now shed another 200 kg, testing resumed at once, and this time Fedrovi was overjoyed. At sea level, the *oblegchenniy* Yak-7DI could routinely manage 505 km/h, and 570 km/h at 5,500 m, while the initial climb was simply superb at 11,02 m/min., and 5,000 m could be reached in 5.5 minutes. In vertical manoeuvres, the Yak-7DI could almost match the Yak-1 *oblegchenniy*, and moreover all of the beautiful handling of the Yak-7 was inherited by the Yak-7DI as a result of its improved vertical and horizontal stabilizers. Aileron response was rapid and of the utmost precision, and due to this, the Yakovlev Pilot-Engineer demonstrated that he could initially out-turn any Yak-1 fighter.

Fedrovi triumphantly turned over the Yak-7DI to the NII VVS for State examinations on 18 July 1942. Though testing lasted until 5 August, the acceptance trials were a mere formality, and it was clear that the Yak-7DI was outstanding. The NII's Yakovlev Evaluation Brigade leader, Stepanets, wrote voluminously about the Yak-7DI prototype, and he concluded that it was the most valuable and versatile fighter in the entire VVS.

It was more than enough for the NKAP, for back in Moscow the wheels of procurement were turning furiously. On 29 August, a sweeping Production Contract was issued by the NKAP for manufacture of the new prototype fighter, based on the *oblegchenniy* variant, as the Yak-9. Yakovlev was instructed to begin re-tooling the production lines at *Zavod* 153, but in such a way that manufacture of the Yak-7 would not be seriously interrupted; a complete disruption in fighter production at this difficult juncture was simply out of the question. At the same time, *Zavod* 166 at Omsk was instructed to discontinue all Tupolev Bureau prototype testing until further notice, and assemble a production line facility for the Yak-9 with all possible speed. Pandemonium at the Omsk facility was near total, and production was not restored until Yakovlev dispatched his most senior Head Designer, Vigant, to redress the situation.

Series manufacture of the Yak-9 commenced at Novosibirsk in October 1942. The production Yak-9 weighed 2,873 kg at take-off, some 34 kg more than the Yak-7DI prototype. The ammunition supply was restored to the usual Yak-7DI *normalniy* configuration, a 120-round box was installed for the ShVAK and 200 cartridges for the single UBS (to port). Power was provided by the 1,180 hp (1,260 hp for take-off and emergency) Klimov M-105PF upright V-12 driving a three metre VISh-61P propeller. The typical early Yak-9 could attain 520 km/h at sea level and 600 km/h at 4,300 m, climbing initially at 1,102 m/min and reaching 5,000 m in only 5.1 minutes. Manoeuvrability was exceptional, and with its superior rate of roll, the Yak-9 could out-turn the lighter Yak-1 *oblegchenniy* through the first full 360 degrees.

The first production batch of 22 Yak-9s was rushed to the Stalingrad Front in December 1942 and went into action at once with the 270 IAP. Once again, German pilots were in for a nasty surprise, and Soviet pilots immediately praised the new type's visibility and handling. Against the Bf 109G, the Yak-9 was superior in every category below 5,000 m, though still lacking in power at higher altitudes, and particularly in close quarters it could out-manoeuvre the Messerschmitt. Its improved rate of roll proved critical against the Fw 190, allowing the Yak to make use of its superior turning circle and vertical abilities to full effect.

Success with the new Yak-9 was immediate. On 5 January 1943, *Kpt.* Ivan M. Kornienko led nine Yak-9s of the 270 IAP over the shattered remains of Stalingrad, whence his *eskadrilya* was attacked by some 15 Bf 109s. Despite being attacked by surprise, and from above, Kornienko's Yaks tore into the German fighters. A bitter contest ensued, and was witnessed by soldiers on the ground from both sides. In the end, eight Bf 109s were destroyed for the loss of two Yak-9s, Kornienko scoring a 'double'. Two weeks later, on the 16th, Kornienko's *eskadrilya* was again in action, this time against Fw 190 fighters. Although, Kornienko did not score personally, his men dispatched six enemy machines without loss.

Production of the Yak-9 at the *Zavod* 166 facility at last got underway in January 1943. Under Vigant's guidance, manufacture of the type was well in hand, though certainly operating at far less capacity than the giant complex at Novosibirsk. Ironically, after 500 aircraft had been completed, production of the initial Yak-9 was to be phased out only months later in favour of two new versions.

The need for greater operational range was a continuing dilemma for Soviet aircraft designers during the GPW. The production Yak-9 had certainly sacrificed range for performance, more than half of the Yak-7DI *normalniy*'s fuel capacity being discarded. Yakovlev and his OKB staff began to feel that the Yak-9, with only 440 litres of fuel, had perhaps gone too far in this regard, and that a tactical 'Frontal' fighter of the type that could take the reigns from the Yak-7 must have a better endurance.

At Novosibirsk, the Yakovlev OKB and factory staff replaced the intermediate outboard fuel tanks into the wing of a production Yak-9, as on the Yak-7DI. Thus, fuel was now contained in four wing tanks, the two innermost cells of 208 litre capacity and the two outermost of 117 litres, giving a total of 650 litres. The supplementary six litre engine oil tank was also replaced below the pilot's chair. The modified Yak-9 was 164 kg heavier than a standard production model, the extra fuel and oil making up all of the increase.

Construction of the aircraft was completed by January 1943, State evaluations commencing immediately on the 14th and lasting until 26 February. Factory-testing of the new Yak-9 with four fuel cells was extremely brief, and the prototype passed immediately to the NII VVS. Not surprisingly, the majority of the examinations centred around the increased weight of the new Yak-9, and the resulting effects on performance. However, to the relief and delight of all parties, the increase in weight did not affect the Yak-9's level speed, though the rate of climb did, naturally, suffer. During early February modifications were made to the reduction gearing driving the VISh-61P airscrew as suggested by LII-testing during the previous winter. With the modified gearing the new Yak-9 was, in fact, even faster than the production model at sea level, and the NII VVS pilot's (Golfastov) report was extremely favourable. In the final test course, 535 km/h was reached at sea level and 591 km/h at 3,650 m, while the initial climb fell to 1,024 m/min. and 6.1 minutes were required to reach 5,000 m.

Simultaneously, work at the Yakovlev OKB centred on the Yak's armament. The successful employment of a cannon as large as the 37 mm gun in the Yak-7-37 was a source of inspiration for the Bureau, and studies were conducted in great detail over possible arrangements for just such a weapon again. Fortuitously, it was just at this juncture that a new 37 mm weapon of outstanding performance was entering mass-production as the NS-37. This new cannon was developed by team lead by Chief Designers A.Nudel'man and A.Suranov, and was not only as powerful as the earlier MPSh-37 cannon, firing the same round, but weighed 100 kg less than it. In combination with what was then the Yak-7DI development, the Yakovlev OKB staff leapt on the concept of mating the new weapon to the improved prototype. In November 1942, a Yak-9 airframe was removed from the lines at *Zavod* 153, and work began on fitting the large gun.

The immediate problem was one of centre of gravity and coping with the increased weight. The Yakovlev staff certainly expected the centre of gravity to move forward, as it had done on the Yak-7-37, but the ad-hoc treatment of the previous prototype was discarded for a more permanent solution. Studying the weight distribution in great detail, Senior Engineer Barsukov worked out that if the Yak-9's *entire* cockpit (and associated assemblies) were moved to the rear only 400 mm it would solve the centre of gravity problem arising from the installation of the NS-37 gun and all sundry equipment. The new prototype's fuselage was thus modified, the cockpit being moved aft along with the radio mast, and resulting in a smaller radio access hatch behind the rear canopy section. Strengthened motor mounts were installed in the forward structure in addition to heavier steel tubing in anticipation of the gun's powerful recoil. A new propeller was required to accept the large muzzle of the NS-37 (which projected some 15 cm beyond the tip of the spinner), and a suitable three metre VISh-105SV was installed. Rearrangement in the engine compartment (oil tank, fuel ducting, etc.) was required to accommodate the large 32-round ammunition box for the 37 mm cannon, and some of the space vacated by the cockpit's rearward placement was utilized to mount a larger box for the 220 rounds of 12.7 mm ammunition as well.

The completed Yak-9-37 prototype rolled out of the factory workshop just before New Year, 1943. The prospect of a fighter mounting such a powerful weapon had been under debate at the GKO from as early as the autumn of 1942. One of the main themes of the State Defence Committee's work centred around the need for an improved aerial anti-tank capability, and much of this emphasis fell on the Ilyushin Il-2 programme. But, a *fighter* with anti-tank armament was also discussed at length, and though the PTAB series of bombs were effective to a degree, a large aerial cannon was seen to be the real answer. On 25 December 1942, the GKO passed a resolution in favour of Yakovlev's just-completed Yak-9-37, and ordered that the prototype be dispatched to the NIPAV immediately upon completion of the factory evaluation.

Factory testing of the completed Yak-9-37 was completed with remarkable speed. The Yak-9-37 immediately showed the accuracy of Senior Engineer Barsukov's calculations, the aircraft's centre of gravity falling to within 2 mm of his projected figure. As a result, handling in the prototype was outstanding and completely unchanged from the production Yak-9. Unexpectedly, the rearward placement of the cockpit actually improved the machine's aerodynamic properties (as would be proved later on at TsAGI), and even with its greater weight the Yak-9-37 was as fast as a production Yak-9 fighter. Ground-taxiing revealed no difficulties despite the great weight of the NS-37 gun, and forward visibility was only slightly reduced forward due to the aft placement of the cockpit.

Thoroughly satisfied, the factory staff turned the Yak-9-37 over to NIPAV on 10 January 1943. The testing range staff were immediately impressed, and found the mounting and mechanical function of the 37 mm cannon to be completely acceptable, although they noted that great care in manufacture would have to be exercised due to the snug fit of the components in the engine bay. If a gun mounting were to come loose or fail, they concluded, recoil could possibly shatter half of the ducting and pipelines in the motor compartment. With little surprise, firing trials revealed that the NS-37 would be devastating – it was capable of penetrating 30 mm of face-hardened steel plate at up to a 45 degree angle from 500 m, and 45 mm of steel plate at 90 degrees. The NIPAV's supply of derelict airframes was also placed into severe jeopardy by the Yak-9-37, every one fired upon by the NS-37 being completely destroyed; even twin-engined bombers like the Il-4 would break up when struck by such a shell.

A summary report from the testing range, filed by telephone on 12 February 1943, was sufficient for the Government. NIPAV was instructed to turn over the Yak-9-37 to the NII VVS *at once* for State Acceptance Trials, these beginning on the 15th. On 18 February the GKO passed yet another resolution, this instructing Yakovlev to replace the current version of the Yak-9 with the new NS-37 armed variant immediately. While under examination by the NII VVS, the Yak-9-37's reduction gearing was modified as had been the *dal'niy* prototype's, which had just completed its evaluation. With this modification, the Yak-9-37 achieved 533 km/h at sea level and 597 km/h at 3,930 m – virtually as fast as the production Yak-9. The Institute Pilots confirmed the outstanding handling of the Yak-9-37 prototype, and noted that the remarkable gun platform properties of the Yak-9 (inherited from the Yak-7) greatly enhanced the use of the big gun. It was found that a burst of more than 2-3 rounds of 37 mm fire would cause the nose to begin to fall, thus spoiling the aim, but that in the Yak-9, individual rounds could be aimed with great precision.

Needless to say, both new Yak-9 prototypes passed their State Acceptance testing with flying colours. On 6 March, the NKAP issued another sweeping Production Contract to *Zavod* 153 which called for the replacement of the current Yak-9 with two new models. The *dal'niy*, ('distant'/long-range) prototype would be produced as the Yak-9D, while the Yak-9-37 would enter series manufacture as the Yak-9T (*tankoviy*, or 'tank' – probably in reference to the GKO resolution). So desirable were the new machines, that interruption of current Yak-9 production was authorized if need be and indeed, it was. Furthermore, once manufacture of the –9D had been established at Novosibirsk, the Yakolev OKB was to assist the staff at Omsk to modify their lines to Yak-9D standard as soon as was practicable. Through Herculean efforts – again playing to the strengths of Yakovlev – the giant *Zavod* 153 complex re-tooled its Yak-9 production lines by the end of the month, even managing to turn out a handful of both new types before 1 April. *Zavod* 166 followed suit in June 1943, but did not fully convert to the Yak-9D until August of that year.

With the advent of mass manufacture, performance did not suffer in the two new Yak-9s. The production Yak-9D was powered by the 1,180 hp M-105PF and weighed 3,117 kg at take-off. A typical Yak-9D could attain 535 km/h at sea level and 591 km/h at 3,650 m, climbing initially at 1,024 m/min. and reaching 5,000 m in 6.1 minutes. With its boosted fuel capacity, the Yak-9D had an remarkable *absolute* range of 1,360 km, but at the more usual cruise of 90 per cent power the figure was 905 km. The production Yak-9T was also powered by the M-105PF and weighed 3,025 kg at take-off. Maximum speed reached 533 km/h at sea level and 597 km/h at 3,930 m, with an initial climb of 1,067 m/min and requiring 5.5 minutes to achieve 5,000 m.

The Yak-9T was first to reach combat service, some 34 machines being supplied to the 16 Air Army's 237 IAD. The 1 GIAP (ex-29 IAP) was the first to fire the Yak-9T's large gun in anger, encountering a flight of Ju 88s on 7 July. Four enemy bombers were destroyed, and although the pilots had yet to fully accustom themselves to the 37 mm cannon, they were more than thrilled with its tremendous striking power. During intensive fighting from 5 June to 6 August, the Yak-9Ts of the 1 GIAP destroyed 49 (44.5 per cent) of the Regiment's confirmed 110 victories for the loss of 12 of their own.

The Yak-9D entered VVS service in August 1943, with *Kmdr.* Golubov's 18 GIAP and completed its first combat on the 17th having

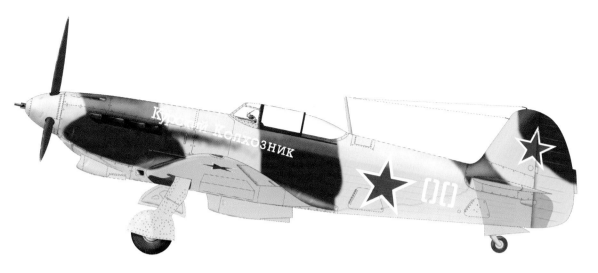

Yak-9T 'White 00'

293 IAP
Pilot unknown
Novosibirsk factory
194

Colours:
AII Brown/Light
Brown/Blue application
from *Zavod* 153

Yak-9T 'White 10'

Unit and pilot unknown
Baltic Front
1945

Colours:
AMT-11/-12/-7 application
from *Zavod* 153

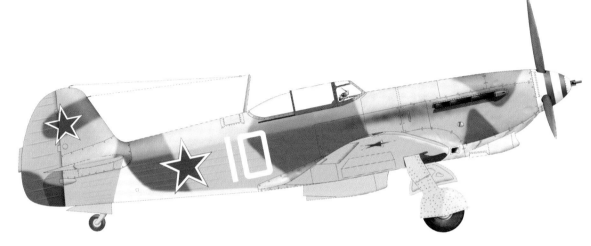

Yak-9T 'White 38'

728 IAP
Aleksandr Vibornov
1944

Colours:
AMT-11/-12/-7 application
from *Zavod* 153

Yak-9T 'White 66'

Location and assignment
uncertain
Summer 1944

Colours:
AMT-11/-12/-7 application
from *Zavod* 153

destroyed one He 111, two Ju 87s, and two Fw 190s for the loss of one Yak-9D. Though the all-up weight had grown 10 per cent over the earlier Yak fighters, the Yak-9D had lost none of its handling. Climbing performance did suffer, of course, due to the extra weight, and it soon became common practice for pilots to fly with the outer fuel cells empty on missions in which the very long-range of the Yak-9D was not required. This was also done because it was discovered that the outer wing tanks were more vulnerable to catching fire than the inner cells, the capacity of the anti-fire system being stretched to its limits. The most successful arrangement, however, was to have a mix of Yak-9 types available in each Regiment. Along every front, the newer Yak-9T and Yak-9D models served side-by-side with older Yak-9s. A typical IAP of late 1943 might include an *eskadrilya* of Yak-9s, one of Yak-9Ts, and one of Yak-9Ds, for example.

The appropriate employment of the Yak-9T fighter, however, and its role within the VVS, soon blew into something of a row. The GKO had conceived of the type as an anti-tank weapon, and was anxious to hear of the Yak-9T's successes in this regard. Many pilots at the front – especially those who had been agitating for increased firepower – saw the Yak-9T as deliverance from above, and began to employ the type as an air superiority machine. At this point, the UVVS would have been expected to step in and decide the matter, but being somewhat caught in the middle, determined that both missions were critical and resolved that Regiments with the Yak-9T should be prepared to take on either the air superiority role or the assault role as the circumstances demanded.

In reality, such an arrangement was not particularly realistic, and in some cases Regiments within the VVS began to specialize. Units like the 274 IAP and 520 IAP soon became experts in the destruction of German armour. During the liberation of the Ukraine in early 1944 their skills were fully demonstrated, and contributed in no small way to the overwhelming defeat of the *Wehrmacht* along the front. With the opening phase of the offensive around Nikopol, on the morning of 9 February, the 274 IAP smashed no fewer than 33 German tanks, 16 of which were Tigers. The 520 IAP, remorselessly pounded German armour trapped in the Korsun-Shevchenkosky pocket. When German forces in the pocket surrendered on 17 February, they had not a single functioning armoured vehicle left; the 520 IAP claimed 44 German vehicles.

In the aerial role, the pilots of *May.* Shinkarenko's 42 IAP led the way. Grigoriy German was brilliant in the air with his Yak-9T in the vicious fighting around Smolensk during September 1943. On the 4th, *Lt* German opened his account by downing a Do 217 bomber; a single round of 37 mm fire tore the wing off the enemy machine. On the 21st, he destroyed two more enemy bombers in similar fashion directly over the head of Marshal Novikov, the Front Commander, and the very next day scored a 'triple' against two Ju 88s and an Fw 190. Other 42 IAP pilots also scored heavily in the Yak-9T, *Kpt.* Brazhnets destroying three Ju 88s in as many firing attempts on 16 September, and on the 28th, A. Legchakov downed two Fw 190 fighters in head-on attacks with his Yak-9T, a procedure regarded as overly dangerous against the Focke-Wulf hitherto.

If one reads the popular press of the GPW period, or the published accounts written thereafter, there is the impression that the Yak-9T was used mainly in the anti-tank role. However, if one accepts an admittedly limited review of the records of two Air Divisions (283 IAD and 240 IAD) as representative of the –9T's utilization in general, the number of aerial combat sorties exceeded that of ground support sorties by a 65:35 ratio. It seems quite likely that the Yak-9T probably was employed chiefly as a fighter, and strongly in a secondary role as a tank-killer, and that its employment in the anti-tank role was highlighted as propaganda by the Government. Regardless of the exact numbers, the Yak-9T was supremely effective in *both* capacities, and served as one of the most important VVS fighters in the inventory until the end of the War.

Back at Novosibirk, the Yakovlev team was hard at work on various developments of the basic Yak-9 airframe. There was a proposed Yak-9P (*pushechniy*, or cannon) in which the 12.7 mm UBS above the

engine was replaced by a 20 mm ShVAK, resulting in an armament of two such weapons. Mass production of this version did not materialize, but the prototype served as a test-bed for installations of ever increasingly powerful weapons, such as the VYa-23, NS-45 (of which, more below), B-20, and even the NS-23. A version of the Yak-9 powered by the M-106 engine was tested during the beginning of 1943, and though performance was quite good in the prototype – 606 km was reached along with a time to 5,000 m of 5.4 minutes – the M-106 was simply too unready at this point to contemplate its introduction into service.

As with the Yak-7 before it, *Razvedchik* (scout) versions of the Yak-9 were built in series as the Yak-9R. At *Zavod* 166 (Omsk), several series of Yak-9R fighters were completed starting in the summer of 1943, and based on the longer-ranged Yak-9D airframe. The early variants retained their normal armament and carried the AFA-IM tactical camera, and RSI-4 radio, and most were also equipped with the RPK-10 radio compass and AGP-2 artificial horizon. In the later months of 1943, the camera equipment was upgraded to the AFA-3S/50 which worked in conjunction with the RPK-10 unit (for both automatic and manual exposures), delivering much improved photography. The usual armament for the newer Yak-9R was reduced to the single ShVAK through the spinner, but versions were also manufactured with the UBS still in place.

One final line of development in the early period of Yak-9 manufacture occurred with the high-altitude Yak-9PD prototypes. The units of the VVS PVO specialized in high-altitude interception, and many of these units were based in and around Moscow. The Yakovlev OKB experimented with many Yak-9 variants designed to fill the needs of the PVO, most of these powered by the M-105PD with various combinations of propellers and supercharger gearing. Many of the Yak-9PD prototypes were stripped of all manner of extraneous weight – airframe No.01-29 weighed only 2,500 kg – and the armament usually comprised only the engine-mounted ShVAK. Most versions of the M-105PD could produce 1,250 hp at about 7,620 m, but often produced all manner of overheating problems, though the M-106PD motor was also utilized. Some of the later M-106PV variants of 1944 incorporated an improved airframe similar to the Yak-9U. Many of the –PD prototypes served for some time with the PVO forces around Moscow. In August 1943, *Podpolk.* Sholokhov successfully intercepted and destroyed a Ju 86R reconnaissance machine at a height of 11,100 m. During April 1944, a limited series of 30 Yak-9PD M-105PDs were manufactured at *Zavod* 301 in Moscow, and served with the PVO forces there until after the GPW.

During the autumn of 1943, a crisis arose within the front line formations operating the Yak-9D. In a number of D models manufactured at *Zavod* 153, the outermost and sealing layer of laminate sheeting on the wings began to crack and fail on service aircraft. The problem was traced immediately to a faulty batch of nitro-cellulose resin supplied by the Frederik Engels factory in Serov (in the Urals), which had been hastily – and improperly – manufactured and shipped to Novosibirsk. The number of Yak-9Ds affected was significant, about 1 in 20 aircraft being defective, and the various Air Armies began to complain vociferously about the situation. As a result, in June 1943, Alexander Yakovlev and NKAP Deputy Commissar Dementiev were hauled in front of an angry Iosif Stalin, in Moscow, who was flanked by no less than Marshals Vasilevsky and Voronov.

In his autobiography, *Life Target*, Yakovlev recalled: "*We at once noticed pieces of cracked wing skinning on the table, and understood what was the matter. The forthcoming conversation promised to be unpleasant.*"

In a tirade of threats and insults, Stalin produced samples of failed laminate skin and pushed them into the faces of Yakovlev and Dementiev. Just before arriving in Moscow, Yakovlev had become aware of the problems, and indeed some discussion had already passed between himself and Dementiev on corrective procedures. When the latter fact was brought to the attention of Stalin, he began to threaten them with charges of 'wrecking' and 'sabotage'. The two men left in fear, especially Dementiev who enjoyed no popularity in Government circles (as did Yakovlev). The dressing-down was unfair, as the defect was caused by the Frederik Engels Factory, and not by *Zavod* 153. Furthermore, factory-testing could not possibly have revealed the problems with the resin, as it failed under extended exposure to moisture; hardly a relevant condition at the factory.

Over the following month, Dementiev worked with furious energy (quite literally to save his life) to rectify the problem in the field. Meanwhile, Yakovlev ensured that all traces of the defective resin were destroyed at Novosibirsk. Through the outstanding work of Dementiev and the NKAP, the problem was largely under control by August, and the crisis passed just in time for the counter-offensive following Kursk.

Having been caught out once before, Yakovlev insisted that all deliveries of resin products to Novosibirsk would be tested by factory staff for quality and consistency. To the plant staff's dismay, however, testing over the following months revealed that while the resin delivered was not actually defective, it was not uniform in strength or adherent properties from batch to batch. With this condition in mind, Senior Engineer Sinel'shikov suggested reinforcing the Yak-9's wing so that the variability of the resin's properties would not be critical. Agreed, and delighted, Yakovlev ordered a production Yak-9D wing to be removed from the lines and thus refinished in the Novosibirsk workshop. The modified wing was skinned in 10 mm (forward section) and 9 mm (aft) *shpon* sheeting, as opposed to earlier 9 mm and 8 mm, and the wing skin was finished with nitro-cellulose resin on both the upper *and* lower skin surfaces, effectively 'gluing' the skin to the longerons. The resulting wing structure was a mere 30 kg heavier than the original, but was fully 10 per cent stronger and impervious to fluctuations in the quality of resin supplied to the factory.

After completion and static testing of the new wing, several production Yak-9s were removed from the lines and modified to the new standard. Both Yak-9Ds and Yak-9Ts were modified during September-October at Novosibirsk, and factory evaluation revealed that performance in both fighters was affected not at all by the small increase in weight. As a result, *Zavod* 153 accepted the new wing design as the standard for manufacture on the entire Yak-9 programme, and it is thought that modified wing examples of both variants left the factory before December 1943. *Zavod* 166 is said to have followed suit, but no information exists on the date or the particulars of its production standard.

It was at this moment that another modification in the Yak-9 programme came under examination. After an analysis of productivity and manufacturing methods in the plant, the *Zavod* 153 Directorate determined that a significant increase might be realized by rationalizing Yak-9 production. Specifically, the manufacture of two different fuselage types was seen to represent a bottleneck of sorts. By the autumn and winter of 1943, several new prototypes were under investigation by the OKB staff, and all of these made use of the new rearward placement cockpit arrangement as on the Yak-9T. The Novosibirsk staff proposed, therefore, that the Yak-9D be modified with the new fuselage, and the old unit be discontinued.

In November 1943, a production Yak-9D was rebuilt in this form using the rear-positioned cockpit. Factory-testing revealed that the modified Yak-9's performance at sea level was unchanged, but at altitude the additional weight of the new fuselage reduced the maximum speed by some 23 km/h. However, in this form it was noted that the current and proposed modifications could be fitted to such an aircraft, thus making them universal on the production lines. After considerable debate, this kind of ability to increase production and also allow for rapid modification of the types under manufacture on any of the lines won the day. The revised Yak-9 with the rearward-placed cockpit was turned over to the NII VVS on 17 December. Testing lasted for 10 days. All of the performance calculations recorded by the factory tests were confirmed, and the new variant passed its examinations the same month.

No particular urgency was seen for the new type by the NKAP, and a Production Contract for the new variant, to be known as the Yak-9M (*modifitsirovanniy*, or modified), was not issued to *Zavod* 153 until February 1944. Only Novosibirsk received instructions to build the new model and *Zavod* 166 continued to produce the Yak-9D until 1946. The contract also forbade significant disruption in Yak-9 production at Novosibirsk during the re-tooling process. Production of the Yak-9M began in May, and it was immediately clear that the new process would result in more fighters delivered per month; 20 Yak-9 aircraft per day was quite common during 1944. The production Yak-9M was powered by the trusty M-105PF driving the Yak-9T's VISh-105SV propeller. The outer wing fuel cells were reduced in size and made less vulnerable, giving a range of 950 km. A slight rearrangement of the ammunition boxes allowed for the removal of the blister fairing of the UBS gun, imparting a smooth look to the aircraft's nose, as on the Yak-9T; the larger 220 round box for the UBS was retained. The Yak-9M weighed 3,095 kg at take-off. At sea level the new variant could reach 518 km/h and 573 km/h at 3,750 m, climbing initially at 1,093 m/min but requiring 6.1 minutes to reach 5,000 m.

By the end of 1943 the need for even greater range was recognized by the Yakovlev OKB, and Senior Engineer Skrzhinskiy was detailed once again to provide an answer. Skrzhinskiy's answer was extremely straightforward and logical – he simply reverted to the six tank wing arrangement of the Yak-7D (885 litres). A suitably re-built wing was then mated to a Yak-9T type airframe with its rearward-position cockpit, and the standard Yak-9D armament package was installed, as well as the supplementary 8 litre oil tank under the pilot. Foreseeing that the machine would be a specialized long-range escort fighter, the OKB staff also installed the navigational aids found on the Yak-9R, namely the RPK-10M radio-compass, AG-2 artificial horizon, and an American SCR-274N radio set with dual transmitters/receivers. The improved instrumentation served both to improve fuel efficiency and ease the pilot's responsibilities during a flight that would often exceed six or more hours.

The new long-range Yak-9 prototype was completed at *Zavod* 153 in April 1944. Weighing fully 3,387 kg, much testing at the factory was concerned with the greatly inflated weight of the new variant. To the astonishment of all concerned, the new prototype demonstrated handling that was virtually unchanged with regard to previous Yak-9 models. Maximum speed fell by a small amount from the Yak-9D, but in fact was superior to the Yak-9M. In the climb, however, the new prototype did show the effects of the extra weight, climbing initially at 951 m/min. and requiring 6.8 minutes to reach 5,000 m. The additional fuel conferred a range of 1,320 km at normal cruise, this ironically being slightly less than the lighter Yak-9D under optimal conditions. A slower cruising speed was the cause of the new machine's shorter range, but its endurance was much improved over the Yak-9D, being able to stay aloft for nearly seven hours. Testing of the new variant was not permitted under ideal conditions, but it was thought that 2,285 km might be reached at an unusually slow cruise.

The official State Acceptance trials eventually took place in June 1944. Without any great urgency a Production Contract was issued to *Zavod* 153 for four Series of the new Yak-9DD (*dal'nevo deystviya*, or 'distance enhanced' for 'extra long-range') on 7 August. However, based on Yakovlev's relationship with the NKAP, manufacture of the Yak-9DD had already commenced at the end of May, some of the first machines being delivered to the 386 IAP for operational evaluation.

In service the Yak-9DD demonstrated its value as a specialized long-range escort fighter. Vertical competitiveness with German aircraft was strictly out of the question, but the Yak-9DD could still outmanoeuvre its opponents in the horizontal plane, and there were many successful pilots on the type. The most outstanding use of the *dal'nevo deystviya* probably occurred in August 1944 when a special *eskadrilya* of Yak-9DDs led by *May*. Ovcharenko was dispatched to Bari, in Italy, to assist the Yugoslav People's Liberation Army across the Adriatic. Following a deployment flight of 1,300 km the Soviet fighters then undertook – to the astonishment of the American and British crews at the base – 155 combat sorties without a single mechanical problem or failure of any kind, and all without mechanical service of any description. Fuel and oil supplies were obtained from the Allied units sharing the field, and great mutual interest was shown by the pilots in their counterparts' aircraft. Of course, being *fighter* pilots, various mock dogfights were arranged between the Yak-9DDs and numerous Allied types, including P-47Ds, P-51Bs, Spitfire MK.Vs and VIIIs, P-40s, P-38s, and Hurricanes. Despite being equipped with the heaviest and least agile of the entire Yak fighter family, the Soviet pilots in their Yak-9DDs bested every Allied fighter they faced, and to the great admiration of their RAF colleagues. One British pilot recalled, '…[we] were very impressed by the Russian pilots and their machines. Some of the aircraft accumulated more than 100 hours of operation at Bari, and we understand that this was after a rather lengthy flight from the Soviet Union. To us, this was unthinkable – a Merlin at 100 hrs. would be removed from our kite and rebuilt in [the] shop. The Russians did not even change a single sparking plug; we changed ours after every sortie. Their fighters are wooden, simple jobs and seem to be lightly armed; but, they have lots of armour protection, are very agile, and we could not outmanoeuvre them in the air…'

Development of the basic Yak-9 airframe continued apace. During the autumn of 1943, Senior Engineer V. Barsukov hit upon an idea to turn the Yak-9 into a high-speed attack bomber, without the need for external racks and other drag-inducing equipment. Planning and development of the new prototype was unusually time consuming, and the calculations for strength and centre of gravity requirements were constantly checked and re-checked during the process. At last, in February 1944 Yak-9D airframe No.14-20 was removed from the *Zavod* 153 lines and modified in the factory workshops. Barsukov's team first moved the radio aft, approximately to a position similar to the Yak-9T type fuselage. Next, four cylindrical tubes were installed vertically at a 75 degree angle just behind the pilot's seat. These tubes were each to accommodate either a 100 kg FAB-100 bomb or a canister of 128 PTAB 2.5 kg munitions. The tubes opened along the bottom of the fuselage through four square trap doors, and the entire assembly was covered over by a lengthened rear canopy section. The radio mast was discarded, and the antenna simply ran from the fuselage to the fin.

The new 'bomber' prototype was completed on 20 March 1944. Factory-testing of the machine was brief, lasting only two days and confirming that no structural defects were present in the new Yak-9. On 23 May, testing of the flight characteristics of the prototype and bombing procedures began in earnest, NII VVS pilots and engineers being present throughout (by 1944, the relationship between the NII VVS and the Novosibirsk factory was quite intimate, and Institute personnel were usually present at the facility). OKB Pilot-Engineer Fedrovi and NII VVS pilot Proshakov shared much of the flying duty, and the 'bomber' Yak-9 prototype's flight properties were examined in great detail.

Fully loaded, carrying four FAB-100s, all-up weight in the 'bomber' Yak-9 reached 3,556 kg. Though this figure was not by itself a source of concern, the dramatic rearward shift in the aircraft's centre of gravity when the rear two tubes were occupied was. Fedrovi and Proshakov were both very experienced pilots, and yet both found the behaviour of the new prototype in this condition to be directionally unstable and quite difficult, and under no circumstances could a landing be recommended carrying four bombs. On the other hand, with only two tubes loaded, the centre of gravity did not shift rearward enough to affect the machine's behaviour to any appreciable degree, and when the stores were discharged, the aircraft reverted to the characteristics of a standard Yak-9D; this was seen to be extremely satisfactory.

With these results in hand, the NKAP issued a limited Production Contract on 10 June 1944 to *Zavod* 153 for the manufacture of a preliminary series of the new 'bomber Yak' as the Yak-9L. However, somewhat amusingly, when the instruction was passed to the *Oktyabrskaya* Line at Novosibirsk to manufacture a run of these machines, the Line Foreman scratched out the designation Yak-9L in the Production Diary and wrote instead, in thick pencil, 'Yak-9

Bombardirovshik' (underlining the 'B' for emphasis), meaning bomber, and the machine was thereafter known to everyone except the Yakovlev OKB and the NKAP as the Yak-9B. The production Yak-9B weighed 3,156 kg without bombs at take-off. Carrying two FAB-100s, maximum speed at sea level was 507 km/h and 562 km/h at 3,750 m, climbing initially at 915 m/min. and reaching 5,000 m in 6.5 minutes. The armament was unchanged from the production Yak-9D, comprising a single UBS and ShVAK firing through the cylinder banks.

The initial batch of 109 Yak-9Bs was delivered to *Maj.* Shinkarenko's 130 IAD on the Third Byelorussian Front during November-December 1944. During intensive operations from 18 December 1944 to 20 February 1945 the Yak-9Bs performed extremely well. In all, 2,494 combat sorties were flown by the Yak-9Bs, dropping a total of 356.5 tons of munitions, and accounting for a confirmed bag of 25 enemy aircraft, the vast majority of which, it should be noted, were Fw 190A fighters. A mere four Yak-9Bs were lost, and four more damaged. Despite this admirable record, the Yak-9B was apparently unpopular with pilots (fighter pilots rarely enjoy being 'relegated' to bombing duties), and service personnel complained about difficulties in loading bombs into the cylinders. Problems were also noted with the operation of the trap doors, and in the final series these units were improved. Operations with four bombs were restricted to all but the most experienced pilots, but with two bombs installed there were no significant accidents or mishaps.

The final project developed from the basic Yak-9 airframe also appeared during the early months of 1944. During the latter half of 1943 the Nudelman-Suronov team had developed a new and heavier 45 mm gun specifically intended to replace the NS-37. The new NS-45 featured a thin-walled barrel and a very ingeniously reduced breech mechanism, these features allowing it to fit in the same space accommodating an NS-37 gun. Understandably, the Yakovlev OKB was enthusiastic to acquire an example of this weapon, and in December 1943 a production Yak-9T was removed from the lines at Novosibirsk and refitted with the NS-45. The new 45mm cannon did fit with the most insignificant changes (a smaller 200 round ammunition box was installed for the UBS). The barrel and muzzle brake projected well beyond the spinner's tip, some 28 cm more than on the Yak-9T.

Factory-testing between 3-5 January produced entirely predictable results, and on the 12th, the Yak-9-45 prototype was passed to the NII VVS for State examinations. The Institute's evaluations were thorough, and twice the machine was sent to NIPAV for firing trials with the NS-45. Predictably, the 45mm cannon was awesome, and could easily punch through 50 mm of face-hardened armour plate at a 45 degree angle and 85 mm of steel plate at 90 degrees from 500 m – enough to defeat any tank in the German inventory. Nudelman and Suranov had provided another fearsome incendiary/fragmentation round and NIPAV determined that any aircraft falling within a blast radius of 10 m from the point of detonation would be destroyed; the fate of an aircraft suffering a direct strike – even by a single round – was beyond question. The NII VVS recorded the all-up weight of the Yak-9-45 at 3,028 kg, almost identical to the Yak-9T. Maximum speed at sea level was recorded as 518 km/h and 573 km/h at 3,750 m, the reduction certainly resulting from the increased drag imparted by the large barrel and muzzle brake.

Having passed NII VVS evaluations, Yakovlev received verbal authorization (there was no Production Contract) from the NKAP to produce a limited 'evaluation' series of the new fighter under the designation Yak-9K (*krupnokaliberniy*, or heavy calibre). Fifty-three Yak-9Ks were completed at *Zavod* 153 from April through to July 1944. During July and August, 44 Yak-9K fighters were distributed to the 274 and 812 IAPs, both units already experienced with the Yak-9T.

A Commission was established to examine the performance of these machines in combat, this was lead by *Gen-Lt.* Savitskiy of the 6 IAK. During two periods of operations – 13 August to 18 September 1944, and 15 January to 15 February 1945 – Yak-9Ks flew a total of 340 combat missions and destroyed a confirmed total of 12 enemy fighters for the loss of one Yak-9K. The 274 IAP excelled in its specialist role of tank destruction, and no fewer than 55 Tigers were claimed during this period with numerous other vehicles, in addition. The 274 IAP's commander, *Polk*. Pologov, reported that not a single German heavy tank survived a strike by the NS-45 cannon.

However, many technical difficulties beset the Yak-9K. The recoil of the NS-45 was ferocious, and in almost every case damage resulted at some point to the ducting and piping in the engine compartment. Many Yak-9Ks were routinely unavailable for operations as a result of such repairs. Furthermore, the NS-45 was prone to jam under high g-loading, and the recoil of the big gun necessitated single-shot firing only. Noting that the Yak-9T was still very satisfactory, Savitskiy's Commission recommended against series manufacture of the Yak-9K. The NKAP accepted these findings, and no further Yak-9Ks were manufactured. Ironically, however, almost every pilot issued with one of these machines adored it, and kept it, and the aircraft continued to see service until the end of the war.

A number of other Yak-9 development projects are worthy of mention. In 1943 there was a proposal for a Yak-9TK variant, this based on the Yak-9T and intended to have the capability of accepting any number of guns mounted to fire through the spinner, the ShVAK, VYa-23, NS-37, NS-45, and B-20 cannon all specifically considered.

A Yak-9 *kurierskiy* (courier) version was proposed in early 1944, this based on the Yak-9DD and fitted with a passenger compartment aft of the pilot. For years, no production was undertaken, but the *kurierskiy* prototype was used by the staff at TsAGI as a swift liaison machine.

In 1944, a version of the Yak-9 powered by the M-105PF2 engine was developed as an advanced trainer. This machine, the Yak-9V (*vivozny*, or introductory), was quite sophisticated and included such refinements as the RPK-10M radio-compass, PAU-22 tactical camera (adjusted to give coverage relevant for training evaluation), AG-2 artificial horizon, and the RSI-6MU radio set. Though completed and ready during 1944, the Yak-9V was not pursued further until after the War, and series manufacture of this variant was launched in August 1945.

Also during 1944 there was a Yak-9S prototype, this also powered by the M-105PF2, and development of this machine led directly to the Yak-9U.

The primary obstacle for Yakovlev in the development of his fighter was the sheer lack of available horsepower. No amount of clever weight-saving or aerodynamic refinement, was a proper substitute for raw thrust. Since 1942, the hopes of many aviation designers had been set on Viktor Klimov's second-generation upright V-12 engine, the M-107. The advancement of the M-107 over the M-105 was analogous to the Rolls-Royce 60-series compared to the -40. The M-107 offered an 8 per cent increase in displacement over its predecessor, and a four-valve head arrangement that allowed for higher compression and intake manifold pressures. As a result, the new motor was rated at 1,500 hp. (1,650 hp. for take-off and emergency) with a two-stage supercharger and 96 octane fuel. But the M-107 was beset by protracted teething difficulties, seemingly of every kind. One motor would pass its 50-hour bench test, only to have the next one throw a rod after minutes, bend and burn its valves, or even burst into flames. Klimov's Design Bureau worked relentlessly to counter each new disaster and produce a suitable improvement.

As early as February 1943, a Yak-9 prototype had flown with an M-107 motor installed. But the M-107 was still beset by cooling difficulties of every description, and on the 23rd one of the most experienced test pilots in the NII VVS, Petr Stefanovskiy, suffered an engine fire in this machine and crashed. Fortunately, Stefanovskiy was not seriously injured, but the Yak-9 M-107 was destroyed.

At last, by the summer of 1943, the M-107A had finally passed its 50-hour testing and was cleared for limited production. However, manufacture was delayed repeatedly as new cooling problems surfaced, and difficulties with the valve arrangement became manifest. By the autumn and winter of 1943, the Yakovlev OKB had made tremendous strides in aerodynamic improvement at Saratov with the Yak-1M, prototype of the Yak-3. These lessons were critical in producing a 'third generation' Yak-9 fighter, and the OKB now set its attention to this task.

With the M-107 still not in a satisfactory condition, several examples of the M-105PF2 motor were obtained, these capable of 1,240 hp (1,320 hp for take-off and emergency). The new Yak-9 was built largely from scratch (though using some components from the Yak-9T) in the Novosibirsk workshops, every aspect of the prototype being open to question and review. The fuselage retained the rearward position of the current Yak-9, but now featured a *shpon*-covered aft section as with the Yak-3 prototypes, the fabric over wire and stringers arrangement being discarded. The entire cooling system of the Yak-1M was installed on the new Yak-9 prototype, this consisting of a greatly improved high-flow transfer radiator, and oil coolers repositioned into the wingroot leading edges, and exiting through vents under the wing centre-section just ahead of the radiator. The engine air intakes were also located in the wingroot alongside the oil cool intakes, giving a completely clean profile to the nose. The vertical and horizontal stabilizers of the Yak-9T were retained.

Voluminous data from the TsAGI wind tunnels were analyzed with regard to other sources of aerodynamic drag. First, the wing tips were given a slightly more rounded shape which produced smaller tip vortices, and thus less drag. The ailerons were replaced by Frise type units of the same size and shape – as on the Yak-1M, to improve response and handling. The radio mast was discarded in favour of a simple wire aerial, as on the Yak-9B. Wind tunnel testing also suggested an improved shape for the rear canopy section, and a suitable rear canopy was installed remarkably similar to that developed for the Yak-9B. The new rear section was lower and longer than the previous unit, and imparted a different and characteristic 'look' to the new Yak-9.

Yakovlev gave much thought to the armament of the new Yak-9. He had hoped to mount a weapon then under final development by Nudelman and Suranov called the NS-23. This cannon fired a shell slightly smaller than the powerful 23 mm VYa-23, but it was much lighter and possessed double the rate of fire. Unfortunately, this weapon was not ready, and Yakovlev's second idea was to install the trusty VYa-23 to fire through the spinner along with two UBS weapons above the engine. This *troika* of weapons gave the new Yak-9 a very heavy punch, but the UVVS was worried that the rate of fire of 450 rpm would be insufficient for a high-performance fighter. Yakovlev countered that this was vastly better than the rate of fire for the NS-37 and NS-45, and the UVVS responded that only a single round of these monstrous anti-tank weapons were required to down an enemy machine. The debate continued in this way for some time.

With the M-107A still not ready, the first of the completed new Yak-9 prototypes would have to go with the back-up. An M-105PF2 engine driving a VISh-105V-01 propeller was thus installed, and the completed aircraft was rolled out of the Novosibirsk workshops during December 1943. Factory-testing began on 2 January 1944, and at once the aerodynamic improvements of the new prototype were obvious. With several NII VVS test pilots in attendance, Fedrovi flew the improved Yak-9-PF2 to 558 km/h at sea level and 620 km/h at 3,850 m, and recording an astonishing initial climb of 1,189 m/min. Handling in the new prototype was, remarkably, even *better* than in a standard Yak-9 with the improved ailerons. Fedrovi could hardly contain himself after the test series, and several NII VVS pilots flew the machine with the same results even before the official examinations began.

Meanwhile, the M-107-powered improved Yak-9 emerged from the factory on 27 December 1943. This machine was outfitted with a revised and lightened armament with a 20 mm ShVAK replacing the big VYa-23 (due to the much increased weight of the M-107 motor). Externally, the M-107-powered prototype could be identified by the appearance of a small scoop above the engine, between the gun breach blister fairings. Readjustments to the radiator were called for when the engine overheated on the ground during taxi trials, and on 5 January 1944 the VK-107A[1] powered prototype at last took to the air under the control of Pilot-Engineer Fedrovi. Several maximum-power flights were made over the course of the next week, and Fedrovi spent much of his schedule tweaking the VK-107 to cool properly. Finally, by the 12th everything seemed to be in order, and Fedrovi flew the machine very hard on four flights during the afternoon. No controlled speed data were taken, but Fedrovi was convinced that he had comfortably beaten 650 km/h. He was quite correct.

On the 18th, the improved Yak-9-VK107 was handed over to the NII VVS for State evaluation. Overheating and various small snags occasionally irritated the Institute staff, but these were quickly mastered and did not interfere with the overall test. On 8 April NII VVS pilot A. Proshakov flew the new prototype to its official State Trials recorded speed of 600 km/h at sea level and 700 km/h at 5,500 m, making it the first Soviet fighter design to date to break the 700 km/h mark. Performance in the climb was equally impressive, the initial value was measured at 1,313 m/min., and 5,000 m was achieved in 4.1 minutes, to the astonishment of all observers. Nothing in the VVS inventory flew like this machine, and the Institute's final report was overwhelmingly enthusiastic.

The inevitable NKAP Production Contract reflected the condition of the NII VVS' report. *Zavod* 82, Moscow, was instructed to begin manufacture of the new VK-107A Yak-9, now called the Yak-9U (*ulyuchshenniy*, or improved), thus terminating its Yak-7 programme. *Zavod* 166 at Omsk was ordered to launch production of the Yak-9U with such priority that construction of the Yak-9D there could *halt* if this facilitated the goal (in the end this was not necessary, but it was an unprecedented order). *Zavod* 153, Novosibirsk, was to add the Yak-9U to its list of current Yak-9 manufacture; both the Yak-9M and Yak-9T programmes would continue.

The production Yak-9U was powered by a VK-107A motor of 1,500 (1,650) hp. driving a new 3.1 m. VISh-107LO propeller. The power plant could be identified externally by a new exhaust stack arrangement, and the appearance of two small intake scoops above the engine. The armament comprised two 12.7 mm UBS guns with 170 cartridges each, and a 20 mm ShVAK cannon firing through the spinner with 120 rounds. Two small blisters appeared above the breeches of the UBS guns on the fuselage top decking. All-up weight at take-off was 3,204 kg, this mainly due to the heavier VK-107A.

Performance in the production Yak-9U was somewhat disappointing. *Zavod* 166 was probably first with its machines to units in the field, and these were found to fall well short of the performance figures in the NII VVS report. In part, the drop in performance related to problems with cooling the VK-107A engine, and to keep the motor within acceptable limits it was not operated at its design maximum rpm (3,200), but rather at a reduced maximum of 3,000 rpm. A typical Yak-9U in this condition could reach only 560 km/h at sea level and 650 km/h at 5,000 m. Aircraft manufactured at *Zavod* 82 were similar; those from *Zavod* 153 were slightly faster.

The first employment of the Yak-9U in combat was with the 163 IAP of *Podpolk*. Ukhanov in October 1944. From 25 August to

25 December, 32 Moscow-built examples were in action around Königsberg. Despite the reduced performance, the Yak-9U was master over any *Luftwaffe* fighter at any but the very highest altitudes. *Lt* Kapustin showed the extraordinary abilities of the Yak-9U by single-handedly engaging two Fw 190s on 12 December, both piloted by high-scoring German aces; Kapustin shot them both down in turn. On the 15th, *Kpt*. N.Konishev and *Lt*. Mankevich led a flight of eight Yak-9Us and encountered a large formation of 50-plus German fighters, promptly engaging the enemy. Despite being heavily outnumbered, seven Messerschmitts were downed without loss.

By the end of 1944 most of the production difficulties had been rectified, and full engine rpm were again possible. The NII VVS tested a production example from *Zavod* 166 in December, and recorded 575 km/h at sea level and 672 km/h at 5,000 m, which was typical. In February 1945 a Novosibirsk Yak-9U was examined at the LII and true-to-form it was faster still, reaching 585 km/h at sea level and 684 km/h at 5,000 m. The result was an even greater disparity in the capabilities between German fighters and the Yak-9U, and Soviet pilots were thrilled with the type.

In the waning months of the war, there was a proposal for a Yak-9UT, with provision for almost any cannon type to be fitted between the cylinder banks, including the ShVAK, B-20, VYa-23, NS-37, or even the new and fearsome NS-23 (a 57 mm anti-armour gun which just missed the War). Furthermore, a Yak-9UV two-seat trainer was also mooted, though in the event neither of these projects came to production. The ultimate member of the Yak-9 family was to be the post-war Yak-9P VK-107A, essentially an all-metal version of the Yak-9U. The Yak-9P was a highly refined interceptor featuring the RPK-10M radio-compass equipment and the PAU-22 tactical camera installation. The Yak-9P was widely exported to Eastern European countries after the war, and often the subject of considerable modification, models with three, or even five, cannon being known. The VK-105PF2 engine was also retro-installed.

By the end of the GPW, some 14,579 Yak-9 fighters of all variants were produced. Indeed, by 1943 the Yak-9 was the most numerous and important fighter in the entire VVS, and remained so until the end of hostilities. Serving brilliantly on all fronts, and in an unprecedented number of roles, the Yak-9 was the workhorse of the victory over the Fascist invaders. In its simplicity, its reliability and ease of maintenance, in its rugged dependability and pilot protection, and in its delightful and crisp handling and manoeuvrability, no other machine could ever quite match the Yak-9; in its element, it was supreme.

1. All engine designations changed in 1944 to the new format made from the Designer's na

	Yak-9	Yak-9D	Yak-9T	Yak-9M	Yak-9R 1943	Yak-9DD
Weights						
Empty:	2281 kg	2355 kg	2303 kg	2432 kg	2287 kg	2350 kg
Loaded:	2873 kg	3617 kg	3025 kg	3095 kg	2890 kg	3387 kg
Wing Area:	17.16 m.sq	17.16 m.sq	17.16 m.sq	17.16 m.sq	17.16 m.sq	17.16 m.sq
Engine	M-105PF	M-105PF	M-105PF	M-105PF	M-105PF	M 105PF
	1180 (1260) hp	1180 (1260) hp	1180 (1260) hp	1180 (1260) hp	1180 (1260) hp	1180 (1260) h
Maximum Speed						
At Altitude:	600 km/h at 4195 m	589 km/h at 3650 m	594 km/h at 3930 m	574 km/h at 3750 m	595 km/h at 4250 m	585 km/h at 3650 m
Sea Level:	521 km/h	532 km/h	531 km/h	516 km/h	518 km/h	523 km/h
Climb						
Initial:	1102 m/min	1024 m/min	1085 m/min	915 m/min	1095 m/min	951 m/min
Time to Height:	5.1 min to 5,000 m	6.1 min to 5,000 m	5.5 min to 5,000 m	6.3 min to 5,000 m	5.2 min to 5,000 m	6.8 min to 5,000 m
Service Ceiling	11125 m	9070 m	10000 m	9450 m	10365 m	9375 m
Armament	1 x UBS	1 x UBS	1 x UBS	1 x UBS		1 x UBS
	1 x ShVAK	1 x ShVAK	1 x NS-37	1 x ShVAK	1 x ShVAK	1 x ShVAK

	Yak-9B (-9L) with 2 bombs	Yak-9K	Yak-9U Early, limited RPM	Yak-9U 1945
Weights				
Empty:	2387 kg	2295 kg	2517 kg	2516 kg
Loaded:	3156 kg	3028 kg	3204 kg	3200 kg
Wing Area:	17.16 m.sq	17.16 m.sq	17.16 m.sq	17.16 m.sq
Engine	M-105PF	M-105PF	VK-107A	VK-107A
	1,180 (1260) hp	1,180 (1260) hp	1,500 (1650) hp	1,500 (1650) hp
Maximum Speed				
At Altitude:	560 km/h at 3750 m.	571 km/h at 3750 m	647 km/h at 5000 m	681 km/h at 5000 m
Sea Level:	505 km/h	516 km/h	556 km/h	582 km/h
Climb				
Initial:	915 m/min	929 m/min	1133 m/min	1280 m/min
Time to Height:	6.5 min to 5000 m	6.5 min to 5000 m	4.8 min to 5000 m	4.1 min to 5000 m
Service Ceiling	8615 m	9980 m	10700 m	11125 m
Armament	1 x UBS	1 x UBS	2 x UBS	2 x UBS
	1 x ShVAK	1 x NS-45	1 x ShVAK	1 x ShVAK
	2 x FAB100			

Yak-9DD wing detail

Yak-9D wing detail

Yak-9

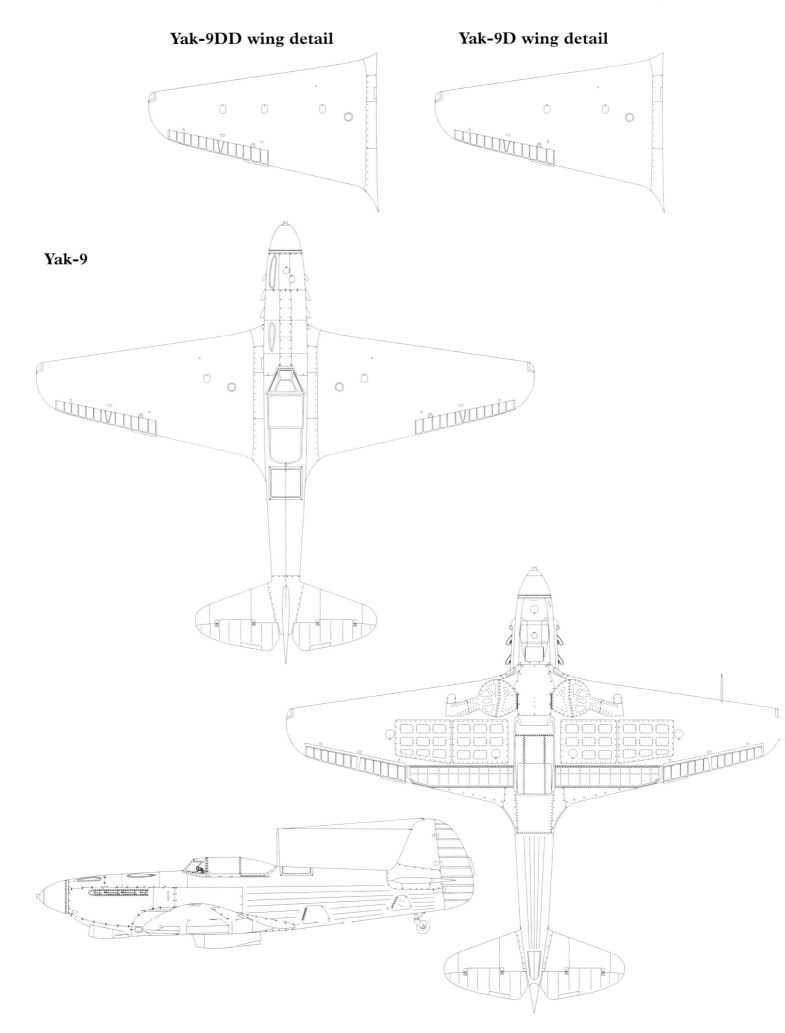

Yak-9B (-9L)

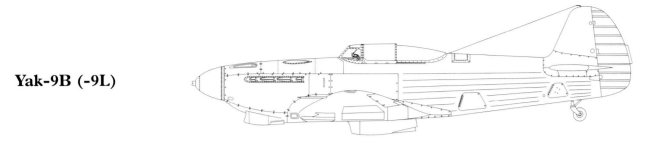

Yak-9K

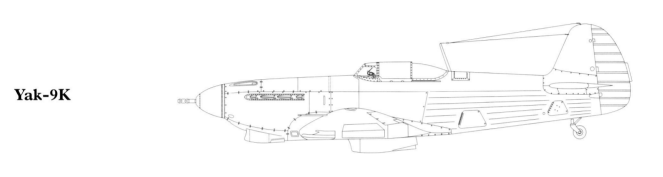

Yak-9M

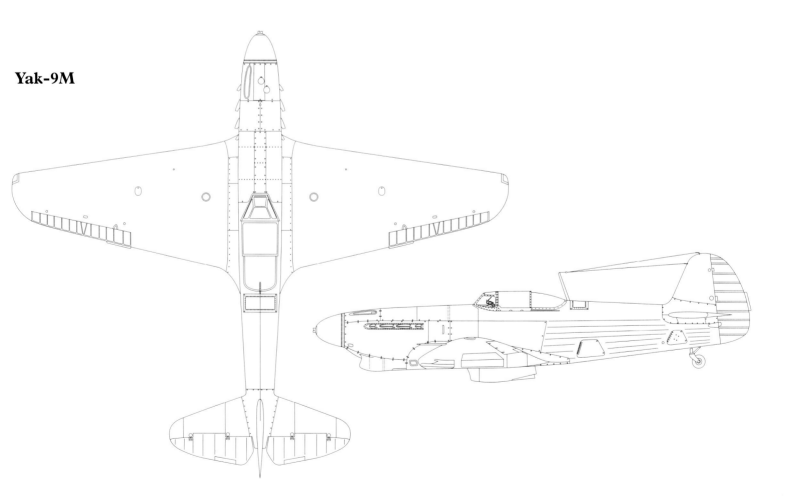

Yak-9T

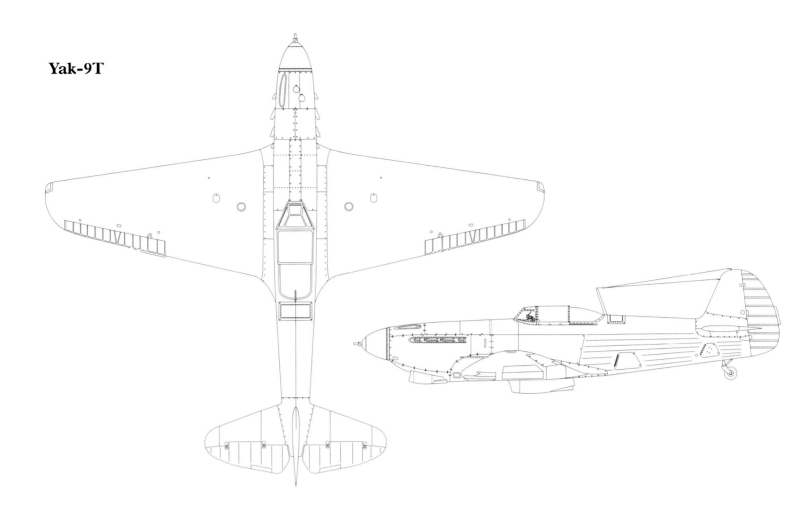

Yak-9U

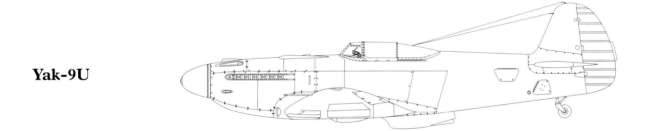

THE DEVELOPMENT OF CAMOUFLAGE ON
THE Yak-9 FIGHTER

The Early Series

Series manufacture of the Yak-9 began in October 1942 at the huge *Zavod* 153 complex at Novosibirsk. At this time, the most common camouflage scheme in use throughout the VVS for fighter aircraft was a Black over Green two-colour disruptive livery. The pattern and application of this scheme varied quite widely between the various factories, and indeed, in some cases within a given factory on different shifts. Likewise, in most cases the interior primer colour was dependent on factory preference, paint stock availability, and (as we shall see) in some cases individual tastes.

The very first series Yak-9s were finished in a camouflage scheme borrowed directly from the Yak-7b machines which they joined on the lines, this comprising AMT-6 Black applied over AMT-4 Green or, less frequently, AII Dark Green over AII Green. The demarcation lines in this scheme were unusually sharp. The undersurfaces were sprayed in the usual AMT-7 or AII Blue, and the demarcation between the upper and lower colours was typically semi-soft (see Fig. 1).

Fig. 1

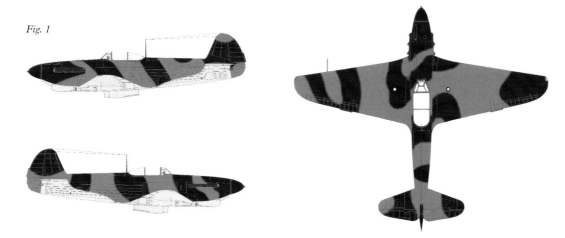

The usual interior finish colour at this juncture consisted of Industrial Metal Use Primer applied on all steel tubing structures, and usually on the armour plate and pilot's seat. Interior wooden surfaces (such as the cockpit sides, floor, etc.) were usually covered in Wood Finishes or Wood *Aerolak*; not infrequently at Novosibirsk during 1943 (and as we have seen, at Saratov), the entire interior was over-coated with this colour. Alternatively, it was common in the early Yak-9 series, in particular, for the cockpit interior to be left entirely unfinished (unpainted), most likely because these machines were being rushed to join the battle at Stalingrad, and were completed with all reasonable speed.

The use of AII varnishes did persist at Novosibirsk, however, and early in the Yak-9 programme a pattern application making use of these older paints could be seen in Dark Green over Green (see Fig. 2).

Fig. 2

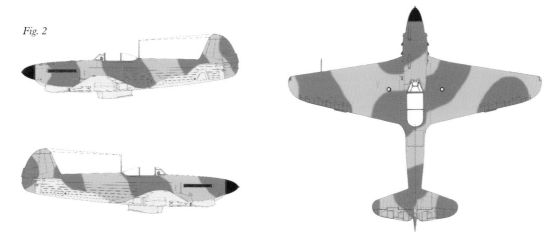

Though clearly simplified in detail over the fuselage, the uppersurface pattern was similar to the contemporary AMT scheme. This pattern quite prefaced in many respects the later NKAP fighter template, and it is possible that it might indeed have been the inspiration for these recommendations. Another interesting difference was the typical use of a 'double' ramp feature aft for the upper/lower colour demarcation line; the first known application of what was to become an icon of the Yak-9's finish.

During the winter of 1942-43, Yak-9s were typically not finished at the factory in a winter livery. Photographs from the period indicate that temperate 'summer' schemes were applied right through the first winter season of Yak-9 manufacture, and despite the fact that contemporary Yak-7 products from the very same factory were finished in a winter application. No explanation of this practice is known, but the answer probably lies in an urgency in building up production of the new fighter.

The Mid-Production Series

With manufacture in stride at *Zavod* 153, several new schemes appeared on the Yak-9 making use typically of AMT colours Black and Green. By the spring of 1943, an extremely striking two-colour disruptive pattern emerged in AMT-6/-4 only; no AII examples have ever been identified (see Fig. 3).

Fig. 3

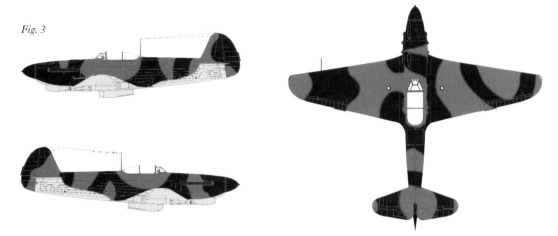

This new scheme was applied with a much more 'typical' semi-soft demarcation between colours, and between the upper and lowersurfaces, and was somewhat similar to a new range of schemes then appearing on the Yak-7 fighter. Indeed, as can be seen, the Yak-7 always influenced the Yak-9's camouflage to an appreciable degree.

In Yak-7 fashion, the new pattern was a semi-'loops' application on the uppersurfaces, while the fuselage patterns were very nicely rendered close-knit forms. The upper/lower colour demarcation was notably irregular in this pattern theme, and sometimes can be seen to extend across the bottom of the rudder.

Also, as on the Yak-7 at this time, a true Bukhanova style 'loops' application was utilized on Yak-9 manufacture during 1943. The preferred colours on the Yak-9 were certainly AMT (or even AII) Green and Black, but examples are known in AII Green and Dark Green, as illustrated here (see Fig. 4).

Fig. 4

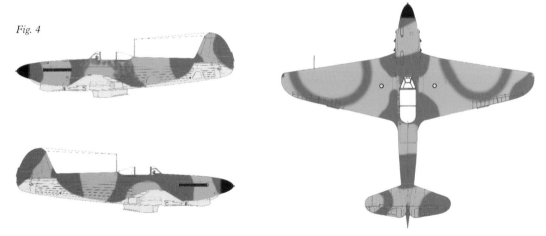

For reasons unknown, a very substantial number of Yak-9 'loops' patterns (and not Yak-7 versions) demonstrate a type of 'mottled' application just below the cockpit area *on the port side only*. Many photographs of this feature are known. No known photograph of a 'loops' scheme shows this type of application to starboard. It is difficult to explain such a practice, but it does seem to be a deliberate feature of this camouflage, and is seen in both AII and AMT versions.

Other Bukhanova patterns were seen on the Yak-9, as well. Her famous patterns involving raised side colour demarcations were occasionally seen, and the frequently noted 'double-ramp' feature for the rearward upper/lower colour demarcation is a hallmark of the Yak-9 programme. Many of the Yak-9 prototypes demonstrate various Bukhanova experimental colouration, including a 'three' colour scheme of black over green, with AMT-4 being used over the forward (metal) areas and AII Green over the rear (largely fabric). Alas, none of these patterns was employed in series manufacture.

During the spring and summer of 1943, production commenced on the Yak-9T, this armed with the 37 mm NS-37 gun. For some reason, this first series – and almost all subsequent batches – of the Yak-9T would feature seemingly outdated camouflage applications. No explanation has ever been given for this practice, but it is patently evident in the photographic record. The very first Yak-9Ts from Novosibirsk were finished in AMT colours in exactly the same manner as early Yak-9s and later Yak-7s had been during the early portion of the year, sometimes even in AII paints (see Fig. 5).

 Fig. 5

At the same time, and to illustrate the point, the most common Yak-9 and Yak-9D pattern application was a simplified scheme usually incorporating AMT lacquers (see Fig. 6).

Fig. 6

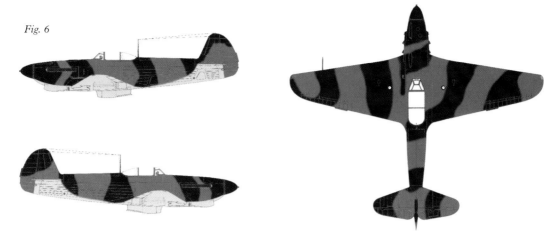

Left: *An AMT-6/-4/-7 scheme on a Yak-9D of an unknown IAP, Ukraine, 1944. The inscription, in Ukrainian, reads 'Berezans'kiy Kolgospnik' ('Berezan' Collective Farm worker'). Note the 'tidy' appearance of these aircraft, despite the fact that they are combat machines in front line service. The crewman on the wing is cleaning the aircraft; it was an axiom for Soviet ground crewmen that a clean aircraft saved lives, and every attempt was made to keep service machines free from dirt. This apparent lack of grime and soot is a phenomenon notable in many photographs of VVS aircraft. (Photo: G.Petrov)*

This pattern was quite straightforward in application, and persisted for several months without modification. The aft upper/lower colour demarcation 'ramp' was interesting in that it represented an older form, was curved, and also followed the rudder hinge line; seemingly a collage of older practices.

It was about this time that a new line supervisor came into service at Novosibirsk, a Lithuanian named F. Rimenich. During his shifts, he apparently forbade the appearance of Metal Use Primer on the interior surfaces of the cockpit, complaining that the colour was so bright as to jeopardize the aircraft's camouflage scheme. Some of his written complaints are part of the Factory records. A substantial number of Yak-9Ds and -9Ts from *Zavod* 153 have been recorded with completely over-painted Wood Finish or Wood *Aerolak* interiors during 1943, and it is curious to note that a similar occurrence took place on the Yak-7 (somewhat predictably, being in the same complex) and also on the Yak-1 programme at Saratov (some distance away). The influence of Rimenich on these practices is unknown, but their similarity in timing seems less than accidental.

During the autumn of the same year the supply stocks of AII Green and Black lacquers appears to have been nearly exhausted at *Zavod* 153, and on the Yak-9 programme no more examples of these paints were to be seen, apart from manufacture of the Yak-9T. At the same time another common application came to the fore, and this pattern was even more simplified in appearance than its predecessors (see Fig. 7).

Fig. 7

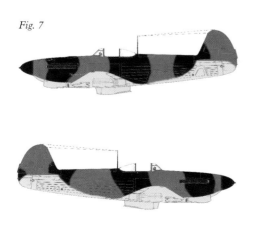

In fact, not only was the new pattern application simplified, but it bore some resemblance to the new 'recommended' camouflage pattern then being discussed by the NKAP. The upper/lower colour demarcation on the aft fuselage was quite up-to-date, being less regular and extending across the rudder. Perhaps even more surprisingly, this is one of the few contemporary schemes applied to the Yak-9T in series manufacture, and examples with this pattern are common (see Fig. 8).

Fig. 8

Above: *Yak-9T 'White 66' of an unknown IAP, date unknown. The NKAP pattern AMT-11/-12/-7 scheme is shown well on this aircraft, which also features an interesting 'chevron' marking, the meaning of which is also unknown. (Photo: G.Petrov)*

Series manufacture of the Yak-9 also got into stride at *Zavod* 166 (Omsk) during late 1943, and it is thought that machines produced here that were finished in Green and Black all conformed to this application (AII lacquers were apparently not used at all). It is not possible in the photographic record to distinguish the products of these two factories. Claim has been made that Omsk manufactured Yak-9s were somewhat poorly finished, but this fact has subsequently been traced to poorly captioned photographs, and pictures of *Zavod* 166 production show no such features.

Throughout 1943, the earlier Yak-9 machines had been replaced on the production lines by the new Yak-9T, -9D, and -9R models. Typically, these machines would be finished in the same schemes employed at the time of their manufacture, according to the current practices. However, the influence of Saratov's superlative Bukhanova could be felt at times throughout the Yak programme, and at Novosibirsk this often took hold on the Yak-9T (after the 'loops' theme, which she invented). Many aircraft of this type received schemes done in AMT lacquers that are unusual, and not in line with series manufacture. These bear all the classic Bukhanova trademarks, and are quite unique in appearance.

Later Series Yak-9s

Once again, the exact timing of the introduction of the new AMT-11/-12 two-tone grey colour scheme at Novosibirsk is a matter of great mystery. There is no doubt that some single-colour grey applications were being applied as early as October/November 1943 (as a well-known photograph demonstrates), but the available photographic evidence is not adequate to determine with which lacquers. It is also unquestionably true that large orders were placed at *Zavod* 30 in Moscow for paints during this time (where the 'old' lacquers seemingly were produced), and nowhere in the Factory records do requests to *Zavod* 36 for paints appear before January 1944. It is the author's *suspicion* that at *Zavod* 153 – as at *Zavod* 292 – the use of AMT greys in a *two-colour* application probably did not come into series manufacture until the beginning of 1944. The concurrent practice at *Zavod* 166, Omsk, is still a mystery. This enterprise might well have used the new two-colour AMT camouflage (given its record), but to date no photograph showing such a scheme occurs before March 1944 in the photographic record.

The classic, single-colour winter 1943-44 application of grey was quite common at Novosibirsk on all models of the Yak-9, though there is written evidence to suggest that some Yak-9T models were completed at the factory in MK-7 White. However, there are striking differences in the appearance of single-colour Yak-9s from Novosibirsk during that winter, and they follow a perplexing pattern. In the first case, the aircraft seem to be finished in a slightly darker shade which appears to be Wood *Aerolak* (see Fig. 9).

Fig. 9

In all cases, the upper/lower colour demarcation line appears to be applied quite low; in the 'old fashioned' style. In other cases a lighter shade is evident, probably AMT-11 – together with a raised, 'double-ramp' feature (see Fig. 10).

Fig. 10

Only one explanation seems to makes sense, and that is that the colours are indeed the different lacquers, and that the 'new' application practices were related to the use of the new grey AMT paints. Further evidence for this case lies in the practices of *Zavod* 166, which, as has been noted, tended to 'follow the book'. Omsk produced only single-colour schemes of the latter format, and one suspects that these had to be in AMT-11.

During the winter of 1943-44, a new two-tone grey camouflage scheme appeared *in addition* to the common single grey colour application on single-seat fighters, presumably at Novosibirsk only. The new winter application consisted of what appears to be Wood *Aerolak* upper surfaces with the lighter Medium

Grey colour applied over this in a disruptive pattern. This 'backwards' practice matches the use of these older lacquers in all other programmes, and seems to have been used in some unknown or haphazard manner alongside the single-colour schemes (see Fig. 11).

Fig. 11

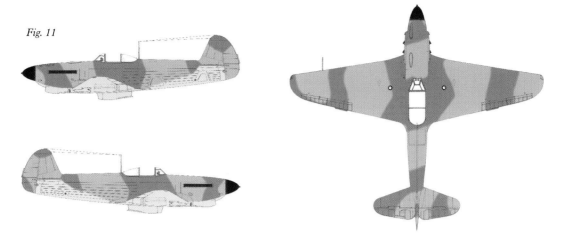

Right: *Yak-9 'Yellow 930' is thought to be wearing the 'backwards' non-AMT grey lacquer scheme of Medium Grey over Wood Aerolak. The aircraft was photographed in service with the 976 IAP during the winter of 1943, and curiously has a grey spinner (black was usual on these applications). There is continued debate as to whether this aircraft may be a later manufacture Yak-7B (the picture angle makes identification difficult); however, the placement of the fuel gauge and filler cap suggests the wing of a Yak-9. (Photo: G.Petrov)*

The spinner was finished in Black, as was typical on earlier camouflage, and the colour demarcations tended to be somewhat soft in all locations. An irregular 'ramp' feature was the norm, in contradiction to existing practices, and the uppersurfaces received a rather angular pattern which appears distinctly out-of-date. This pattern application was also seen on the Yak-9T (see Fig. 12).

Fig. 12

1944

During the spring of 1944, the new AMT-11/-12/-7 camouflage scheme – as adopted by the VVS for use on all single-seat fighters – at last appeared on the Yak-9 as the standard colour application. The new scheme consisted of a two-tone disruptive pattern that complied quite closely to the NKAP pattern, as laid down in the summer of 1943 (see Fig. 13).

Fig. 13

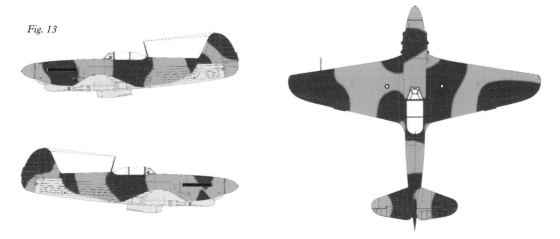

Above: *Possibly the most widely circulated photograph of GPW-era aircraft over the last 60 years, Mikhail Grib's Yak-9D '22' demonstrates a typical finish for 1944. This still was taken from a roll of 16 mm movie film and shows such properties– the underside blue is not washed-out, as on K-16/39 35 mm film. Grib's '22' wears a modified NKAP Template camouflage with an unusual 'W' feature on the port wing, and features Guards and Red Banner emblems on both sides of the nose. (Photo: G.Petrov)*

Left: *This unfortunate Yak-9 wears the NKAP two-tone grey scheme, somewhat modified on the uppersurfaces. '18' was photographed in August 1944 having been in service with the 29 GIAP. (Photo: G.Petrov)*

Left: *Another example of the NKAP template AMT-11/-12/-7 application, this time on Aleksandr Vibornov's (later Hero of the Soviet Union) Yak-9T, 'White 38' of the 728 IAP in 1944. Twenty victory markings adorn the fuselage and the inscription reads 'A.I.Vibornovu ot Kashirskikh Shkol'nikov' ('To A.I.Vibornov from the schoolchildren of Kashira'). A close examination of the fuselage national marking indicates that it might be a 'Kremlin'-type star. (Photo: G.Petrov)*

This camouflage was so ubiquitous, and applied to so many aircraft, that variations on the theme are absolutely legion. Indeed, the illustration here should be considered to be 'typical', but by no means prototypical. Different upper/lower colour demarcation ramps were common – irregular, extending across the rudder, and old fashioned 'ski' type (as seen) all being known. Variations on the starboard and (less frequently) port side uppersurfaces were also known. This application theme was common on all models of the Yak-9 from 1944 onwards, and from products at all factories manufacturing the fighter (here on the Yak-9U) (see Fig. 14).

Fig. 14

Two other applications were known to be common, both seen during 1944-45 at various intervals, though certainly less common that the previous application. The first has been identified only on Yak-9s from Novosibirsk (most famously on Yak-9Bs), and is interesting in a number of ways (see Fig. 15).

Fig. 15

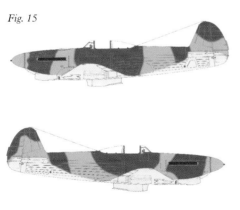

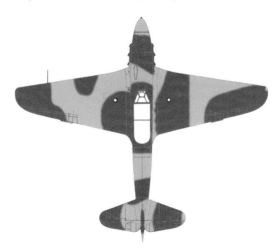

Below: *A Yak-9B of the 130 IAD 'Moscow' Regiment (see the inscription: Moskva) in the Moscow region in 1944. The 'half-round' AMT-11/-12/-7 lacquer scheme is clearly shown here. (Photo: G.Petrov)*

Below: *A line-up of Yak-9Bs of the 130 IAD, at the Novosibirsk factory, 1944. The funds for these aircraft were donated by the employees of the Little Theatre in Moscow, and the inscription states 'Maliy Teatr Frontu' ('From the Little Theatre to the Front'). This photograph affords another fine view of the 'half-round' Novosibirsk scheme. (Photo: G.Petrov)*

The scheme seems to be clearly related to the NKAP pattern, but features a number of different elements, the most fascinating of which appear to starboard. In this case, the fuselage pattern does not reach the right wing uppersurface, but rather terminates below the cockpit in a half-round shape. The darker AMT-12 colour also follows quite scrupulously a significant panel line (as was seen often in Soviet VVS camouflage), not crossing onto the wing root fillet. The spinner was painted AMT-11, even in cases where the AMT-12 area around the nose clearly abutted the spinner hub.

The next pattern appears less frequently in the photographic record until 1945, and it was applied to Yaks leaving the Omsk facility in addition to Novosibirsk. This application's most notable feature is the trademark 'zigzag' area on the port forward fuselage, much as one sees on the La-5 programme (see Fig. 16).

Fig. 16

This application was a favourite at Omsk on the Yak-9U, and continued to be used for this purpose well after the War. While the upper surface application was basically unchanged, some of the patterns along the sides of the fuselage were slightly modified, in fact, almost 'shifted' (see Fig. 17).

Fig. 17

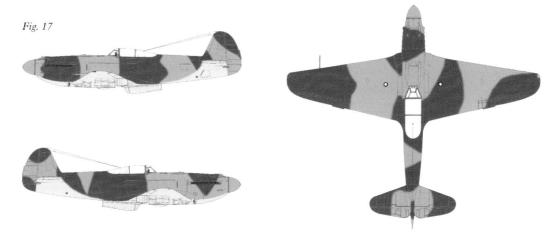

Unusual Yak-9 Schemes

There has always been speculation that some of the early Yak-9s produced at *Zavod* 153 might have been completed in that factory's eccentric AII Black over Tractor Green scheme. This would seem entirely possible, but no photographs have yet surfaced of such a machine with these colours.

Several entire series of Yak-9s (-9D, -9T, and -9Ms) were completed at *Zavoda* 153 and 166 for use in the South (in one case, to replace the losses of the 252 IAP in 1944). As was the standard practice in such cases, these machines were completed at the factory in a camouflage suitable for the intended destination. During 1943, the Novosibirsk Production Diary states that a Black and Light Brown scheme was used for these 'South Front' machines, but the best-known of the southern Yak-9s are a block manufactured in AII Brown and Light Brown during 1943 (see Fig. 18).

Fig. 18

During 1944, a number of Yak-9R machines were, inexplicably, finished in the old Yak-9D AMT Black/Green pattern application of 1943 at *Zavod* 166. No explanation for this retro-scheme has ever surfaced.

Left: *A fine aerial photograph of an early Yak-9T seen in 1943, probably photographed during factory-testing. This aircraft is wearing an AMT lacquer scheme of early 1943 arrangement and has outdated black-bordered national markings. (Photo: G.Petrov)*

Below: *Another view of the same Yak-9T, from the port side. The lack of Regimental markings (trim, tactical number, emblems) may indicate that the aircraft is undergoing factory acceptance tests. (Photo: G.Petrov)*

Left: *Yak-9Ts and Yak-9Ms in the Zavod 153-applied South Front camouflage of AII Brown/Light Brown. These machines were donated by the Kursk Collective Farm (inscription Kurskiy Kolkhoznik), and were photographed outside the Novosibirsk factory in 1944 before being handed over to – it is believed – the 293 IAP on the North Caucasus Front. The two Yak-9Ms seem to sport white spinners, while the Yak-9T's appears to be finished in Light Brown. (Photo: G.Petrov)*

Right: *A South Front camouflaged Yak-9D at the Omsk factory (Zavod 166) in 1944. The Omsk factory records do not mention the colours used, but the appearance is identical to Yak-9Ts and Yak-9Ms completed at the same time in Novosibirsk, where the paints are known to have been AII Brown over AII Light Brown (factory records refer to paints 'red-ochre' and 'sand'). (Photo: G.Petrov)*

Below: *A Yak-9M of the Moscow PVO forces in 1944. The tactical number '21' is thought to be a dirty white colour, as is the small numeral '10' on the rudder; the flash appears to be white. The spinner is probably red, expertly trimmed with white bands. (Photo: G. Petrov)*

Above: *The colourful Yak-9 of Ivan Stepanenko (later twice Hero of the Soviet Union), of the 4 IAP seen near Kursk in 1943. Forgiving the poor quality of this photograph, the lightning bolt is thought to be in red, while the number '17' is in white. The tiger figure seems to be chasing a stylized Goebbels or Himmler figure, complete with microphone. (Photo: H. Seidl)*

Left: *This dramatic, shark-mouthed Yak-7B is thought to have belonged to the 431 IAP during 1944 near Velikie Luki. The identities of the pilots in the foreground are not known. Though the 'shark-mouth' motif is often associated with units of Western air forces, in fact, the Soviet VVS employed this type of decoration much more than any Western air force, and indeed it could be said that it was somewhat obsessed with it. The spinner and propeller are also colourfully marked. Number '70', behind, is described on the caption to this photograph as wearing the inscription, 'za Vadima' ('for Vadim'). (Photo: G. Petrov)*

Below: *Yak-9U 'Yellow 50' of an unknown unit was probably photographed during 1945. This aircraft wears a very badly applied (and worn) yellow band on the fuselage, and a small number '2' on the rudder. Other caption information dates the photograph to 1947, which is possible. (Photo: G. Petrov)*

Left: *Yak-9Ms of the 21 IAP VVS KBF photographed during the summer of 1944. The spinners and rudders of these machines are all-white, but the numerals and national marking borders on '15' seem to be rendered in yellow (the star border is distinct against the rudder). (Photo: G.Petrov)*

Below: *A rather poor photograph of a spectacularly-marked Yak-9 in Poland, 1944. On the strength of other photographs from this series, the scheme is thought to be a usual NKAP Template, but the striped spinner is clear in this view, and the numeral appears to be in white. The inscription exclaims 'S Pobedoy!' ('With Victory!'), and the badge below appears to be the Order of Suvorov. (Photo: G.Petrov)*

Left: *A close-up of one of the Yak-9Bs of the Maliy Teatr Frontu Regiment, 130 IAD. (Photo: G.Petrov)*

Right: *Striped spinners (possibly in red and white) adorn these Yak-9Ts and Yak-9Ms along the Baltic Front in 1945. The colouration of some of these machines is a matter of extended debate; the film type utilized in this photograph is unknown. No agreed explanation exists for the curious pattern application, and the difference in tone from fore to aft on the fuselage. Some authors claim that the foremost aircraft might, in fact, feature three-colour camouflage as opposed to the usual two-colour, but no further evidence exists to support this theory. The second machine in line, 'White 10', is shown in another photograph taken with K-39 film, and is clearly wearing a modified NKAP Template scheme in AMT-11/-12/-7. (Photo: G.Petrov)*

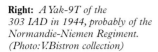

Right: *A Yak-9T of the 303 IAD in 1944, probably of the Normandie-Niemen Regiment. (Photo: V.Bistron collection)*

Above: *A Yak-9P at the NII VVS. This machine is thought to wear a single-colour AMT-12 livery. (Photo: G.Petrov)*

Below: *The demise of this Yak-9 offers a good view of the aircraft's camouflage scheme as seen in 1944. In this case, we have a classic NKAP Template example, possibly from Zavod 166. Note the white stripes on the fin/rudder. The trim around the tactical number '25' is quite dark, and might be blue. (Photo: G.Petrov)*

Above: *Yak-9Ts of the 29 GIAP, Leningrad Front, 1944. Note the outboard position of the fuel filler cap on this aircraft. Upon such evidence it is thought that later examples of the Yak-9T featured the revised wing fuel cell arrangement of the Yak-9M variant. (Photo: G.Petrov)*

Yakovlev Yak-3

Chapter 9

Yakovlev Yak-3

From as early as 1941, Alexander Yakovlev had been considering various ways whereby he might extract maximum performance out of the basic I-26 design. With the prospect of greater horsepower moving ever further away – the result of teething troubles with the Klimov M-107 – Yakovlev was forced to rely on the considerable aerodynamic and structural engineering skills of his design staff. The fruits born of this work would be extraordinary, for in looking back on the Yak-3, the designers of the Yakovlev OKB produced an aircraft which seems beyond comprehension. That a tiny 1,260 hp wooden fighter could be the unmitigated master of all before it – of designs with twice the size, weight, complexity, and power – defies conventional aeronautical logic. But in the Yak-3, incredibly, it is true.

The year 1942 at Saratov had seen triumphs in aerodynamics and frustration in the search for new and more powerful engines. To Yakovlev, it seemed to be the same old story – the M-106 engine was tested extensively in the Yak-1 at the end of the year, but it failed once more to supply a source of increased power. That this motor was supposed to have powered the *original* I-26 prototype, *three years ago*, was central in Yakovlev's mind. On the other hand, time and again his brilliant design staff had found ways to improve the structure, reduce the weight, and generally enhance the family of Yak fighters even without a major engine change. The year 1943 looked to be similar.

Throughout the latter half of the year, there had been voluminous exchanges with the staff at TsAGI. The irrepressible and indefatigable Prof. Polinovski had been very hard at work at TsAGI's wind tunnels testing all manner of aerodynamic refinements, and later in the year in collecting data on aerofoil shapes. This latter data was critical for the Yakovlev OKB in particular. Senior Engineer Grigor'ev and Head Designer Vigant were working on a major theoretical paper relating to the wing of the Yak-1 fighter. In this work there was a daily exchange of information between the two organizations as Polinovski – also assisted by TsAGI Engineers Novikov and Vindant – tested new shapes and planforms proposed by Grigor'ev and Vigant and reported the results in detail, whereupon the two OKB Designers would work often through the night reformulating their calculations to propose a new wing section, and the process would begin again.

It is impossible to overestimate the importance of this work. In his surviving papers, easily one-third of Yakovlev's entire collection – thousands of pages – are the reams of documents relating to these wing calculations. It is quite clear that Yakovlev was overseeing these discussions, and had shrewdly 'steered' his designers into forming something of a human computer. It was another Yakovlev masterstroke. By December 1942 the work was complete, and Grigor'ev and Vigant had designed an entirely new wing, one that was *smaller* than the current Yak-1 ten metre wing. Its details were extremely clever, and showed the influences of tremendous wind tunnel testing. The proposed new wing would have a span of 9.2 m, and to save additional weight the spar and formers would be of dural construction, as on the Yak-9. The wing's Clark YH aerofoil section was retained, but the aspect ratio of the wing was reduced some 5 per cent, again to save weight. The general planform was unchanged, but improved Frise type ailerons were proposed to improve the roll response.

In January 1943 Yak-1 airframe No.111-04 was removed from the production lines and rebuilding commenced. The fuselage, as a Series 111, already incorporated all of the weight savings and improvements of the Yak-1 programme, and work was concentrated on building the new wing. However, the oil cooler intake was modified, being made more shallow in appearance. The air intakes for the engine were moved – as per TsAGI recommendation – into the wing root, and a Yak-9 radiator replaced the original type, though it was mounted as per the latter, aft, below and behind the cockpit.

The new prototype was completed in February 1943 and was immediately dubbed the Yak-1M. The completed Yak-1M prototype weighed 2,655 kg, 227 kg less than a production Yak-1B. It was, of course, the new wing that accounted for most of this saving, and there was great anticipation to see if it would, indeed, perform as had been calculated. Following excellent taxiing trials, Senior Pilot-Engineer Fedrovi took off in the Yak-1M for the first time on 28 February. To the relief of the entire OKB staff, the Yak-1M handled magnificently. Despite the reduction in wing area, the new wing's loading was actually lower than the original unit, decreasing the Yak-1M's turning circle. The new Frise type ailerons gave outstanding response, and the rate of roll was almost beyond belief. Control harmony was good, the lightness of the structure generally contributing to superior handling. The new wing also provided much reduced drag, and this was reflected in the speed performance recorded on 1 March when Fedrovi reached 545 km/h at sea level and 632 km/h at 4,750 m.

Following some modifications to the M-105PF engine, the Yak-1M was turned over to the NII VVS on 7 June 1943. The engine modifications were undertaken following conversations with Klimov's OKB, and reflected the changes that would be incorporated into the M-105PF2 motor that was just about to reach production, minus the revised supercharger. NII VVS testing was very successful, and the Institute pilots were delighted with the Yak-1M. Handling in the new prototype was essentially unchanged from that of the Yak-1 in terms of safety and ease of operation, save for the stall under high-g loading. The stall in the Yak-1 came on gently, and with plenty of warning through aileron buffeting, but with the new wing and Frise ailerons the approaching buffet was reduced, and a serious stall could develop at very high loading. Happily, the Yak-1M would not remain in a spin unless deliberately made to do so, and no significant safety issues were seen to arise. On the other hand, this minor annoyance was accompanied by breathtaking improvements in manoeuvrability overall. The NII VVS determined that the Yak-1M's rate of roll was equal to that of the German Fw 190, hitherto unmatched. The turning circle was smaller than any contemporary VVS fighter, and the rate of climb was phenomenal.

Despite this impressive showing, Yakovlev was convinced that the Yak-1M could be developed further. During the summer, Senior Engineer Grigor'ev worked at nothing else, and much of the Saratov staff was dedicated to the programme. Construction of a second Yak-1M prototype, nick-named *dubler* (actor's double), was completed by 9 September. The *dubler* featured many additional refinements, the most obvious being a revised rear fuselage. The Yak-1 construction method – a traditional fabric and wire over formers design – was replaced by a sheet of *shpon* skinning. Power was provided by the new 1,260 hp (1,320 hp for take-off and emergency) M-105PF2, this driving an improved VISh-105SV-01 propeller. Yakovlev was convinced that the current Yak-1 armament was inadequate, and many possible gun arrangements were proposed. The lightweight ShA-20M cannon was not yet available, as was neither the B-20, and in the end two 12.7 mm UBS guns were installed above the engine, the cannon

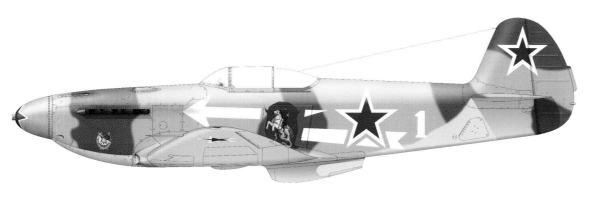

Yak-3 'White 1'

303 IAD
Georgiy Zakharov
1944

Colours:
AMT-11/-12/-7 unknown
or field application

Yak-3 'White 2'

7 GIAD
Podpolk. G. Lobov
1945

Colours:
AMT-11/-12/-7
field application

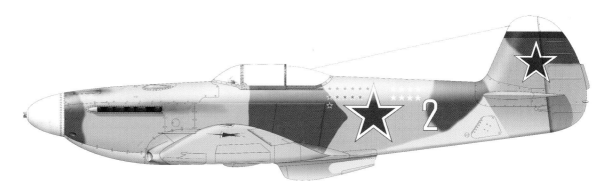

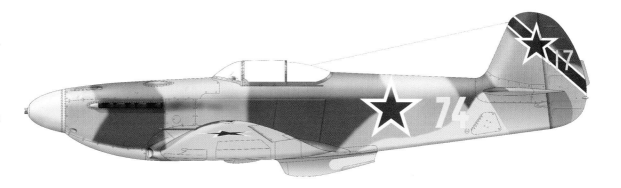

Yak-3 "White 19",

Unit and pilot uncertain
ca. 1945.

Colours:
AMT-11/-12/-7 unknown
or field application.

Yak-3 'Yellow 74'

Location and assignment
uncertain

Colours:
AMT-11/-12/-7 application
from *Zavod* 31

Yak-3 'White 100'

Unit and pilot unknown,
1945

Colours:
AMT-11/-12/-7 field
application

through the spinner remaining a 20 mm ShVAK. Cooling was improved by the installation of an automatic ART-41 radiator control unit, this also making operation of the aircraft easier for the pilot. An RSI-4 radio was installed, and an improved aerial with no radio mast was devised which not only reduced drag considerably, but even improved transmission range. The M-105PF2 was paired with revised exhaust stacks with improved thrust-giving properties. Improvements were also made to the fuel cells in the wing, these now being sealed in anoxic compartments to reduce their vulnerability even further.

Technically, the most challenging modification on the *dubler* was the repositioning of the oil cooler intake. Following intensive testing at TsAGI, a new system was devised wherein the oil cooler's intake was split in two, and repositioned into the wing roots. The resulting exhaust from the unit was then vented aft through slit channels which exited just before the radiator, thus providing thrust. The new Yak-1M was rebuilt with this modification installed; the resulting smooth profile to the nose of the prototype became the hallmark of the Yak-3.

Factory evaluation of the Yak-1M *dubler* began on 20 September. Once again, Fedrovi was delighted with the new prototype. Despite the addition of another UBS gun, the overall weight of the *dubler* – through careful weight savings – rose by only 5.45 kg. Engine cooling with the new radiator and ART-41 apparatus was outstanding, and no difficulty whatever was encountered in operating the M-105PF2 at continuous maximum RPM until the fuel was exhausted. The modest increase in power provided by the -PF2 engine only increased the Yak-1M's performance, and 570 km/h was achieved at sea level, while 651 km/h was reached at 4,300 m. So impressive was the *dubler*'s turning capability – both in turning circle and extended turning ability – that it was increasingly compared to biplanes like the I-153. Perhaps most shattering of all, the new Yak-1M could achieve 5,000 m in only 4.1 minutes and climb at 1,555 m/min, a rate which surpassed all other Soviet designs.

The NII VVS report on the Yak-1M *dubler* could not have been more enthusiastic. Upon the completion of State trials in October 1943, the NKAP responded immediately with a Production Contract for a new fighter based on the Yak-1M *dubler* as the Yak-3. Manufacture of the Yak-1 at Saratov was critically necessary for the VVS, and under no conditions was production of this machine to suffer while bringing the Yak-3 on-line. *Zavod* 31 at Tbilisi, which was then reaching the end of the LaGG programme, was also instructed to manufacture the Yak-3, and Yakovlev was to provide assistance in that undertaking.

The difficult conditions of the NKAP Contract meant that the lines, tools, and jigs required for Yak-3 production were assembled slowly, and it was not until 1 March 1944 that the first production Yak-3 left the lines at Saratov. *Zavod* 31 followed suit in April, but never at the copious rate of the advanced *Zavod* 292 (Saratov). The production Yak-3 weighed 2,123 kg at take-off, virtually unchanged from the prototypes. Maximum speed at sea level was 567 km/h and 646 km/h could be reached at 4,400m, a small sacrifice to mass-production methods being in evidence. The production machine could climb to 5,000 m in 4.5 minutes, and initial climb was reduced to 1,357 m/min, still an impressive figure. The standard armament was two 12.7 mm UBS guns above the engine, each with 150 rounds, and the usual 20 mm ShVAK firing through the spinner with 120 rounds. However, due to a misleading statement in the Production Contract, the first 197 Yak-3s were delivered with the original Yak-1 armament, a single UBS above the engine and the motor-mounted ShVAK. The error was quickly realized, and a kit was issued from *Zavod* 292 designed to re-fit aircraft still in service with a single gun with two synchronized weapons.

The first examples of the new Yak-3 began to reach VVS regiments during the summer of 1944. *Podpolk*. Kovalev's 91 IAP was probably first into action with the type, and between June-July the Regiment destroyed 20 German fighters and three Ju 87s for the loss of two Yak-3s. Soviet pilots soon discovered that no *Luftwaffe* fighter could evade them; in no category save at the *very* maximum service ceiling could the Yak-3 be bettered. For their part, German pilots were soon dumbstruck by the little Yak, and reported that it could turn tightly and could climb vertically for an unnaturally long period of time.

Soviet pilots would add to this that its control forces remained light and crisp at the highest of airspeeds, and control harmony was exemplary. On 16 June, a large contest ensued over Nesterov, near Lvov, when 18 Yak-3s of the 91 IAP encountered some 25 *Luftwaffe* fighters; 15 German machines were confirmed destroyed (three by *Kpt*. Pomov) for the loss of a single Yak-3.

As the number of Yak-3 fighters proliferated across the operational fronts during the latter half of 1944, it was clear that the *Luftwaffe* was hopelessly outclassed. Although the Germans continued to deploy very large numbers of fighters (the odds in the 16 June battle were not at all uncommon) the history of the Yak-3 is replete with incidents of small numbers of Yaks eliminating whole formations of German aircraft. Indeed, so horrified were the Germans, and so desperate had the situation become, that OKL (*Luftwaffe* High Command) issued a directive instructing its units to "*...avoid combat below 5,000 m with Yakovlev fighters lacking an oil cooler under the nose*"!

Yak-3s were also received during the summer by another unit, the French *Normandie-Niemen* Regiment. Flying within the illustrious 303 IAD, the French pilots had been very successful hitherto in their Yak-1s and Yak-9s. However, with the receipt of a number of Yak-3s, a new period of unmitigated disaster struck the *Luftwaffe* wherever they operated. During October 1944, the *Normandie-Niemen* Regiment destroyed, on successive days, 29 enemy aircraft without loss, and then 12 more the following day for the loss of two Yak-3s. More successes of the same order continued throughout the month – 11 without loss (18th); 14 without loss (23rd); nine without loss (24th). The carnage went on, and within that single month, the French had destroyed more than 100 German aircraft for the loss of three Yak-3s and one pilot. Little wonder, indeed, that when the *Normandie-Niemen* was offered its choice of *any* Allied fighter (including those from Britain and America) in 1944, they chose the Yak-3.

As production continued through 1944, several difficulties emerged in the Yak-3 programme. In haste to build up very large-scale production of the Yak-3 at the earliest moment, the gross weight of machines built at Saratov began to creep upwards. Standards of finish fell, too, and by September, units in the field began to complain. A Joint Committee was established with members from the NII VVS, LII, and TsAGI to investigate the matter. Very quickly, it was found that some of the Yak-3s manufactured at *Zavod* 292 were as much as 136 kg overweight, and some were subject to such drag that the maximum speed fell by some 32 km/h. Ironically, even in this condition the affected Yak-3s were superior to their German counterparts, but clearly the situation was intolerable.

The cause was discovered to be, to no surprise, the extremely rapid build-up of manufacture at Saratov. In only a few months output, the Yak-3 had replaced the Yak-1 completely. This astonishing achievement in industry was followed by the inevitable decline in quality control, and measures were immediately taken at the factory to redress the problems. By October, machines of proper weight and performance were once again pouring out of *Zavod* 292. *Zavod* 31, interestingly, had never been in a position to produce fighters in such numbers, and so manufacture at that plant was never beset by a fall in quality. Machines made at Tbilisi were typical in performance, matching the initial production runs throughout.

In November 1944, yet another and more serious episode beset Yak-3 manufacture at Saratov. In a replay of the fiasco at Novosibirsk with the Yak-9, a shipment of sub-standard resin was sent to the factory and manufacture of almost 800 fighters was completed before the situation was brought to light. The resin bonding the outermost layer of the wing skin laminate failed in precisely the same manner – i.e. when exposed to moisture and cold – as on the Yak-9 wings, and the Commander of the VVS, *Marshal* A.Novikov, was forced to withdraw all Yak-3s from service near the end of the year. It was quickly realized that only Saratov-built examples were affected, and all Tbilisi machines were reinstated shortly thereafter. The defective machines were dispatched to the nearest PARM for repairs, and through heroic efforts the majority had been fixed and returned to service by the end of January 1945.

Yak-3s served prominently and well during the Soviet offensives of 1945. The 18 GIAP, also a member of the 303 IAD, was notable in the fighting in East Prussia, destroying 67 enemy aircraft in one month (all Bf 109s and Fw 190s) without loss. On the approaches to Berlin the 744 IAP, almost entirely equipped with Yak-3s, terrorized the *Luftwaffe*. Over a two month period, 102 German fighters and 13 bombers were destroyed for the loss of two Yak-3s. Over Berlin, the truculent *May*. Arseniy Vorozheykin used a Yak-3 to destroy an Ar 234 jet in April, as did *St.Lt* Pavel Brulov of the 66 GIAP on 1 May.

The basic Yak-3 airframe was developed during the last months of the War in much the same way as its predecessors had been. A handful of Yak-3PD high-altitude prototypes were completed at *Zavod* 292, these powered by the VK-105PD and -105PV motors of 1,160 hp. There was a Yak-3T prototype, mounting the improved and lightened Nudelman N-37 cannon through the propeller spinner. Based on the Yak-3 airframe, the Yak-3T had a rear-positioned cockpit similar to that of a Yak-9U, though it retained the 9.20 m wing. No production of the Yak-3T materialized, despite its fine handling and performance. The final VK-105-engined variant was the fearsome Yak-3P (*pushechniy*, or cannon), armed with three of the new 20 mm B-20 lightweight cannons, each with 130 rounds of ammunition. Unfortunately, the type just missed the end of hostilities in Europe, though two squadrons were operational against the Japanese from 8 August. These were untouchable, and the Yak-3P was said, when attacking, to cut even modern and protected Japanese aircraft (such as the Ki-84 and Ki-61) in half like a buzz-saw.

As the war against Germany drew to a close, a new generation of Yak-3 machines was under development. In early 1944 a prototype was constructed powered by the VK-107A engine. The cockpit was moved aft 400 mm (as on the later Yak-9s) to stop the displacement of the centre of gravity, the VK-107 being rather heavier than the VK-105. Additional fuel capacity was installed since the VK-107 was a much thirstier proposition than the VK-105PF2. Armament comprised two lightweight B-20 cannon, one mounted above and the other through the engine. Despite the increase in all-up weight to 2,346 kg, the VK-107-powered Yak-3 was light and possessed of excellent power-to-weight properties, and could achieve 720 km/h. However, cooling difficulties doomed the prototype, and a new all-metal winged VK-107 powered prototype was built.

The new wing was completed in May 1944. The aerofoil was entirely similar to the original Yak-3 unit, but constructed of metal and with dural sheet skinning. The anticipated weight saving from the wing were not realized, however, and the metal-wing VK-107A prototype weighed *more* than its wooden-winged predecessor. Predictably, performance was reduced, and development of this version came to a halt. An all-metal Yak-3 prototype then followed, and although the weight was reduced to that of the original wooden prototype, performance was much inferior due to the increased drag of the dural skinning. Curiously, after the War

in 1946 a few of each model were produced under great confusion and internal political manoeuvring between the Saratov and Tbilisi staffs, but the resulting machines were declared to be full of defects and quickly discontinued.

The two last Yak-3 development proposals were for an improved airframe mounting more powerful engines. A Yak-3 airframe with the aft-positioned cockpit modification was fitted with the 1,500 hp (1,710 hp for take-off and emergency) VK-108 engine. Though the level speed performance was excellent – 745 km/h was reached – the VK-108 was certainly in no condition to permit service usage, and its most usual operation was to emit thick oil-smoke and overheat badly. When this behaviour was coupled with its incessant vibration, the VK-108-powered prototype was abandoned.

The final project made use of the excellent ASh-82FN radial. The OKB staff wondered if the powerful 1,850 hp 14-cylinder radial could be handled by the Yak-3's small airframe, but in the end their misgivings were unfounded. Dubbed the Yak-3U, the new model was built around a revised wing of 9.4 m span with larger chord, this mounted forward on the fuselage some 21.9 cm to improve the centre of gravity. The pilot's seat was also moved aft slightly in the same vein, but apart from that the rear fuselage was essentially similar to a standard Yak-3. Testing of the Yak-3U was very successful. Performance in the new variant was blistering – it could achieve 710 km/h at 5870 m, and climb initially at the unheard of rate of nearly 1,768 m/min. Manoeuvrability was astonishing in the Yak-3U, and no known fighter could stay with the type in combat flight. Indeed, the prototype was retained by the Yakovlev OKB staff in flyable condition for years after the War, and they delighted in pitting the Yak-3U against both domestic and foreign aircraft; no machine ever came close to matching it. However, the costs associated with production of this highly revised prototype in light of the end of the War meant that production was not ordered, despite its obvious potential. Yakovlev's new role was to design jet fighters, and so the formidable Yak-3U remained a single prototype.

In all, the Yak-3 proved to be a tremendously safe, reliable and robust machine, thriving under the harshest of conditions and constantly outperforming its enemies. Given the lack of available horsepower, the severe operating conditions at the front, and the need for extreme urgency, the Soviet designers produced an aircraft that, in retrospect, humbles even the most advanced modern aircraft designer. Indeed, this tiny lightweight fighter may have been one of the most impressive aeronautical achievements of the entire age. And it was, certainly, a testimony to the monumental contributions of its designer, Yakovlev, and his staff, and their remarkable family of I-26 fighters, which, as a group, laboured more widely and more faithfully than any other aircraft of the GPW, and served the Russian people wonderfully in their hour of peril. If the Yak fighter is, indeed, an icon in Russia – as the Spitfire is in England and the Mustang in the USA – it is truly warranted.

	Yak-3 1944	Yak-3P 1945	Yak-3 VK-107 1946	Yak-3U
Weights				
Empty:	2132 kg	2134 kg	2377 kg	2278 kg
Loaded:	2702 kg	2709 kg	2995 kg	2798 kg
Wing Area:	14.85 m.sq	14.85 m.sq	14.85 m.sq	17.16 m.sq
Engine	VK-105PF2	VK-105PF2	VK-107A	ASh-82FN
	1,250 (1320) hp	1,250 (1320) hp	1,500 (1650) hp	1,850 hp
Maximum Speed				
At Altitude:	645 km/h at 4300 m	645 km/h at 4300 m	703 km/h at 5870 m	706 km/h at 5870 m
Sea Level:	565 km/h	565 km/h	602 km/h	603 km/h
Climb				
Initial:	1357 m/min	1357 m/min	1479 m/min	1768 m/min
Time to Height:	4.5 min to 5000 m	4.5 min to 5000 m	4.25 min to 5000 m	3.9 min to 5000 m
Service Ceiling	10400 m	10400 m	11050 m	11250 m
Armament:	2 x UBS 1 x ShVAK	3 x B-20	2 x UBS 1 x ShVAK	2 x B-20

**Yak–3
standard production**

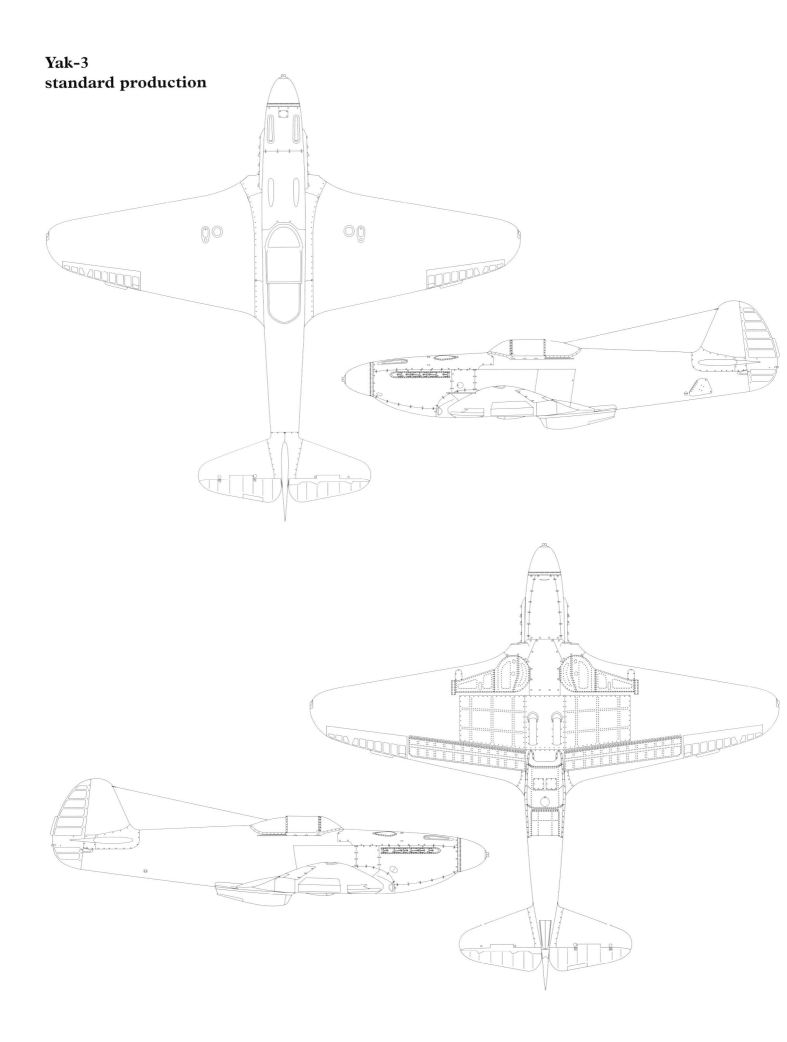

THE DEVELOPMENT OF CAMOUFLAGE ON
THE Yak-3 FIGHTER

The Saratov Wonder

At the beginning of 1944, the VVS acquired a new fighter, one that was to achieve immortality. Developed as the result of intensive weight-savings and aerodynamic refinement, the Yak-3 was the crowning achievement of the Yakovlev Bureau during the Great Patriotic War.

However, as a machine reaching production in 1944, the Yak-3 programme was not characterized by great innovations in camouflage. By that date, the NKAP had decided on new colours for VVS fighters, these standardizing on AMT-12 over AMT-11 in a two-colour scheme on uppersurfaces, with undersurfaces finished in AMT-7 Blue. A 'general' pattern had been recommended and factories were essentially free to either follow this suggestion or not. Many chose 'not'; others followed the pattern as if stainless steel templates had been issued. The Yak-3 gives a hint of both practices.

Saratov

Yak-3 production at Saratov (*Zavod* 292) commenced in the late spring of 1944. From the outset, the camouflage pattern of the aircraft produced there was not a source of great diligence and from photographs are usually distinguishable from Yak-3s manufactured at Omsk. The reason is that Saratov-built examples had widely variable, and not particularly smartly, applied finishes. Colour demarcation lines could range from semi-soft to soft, and the pattern in use was haphazard. It somewhat resembled the NKAP recommendation in the broadest sense, but rarely in the specific sense. Patterns vary widely from machine to machine. Upper/lower colour demarcations were especially fluid, and 'ramp' features run the full gambit of possibilities.

The following schemes must be seen as representative, only. The colours are the standard AMT-12 over AMT-11 uppers, with AMT-7 undersurfaces (see Figs. 1 and 2).

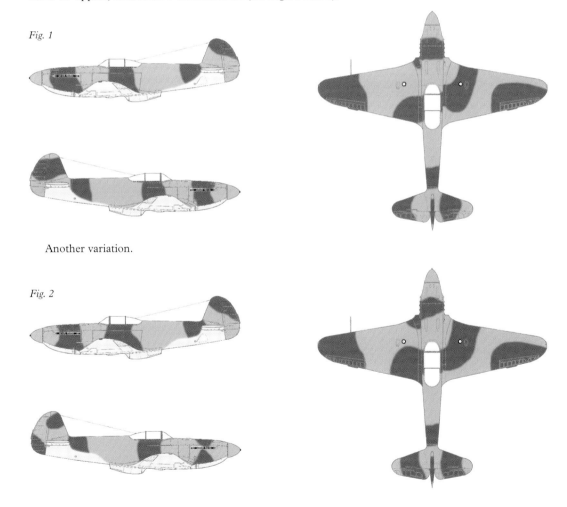

Fig. 1

Another variation.

Fig. 2

The uppersurface pattern did seem near to the NKAP recommendation, but the fuselage applications did tend to form simple bands, and no excessive effort was expended to create intricate patterns. This type of 'casual' execution of the camouflage is very typical of *Zavod* 292-built Yak-3s.

Tbilisi

Zavod 31 at Tbilisi was another proposition altogether. Staffed with current and ex-Moscow bureaucratic notables like Vladimir Gorbunov and Mikhail Komelkov, the factory was seen as something of an 'exemplary' enterprise (similar to Omsk and Gor'ki). As such, *Zavod* 31 sought to apply camouflage patterns to its Yak-3s that were uniform in appearance, and as close to the NKAP recommendations as possible. A quick look at the NKAP pattern [see Appendix] demonstrates that *no* VVS camouflage looks entirely like it, but certainly specific features are identifiable.

At the factory, the resulting pattern was distinctive. The application was fairly uniform, and all colour demarcation lines were semi-soft (see Fig. 3).

Fig. 3

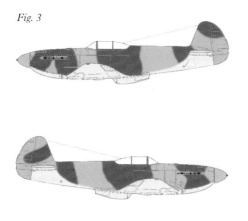
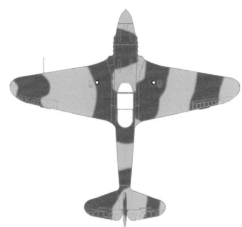

Left: *The Victor and the Vanquished. This colourful Yak-3 of an unknown unit was photographed in Germany in 1945. The lightning bolt suggests that this machine belonged to the 212 GIAP (ex-483 IAP), or perhaps another unit within the 303 IAD. (Photo: G.Petrov)*

1945

During the winter of 1944-45, a single-colour AMT-11 application was common for all Yak-3s. Interestingly, a large number but not all, of these applications demonstrated a 'double-ramp' upper/lower colour demarcation on the rear fuselage (see Fig. 4).

Fig. 4

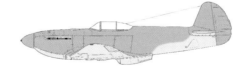

Below: *Yak-3 'White 10' is thought to have belonged to pilot Yu. Antipov in 1945. This fine photograph shows a common Saratov AMT-12/-11/-7 application scheme. (Photo: G.Petrov)*

However, in the Yak-3 programme it also seems to have been quite typical to use AMT-12 in this manner, at least during the winter months (see Fig. 5).

Fig. 5

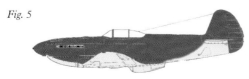

Many Yak-3s continued to be finished in this single-colour livery well into 1945. Two-tone camouflage did return before the end of the War, but at this point it became notably less like those of the previous year. Indeed, even at Tbilisi the pattern

'relaxed' somewhat, and although examples were certainly seen from that factory resembling the 1944 application, many also began to look like products from Saratov (see Fig. 6).

Fig. 6

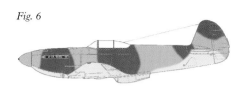

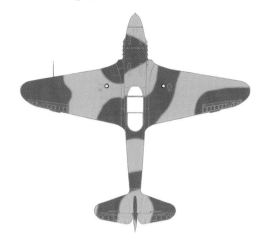

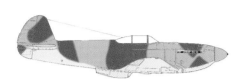

Above: *Podpolkovnik (later General-Major) G. Lobov, Commander of the 7 GIAD seen in 1945. His Yak-3 'White 2' carries 20 victory markings, variously applied. Note the most unusual hard-edged colour demarcations around the cockpit, and on the wing. It is possible that this was an in-the-field appliqué, as was seen in the spring of 1945 on Yak-3s originally finished in a single-colour AMT-11 livery. (Photo: G.Petrov)*

Above: *Post-war Yak-3s at the Moscow Central Aerodrome in 1946. These machines demonstrate the solid-colour uppersurface AMT-12 colouration. (Photo: G.Petrov)*

Unusual Yak-3 Schemes

In the *Normandie-Niemen* Regiment, several Yak-3s were repainted – apparently deliberately – in a very 'clumsy' manner. AMT-12 and AMT-11 were used, but the 'pattern application', such as it was, is inexplicable.

Left: *The colourful Yak-3 'White 3' of Hero of the Soviet Union, Ivan Maslov of the 157 IAP seen during the approach to Berlin, 1945. The spinner appears to be painted red, and the inscription reads 'Kolkhoz Krasniy Oktyabr' ('Collective Farm Red October'). There is some type of inscription ahead of the national star, but unfortunately no clear view exists of this feature. (Photo: G.Petrov)*

Left: *Yak-3s on parade just after the Victory, 1945. Upon study, the tactical number '74' appears to be rendered in yellow, as is the spinner and the numeral '17' on the rudder. A red band with white trim is evident under the national marking on the fin/rudder. (Photo: G.Petrov)*

Below: *A line-up of Yak-3s seemingly finished in a single-colour application, in 1944. The choice between AMT-11 and -12 is difficult to determine, and as a still from a roll of 16 mm film, there is no negative available to analyze. The spinner colour is unknown. (Photo: G.Petrov)*

Above: *The Yak-3 of Hero of the Soviet Union, G. Balashov of the 402 IAP in 1944. 'White 10' wears a 'winged-sword' emblem (which has been inexplicably obscured with scratches on the negative, resulting in black lines) similar to the 274 IAP's marking, and features a red spinner. (Photo: H.Seidl)*

Left: *General Georgiy Zakharov (later Hero of the Soviet Union), Commander of the 303 IAD and his Yak-3 'White 1' in 1945. Despite being a General, Zakharov flew combat missions whenever possible and finished the War with 10 confirmed victories. (Photo: G.Petrov)*

Right: *Yak-3s of the 402 IAP, 1944. These machines wear the Regiment's 'winged-sword' emblem, and 'White 100' features a white spinner and fin/rudder flash. The pilot, foreground, has not been identified. (Photo: G.Petrov)*

Below: *M. Roger Sauvage of the Normandie-Niemen Regiment of the 303 IAD, 1944. 'White 5' is finished in a typical Saratov AMT-11/-12/-7 application. (Photo: H.Seidl)*

Below: *A presentation Yak-3 to Boris Eremin in 1944. The inscription reads 'Ot Feraponta Petrovicha Golovatova 2-oy samolet na okonchatel'niy razgrom vraga' ('From Ferapont Petrovich Golovatov, the 2nd aircraft for the final defeat of the enemy'). Eremin must surely have set a record for the number of Yak fighters to have featured a dedication inscription; to date, seven are known in the photographic record, and more are suspected through anecdotal evidence. The spinner is trimmed with a red and white star. (Photo: G.Petrov)*

Above: *A still taken during 1945 with French 16 mm movie film of the Normandie-Niemen Yak-3s in Paris. (Photo: Author's collection)*

Above: *A close-up view of a Yak-3 in Paris. (Photo: Author's collection)*

Appendices

Notable Prototypes and Developmental Aircraft

During the GPW period a number of significant prototypes appeared which just missed entering series manufacture. Some of these machines were even ordered into production, but at the last minute were withdrawn for various reasons. Virtually all of the significant Design Bureaux had projects of this type, and some of these will be familiar and well-known.

Right: *BI rocket-fighter prototype No.5 fitted with ski landing gear in 1943. The aircraft wears an interesting AMT-6/-4/-7 camouflage. (Photo: G.Petrov)*

BEREZNYAK-ISAEV BI

Nazi Germany has long been regarded as having been in the lead of many highly technical endeavours during the Second World War. From the Soviet point of view however, Germany was simply less responsible and more unrealistic in its pursuit of technology, wasting much effort on weapons that were 'scientific toys.' Nowhere is the contrast between these differing views on military technology more evident than with the case of the BI rocket fighter.

In the immediate pre-war years designers from the Bolkhovitinov OKB led by Senior Engineers A. Bereznyak and A. Isaev worked determinedly on rocket engines suitable for aircraft. By 1941, the D-1-A engine was perfected, this weighing a mere 220 kg but producing 1,100 kg of thrust. The D-1-A was powered by kerosene and utilized a nitric acid oxidizer, these contained in pressurized bottles with a full nitrogen flooding system for the delivery lines, preventing the sort of catastrophic explosions which routinely beset other nations' rocket fighters.

Simultaneously, a tiny interceptor airframe was developed to be powered by the engine. The BI was a small and light aircraft of 6.5 m span. The wings were constructed of wooden formers and spars with *shpon* skinning, while the fuselage was a wooden semi-monocoque with plywood covering. All control surfaces were metal framed with fabric covering. The conventional landing gear was retractable, and armament consisted of two 20 mm ShVAK cannon in the extreme nose. Weighing only 805 kg empty, its flight weight was fully twice that at 1,650 kg.

Following gliding trials in 1941 and early 1942, the BI was ready for powered flight. On 15 May 1942 the BI first took to the air under rocket power. The flight was entirely successful, and the handling of the little fighter was discovered to be excellent. The D-1-A engine functioned flawlessly, and offered the fully-rated power of 1,100 kg thrust on the very first attempt. By the end of May, the BI had achieved 790 km/h at 1,000 m and the anticipated speed at 6,000 m was 890 km/h.

The NKAP gave considerable thought to mass production of the BI. With this possibility in mind, six pre-production BIs were completed, one of which – the No.5 prototype – carried ski landing gear. Ironically, a rocket-powered fighter was suitable only for point defence duties, and by the summer of 1942 any threat to Moscow – the obvious defensive point in mind – from the *Luftwaffe* had been largely dismissed. As a result, no series production ensued, but testing and development of the BI continued until 1943 when Test Pilot Bakchivandzhi was killed in a crash.

The reality, however, was that by mid-1942, the Soviet Union could have placed into mass-production and successfully fielded the BI. Not only was this a full *two years* before the operational deployment of the German Me 163 rocket fighter, and of similar performance, but the Messerschmitt was a vastly inferior design that generated casualties almost exclusively to its operators, and not to its intended targets. No explosion nor fuel-related casualty ever beset the BI programme, which was basically safe and operable under service conditions.

Left: *MiG-3 M-82 at the Kuibishev factory, 1942. The aircraft's colouration is probably AII Green, despite the dark appearance of the photograph. (Photo: G.Petrov)*

MIKOYAN i GUREVICH MiG-3 M-82

After the termination of the MiG-3 fighter towards the end of 1941, Head Designers Mikoyan and Gurevich did not fade into the background. Just after the evacuation of *Zavod* 1 to Kuibishev, five examples of the MiG-3 powered by the M-82 radial were completed and dispatched to Moscow for evaluation by the NII VVS. During August 1941, the results of the factory-testing of the prototype were confirmed by the NII VVS, and with boosted flight possible, 616 km/h was attained at 5,850 m. The five MiG-3 M-82s (the MiG-9 designation would have been used had series manufacture ensued) were subsequently distributed to the PVO forces around Moscow, and served with operational Regiments through the year. No Contract for series manufacture was issued, however, and so development continued with the I-211.

MIKOYAN i GUREVICH I-211E

A further development of the MiG-3 with the M-82 radial was realized in 1943. The I-211E was a tremendously streamlined aircraft powered by the M-82FN radial. The basic MiG-9 airframe was retained, but the attention paid to engine cowling streamlining was meticulous. Despite all of these efforts, performance in the I-211E was not overly exciting, and 670 km/h was attained at 7,000 m. Handling was somewhat poor, and with the level-speed performance no more than the La-5FN prototype, no production was attempted.

MIKOYAN i GUREVICH MiG-3U (I-230)

Development of the in-line-engined MiG-3 also continued after the evacuation of *Zavod* 1. The Mikoyan and Gurevich OKB was reorganized at *Zavod* 155 in Moscow, and developmental ideas on the MiG-3 again returned to the AM-38 engine. During 1942 and 1943, the OKB concentrated on their Type D fighter (I-230). The final Type D was powered by a specially-modified AM-38 engine with flat cylinder heads and a four-valve arrangement, somewhat similar to the AM-38F, and driving an experimental AV-5L-126A propeller. The internal structure was all dural, save for the wooden monocoque fuselage, while the skinning on the wings was *shpon* sheet. The fuselage structure was not covered with *shpon*, but rather a sandwich of three plywood sheets bonded with lacquer.

Above: *The I-211E prototype in Moscow, 1943. The uppersurfaces seem to be a solid-colour AMT-4 application. (Photo: G.Petrov)*

Many detailed improvements were applied to the Type D. The landing gear was improved and strengthened, but smaller mainwheels were utilized. The armament comprised two 20 mm ShVAK cannon above the engine with 170 rounds apiece. A fire-resistant bulkhead separated the cockpit from the main fuel cell. Lastly, the horizontal stabilizer was repositioned some 200 mm higher on the fuselage to improve response.

Testing at the NII VVS during July 1943 was conducted under the designation MiG-3U (*uluchshenniy*, or improved). The MiG-3U attained 526 km/h at sea level and 656 km/h at 7,000 m, but requiring fully 6.2 minutes to reach 5,000 m. Handling in the MiG-3U was poor, and all of the old instabilities of the MiG-3 accompanied the new prototype. The type's landing behaviour was particularly alarming, and spinning trials could not be successfully completed. The NII VVS did not pass the MiG-3U for its State evaluation trials.

Nevertheless, *Zavod* 155 completed six prototypes, largely on its own initiative. These were subsequently rejected by the NKAP, but Mikoyan used his political influence to have four of the

Right: *One of the sleek MiG-3U prototypes in service with the 12 GIAP, Moscow, late 1943. The film type used in this photograph is unknown, and therefore the colours in use are a mystery. The scheme, which appears to be a unique pattern, is probably finished in AMT lacquers, but whether it is an AMT–6/-4 or an AMT–12/-11 combination is indeterminate. (Photo: G.Petrov)*

prototypes dispatched to the 12 GIAP around Moscow for 'service trials'. The pilots of the 12 GIAP operated these MiG-3Us for several months, but with a notable lack of success, and they were returned to *Zavod* 155 after two of the machines were wrecked in landing mishaps. No further development of the MiG-3 aircraft was undertaken.

MIKOYAN i GUREVICH I-220 SERIES

Following the failure of its radial-engined developments, the MiG OKB turned its attention to high-altitude fighters. A series of machines soon materialized powered by the Mikulin AM-39 engine of 1,500 hp (1,700 hp for take-off and emergency). The I-220 was a graceful low-wing monoplane with a rear-set cockpit, resembling the MiG-3. The wing was of similar three-piece construction with wooden outer sections, the spars being of dural manufacture. The fuselage was built up around a steel tube truss with wooden formers and ply skinning, and the vertical and horizontal stabilizers were all-wooden. The engine was carefully streamlined into the nose, which was covered with dural sheet panels.

During NII VVS testing in August 1944, the I-220 reached the impressive speed of 697 km/h at 7,800 m. Handling was found to be adequate from a safety standpoint, but manoeuvrability was poor, and even higher operating altitudes were hoped for by the UVVS. With this goal in mind, emphasis was shifted to the turbo-supercharger-equipped I-222.

The I-222 prototype largely resembled the I-220, but featured an extended wingspan for high-altitude flight. Powered by the AM-39B-1 engine coupled with a TK-300B turbo-supercharger, the combination was rated to produce 1,860 hp at take-off and 1,430 hp at 13,200 m. The new prototype showed remarkable high-altitude performance, 691 km/h being achieved at 12,500 m during NII VVS testing during May 1944. However, the MiG OKB was already at work on improved versions of this aircraft, and the I-224 could achieve 695 km/h at the same height.

The final aircraft of this series was the I-225, based on the I-220 airframe. Now powered by the AM-42FB engine with the TK-300B turbo-supercharger producing 2,000 hp, the I-225 could climb to 14,500m. Maximum speed was measured at 704 km/h at 7,800 m, a superb high-altitude performance. However, testing of the I-225 was not complete until April 1945, by which time the War was almost over, and no series production of the type was undertaken.

SHEVCHENKO-NIKITIN IS

Easily one of the most intriguing aircraft ever conceived and built, the IS fighter prototype was of a class of aircraft unknown outside of the USSR. At the very height of the biplane-versus-monoplane debate within the UVVS, Pilot Engineer Vladimir Shevchenko, along with Designer Vasily Nikitin sought to placate both points of view with a *folding* fighter, one which could operate as *both* a biplane *and* a monoplane. This extraordinary concept took shape in the IS (*istrebitel' skladnoy*, or folding fighter) prototype of 1940. The IS was an all-metal monocoque aircraft of very advanced construction. The fixed upper main wing featured a gulled *Chaika* centre-section, placed directly in front of the pilot who sat well-aft. The lower wings were hinged to the bottom of either side of the fuselage, and carried the landing gear members. Upon retraction, the entire wing and gear combination would fold up to lie flush within both the fuselage side (gear), and into recesses in the upper wing undersurface (wing).

Operation of this contraption seemed most improbable. Remarkably however, the folding mechanism worked outstandingly well. Not only were there no difficulties or unusual aerodynamic forces nor disturbances encountered during retraction or extension, but the lower wing could be left in any intermediate condition (simulating a failure of the retracting mechanism) with no difficulties of any kind. The operational concept was to have the IS take-off as a biplane – enjoying the short run and

Left: *The extraordinary Shevchenko-Nikitin IS-1, photographed in 1941. Note the US-made Hamilton Standard three-bladed propeller, and the closed cooling shutters on the cowl face. (Photo: G.Petrov)*

rapid climb-out of that type – and then to transform into a parasol monoplane for cruise and combat. However, so good was the lower wing retraction mechanism, that pilots would have been able to drop these at any time in combat and manoeuvre like a biplane.

The IS-1 was powered by the 930 hp M-63 radial, and its cowling very much resembled that of the I-153. With this engine the IS-1 could achieve 453 km/h, roughly equivalent to an I-16. The upper wing carried four ShKAS guns, and sufficient fuel for 600 km was contained in its single fuel cell. The re-engined IS-2 was powered by the 1000 hp M-88 radial and featured improved streamlining but even so, the maximum speed did not exceed 502 km/h. With performance inferior to the new Yak-1, MiG-1, and LaGG-3 the IS did not reach production.

POLIKARPOV I-180

Having exhausted all possible avenues of advancement with the M-25 radial-powered I-16, Polikarpov turned his attention to new aero engines. During 1938, the Polikarpov OKB constructed the I-180 prototype, this powered by the twin-row M-88 radial of 960 hp. The I-180, however, was a significant re-design of the TsKB-12 airframe. The rear fuselage resembled an I-16 fighter, but the I-180's fuselage was longer, and the engine cowling necessarily larger and of increased diameter. The wing was built similarly to the TsKB-12, and attached to the all-metal centre-section were two wooden outer wing sections, these of radically different planform. The aerofoil section remained of the Clark YH type, but the leading edges were completely straight and perpendicular to the fuselage, while the trailing edges tapered dramatically to the pointed tips.

Prior to the completion of the I-180, representatives of TsAGI had sent a very strongly worded letter to Polikarpov. The letter contain factual data obtained at the T-101 wind tunnel on a wing shape of exactly the type Polikarpov was proposing on the I-180. In TsAGI's view, the wing was efficient but unstable, and too dangerous for inclusion on a service fighter. Polikarpov was requested to drop or modify the proposed wing. At the same time, much bad blood had developed between Polikarpov, his OKB staff, and certain members of the testing fraternity, including NII VVS Director Filin, and even its own Chief Test Pilot, Valeriy Chkalov. Chkalov – a long-time servant of Polikarpov and his designs – had become increasingly critical of the Head Designer's new direction in aircraft development, noting that his prototypes were increasingly dangerous and ill-behaved, and that Polikarpov seemed to be indifferent to this condition. Indeed, Chkalov's concerns were well-warranted, as he was nearly killed by the TsKB-29 in 1936, and by the I-17 the next year. The I-180 was yet more of the same, and it featured the similarly dangerous wing as the TsKB-25.

With these factors in mind, the I-180 project was sitting on a powder keg. The initial flight of the I-180 prototype took place on 15 December 1938 with Chkalov at the controls. After three circuits of the field, the I-180's engine suddenly stopped. Failed motors were hardly unknown in prototype testing, and a pilot of Chkalov's immense experience should have been able to regain the field and make an emergency landing. What happened next, however, horrified all who witnessed it – the I-180 plunged out of control into a hanger where it exploded, killing Valeriy Chkalov. Innumerable theories – conspiracy, and otherwise – have arisen in Russia (and elsewhere) about Chkalov's death – the possibility of sabotage, and all manner of technical minutiae.

With the death of the most beloved aviation hero in the history of the nation, public outcry after the tragedy was enormous. This, in combination with Stalin's oppressive regime, led to the inevitable arrests and trials. A number of leading figures in Polikarpov's Bureau were arrested, including his Deputy, Tomashevich. Polikarpov, himself, just managed to avoid arrest on the basis that he did not sign the type-readiness form for the flight (as should have been done), and so was able to claim that he did not authorize it.

To Polikarpov's great discredit, his behaviour over the following weeks was shabby, never once considering the death of Chkalov, but instead worrying about how the event might affect his fighter programme. Development of the I-180 did proceed, but only after extended lobbying from Polikarpov. In the end, the NII VVS confirmed the suspicions of the TsAGI, and it was clear that the I-180 behaved very poorly and was much too dangerous for service introduction. The type was subsequently rejected by the NKAP and dropped altogether.

POLIKARPOV I-185

Responding to the loss of the I-180 and the warnings of the TsAGI, Polikarpov's OKB next turned its attention to the I-185. Polikarpov's surreptitious awareness of his own guilt in the matter is clear in the I-185, which abandoned the previous airframe. A completely new design, the I-185 prototype was developed around the 2,000 hp M-90 twin-row radial. The I-185 was a classic Polikarpov design featuring mixed construction, a three-piece wing (where the central section was integral with the fuselage), an aft location for the cockpit, and *shpon*-covered semi-monocoque rear fuselage. The wing had a very short span, and was fitted with high-lift devices such as Handley-Page type leading edge slats.

In the event, the M-90 engine was not ready for installation into the I-185, and so a Shvetsov M-82A was fitted instead. Armament in the new prototype was heavy, three 20 mm ShVAK cannon being disposed around the cowling. Despite the presence of these weapons, the cowl was very tightly formed, and gave a streamlined appearance. In April 1942, the I-185 reached 549 km/h at sea level and 615 km/h at 6,470 m, climbing to 5,000 m in 5.8 minutes. The NII VVS' pilots found the I-185 to have good handling and flight characteristics, without any serious vices. Horizontal manoeuvrability was poor, however, the machine's rather high wing loading leading to a large turning circle, though the control surfaces were fairly well co-ordinated.

However, the M-82 powered I-185 did not live up to the claims made by the Polikarpov OKB, and a search for more power resulted in the adoption of the 1,625 hp (1,900 hp for take-off and emergency) M-71 radial. The M-71 was larger and heavier than the M-82, and therefore a much larger cowling was installed on the third I-185 prototype. During the Autumn of 1942 the I-185 M-71 was examined by the NII VVS, the handling and safety characteristics being found to be unchanged. With the M-71, the prototype reached 556 km/h at sea level and 630 km/h at 6,170 m, climbing initially at 3,700 ft./min and attaining 5,000 m in only 5.2 minutes.

The performance, firepower, and generally good handling of the I-185 certainly justified series production, just as the NII VVS report indicated. The political situation with regard to Polikarpov, however, meant that Moscow showed no interest in designs emanating from his Bureau. The NKAP responded to the successful State examinations of the I-185 by insisting that Polikarpov hand over the various technical data relating to his design to both the Yakovlev and Lavochkin Bureaux, rather than by launching the type into production. Despite Polikarpov's constant lobbying, the NKAP delayed and deflected all discussion about series manufacture, and in the end none was undertaken.

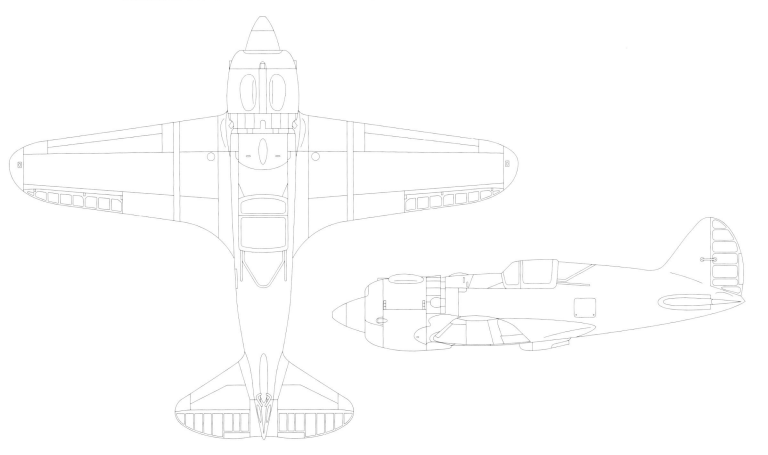

POLIKARPOV ITP

During 1940-41, the Polikarpov OKB developed another fighter prototype based on in-line aircraft engines. The ITP (*istrebitel tyazhelyi pushechni*, or heavy gun fighter) was initially developed around the Klimov M-107 of 1,500 hp. The ITP was very sleek and streamlined, externally resembling the MiG I-200 series. The nomenclature ITP derived from the intention to install a 37 mm cannon between the engine cylinder banks, but in the end difficulties with the M-107 prevented the initial ITP from being completed. A second ITP was completed in 1942 with the Mikulin AM-39 engine of 1,600 hp. In the No.2 prototype, the armament was modified to comprise three 20 mm ShVAK cannon, two above the engine and the third engine-mounted weapon firing through the spinner. Incessant delays were experienced with regard to testing the ITP AM-39 (once again the result of Polikarpov's political ills), and in fact proper evaluations were not carried out until the end of 1943. By that late date, the ITP's maximum speed of 650 km/h, poor manoeuvrability and uninspiring rate of climb did not recommend the type for series manufacture, and the programme was terminated.

TOMASHEVICH '110'

During the late 1930s and early 1940s, a design bureau existed within Moscow that was like no other in the USSR. The NKVD operated an aviation design programme within the former KOSOS offices that was officially known as 'TsKB-29'. This design bureau was staffed by political prisoners of the Stalinist regime, in particular head designers who had fallen into disfavour for one reason or other. Many illustrious aircraft emanated from this Bureau, including Samolet 100 (aircraft No.100—the Designer's name was never used from this facility) which became the superb Pe-2, and Samolet 103, which became the equally outstanding Tu-2.

One of the designers so detained at TsKAB-29 was Dmitri Tomashevich, former Deputy to Polikarpov. After the catastrophe with the I-180 and the death of Valeri Chkalov, Tomashevich was imprisoned for 'Wrecking' (essentially, a charge of criminal negligence). The philosophy at TsKB-29 was that the 'inmates' had literally to 'design' their way out of the institution: Petlyakov was released with the success of the Pe-2; Tupolev for the Tu-2; Turmanski for his successful work on aero engines, and so on. Tomashevich worked on several projects, but the first to reach prototype status was the '110'.

The Tomashevich '110' was a low-wing fighter aircraft of mostly wooden construction. The wing spar was dural, but all skinning was *shpon* laminate. For power, the Klimov M-107 engine was installed, this supported by a very large 'chin' radiator giving the '100' a profile somewhat like a Curtiss P-40 N. The wings formed a three-piece unit very much resembling, perhaps not surprisingly, those of the MiG-3, or any other Polikarpov design.

The '110' was evaluated at the end of 1942 by Petr Stefanovski. The prototype possessed very poor handling and manoeuvrability, and while it was capable of 610 km/h, the rate of climb was quite poor owing to the overweight structure. Although no production order ensued, work on the '110' was instrumental in assisting the M-107 engine to reach a state where series manufacture could be contemplated.

APPENDIX II

NKAP Painting Template

This three-view demonstrates the 1943 NKAP painting recommendation template for all Soviet single-engined fighters. The pattern was to accompany the new aerolacquers AMT-11 and AMT-12. From the artwork it is clear that no VVS camouflage ever matched such an application, this being altogether far too linear and 'rigid' for the aircraft industry and the Air Force. Some features of this pattern were seen but almost never with such angular form.

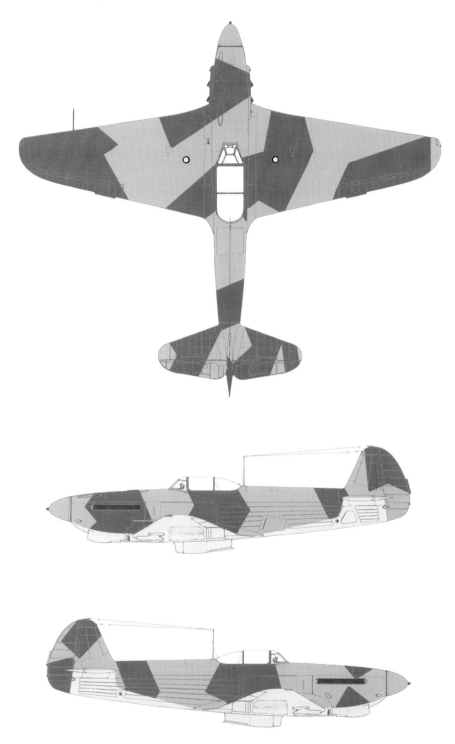

APPENDIX III

VVS National Markings

 Plain Red Star

This marking was common in the pre-War era, and had been relatively standard for many years dating from the 1920s. The plain star remained in use well into 1942, and into 1943 in cases, but was rarely seen thereafter.

 Circle Star

This permutation of the bordered star came into vogue several times during the 1920s and 1930s, and was seen occasionally on aircraft in the early GPW period that had been manufactured in 1937-39.

 Black Bordered Star

A national star with a thin black border very popular in the 1941-43 period, particularly with certain aircraft programmes (for example on Yak fighters). This type of star fell out of use during 1943, and was not usually seen thereafter.

White Bordered Star

A white border of varying sizes was applied to many national star markings. Initially, the borders tended to be quite thin, as with their black bordered counterparts. By 1942 the borders were usually slightly thicker, and this trend continued into 1944-45 when they could become thicker still. Some rare examples of this type of marking are known even from the pre-War era, but mainly this star was common from the latter half of 1942 onwards.

 Yellow Bordered Star

Stars with a yellow border were never especially common, and seemed to have been a decorative substitute for white borders. However, such markings were seen from 1942 right through to 1945, and tended to have medium-thick outlines.

Kremlin Star

These three dimensional stars were inspired by those of the Kremlin's various spires, and thus so-named. Some unbordered Kremlin stars were known, but these were rare, and usually from the pre-War period. From 1942-45, these types of stars featured the border of the period, that being white until 1944, and thereafter an outline type as well.

Victory Star

Also called the 'outline' star, the phrase 'Victory Star' was actually coined in the 1950s. This star is essentially that of the modern Russian (and Soviet, previously) VVS, and features a thin outline to the white border. Such markings were seen very rarely before 1944, but seem really to have appeared in quantity at some time early in the year. During 1945 these markings seemed to have become the agreed standard and largely supplanted all other national star types, and have remained so to the present time.

APPENDIX IV

Pilots

Above: *Hero of the Soviet Union Sultan Amet Khan stands next to his colourful Yak-7B, 'Red 28', in 1942. This aircraft appears to be finished in an AMT-6/-4/-7 scheme. (Photo: H.Seidl)*

Above: *Pilot N. Denchik (later Hero of the Soviet Union) of the 64 GIAP, 1943. The photograph is not of the highest quality, but Denchik's Yak-9 appears to wear an AMT-6/-4/-7 scheme typical of 1943. The inscription beginning with 'Za' ('Za Rodinu!' – 'For the Motherland!') is just evident aft of the 'kill' star markings. The tactical numeral has been suggested as 'White 3'. (Photo: H.Seidl)*

Left: *The LaGG-3 'White 6' of Kpt. G. Grigorev of the 178 IAP in 1942. His aircraft appears to be finished in a Gor'ki AMT-6/-4/-7 'Meander' scheme, and features black-bordered national insignia. (Photo: H.Seidl)*

Below: *Pavel Likholetov in front of his La-5F, 1943. (Photo: H.Seidl)*

Right: *St.Lt. Tikhonov in front of his LaGG-3-37 'White 90', August 1942. Tikhonov served in May. Shinkarenko's 42 IAP, a unit which routinely tested Yak and LaGG fighters with large-calibre cannon. The camouflage scheme of '90' is not known at the time of writing. (Photo: H.Seidl)*

Right: *A close-up of Hero of the Soviet Union Mikhail Baranov's aircraft of the 183 IAP in 1942. The inscription on both sides of the fuselage reads 'Groza Fashistov M.D. Baranov' ('Threat to Fascists, M.D. Baranov').*
(Photo: Author's Collection)

Left: *A VVS ace on the wing of his well-marked Yak-9 (or Yak-7B) fighter. The pilot is said to be Nikolai Kozlov, eventual commander of the 907 IAP. If true, this photograph must date from the period immediately before Kursk when he was serving with the 788 IAP. The scheme is certainly AMT-6/-4/-7, but a wider view is needed to determine the application pattern. (Photo: G.Petrov)*

Right: *Lt. Serikh of the 21 IAP stands in front of his Yak-9 (Yak-9T or, more likely, Yak–9M) on 15 October 1944. Considerable repainting seems to be evident around the cockpit and number '48'. The tactical number and fuselage star borders look to be in white, while the Victory star on the rudder appears to be trimmed in yellow. (Photo: H.Seidl)*

APPENDIX V

Performance Tables (Imperial)

Lavochkin LaGG-3

	LaGG-3 1941 Zavod 23	LaGG-3 1941 early	LaGG-3 1941 mid	LaGG-3 1941 Zavod 153	LaGG-3-37 1941	LaGG-3 1942
Weights						
Empty:	5580 lbs	5672 lbs	5753 lbs	5665 lbs	5890 lbs	5579 lbs
Loaded:	7179 lbs	7376 lbs	7231 lbs	7370 lbs	7515 lbs	6834 lbs
Wing area:	188.4 sq.ft	188.4 sq.ft	188.4 sq.ft	188.4 sq.ft	188.4 sq.ft	188.4 sq.ft
Engine	M-105P 1050 (1100) hp	M-105P 1050 (1100) hp	M-105P 1050 (1100) hp	M-105P 1050 (1100) hp	M-105PA 1050 (1100) hp	M-105PA 1050 (1100) hp
Maximum Speed						
At altitude:	357 mph at 16500 ft	332 mph at 16500 ft	335 mph at 16500 ft	330 mph at 16500 ft	330 mph at 16500 ft	341 mph at 16500 ft
Sea level:	309 mph	284 mph	289 mph	281 mph	285 mph	292 mph
Climb						
Initial:	2953 ft/min	2719 ft/min	2780 ft/min	2700 ft/min	2750 ft/min	2880 ft/min
Time to height:	6.8 min to 16500 ft	8.5 min to 16500 ft	7.9 min to 16500 ft	8.7 min to 16500 ft	8.2 min to 16500 ft	7.1 min to 16500 ft
Service Ceiling	27950 ft	30500 ft	30500 ft	30500 ft	28100 ft	30500 ft
Armament	2 x UBS 2 x ShKAS 1 x BK	1 x UBS 2 x ShKAS 1 x VYa-23	1 x UBS 2 x ShKAS 1 x ShVAK	1 x UBS 2 x ShKAS 1 x ShVAK	1 x UBS 1 x Sh-37	1 x UBS 1 x ShVAK 6 x RS-82

	LaGG-3 1942 Lightened	LaGG-3 194 Lightened	LaGG-3 1942 Boosted and Lightened	LaGG-3-37 1942	LaGG-3 1943, Improved and Lightened	LaGG-3 Type 105
Weights						
Empty:	5012 lbs	5579 lbs	5108 lbs	6243 lbs	4898 lbs	4742 lbs
Loaded:	6316 lbs	6834 lbs	6405 lbs	7414 lbs	6110 lbs	6060 lbs
Wing area:	188.4 sq.ft	188.4 sq.ft	188.4 sq.ft	188.4 sq.ft	188.4 sq.ft	188.4 sq.ft
Engine	M-105P 1050 (1100) hp	M-105PF 1180 (1260) hp	M-105PF 1180 (1260) hp	M-105PF 1180 (1260) hp	M-105PF 1180 (1260) hp	M-105PF-2 1240 (1310) hp
Maximum Speed						
Sea level:	354 mph at 12500 ft	350 mph at 16500 ft	357 mph at 16500 ft	347 mph at 16500 ft	371 mph at 12500 ft	384 mph at 11200 ft
At altitude:	290 mph	309 mph	319 mph	311 mph	338mph	344 mph
Climb						
Initial:	3150 ft/min	3220 ft/min	3455 ft/min	3340 ft/min	3680 ft/min	3800 ft/min
Time to height:	6.7 min to 16500 ft	6.6 min to 16500 ft	6.0 min to 16500 ft	6.4 min to 16500 ft	5.1 min to 16500 ft	4.8 min to 16500 ft
Service Ceiling	30500 ft	33500 ft	33500 ft	33500 ft	35100 ft	36800 ft
Armament	1 x UBS 1 x ShVAK	1 x UBS 1 x ShVAK 6 x RS-82	1 x UBS 1 x ShVAK	1 x UBS 1 x NS-37	1 x UBS 1 x ShVAK	1 x UBS 1 x Vya-23

Lavochkin La-5, La-5FN, La-7

	LaG-5 1942	LaG-5 1942, Standard	La-5F 1943, Early Series	La-5F 1943, Type 39	La-5FN 1943, Early Series	La-5FN 1943, Standard
Weights						
Empty:	5910 lbs	5889 lbs	5731 lbs	5709 lbs	5903 lbs	5841 lbs
Loaded:	7407 lbs	7385 lbs	7405 lbs	7098 lbs	7318 lbs	7323 lbs
Wing area:	188.4 sq.ft	188.4 sq.ft	188.4 sq.ft	188.4 sq.ft	189.3 sq.ft	189.3 sq.ft
Engine	M-82A 1330 (1510) hp	M-82A 1330 (1510) hp	M-82F 1350 (1700) hp	M-82F 1350 (1700) hp	M-82FN 1470 (1850) hp	M-82FN 1470 (1850) hp
Maximum Speed						
At altitude:	360 mph at 20500 ft	363 mph at 20500 ft	371 mph at 20500 ft	380 mph at 19000 ft	383 mph at 19000 ft	394 mph at 19500 ft
Sea level:	316 mph	324 mph	342 mph	345 mph	350 mph	356 mph
Climb						
Initial:	3225 ft/min	3350 ft/min	3690 ft/min	3745 ft/min	3850 ft/min	3980 ft/min
Time to height:	6.0 min to 16500 ft	5.9 min to 16500 ft	5.4 min to 16500	5.0 min to 16500 ft	4.8 min to 16500 ft	4.6 min to 16500 ft
Service Ceiling	31000 ft	31000 ft	31250 ft	33100 ft	35000 ft	36100 ft
Armament	2 x ShVAK	2 x ShVAK	2 x ShVAK	2 x ShVAK	2 x ShVAK	2 x ShVAK

	La-7 1944, Early Series	La-7 1944 Standard	La-7 1945,
Weights			
Empty:	5779 lbs	5822 lbs	5811 lbs
Loaded:	7164 lbs	7308 lbs	7310 lbs
Wing area:	189.3 sq.ft	189.3 sq.ft	189.3 sq.ft
Engine	ASh-83FN 1470 (1850) hp	ASh-83FN 1470 (1850) hp	ASh-83FN 1470 (1850) hp
Maximum Speed			
At altitude:	409 mph at 20200 ft	420 mph at 20200 ft	420 mph at 20200 ft
Sea level:	361 mph	381 mph	381 mph
Climb			
Initial:	4000 ft/min	4300 ft/min	4300 ft/min
Time to height:	4.6 min to 16500 ft	4.2 min to 16500 ft	4.2 min to 16500 ft
Service Ceiling	30500 ft	34250 ft	34250 ft
Armament	2 x ShVAK	2 x ShVAK	3 x B-20

Mikoyan and Guryevich I-200, MiG-1, MiG-3

	MiG-1 1940	MiG-3 1941 (early)	MiG-3 1941 (Standard)	MiG-3 1941 5-gun Variant	MiG-3 1941 Lengthened Version
Weights					
Empty:	5931 lbs	6105 lbs	6090 lbs	6128 lbs	5903 lbs
Loaded:	7288 lbs	7441 lbs	7299 lbs	7385 lbs	7272 lbs
Wing area:	187.7 sq.ft	187.7 sq.ft	187.7 sq.ft	187.7 sq.ft	187.7 sq.ft
Engine	AM-35A 1200 (1350) hp	AM-35A 1200 (1350) hp	AM-35A 1200 (1350) hp	AM-35A 1200 (1350) hp	AM-35A 1200 (1350) hp
Maximum Speed					
At altitude:	377 mph at 23600 ft	371 mph at 23600 ft	374 mph at 23600 ft	364 mph at 23600 ft	382 mph at 25000 ft
Sea level:	288 mph	280 mph	287 mph	279 mph	289 mph
Climb					
Initial:	3200 ft/min	3000 ft/min	3000 ft/min	2900 ft/min	3100 ft/min
Time to height:	6.3 min. to 16500 ft	7.2 min. to 16500 ft	7.2 min. to 16500 ft	7.5 min. to 16500 ft	7.1 min. to 16500 ft
Service Ceiling	36500 ft	36500 ft	36500 ft	35000 ft	39500 ft
Armament	2 x ShKAS 1 x UBS	2 x ShKAS 1 x UBS	2 x ShKAS 1 x UBS	2 x ShKAS 1 x UBS 2 x UBS	2 x ShKAS 1 x UBS 6 x RS-82

MiG-3
Final Variant

Weights
Empty: 5950 lbs
Loaded: 7290 lbs
Wing area: 187.7 sq.ft

Engine AM-35A
1200 (1350) hp

Maximum Speed
At altitude: 397 mph at 25000 ft.
Sea level: 295 mph

Climb
Initial: 3225 ft/min
Time to height: 6.5 min to 16500 ft

Service Ceiling 39500 ft

Armament 3 x UBS
6 x RS-82

Polikarpov I-15, I-152, I-153

	I-15	I-15 M-25A	I-152	I-153 M-25V	I-153 M-62 (early Series 1939)
Weights					
Empty:	2438 lbs	2683 lbs	3026 lbs	2949 lbs	3187 lbs
Loaded:	3119 lbs	3439 lbs	3747 lbs	3703 lbs	3884 lbs
Wing area:	253.0 ft.sq	253.0 ft.sq	242 ft.sq	261 ft.sq	261 ft.sq
Engine	M-22 480 hp	M-25A 725 hp	M-25V 750 hp	M-25V 750 hp	M-62 800 (920) hp
Maximum Speed					
At altitude:	214 mph at 9825 ft	231 mph at 9450 ft	228 mph at 9500 ft	268 mph at 12000 ft	270 mph at 9800 ft
Sea Level:	177 mph	207 mph	202 mph	229 mph	231 mph
Climb					
Initial:	1380 ft./min.	2160 ft./min.	1535 ft./min.	2300 ft./min.	2700 ft./min.
Time to height:	11 min to 16400 ft	7.0 min to 16400 ft	7.3 min to 16400 ft	6.9 min to 16400 ft	6.1 min to 16400 ft
Service Ceiling	24700 ft	28500 ft	29800 ft	28500 ft	32100 ft
Armament	2 x PV-1	4 x PV-1	4 x PV-1 2 x FAB-50 2 x AO-25	4 x ShKAS	4 x ShKAS

	I-153 M-62 (standard Series 1940)	I-153 M-63 (with skis)	I-153 M-63 (1940 Series)
Weights			
Empty:	3210 lbs	3415 lbs	3288 lbs
Loaded:	3951 lbs	4193 lbs	4076 lbs
Wing area:	261 ft	261 ft	261 ft
Engine	M-62 800 (920) hp	M-63 950 (1100) hp	M-63 950 (1100) hp
Maximum Speed			
At altitude:	263 mph at 9200 ft	266 mph at 11500 ft	272 mph at 11500 ft
Sea level:	226 mph	228 mph	230 mph
Climb			
Initial:	3000 ft/min.	3000 ft/min	3100 ft/min.
Time to height:	5.0 min to 16400 ft	5.1 min to 16400 ft	5.0 min to 16400 ft
Service Ceiling	24700 ft	29800 ft	28500 ft
Armament	4 x ShKAS OR 2 x UBS	4 x ShKAS 2 x FAB-50 2 x AO-25	4 x ShKAS 8 x RS82

Polikarpov I-16

	I-16 Type 4	I-16 Type 5	I-16 Type 10	I-16 Type 12	I-16 Type 17	I-16 Type 18
Weights						
Empty:	2355 lbs	2524 lbs	2945 lbs	2784 lbs	3141 lbs	3108 lbs
Loaded:	2979 lbs	3373 lbs	3805 lbs	3738 lbs	3990 lbs	4069 lbs
Wing area:	156.5 sq.ft	156.5 sq.ft	156.5 sq.ft	156.5 sq.ft	156.5 sq.ft	156.5 sq.ft
Engine	M-22 480 hp	M-25A 725 hp	M-25V 750 hp	M-25A 725 hp	M-25V 750 hp	M-62 800 (920) hp
Maximum Speed						
At altitude:	214 mph at 9870 ft	276 mph at 9000 ft	278 mph at 10400 ft	268 mph at 8000 ft	264 mph at 9000 ft	285 mph at 10500 ft
Sea level:	223 mph	242 mph	247 mph	244 mph	239 mph	255 mph
Climb						
Initial:	1300 ft/min	2350 ft/min	2100 ft/min	2045 ft/min	1800 ft/min	3400 ft/min
Time to height:	9.9 min to 16400 ft	7.8 min to 16400 ft	8.2 min to 16400 ft	8.3 min to 16400 ft	9.0 min to 16400 ft	5.4 min to 16400 ft
Service Ceiling	24400 ft	27250 ft	27000 ft	27400 ft	27000 ft	31000 ft
Armament	2 x ShKAS	2 x ShKAS	4 x ShKAS	2 x ShVAK	2 x ShKAS 2 x ShVAK	4 x ShKAS 6 x RS-82

	I-16 Type 27	I-16 Type 28 with revised supercharger gearing	I-16 Type 24	I-16 Type 29
Weights				
Empty:	3280 lbs	3364 lbs	3167 lbs	3406 lbs
Loaded:	4305 lbs	4588 lbs	4140 lbs	4210 lbs
Wing area:	156.5 sq.ft	156.5 sq.ft	156.5 sq.ft	156.5 sq.ft
Engine	M-62 800 (920) hp	M-63 930 (1100) hp	M-63 930 (1100) hp	M-63 930 (1100) hp
Maximum Speed				
At altitude:	272 mph at 10500 ft	287 mph at 6560 ft	285 mph at 15470 ft	290 mph at 14695 ft
Sea level:	251 mph	265 mph	253 mph	259 mph
Climb				
Initial:	3000 ft/min	2520 ft/min	3250 ft/min	3425 ft/min
Time to height:	6.9 min to 16400 ft	7.3 min to 16400 ft	6.0 min to 16400 ft	5.8 min to 16400 ft
Service Ceiling	29520 ft	30500 ft	35500 ft	32000 ft
Armament	2 x ShKAS 2 x ShVAK	2 x ShKAS 2 x ShVAK 6 x RS-82	4 x ShKAS 6 x RS-82	2 x ShKAS 1 x UBS 6 x RS-82

Yakovlev Yak-1

	Yak-1 1940-41	Yak-1 1941	Yak-1 1941 w/ rocket rails	Yak-1 1941 w/skis	Yak-1 1942 massoviy	Yak-1 1942 M-105PF
Weights						
Empty:	5213 lbs	5280 lbs	5354 lbs	5299 lbs	5277 lbs	5279 lbs
Loaded:	6300 lbs	6348 lbs	6430 lbs	6425 lbs	6355 lbs	6393 lbs
Wing area:	184.6 sq.ft	184.6 sq.ft	184.6 sq.ft	184.6 sq.ft	184.6 sq.ft	184.6 sq.ft
Engine	M-105P 1050 (1100) hp	M-105PA 1050 (1100) hp	M-105PA 1050 (1150) hp	M-105PA 1050 (1150) hp	M-105PA 1050 (1150) hp	M-105PF 1180 (1260) hp
Maximum Speed						
At altitude:	358 mph at 16250 ft	348 mph at 15750 ft	331 mph at 16250 ft	331 mph at 16250 ft	350 mph at 15900 ft	355 mph at 12500 ft
Sea level:	298 mph	291 mph	276 mph	274 mph	297 mph	317 mph
Climb						
Initial:	3280 ft/min	3010 ft/min	2890 ft/min	3000 ft/min	3400 ft/min	3515 ft/min
Time to height:	5.7 min to 16400 ft	6.3 min to 16400 ft	6.8 min to 16400 ft	6.3 min to 16400 ft	5.9 min to 16400 ft	6.0 min to 16400 ft
Service Ceiling	30500 ft	32500 ft	32500 ft	32500 ft	34000 ft	36100 ft
Armament	2 x ShKAS 1 x ShVAK	2 x ShKAS 1 x ShVAK	2 x ShKAS 1 x ShVAK 6 x RS-82	2 x ShKAS 1 x ShVAK	2 x ShKAS 1 x ShVAK	2 x ShKAS 1 x ShVAK

	Yak-1(Obl.) 1942 M-105PF	Yak-1 1943 ('Yak-1b')
Weights		
Empty:	5180 lbs	5195 lbs
Loaded:	6128 lbs	6358 lbs
Wing area:	184.6 sq.ft	184.6 sq.ft
Engine	M-105PF 1180 (1260) hp	M-105PF 1180 (1260) hp
Maximum Speed		
At altitude:	368 mph at 12500 ft	368 mph at 12500 ft
Sea level:	327 mph	330 mph
Climb		
Initial:	3715 ft/min	3650 ft/min
Time to height:	4.7 min. to 16400 ft	5.2 min. to 16400 ft
Service Ceiling:	37500 ft	36100 ft
Armament	2 x ShKAS 1 x ShVAK	1 x UBS 1 x ShVAK

Yakovlev Yak-7, UTI-26

	Yak-7	Yak-7A	Yak-7B	Yak-7-37	Yak-7B M-105PF 1942	Yak-7B M-105PF 1943
Weights						
Empty:	5460 lbs	5401 lbs	5689 lbs	5939 lbs	5489 lbs	5415 lbs
Loaded:	6525 lbs	6470 lbs	6898 lbs	7130 lbs	6635 lbs	6590 lbs
Wing area:	184.6 sq.ft	184.6 sq.ft	184.6 sq.ft	184.6 sq.ft	184.6 sq.ft	184.6 sq.ft
Engine	M-105PA 1050 (1150) hp	M-105PA 1050 (1150) hp	M-105PA 1050 (1150) hp	M-105PA 1050 (1150) hp	M-105PF 1180 (1260) hp	M-105PF 1180 (1260) hp
Maximum Speed						
At altitude:	347 mph at 16400 ft	355 mph at 16400 ft	358 mph at 12750 ft	350 mph at 15500 ft	350 mph at 12000 ft	361 mph at 12000 ft
Sea level:	292 mph	308 mph	309 mph	301 mph	303 mph	319 mph
Climb						
Initial:	2900 ft/min	3000 ft/min	2850 ft/min	2600 ft/min	3200 ft/min	3310 ft/min
Time to height:	6.8 min. to 16400 ft	6.4 min. to 16400 ft	6.5 min. to 16400 ft	7.2 min. to 16400 ft	5.8 min. to 16400 ft	5.7 min. to 16400 ft
Service Ceiling	30250 ft	31000 ft	32500 ft	27000 ft	32500 ft	33400 ft
Armament	2 x ShKAS 1 x ShVAK 6 x RS-82	2 x ShKAS 1 x ShVAK 6 x RS-82	2 x UBS 1 x ShVAK	2 x UBS 1 x MPSh-37	2 x UBS 1 x ShVAK	2 x UBS 1 x ShVAK

	Yak-7 Razvedchik
Weights	
Empty:	5490 lbs
Loaded:	6485 lbs
Wing area:	184.6 sq.ft
Engine	M-105PA 1050 (1150) hp
Maximum Speed	
At altitude:	356 mph at 15550 ft
Sea level:	314 mph
Climb	
Initial:	3050 ft/min
Time to height:	5.9 min. to 16400 ft
Service Ceiling	32500 ft
Armament	1 x ShVAK

217

Yakovlev Yak-9

	Yak-9	Yak-9D	Yak-9T	Yak-9M	Yak-9R 1943	Yak-9DD
Weights						
Empty:	5019 lbs	5180 lbs	5066 lbs	5352 lbs	5031 lbs	5171 lbs
Loaded:	6320 lbs	6857 lbs	6655 lbs	6809 lbs	6358 lbs	7451 lbs
Wing area:	184.6 sq.ft	184.6 sq.ft	184.6 sq.ft	184.6 sq.ft	184.6 sq.ft	184.6 sq.ft
Engine	M-105PF	M-105PF	M-105PF	M-105PF	M-105PF	M-105PF
	1180 (1260) hp	1180 (1260) hp	1180 (1260) hp	1180 (1260) hp	1180 (1260) hp	1180 (1260) hp
Maximum Speed						
At altitude:	372 mph at 13760 ft	365 mph at 11970 ft	368 mph at 12890 ft	356 mph at 12300 ft	369 mph at 13950 ft	363 mph at 11970 ft
Sea level:	323 mph	330 mph	329 mph	320 mph	321 mph	324 mph
Climb						
Initial:	3615 ft/min	3360 ft/min	3560 ft/min	3000 ft/min	3590 ft/min	3120 ft/min
Time to Height	5.1 min to 16400 ft	6.1 min to 16400 ft	5.5 min to 16400 ft	6.3 min to 16400 ft	5.2 min to 16400 ft	6.8 min to 16400 ft
Service Ceiling	36500 ft	29750 ft	32750 ft	31000 ft	34000 ft	30750 ft
Armament	1 x UBS	1 x UBS	1 x UBS	1 x UBS	1 x ShVAK	1 x UBS
	1 x ShVAK	1 x NS-37	1 x ShVAK	1 x ShVAK	1 x ShVAK	

	Yak-9B (-9L) with2 bombs	Yak-9K	Yak-9U Early, limited RPM	Yak-9U 1945
Weights				
Empty:	5251 lbs	5050 lbs	5537 lbs	5535 lbs
Loaded:	6943 lbs	6662 lbs	7049 lbs	7040 lbs
Wing area:	184.6 sq.ft	184.6 sq.ft	184.6 sq.ft	184.6 sq.ft
Engine	M-105PF	M-105PF	VK-107A	VK-107A
	1180 (1260) hp	1180 (1260) hp	1500 (1650) hp	1500 (1650) hp
Maximum Speed				
At altitude:	347 mph at 12300 ft	354 mph at 12300 ft	401 mph at 16400 ft	422 mph at 16400 ft
Sea level:	313 mph	320 mph	345 mph	361 mph
Climb				
Initial:	3000 ft/min	3050 ft/min	3715 ft/min	4200 ft/min
Time to height:	6.5 min to 16400 ft	6.5 min to 16400 ft	4.8 min to 16400 ft	4.1 min to 16400 ft
Service Ceiling	28250 ft	32730 ft	35100 ft	36500 ft
Armament	1 x UBS	1 x UBS	2 x UBS	2 x UBS
	1 x ShVAK	1 x NS-45	1 x ShVAK	1 x ShVAK
	2 x FAB100			

Yakovlev Yak-3

	Yak-3 1944	Yak-3P 1945	Yak-3 VK-107 1946	Yak-3U
Weights				
Empty:	4691 lbs	4695 lbs	5230 lbs	5011 lbs
Loaded:	5945 lbs	5960 lbs	6590 lbs	6155 lbs
Wing area:	159.8 sq.ft	159.8 sq.ft	159.8 sq.ft	184.6 sq.ft
Engine	VK-105PF2	VK-105PF2	VK-107A	ASh-82FN
	1250 (1320) hp	1250 (1320) hp	1500 (1650) hp	1850 hp
Maximum Speed				
At altitude:	400 mph at 14100 ft	400 mph at 14100 ft	436 mph at 19250 ft	438 mph at 19250 ft
Sea level:	350 mph	350 mph	373 mph	374 mph
Climb				
Initial:	4450 ft/min	4450 ft/min	4850 ft/min	5800 ft/min
Time to height:	4.5 min to 16400 ft	4.5 min to 16400 ft	4.25 min to 16400 ft	3.9 min to 16400 ft
Service Ceiling	34150 ft	34150 ft	36250 ft	36900 ft
Armament	2 x UBS	3 x B-20	2 x UBS	2 x B-20
	1 x ShVAK		1 x ShVAK	

BIBLIOGRAPHY

Due to the extraordinary size of the full bibliography for this work, comprising some 15 years' worth of reading and research, the following may be regarded as a cursory listing of the most important materials. The selection of the sources to be included are mine, alone, and I apologize for any crucial or important omissions in this list.

PRIMARY ARCHIVAL SOURCES

Records from the Production Diary of State Aviation Factory No. 1

Tsentralnoe Statisticheskoe Upravlenie, GOSPLAN, iz del GOSSNAB II-IV

GOSSNAB, *fond* 29, *opis'* 1121, *delo* 8, *list* 8-116 (inclusive), *list* 121-190 (inclusive)

GOSSNAB, *fond* 29, *opis'* 1121, *delo* 10, *list* 36-56 (inclusive), *list* 67-150 (inclusive), *list* 189-204 (inclusive)

GOSSNAB, *fond* 29, *opis'* 1121, *delo* 11, *list* 1-9 (inclusive), *list* 20-45 (inclusive)

GOSSNAB, *fond* 404, *opis'* 1, *delo* 1, *list* 1-243 (inclusive)

Tsentralniy Gosudarstvenniy Arkhiv Moskovskoi Oblasti

Fond 4610, *opis'* 1, *delo* 295, *list* 1-31 (inclusive)

Fond 8328, *opis'* 1, *delo* 1328, *list* 2-16 (inclusive)

Records from the Production Diary of State Aviation Factory No. 18 *imeni Voroshilova*

Tsentralnoe Statisticheskoe Upravlenie, GOSPLAN, iz del GOSSNAB II-IV

GOSSNAB, *fond* 125, *opis'* 96, *delo* 22, *list* 5-13 (inclusive)

GOSSNAB, *fond* 127, *opis'* 9, *delo* 1, *list* 1-19 (inclusive), *list* 28-56 (inclusive), *list* 59-88 (inclusive), *list* 105-166 (inclusive)

GOSSNAB, *fond* 127, *opis'* 10, *delo* 1, *list* 51-100 (inclusive), *list* 133-206 (inclusive)

GOSSNAB, *fond* 127, *opis'* 13, *delo* 60, *list* 8-91 (inclusive), *list* 102-122 (inclusive), *list* 180-200 (inclusive)

GOSSNAB, *fond* 127, *opis'* 17, *delo* 66, *list* 1-243 (inclusive)

Tsentralniy Gosudarstvenniy Arkhiv Sovietskoi Armii

TsGASA, *fond* 29, *opis'* 10, *delo* 655, *list* 5-31 (inclusive), *list* 104-165 (inclusive)

Records from the Production Diary of State Aviation Factory No. 19 *imeni Stalina*

Tsentralnoe Statisticheskoe Upravlenie, GOSPLAN, iz del GOSSNAB II-IV

GOSSNAB, *fond* 416, *opis'* 991, *delo* 2, *list* 1-113 (inclusive)

Records from the Production Diary of State Aviation Factory No. 21 *imeni Ordzhonikidzhe*

Tsentralnoe Statisticheskoe Upravlenie, GOSPLAN, iz del GOSSNAB II-IV

GOSSNAB, *fond* 191, *opis'* 101, *delo* 65, *list* 9-31 (inclusive), *list* 56-63 (inclusive), *list* 70-79 (inclusive), *list* 108-144 (inclusive), *list* 153-202 (inclusive), *list* 207-219 (inclusive), *list* 277-300 (inclusive), *list* 376-388 (inclusive), *list* 393-409 (inclusive), *list* 415-427 (inclusive)

GOSSNAB, *fond* 191, *opis'* 188, *delo* 7, *list* 1-13 (inclusive), *list* 60-70 (inclusive), *list* 115-138 (inclusive)

GOSSNAB, *fond* 191, *opis'* 190, *delo* 3, *list* 1-51 (inclusive)

GOSPLAN TsSU, *fond* 74, *opis'* 2, *delo* 2, *list* 1-39 (inclusive)

Records from the Production Diary of
State Aviation Factory No. 22

Tsentralnoe Statisticheskoe Upravlenie, GOSPLAN, iz del GOSSNAB II-IV

GOSSNAB, *fond* 336, *opis'* 1002, *delo* 65, *list* 90-117 (inclusive), *list* 156-218 (inclusive), *list* 243-270 (inclusive)

Records from the Production Diary of
State Aviation Factory No. 30
(*incl. GAZ 16 Aerolak*)

Tsentralnoe Statisticheskoe Upravlenie, GOSPLAN, iz del GOSSNAB II-IV

GOSSNAB, *fond* 53, *opis'* 1099, *delo* 78, *list* 84-122 (inclusive), *list* 145-190 (inclusive) , *list* 212-230 (inclusive)

GOSSNAB, *fond* 53, *opis'* 1343, *delo* 9, *list* 1-8 (inclusive), *list* 20-40 (inclusive), *list* 60-75 (inclusive), *list* 100-123 (inclusive), *list* 130-140 (inclusive)

Records from the Production Diary of
State Aviation Factory No. 99

Tsentralnoe Statisticheskoe Upravlenie, GOSPLAN, iz del GOSSNAB II-IV

GOSSNAB, *fond* 31, *opis'* 552, *delo* 1, *list* 1-36 (inclusive)

GOSSNAB, *fond* 31, *opis'* 552, *delo* 4, *list* 5-25 (inclusive), *list* 37-77 (inclusive), *list* 100-142 (inclusive), *list* 158-195 (inclusive)

Records from the Production Diary of
State Aviation Factory No. 153

Tsentralnoe Statisticheskoe Upravlenie, GOSPLAN, iz del GOSSNAB II-IV

GOSSNAB, *fond* 28, *opis'* 441, *delo* 22, *list* 3-107 (inclusive)

GOSSNAB, *fond* 28, *opis'* 451, *delo* 1, *list* 85-239 (inclusive)

GOSSNAB, *fond* 28, *opis'* 499, *delo* 19, *list* 1-13 (inclusive), *list* 200-271 (inclusive)

GOSSNAB, *fond* 206, *opis'* 55, *delo* 20, *list* 5-54 (inclusive), *list* 90-114 (inclusive), *list* 133-166 (inclusive), *list* 172-201 (inclusive), *list* 230-246 (inclusive), *list* 263-291 (inclusive), *list* 330-348 (inclusive), *list* 361-387 (inclusive), *list* 391-399 (inclusive)

GOSSNAB, *fond* 206, *opis'* 114, *delo* 1454, *list* 1-25 (inclusive)

GOSSNAB, *fond* 206, *opis'* 899, *delo* 30, *list* 6-19 (inclusive), *list* 117-209 (inclusive)

GOSSNAB, *fond* 331, *opis'* 13, *delo* 13, *list* 9-71 (inclusive), *list* 100-120 (inclusive), *list* 137-155 (inclusive)

GOSSNAB, *fond* 331, *opis'* 17, *delo* 1, *list* 1-15 (inclusive), *list* 39-69 (inclusive), *list* 78-122 (inclusive), *list* 156-181 (inclusive)

GOSPLAN TsSU, *fond* 5613, *opis'* 9, *delo* 112, *list* 1-50 (inclusive), *list* 100-200 (inclusive)

Records from the Production Diary of
State Aviation Factory No. 166

Tsentralnoe Statisticheskoe Upravlenie, GOSPLAN, iz del GOSSNAB II-IV

GOSSNAB, *fond* 99, *opis'* 867, *delo* 8, *list* 1-21 (inclusive), *list* 61-91 (inclusive), *list* 105-128 (inclusive), *list* 134-176 (inclusive), *list* 188-193 (inclusive)

GOSSNAB, *fond* 99, *opis'* 867, *delo* 9, *list* 1-71 (inclusive)

GOSPLAN TsSU, *fond* 702, *opis'* 400, *delo* 6, *list* 3-50 (inclusive)

Records from the Production Diary of State Aviation Factory No. 292

Tsentralnoe Statisticheskoe Upravlenie, GOSPLAN, iz del GOSSNAB II-IV

GOSSNAB, *fond* 16, *opis'* 188, *delo* 54, *list* 1-100 (inclusive), *list* 124-157 (inclusive)

GOSSNAB, *fond* 16, *opis'* 188, *delo* 79, *list* 4-10 (inclusive) , *list* 31-67 (inclusive), *list* 99-117 (inclusive), *list* 144-166 (inclusive), *list* 180-194 (inclusive)

GOSSNAB, *fond* 16, *opis'* 188, *delo* 80, *list* 71-185 (inclusive)

GOSSNAB, *fond* 16, *opis'* 188, *delo* 82, *list* 1-73 (inclusive), *list* 101-145 (inclusive)

GOSSNAB, *fond* 16, *opis'* 205, *delo* 1, *list* 9-116 (inclusive)

Arkhiv Museya Staratovskogo Aviatsionnogo Zavoda

Fond "Material Yakovlova", delo 9, list *84-131 (inclusive)*, list *157-179 (inclusive)*

Material and Data Statistics on NKAP Production Contracts

Tsentralniy Gosudarstvenniy Arkhiv Narodnogo Khozyaystva SSSR

Fond *1318*, opis' *12*, delo *59*, list *1-20 (inclusive)*

Fond *1737*, opis' *4*, delo *169*, list *7-63 (inclusive)*

Fond *1737*, opis' *34*, delo *8*, list *86-121 (inclusive)*, list *145-168 (inclusive)*

Fond *2686*, opis' *7*, delo *5*, list *1-55 (inclusive)*

Fond *2915*, opis' *1*, delo *1*, list *1-109 (inclusive)*, list *122-154 (inclusive)*, list *168-177 (inclusive)*

Fond *3551*, opis' *3*, delo *2*, list *66-130 (inclusive)*

GENERAL ARCHIVE RESOURCES

Tsentralniy Gosudarstvenniy Arkhiv Sovietskoi Armii *(TsGASA)*
   [Central State Archive of the Soviet Army]

Arkhiv Muzeya Voenno-Vozdushnikh Sil Rossii imeni Frunze (Monino)
   [Frunze Archive of the Military Air Forces of Russia]

Fond *29* Upravlenie Voenno-Vozdushnikh Sil SSSR
   [Collection 29 of the Directorate of the Military Air Forces of the USSR]

Tsentralniy Dom Aviatsii i Kosmonavtiki (Moscow)
   [Central House of Aviation and Cosmonautics]

Tsentralniy Arkhiv Ministerstva Oboroni (TsAMO)
   [Central Archives of the Ministry of Defense]

Tsentralniy Gosudarstvenniy Istoricheskiy Arkhiv Goroda Moskvi
   [Central State Historical Archives of Moscow City]

Arkhiv OKB Yakovleva (Moscow)
   [Archive of the Yakovlev Design Bureau]

SELECTED BOOKS

Abanshin, M.E.   *Fighting Lavochkin*
         [1993] ; Aviation International (Washington, USA)

Abanshin, M.E.   *Fighting Polikarpov*
         [1994] ; Aviation International (Washington, USA)

Andersson, L.   *Soviet Aircraft and Aviation 1917-1941*
         [1994] ; Naval Institute Press (Annapolis, USA)

Arlazorov, M.S.   *Front Idet Cherez KB*
         [1975] ; Znanie, 2nd Edition (Moscow)

Bock, R.   *Monografie Lotnicze No.13; Yak-1 Yak-3*
         (Aircraft Profile No. 13; Yak-1 Yak-3)
         [1995] AJ Press (Gdansk, Poland)

Bock, R.   *Monografie Lotnicze No.47; Yak-7 Yak-9*
                         (Aircraft Profile No. 47; Yak-7 Yak-9)
                         [1999] AJ Press (Gdansk, Poland)

Bursch, E. F.   *Vozdushnaya Voina i Voennaya Maskirovka*
                         (Air War and Military Camouflage)
                         [1938] ; (Moscow)

Duz', P.D.   *Istoriya Vozdukhplanovanniya i Aviatsii v Rossii*
                         (The History of Aeronautics and Aviation in Russia) [1986] ; Nauka (Moscow)

Gordon, E. Khazanov, D.
                         Soviet Combat Aircraft; Volume One: Single Engined Fighters
                         [1998] ; Midland Publishing, Ltd. (Leicestershire, U.K.)

Gordon, E., Zenkin, V., Titov, V.
                         I-5, I-15, I-15bis; Istrebitel-biplan N.N. Polikarpova
                         (I-5, I-15, I-15bis; Fighter-Biplanes of N.N. Polikarpov) [1992] ; Polygon (Moscow)

Guest, C-F., Keskinen, K., Stenman, K.
                         Red Stars— Soviet Air Force in World War Two
                         [1993] ; Kustantaja Ar-Kustannus Oy (Kangasala, Finland)

Hardesty, Von.   *Red Phoenix— The Rise of Soviet Air Power 1941-1945*
                         [1982] ; Smithsonian Institution Press (Washington D.C.)

Karpovich, M.D.   *Sovietskie Letchiki v Velikoy Otchestvennoy Voine*
                         (Soviet Pilots in the Great Patrotic War) [1951] ; DOSAAF (Moscow)

Kazarinova, M.A.   *V Nebe Frontovom—Sbornik Vospominaniy Sovetskikh Letchitsuchastnits Velikoy
                         Otchesvennoy Voini*
                         (In the Skies Over the Front—A Collection of Recollections of Soviet Women Pilots in
                         the Great Patriotic War) [1962] ; Molodaya Gvardiya (Moscow)

Kuznetsov, S.   *Perviy Yak*
                         (First Yak) [1995] ; "Beloved Books" Press (Moscow)

Leypnik, D.L.   *Yak-9: Radovie Nebes*
                         (Yak-9: Soldier of the Sky) [2000] ; Arkhiv Press (Kiev)

Maslov, M.   *Istrebitel' I-16*   (I-16 Fighter) [1997] ; M-Hobby (Moscow)

Maslov, M.   *I-153*
                         (I-153) [2001] ; "Technical-Youth" Publishing House (Moscow)

Michulec, R.   *Monografie Lotnicze No.22; Il-2 Il-10*
                         (Aircraft Monograph No.22; Il-2 Il-10) [1995] AJ Press (Gdansk, Poland)

Michulec, R.   *Kampanie Lotnicze No.7; Stalinowskie Sokoly*
                         (Air Campaign No.7; Stalinist Falcons) [1995] AJ Press (Gdansk, Poland)

Ozerov, G.A.   *Tupolevskaya Sharaga*
                         (The Tupolev Political-Internment Bureau) [1971] ; Possev-Verlag (Frankfurt-am-Main,
                         DDR)

Ponomarev, A. N. *Sovietskie Aviatsionnie Konstruktori*
                         (Soviet Aviation Designers) [1980] ; Voenizdat 2nd Edition (Moscow)

Pospelov, P.N.   *Istoriya Velikoy Otchestvennoy Voyni Sovetskogo Soyuza, 1941-45*
                         (The History of the Great Patriotic War of the Soviet Union, 1941-45) [1965] ;
                         Voenizdat (Moscow)

Pshenyanik, G.A.   *Sovetskie Voenno-Vozdushnie Sili v Bor'be s Nemetsko-Fashistskoy Aviatsiey v Letne -
                         Osenney Kampanii 1941 g.*
                         (Soviet Military Air Forces in the Struggle Against Fascist-German Aviation in the
                         Summer Campaign in 1941) [1961] ; Voenizdat (Moscow)

Rudenko, S.I.,   editor. *Sovietskie Voenno-Vozdushnie Sili v Velikoy Otchestvennoy Voine 1941-45 gg*
                         (The Soviet Military Air Forces in the Great Patriotic War 1941-45) [1968] ; Voenizdat
                         (Moscow)

Saukke, M.   *Samoleti Tupoleva; ANT-1 – ANT-15*
                         (Tupolev Aircraft; ANT-1 to ANT-15) [1995] ; Libri (Moscow)

Seidl, H. D.   *Stalin's Eagles; An Illustrated Study of the Soviet Aces of WWII and Korea*
                         [1998] ; Schiffer (Pennsylvania, USA)

Shadiskiy, P.   *Sovietskaya Aviatsiya v Boyakh za Rodinu*
                         (Soviet Aviation in the Battle for the Motherland) [1966] ; DOSAAF, 2nd Edition
                         (Moscow)

Shavrov, V.B.   *Istoriya Konstruktsiy Samoletov SSSR do 1938 g*
                         (The History of Aircraft Construction of the USSR to 1938) [1978] ; Machinostroenie
                         Press (Moscow)

Shavrov, V.B. *Istoriya Konstruktsiy Samoletov SSSR 1938-1950 gg*
(The History of Aircraft Construction of the USSR from 1938-1945) [1979] ;
Machinostroenie Press (Moscow)

Shipilov, I.F., editor. *Zvezdi na Kril'yakh—Vospominaniya Vetreranov Sovetskoy Aviatsii*
(Stars on the Wings—Recollections of Soviet Aviation Veterans) [1959] ; Voenizdat
(Moscow)

Skomorokhov, N.M.
Semdesetaya Vozdushnaya Armiya v Boiyakh ot Stalingrada do Veni
(17th Air Army in Battle from Stalingrad to Vienna) [1977] ; Voenizdat (Moscow)

Skulski, P., Bargiel, J., Cisek, G.
Asy Frontu Wschodniego
(Aces of the Eastern Front) [1994] Ace Publications (Wroclaw, Poland)

Stepanets, A.T. *Istrabiteli Yak Perioda Velikoy Otechestvennoy Voyni*
(Yak Fighters From the Period of the Great Patriotic War) [1992] ; Machinostroenie
Press (Moscow)

Vestsik, M. *Lavockin La-7*
(Lavochkin La-7) [2000] MBI (Prague)

Vazhin, F.A. *Vozdushniy Taran*
(Air Ramming) [1962] ; Voenizdat (Moscow)

Vladimirov, D., Yur'evich, K.
Samoleti Stalinskikh Sokolov
(Aircraft of Stalin's Falcons) [1992] ; Aeromuseé Publications (St.Petersburg)

Voronin, V., Kolesnikov, P.
Sovetskie Istrebiteli Velikoy Otechestvennoy Voyni – MiG-3, LaGG-3, La-5
(Soviet Fighters of the Great Patriotic War – MiG-3, LaGG-3, La-5) [1986] ; DOSAAF
(Moscow)

Yakovlev, A.S. *50 Let Sovietskogo Samoletstoenniya*
(50 Years of Soviet Aviation Accomplishment) [1981] ; Nauka/DOSAAF, 3rd Editon
(Moscow)

Yakovlev, A.S. *Rasskazi Aviakonstruktora*
(Stories of an Aircraft Designer) [1974] ; Detskaya Literatura (Moscow)

Zhabrov, A. A. *Annotirovanniy Ukazatel' Literaturi na Russkom Yazike po Aviatsii i Vozdukhoplvanniyu za
50 Let, 1881-1931* (Annotated Guide to Russian Language Literature on on Aviation
and Aeronautics for 50 years, 1881-1931) [1931] ; (Moscow)

ARTICLES, ACADEMIC PAPERS AND OTHER VARIOUS SOURCES

Stanovlenie Aviastroeniya v SSSR, 1916-1947 gg
(Development of Soviet Aviation Manufacture in the USSR), Chapters 1-31 (inclusive) Ivan I.
Rodinov (1997)

Somoleti i Nauka; Ispitatelnie Poleti NII VVS Perioda Velikoy Otechestvennoy Voyni
(Aircraft and Science; NII VVS Flight Testing During the Great Patriotic War) Viktor Belov (1969)

Periodicals and Magazines

General Reference

Aviamaster

Aviatsiya i Vremya

Aviatsiya i Kosmonavtika

Istoria Aviatsiya

Krilya Pobedi

Krilya Rodini

Mir Aviatsii

Modelist-Konstruktor

ADDITIONAL RESOURCES

ARTICLES

Arsenev, E. Samoleti OKB Imeni A.N. Mikoyana
Aviatsiya i Kosmonavtika

Lurance, Z. Samolot Mysliwski; Yak-1M
Skrzydla w Miniaturze 2/91

Vakhlamov, V., Orlov, M. Tsveta Sovietskoy Aviatsii, Chast' 1
M-Hobby Magazine No. 9/97

Vakhlamov, V., Orlov, M. . Tsveta Sovietskoy Aviatsii, Chast' 2
M-Hobby Magazine No. 1/99

Vakhlamov, V., Orlov, M. Tsveta Sovietskoy Aviatsii, Chast' 3
M-Hobby Magazine No. 2/99

Vakhlamov, V., Orlov, M. Tsveta Sovietskoy Aviatsii, Chast' 4
M-Hobby Magazine No. 3/99

Vakhlamov, V., Orlov, M. Tsveta Sovietskoy Aviatsii, Chast' 5
M-Hobby Magazine No.

Vakhlamov, V., Orlov, M. Tsveta Sovietskoy Aviatsii, Chast' 6
M-Hobby Magazine No.

MUSEUMS

Frunze Museum of the Military Air Forces of Russia, Monino

Central Aero-Hydrodynamics Institute, Moscow

Central House of Aviation and Cosmonautics, Moscow

Museum of the Yakovlev OKB, Moscow

Museum of the Il'yushin OKB, Moscow

Museum of Saratov Aircraft Production, Saratov

Central Naval Military Museum, St.Petersburg

State Museum of Aviation, St.Petersburg

The Aviation Museum, Kbely (Prague)

Polish Aviation Museum, Krakow

Polish Military Museum, Warsaw

Musee de l'Air, Paris

National Military Museum, Bucharest

INDEX